METROPOLITAN POLITICS
A Reader

METROPOLITAN POLITICS
A Reader

EDITED BY

MICHAEL N. DANIELSON

LITTLE, BROWN and COMPANY

Boston

LIBRARY OF CONGRESS CATALOG CARD NO. 66-15459

THIRD PRINTING

Published simultaneously in Canada
by Little, Brown & Company (Canada) Limited

PRINTED IN THE UNITED STATES OF AMERICA

PREFACE

One consequence of the explosive growth of metropolitan areas in the United States has been a vast outpouring of books, articles, pamphlets, and official documents treating the governmental and political aspects of urban growth and change. From the metropolitan study commissions, civic associations, planning groups, and university bureaus of public administration come an apparently inexhaustible flow of reports dealing with governmental structure and the provision of public services in our burgeoning metropolitan areas. Mounting concern with the problems of urban growth and change also has stimulated a rising tide of popular literature preoccupied with the sickness of the city and the maladies of the metropolis. Last, but certainly not least important, is the rapidly growing body of analytical studies of political behavior in metropolitan areas, one of the prime products of the rediscovery of the city in the past decade by political science.

This torrent of studies, surveys, and reports threatens to overwhelm the student of metropolitan politics, to say nothing of severely taxing the resources of the librarian responsible for the reserve reading room. In this volume, I have brought together thirty-seven selections from this mushrooming literature which I have used with profit in courses in state and local government, metropolitan politics, and urban development.

Each of the seven chapters begins with an introductory essay which sets forth the central theme around which the chapter is organized, provides continuity, and underscores matters of particular interest to the student of metropolitan politics. In addition, these introductory sections offer a general analysis of the development, operation, and prospects of the metropolitan political system. Some of the readings document or reinforce the editor's interpretation; others challenge it or introduce discordant notes.

Unlike much of the literature dealing with government in metropolitan areas, this volume's primary objective is the analysis of the

160158

political system of the metropolis rather than its reform. Therefore, the main focus is political behavior rather than institutional structure. From a wide range of perspectives, the readings examine the distribution of influence in the metropolis and the impact on this distribution of the forces of urban growth and change. In so doing, considerable attention is given to the attitudes, perceptions, capabilities, and activities of the various participants in the metropolitan political system.

As a consequence of this central concern with what *is* rather than what *ought to be*, this collection of readings draws heavily from the work of a group of political scientists—including Robert C. Wood, Edward C. Banfield, Scott Greer, York Willbern, Norton E. Long, and Charles R. Adrian—who in the past decade have concerned themselves with the workings of metropolitan political systems. The doctrines of metropolitan reform which so long dominated the study of government in urban America, on the other hand, are not afforded a privileged place in this book. Instead, the views and activities of the forces of metropolitan reform, like those of other influential participants in the politics of the metropolis, are examined in the context of their role in the metropolitan political process.

Students of metropolitan politics frequently restrict their attention to political activity arising from efforts to create, maintain, and operate metropolitan governments. In this volume, however, metropolitan politics is not defined in this narrow fashion. Selections cover the entire spectrum of issues and political activity which shape and are shaped by the patterns of metropolitan politics. Thus, the readings examine the politics of transportation, water supply, planning, race relations, special districts, interlocal agreements, and state and federal involvement in metropolitan problems, as well, of course, as the politics of metropolitan government.

Inevitably a number of debts are incurred in the preparation of a collection of readings. First, I am grateful to the authors and their publishers for kindly permitting me to reprint the material included in this volume. Second, I want to thank the students who have read and evaluated many of these selections in my undergraduate and graduate courses at Princeton University. I also am indebted to two Princeton colleagues, Jameson W. Doig and John H. Strange, who read the manuscript and offered numerous suggestions for improvement. Richard M. Cion, my research assistant for the past year, provided invaluable assistance in the collection of the contents of this

volume and their preparation for publication. Finally I owe a special
debt to Donald R. Hammonds and Alfred E. Browne of Little, Brown
and Company for their advice, encouragement, and persistence. To
all of these people, as well as to my wife Patti, I acknowledge with
thanks your contributions while assuming full responsibility for any
errors of omission or commission.

Michael N. Danielson

Princeton, N. J.
September, 1965

CONTENTS

1

THE IMPACT OF URBANIZATION ON THE POLITICAL ENVIRONMENT

2

THE POLITICAL SYSTEM OF THE METROPOLIS

3

METROPOLITAN PROBLEMS AND
THE ROLE OF GOVERNMENT

4

METROPOLITAN GOVERNMENT:
THE POLITICS OF REVOLUTION

5

THE ADAPTIVE METROPOLIS:
THE POLITICS OF ACCOMMODATION

6

THE METROPOLIS AND THE FEDERAL SYSTEM

Introduction   299

7

THE FUTURE METROPOLIS

METROPOLITAN POLITICS
A Reader

1

THE IMPACT OF URBANIZATION
ON THE POLITICAL ENVIRONMENT

Essential to an understanding of political behavior in the American metropolis is an examination of the process of urban growth and change. The social, economic, and technological forces which have interacted to produce the sprawling, dynamic metropolitan areas of the 1960s have left an indelible imprint on urban political systems. We have been transformed into a nation of suburbanites almost before we realized that we had become a nation of urban dwellers. Older technologies such as those of the trolley car and the downtown factory loft have been swept away by the automobile and the industrial park. The poor, the Negro, and the Puerto Rican have been concentrated in the older cities while a burgeoning middle class has spread far beyond the city limits. Political power in the extended metropolis has been fragmented as geographic and functional units of government have proliferated. Differences in constituency, capabilities, and the impact of urban change have produced a widening gulf between city and suburb, and sizeable disparities among suburbs. With growth and change have come pyramiding demands on government for more and better services, as well as intensified pressures for the resolution of conflicts arising from a complex, fragmented, and differentiated urban society.

1

More and more Americans are becoming aware of the basic dimensions of the urbanization of their society. A rapidly growing population increasingly is concentrated in metropolitan areas. In 1960, 113 million of the United States' 179 million inhabitants lived within the nation's 212 metropolitan areas. Approximately half of this metropolitan population was located in the two dozen regions with a million or more residents. Metropolitan areas accounted for 84 per cent of the population growth of the United States between 1950 and 1960; and almost 97 per cent of this increase occurred at the outer reaches of the metropolis. Many of the older cities, particularly in the larger metropolitan areas of the Northeast and the Midwest, either failed to grow or lost population in the past decade. Equally important, a massive exodus of white families from the cities and migration to the cities from the black belts of the South and depressed areas such as Appalachia have produced significant changes in the composition of the population of older urban centers such as New York, Philadelphia, Cleveland, and Chicago.

The underlying causes of the growing dominance of a metropolitan way of life and its spread outward from the traditional urban centers also are readily apparent. The components of a complex, modern economy gravitate to the metropolis. While metropolitan areas encompass approximately two-thirds of the population, they account for three-quarters of the nation's bank deposits and industrial jobs. Agricultural mechanization generates a steady stream of rural migrants to the city. Economic stability and growth provides an increasing proportion of the population with the capital needed to partake in the outward march from the city. Prosperity also encourages larger families which quicken the quest for enlarged living space. By liberating urban development from the constraints of fixed transportation systems, the automobile and the public highway have opened vast tracts of land to new settlement. The movement of jobs also has been centrifugal. Retail and service establishments have followed the population outward. Technological innovation and the transportation revolution have produced voracious space demands for manufacturing facilities which the older industrial areas have been unable to satisfy. The result has been the creation of a new kind of urban society, a world of the housing development, the shopping center, and the industrial park, a world tied together by the automobile and the expressway, and a world increasingly oblivious to the urban core.

Many voices have been raised in protest over the outward thrust of the metropolis and the decay of the inner city. The transformation of the economic, social, cultural, and intellectual centers of the nation into drab neighborhoods for the impoverished and the non-white is an appalling prospect to a wide range of urban activists. Social critics decry the conformity and monotony of the mass produced, homogeneous suburb. Conservationists condemn the greedy consumption of land by subdevelopments, shopping centers, and superhighways. Civic leaders in New York City despair at the prospect of an auto-dominant "spread city" twice the size of the present 7,000 square mile New York region. California planners nervously watch bulldozers turn orchards and citrus groves into vast, formless "slurbs."

Partisans of the city insist that there are alternatives to the emerging diffused metropolis. The revitalization of the central city is sought through massive programs of urban renewal and rail transit improvement. The decentralized political system is viewed as a primary cause of unplanned growth, fiscal inequities, spreading slums, deteriorating public transportation, and practically every other ill of the metropolis. To overcome the shortcomings of the existing political system, as well as to redirect the development of the metropolis, urban reformers seek metropolitan planning to control land use and coordinate developmental activities, and regional government to tackle areawide problems and equalize the resources of city and suburb.

What are the prospects of reversing, or even checking, the present trend of urban development? Practically nonexistent, argues York Willbern in his analysis of urban growth and metropolitan dispersal. Once set in motion, the forces of decentralization appear inexorable to Willbern. In the absence of evidence that governmental policy can reverse the choices of the marketplace, choices which overwhelmingly favor continued dispersion, he questions the significance of the political system as a factor in the shaping of the urban environment. The result of the interplay of the forces of dispersion, Willbern concludes, is the withering away of the city conceived as the central focus of urban activity.

For Lewis Mumford, the city and its culture are unique, indispensable, and irreplaceable. He agrees that the city as traditionally conceived is in danger, but refuses to accept the inevitability of its decline. The past, he argues, is not a reliable guide to the future because men, reacting to what has happened, can change their behavior patterns. And Mumford is confident that urban Americans will alter their habits as the manifest inadequacies of life in the spreading and culturally barren metropolis become increasingly apparent. As more and more people realize that the city is essential to civilization, Mumford believes that the political system will respond, that policies will be changed, and that the formless and dehumanized metropolis will give way to the clustered, variegated city of man.

To Raymond Vernon, an economist who directed the ambitious New York Metropolitan Region Study, Mumford's predicted reawakening is no more than the characteristic wishful thinking of that small minority of Americans who value the city. In Vernon's view, the public by and large ignores the prophets of metropolitan doom because it correctly associates the emerging metropolis with personal betterment. Only the economic, social, and intellectual elites, with their close ties to the traditional city, he contends, have been seriously disadvantaged by the changing pattern of urban growth. While the protests of a small but articulate minority dominate the debate on the metropolis, the vast majority quietly adjusts and advances. As a result, pressures on the political system for more of the same are likely to be far more influential than the cries in the wilderness for a halt to the outward march of urban development and a rebirth of the city.

None of the forces altering the urban landscape has more significance for metropolitan politics than race. In his discussion of the racial aspects of growth and change in the larger metropolitan areas, John H. Strange echoes the pessimism of Willbern and Vernon concerning possibilities for significant alterations in the pattern of urban development originating in the political system of the metropolis. But he is less sanguine than Vernon about the prospects of the urban poor, or at least the majority of them who are Negroes. For the Negro who has followed the Irishman, the Italian, and the Pole into the city, the second stage of metropolitanization — the move to suburbia — is practically non-existent. As Strange indicates, the containment of the Negro in the ghettos of the central city has extremely important implications for the politics of the city, the suburbs, and the metropolis as a whole.

<hr />

YORK WILLBERN

The Transformation of the Urban Community

The linguistic and historical relationship between the words "city" and "civilization" have often been noted. The present state of American cities and that great part of the civilization of this country which revolves around their functioning and well-being, have provoked a rapidly growing volume of interest and concern.

Reprinted from *The Withering Away of the City* (University, Alabama: University of Alabama Press, 1964), pp. 9-33, with the permission of the author and the publisher.

Most literate people are reasonably familiar with the gross outlines of urban population movements. They know that urban areas
have increased in population much more rapidly than rural areas,
that the great bulk of this growth has been in areas of metropolitan
character, and that suburban areas have been growing much more
rapidly than have central cities. None of us, however, yet understands adequately the implications and consequences of these massive redistributions of the population.

We are participating, in my opinion, in two revolutions, one imposed upon the other, and the meaning of the second is partially
obscured by the fact that the first, much older, revolution is continuing even as the second develops.

The first of these revolutions, of course, is the rise of an urban
way of life. The second is its diffusion and dispersal over the countryside. The first has been in the making in Europe and in this country for several hundred years. It was in nearly full flower when
Johnson and Boswell were enjoying the fleshpots of eighteenth century London. This revolution was based on the rise of trade and on
the growth of industry. The new technologies which promoted specialization, manufacturing, and great increases in the interchange
of goods and services have continued and been accelerated in the
last two generations. They are now world-wide in their impact; the
non-Western world as well as the West is struggling today with
the gains and costs of these changes. Those who are staggered by the
problems of urbanization in this country are really shaken when
they see Tokyo or Calcutta. Tokyo, the world's most populous city,
has no sewerage for eighty percent of the metropolitan area. In Calcutta two-thirds of a million people have no home but the public
streets and alleys.[1]

These urbanizing forces continue unabated in this country. The
proportion of the national population living in areas defined by the
Census Bureau as "metropolitan" increased from 58 percent in 1950
to 63 percent in 1960. The proportions continue to grow and will
probably reach 70 or 75 percent before the Census Bureau decides
that it is unable any longer to fabricate definitions to demarcate a
population which is almost universally metropolitanized.

[1] *New York Times,* Dec. 17, 1961, p. 40; Paul N. Ylvisaker, address to
the World Traffic Engineering Conference, Washington, D.C., Aug. 21,
1961.

The second revolution is much newer and has been much more strongly felt in this country than anywhere else. This is the outward explosion of our urban centers. It has several causes, of course. One is the desire of families, particularly families with children, for detached dwellings on substantial plots of land. Sir Frederic J. Osborn, dean of British planners and editor of *Town and Country Planning,* emphasized this desire in a recent address to American planning officials, and in so doing raised a question of crucial importance to the continuation and welfare of large cities. He indicated that the most disastrous shortcoming associated with city size is "the lack of sufficient space inside cities for good family dwellings with private yards or gardens, for recreation, for industrial efficiency, and for the vegetative surroundings and the quiet and simple beauty man needs and desires for the fullness of life."

> Relative unconsciousness of this aspect of the urban problem surprises me in all countries, including my own, because the most conspicuous cause of the "metropolitan explosion" is the spontaneous quest by more and more urban families, as net incomes rise, for the family house standing in its own yard. The outward movement of the well-off is nothing new; what is new is the spread of wealth to far more numerous classes who can afford what Susannah's husband provided for her in Babylon and great senators took for themselves in ancient Rome — a suburban home in a garden. . . . such environments reflect a universal natural desire that man indulges wherever and whenever he becomes prosperous and free.
>
> Admittedly, there are some genuine addicts of high urban culture to whom space and green surroundings make little appeal — types who like to live in city centres with their rich assemblies of theatres, concert halls, art galleries, restaurants, night clubs, snack bars, and hamburger stands — and are reassured by the bustle of crowds, traffic noises, flashing signs, and the insistent impact on their senses of commercial vitality. I do not deplore the existence of these types, though I suspect that their contribution to our culture is over valued. But they are a tiny minority. . . .[2]

This view is, of course, greatly at odds with that suggested by Mrs. Jane Jacobs in a book which is currently attracting a great deal of attention among students of urbanism.[3] If the figures on popula-

---

[2] Frederic J. Osborn, "The Conqueror City," *Town and Country Planning,* XXIX (Apr., 1961), 141.
[3] Jane Jacobs, *The Death and Life of Great American Cities* (New York: Random House, 1961).

tion movement are an accurate indication of the desires of people
for home environments, the evidence certainly supports Sir Frederic's view much more strongly than that of Mrs. Jacobs.

A good many technological developments have made this dispersion of urban housing relatively easy. Reliance upon electric power
and the ease of power transmission, telephone lines, septic tanks
and similar developments bring to widely scattered houses many
of the conveniences and amenities once possible only in very closely
settled cities.

A development of social technology — the long-term, monthly pay-
ment mortgage loan with low interest rates — has greatly facilitated
the spread of American families into single-family detached dwellings. The growth of credit arrangements of this type has certainly
been encouraged and fostered by national legislation. It can be argued that the nature of the urban residential patterns of this generation has been shaped very substantially by FHA and similar governmental programs. The overwhelming political support for these
programs, however, and the existence of parallel non-governmental
developments indicate clearly that these credit socialization devices
have probably been more the product than the cause of the social
and economic forces at work.

If the basic desire for detached dwellings and space is one cause
of the dispersion, another and very important cause is the appearance and practically universal use of the automobile in this country.
We now have available, for most individuals, personalized rapid
transit. The customary reaction to the automobile of Mrs. Jacobs
and others who admire the congestion of dense urban settlement
is to wish it would go away.

The impact of the automobile revolution is newer than many of
us realize; its outlines are only now beginning to emerge. The last
decade was the first in which it was fully operative; the 1960 census
returns gave figures which indicate some of the results on a nationwide basis. Automobiles began to be widespread in the 1920's, but
too little time had as yet passed for really basic changes in ways of
living and spatial relationships. In the 1930's the great economic
depression overshadowed and hampered adjustments to the new
technology; the 1940's brought another overpowering circumstance,
the war and its aftermath, to mask and postpone the basic changes.
They hit us full force in the 1950's, but a decade is a short time for
a social revolution. The greatest public works enterprise in the his-

tory of mankind, our national system of expressways, which will probably give the automobile age its greatest boost since the Model T Ford, is just beginning. I am indebted to Harlan Cleveland for a statistic which he considered the most interesting of a recent year: we now have enough automotive vehicles in operation in this country for every man, woman, and child in the population to ride comfortably and simultaneously in the front seats.

It is difficult for us to realize that this new revolution may have a social impact comparable to that of the first. The basic purpose of a city is the facilitation of interchange — the interchange of goods through trade and merchandising, of labor and services in industrial and service enterprises, of messages and ideas in financial and political and cultural activities. When the means of interchange are drastically altered, the nature of the city must also be drastically altered.

In the large cities of a century ago, population was tightly concentrated. Concentration was necessary, in order for people to get from home to work and school and shop and engage in the other complex exchanges of a city. When each individual and most of the goods move from place to place within the urban environment in a vehicle weighing more than a ton and capable of moving economically at the rate of a mile a minute, the old patterns of settlement are technologically obsolete and will inevitably be changed. To achieve for a given population the same facility of circulation that the older concentrated cities had for pedestrian, horse-drawn, or even rail traffic, the modern city requires a land area many times greater. When movement and interchange were pedestrian and horse-drawn, an efficient area for a population of 200,000 might be about four square miles,[4] for 200,000 people now, on a one or two persons per car basis (increasingly the normal pattern), the most efficient area might well be 100 square miles.

Many of the great cities of the world outside the United States are experiencing the integrating revolution, with relatively little evidence yet of the disintegrating one. Perhaps they may avoid the second. A Soviet economist, watching Americans coming to work one-in-a-car is supposed to have said "we'll never make that mistake — that is, if we can help it."[5]

[4] In 1850 Philadelphia had a population of 121,000 and an area of two square miles.
[5] Ylvisaker, p. 18.

In this country, however, disintegrating forces are moving at a
rapid pace. The area north of the Ohio River and east from Chicago
and St. Louis contains the urban heart of the United States. There
were in this area in 1950 a dozen cities with more than half a million
inhabitants each. What happened to the population of these cities
in the decade of the 1950's, a decade in which urbanization continued apace? Every one of them lost, rather than gained, in population. While the urban area, the metropolitan area, in each case
grew very substantially in population, not a single one of the large
central cities in this area increased. If this is what is happening to
the oldest, best established American cities, will Birmingham and
Indianapolis, or even Houston and Los Angeles, be far behind?

The famous Regional Plan of 1929 for the New York metropolitan
area projected a population by 1965 of 21 million people living in
approximately 1,000 square miles of the region. In 1960, five years
before the projected date, there were actually only 16 million people, but the urbanized area constituted 2,000 square miles, twice the
projected amount.[6]

CHANGE IN POPULATION, 1950-1960, MAJOR CITIES IN NORTHEAST AND MIDWEST

	1950	1960	Amount Change
Baltimore	949,708	939,024	− 10,684
Boston	801,444	697,197	−104,247
Buffalo	580,132	532,759	− 47,373
Chicago	3,620,962	3,550,404	− 70,558
Cincinnati	503,998	502,550	− 1,448
Cleveland	914,808	876,050	− 38,758
Detroit	1,849,568	1,670,144	−179,424
New York	7,891,957	7,781,984	−109,973
Philadelphia	2,071,605	2,002,512	− 69,093
Pittsburgh	676,806	604,332	− 72,474
St. Louis	856,796	750,026	−106,770
Washington, D.C.	802,178	763,956	− 38,222

Source: *Statistical Abstract of the United States*, 1962, pp. 22-23.

[6] Paul Windels, "The Region — Past, Present, and Future," *Metropolis
1985*, p. 21, a report from a conference held at Arden House, March 1,
1961.

The most recent major study of the New York metropolitan area, which Raymond Vernon and his associates made for the same Regional Plan Association, came to the following conclusion:

As one surveys the outward shift of the population in the New York Metropolitan Region and of the consumer activities tied to them, the forces behind the shift seem near-inexorable. Basic technological developments in transportation and deepseated changes in consumer wants appear to lie behind the phenomenon. Here and there one sees evidences of preferences which breast the main tide; the occasional reappearance of a disillusioned exurbanite in his former city haunts, the gradual growth of apartments-in-the-city for the very rich — these are phenomena whose impact cannot be overlooked. The bigger risk, however, is that their implications for the future will be exaggerated rather than overlooked. Short of some fundamental alteration in consumer outlook or in urban environment, the trends for the future seem likely to represent a continuation — even a speed up — of the dispersive tendencies of the past.[7]

This is what they predict in the text of the book. After coming to this conclusion, however, Mr. Vernon inspected the 1960 census returns and found that he had been short of the mark. The city core has declined in population more than he anticipated, and the outlying areas have expanded more rapidly. In a footnote attached after the report was completed, but before the volume was finally published, he confessed that "in general, the dispersive population forces in the Region seem even stronger than those built into our model."[8]

Even the census figures summarizing the growth in the outlying portions of metropolitan areas and the losses or much slower growth in the urban core may understate the dispersion. For example, the Census Bureau defines the Indianapolis metropolitan area as Marion County. This area increased in population by 24 percent between 1950 and 1960, a very substantial rate of growth. But the counties immediately to the north, east, south, and west of Marion County, not included in the census-defined metropolitan area, had rates of growth of 40, 30, 67, and 65 percent, respectively. The growth of these counties immediately beyond the census metropolitan area limits is not considered in the statistics to be suburban growth, but

[7] Raymond Vernon, *Metropolis 1985* (Cambridge: Harvard University Press, 1960), p. 165.
[8] *Ibid.*, p. 222.

the percentage growth has often been even greater than that of the suburban areas *within* the official metropolitan area.

During the decades when the urbanizing forces were strongest, and before the forces of dispersal had begun to accumulate, the percentage of the population living in the central city of an urbanizing area increased substantially. This percentage has tended to decrease as the second revolution has become mixed with the first. In the accompanying chart are some representative figures from three cities at which I have been looking intensively.

PERCENTAGE OF COUNTY POPULATION IN CENTRAL CITY
THREE CITIES, 1850-1960

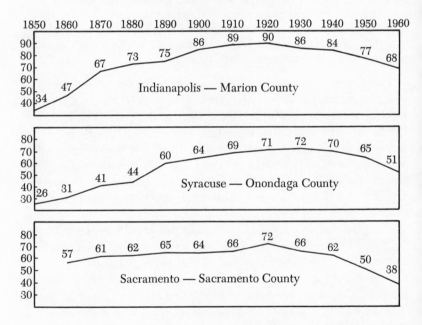

In each of the three cities the central city reached its peak percentage in 1920 or 1930, along with the initial surge of the automobile revolution, and has since declined at a rapid and ordinarily accelerating rate. New York City constituted the largest percentage, in population, of the counties composing its metropolitan area in *1910*; the percentage has been dropping ever since. The peak in Birmingham was *1930*.

In gross national figures the greatest concentration of metropolitan population inside central cities occurred between 1920 and 1930. Until 1920 the central cities were growing faster than their metropolitan rings; beginning with the census of 1930, the fringe growth has been faster than the central growth, and the gap widens with each census. During the 1950-1960 decade, the central cities of the 212 metropolitan areas of the country increased 1.5 percent in population within their 1950 boundaries, and added another 9.2 percent by annexation, for a total increase of 10.7 percent, and, as I have indicated, many of the biggest and oldest actually lost population. The remaining, or fringe portion of the metropolitan areas, increased 48.6 percent. The more than ninety percent of the land area outside the metropolises saw its population increase by eleven percent.

It is roughly accurate to say that one-third of the American population is within the central cities of metropolitan areas, and this segment is increasing at the rate of one percent per year, almost entirely by annexation. (This increase, as we shall see, is concentrated in a few states.) Another third is in the metropolitan fringes, and here the rate of increase is four percent per year, in spite of the bites taken from it by annexation into the central cities. The remaining third of the population is in the rest of the country, and this segment also is increasing at the rate of about one percent per year.

Nor is this diffusion of urban life over the countryside to be limited by the commuting range, expanding though that range may be through massive expenditures on expressways. We are not witnessing a pattern in which people seek out spaciousness for living, but return to a congested core each day for work. The jobs also seek space, and manufacturers want space as well as home builders.

In recent years, manufacturers in the New York Metropolitan Region have dramatically increased their use of land. Our surveys indicate that the amount of plot space per worker in the post war suburban plants of the Region is over four times as great as in suburban plants built before 1922. In the new plants more than an acre of land is used for every ten workers.[9]

The service activities, of course, follow the population. The spectacular growth of shopping centers, the great demands for extensive sites for new schools, the need to locate all kinds of enterprises

[9] *Ibid.*, pp. 116-117.

where there is ample parking space, are indications of dispersion
in economic activity. Even in New York, which has peculiar reasons
for concentration because its central business district serves in large
measure as the central business district of the nation, the jobs are
moving out about as fast as the people, according to the Vernon
studies.[10] Frank W. Herring, Deputy Director of Comprehensive
Planning of the Port of New York Authority, says that "growth in
journey-to-work travel is no longer focused on the Central Business
District, but rather is characterized by intersuburban travel, reverse
commuting and the like."[11]

The net flow of commuting is, of course, still toward the center,
and it will probably continue to be for a long time. The Vernon
studies indicate that the core of the New York area now has about
half the population of the region and two-thirds of the jobs. According to their projections, by 1985 the core will have only one-
third the population but will probably still have half the jobs.

The dispersion of employment may be greater in other centers
than in New York. In the Chicago area (where the city of Chicago
constitutes a larger portion of its metropolitan area than does New
York), the city's share of manufacturing employment in the area fell
from 84 percent in 1920 to 81 percent in 1940 and to 72 percent in
1957.[12] A continuation of this accelerating trend would suggest that
the city of Chicago now has less than 70 percent of the industrial
jobs in the area, compared to about 58 percent of the people.

> Dispersal of manufacturing activity from the inner zones of the cen-
> tral city was the dominant trend in plant location throughout the
> United States in 1950-1960. In Chicago, typically, the greatest gains
> in activity took place in an arc ten to fifteen miles from the central
> business district. The greatest losses occurred within five miles of

[10] New York is to be contrasted to London and Tokyo, its two largest
competitors as world urban centers. In both of these, the population increase is at the edges while the jobs continue to be relatively concentrated
in the center. Paul Ylvisaker reports that land in the heart of Tokyo is
four times as expensive as land in the heart of Manhattan. The chief reason for the difference is almost certainly the difference in the state of the
automotive revolution.
[11] "Metropolitan Growth and Metropolitan Travel Patterns," a paper
presented at the annual meeting of the Highway Research Board, Committee on Urban Research, Jan. 12, 1961.
[12] Northeastern Illinois Metropolitan Area Planning Commission, *Social
Geography of Metropolitan Chicago* (Chicago, 1960), p. 20.

the core. Warehouses, in particular, moved from inner zones to the periphery, situating themselves close to areas of population growth and expanded manufacturing activity. To call this process suburbanization may be too much of a simplification.[13]

In many cities of smaller size, the great developments in industrialization, and in jobs, occur beyond the city limits. The new industries tend to locate in industrial parks, or on spacious sites well outside the cities. In Syracuse, New York, for example, the city's proportion of the population of Onondaga County has been declining for more than twenty years, but its proportion of the assessed valuation of the county has been declining even more rapidly than its proportion of the population, indicating that productive property, which has higher assessments than residences, has been growing faster outside the city than inside.[14]

Some observers argue that the tide of movement out of central cities into suburban and rurban areas can be checked and reversed by improved mass transit, renewal of the older urban areas, and various other remedial measures. Efforts in this direction may be expected to continue. It seems likely that policy changes may affect the character of the movement somewhat, but the overwhelming bulk of the evidence makes the outward movement seem, as Vernon and his associates put it in their study of New York, "inexorable."

Most of our accumulated physical capital is in urban areas. The sweeping changes in the technology of settlement and interchange which have resulted in the shifting populations have a great impact on the maintenance and utility of these accumulated investments. The existence of these great investments, both in physical facilities and in skills and habits, constitutes a great drag upon adaption to technological innovation. Farm homes and land holdings and habits of work have continued long after becoming technologically obsolescent; this is the basic cause of our so-called "farm problem." We now have similar lags because of the investments in outmoded urban plants. We live, however, in a relatively affluent age, an age when we can make massive continuing new investments, even at

[13] Mark Reinsberg, *Growth and Change in Metropolitan Areas and Their Relation to Metropolitan Transportation: A Research Summary* (Evanston, Ill.: The Transportation Center, Northwestern University, 1961), p. 10.
[14] Roscoe C. Martin, Frank Munger, and others, *Decisions in Syracuse* (Bloomington: Indiana University Press, 1961), pp. 23 and 29.

the price of losing full use of much of the old. Furthermore, our society is increasingly mobile, not only geographically but in capacity to shift patterns of behavior. Substitution of investment for many reasons, in addition to the changing technology of communication and movement, goes on continually.

With new investments being made as a matter of course, the investors (whether in productive plant, or in patterns of service, or in housing and ways of life) are able to locate in better conformity to the technological patterns of the present and future. The pressures to maintain and adapt and renew the center which have characterized European cities for many generations are far less demanding here. A merchant who sees opportunities for growth in an expanding urban environment, and who has or can get capital to invest, is much less likely to use it in rebuilding or refurnishing and improving a downtown store location. Instead he will join a new regional shopping center near a freeway interchange where there can be six square feet of parking space for every square foot of selling space.

So far, in this country the forces of the second, suburbanizing revolution have been balanced in large measure by the continuing forces of the first, urbanizing revolution. The massive forces for dispersal of investment have been accompanied by such great need for the use of all the possible capital available in urban areas that both the new and much of the old have been necessary.

The physical decay and obsolescence of the older investment have not yet resulted in great decreases in property values. In the last thirty years the rate of investment in new housing units and new industrial and business sites in urban areas has not exceeded the rate of influx from the remote rural communities. To be more explicit, although over a million housing units a year have been built in urban fringe areas for the last decade, as yet comparatively few vacancies have appeared in the deteriorating housing units of the central cities. The new units serve as additions to the total urban supply, not as replacements. The accumulated overcrowding of the depression and war years and the continuing immigration from rural parts of the country have kept the demand for housing units at a sufficient intensity that rental income from slum property is still highly remunerative. As fast as the inhabitants of the gray area (or "mice country," as Robert Wood calls it) have moved out to the suburbs, the Negro, Puerto Rican, and hill country farm people have crowded in to the decaying houses of the old city. Reductions in population of the central cities, now definitely begun, have made it possible so far only to clear some land to provide more room for automobiles to maneuver and be stored and to reduce somewhat the doubling up and overcrowding; vacancy rates in slum housing are still not high enough to worry the landlords.

There are some indications that new housing construction has begun to catch up with the urban population growth. As to the deteriorating central city housing in New York, Vernon suggests that "no projection which we would consider realistic contemplates an increase in the demand for such housing in the Region anywhere near as great as the prospective increase in supply."[15] If vacancies in the slums begin to mount (as is already true in some decaying commercial and industrial properties) reductions in income potential may cause the values of the decaying central city properties to fall significantly.

Some forces do exist which tend to offset the disintegrated effects of transportation changes and the desire of people for detached dwellings. One is the great value for many small enterprises of what the economists call "external economies." These are the specialist services which a large enterprise may provide for itself but which a small enterprise can best get from other suppliers. Although these may be interchanged even in a dispersed, less congested locational pattern, there remain some advantages in the greater proximity of denser locations.

Second, and much more important, some activities in our complex society are best carried on where there is frequent and convenient opportunity for face-to-face contact with a variety of other people: the financial institutions, for example; the central corporate offices; the advertising business. Here, intelligence is perhaps the chief item of exchange, and it can best be exchanged on the basis of frequent conferences, luncheons, and personal contacts. For this reason the shining towers of central Manhattan continue to rise although much of the surrounding area is deteriorating.

The central business district of New York has peculiar advantages, of course, because it performs so many of these functions for the whole nation and even the world. At the same time, the proportion of our society engaged in the white-collar, highly interpersonal communication activities is increasing so extensively that there are

[15] Vernon, p. 154.

good economic prospects for the core of central business districts of many of our cities, even though the fabrication and distribution of goods may be continually dispersed.

Third, some industries need large quantities of relatively low-wage labor. Since the lowest income groups tend to live in the central city, and relatively near the center, and since these groups are somewhat less mobile, it is sometimes advantageous for lower-wage industries to stay near the population and transit center. In Chicago the industries showing the lowest decentralizing tendencies (though even here the net movement was outward) were textiles and apparel, lumber and furniture, and food products, all of which are comparatively low-wage operations.[16]

A fourth centralizing factor may be suggested, but its actual impact is not easy to predict. This is the almost certain great increase in the number of two-house families. Two-car families are now commonplace in this country, and two-house families are expected to become so. Already perhaps a million of the fifty million family units have more than one place of residence, and these million tend to be the high-income, high-status families whose patterns of life are copied by others as quickly as they can afford it. If one residence offers almost complete isolation, many families may plump in favor of the attractions and conveniences of high-density living for the other residence and use their automobiles as much or more for week-end as for daily commuting. The apparent preference of people with children for detached dwellings, however, along with the continually growing reliance upon the automobile even for frequent movements during the day, leads to considerable doubt that the rise in dual dwellings will result in more than a marginal integrating force.

How much can public policy shape and guide and direct these patterns of investment and of settlement? Was it government's cheap land policy which led to the rapid agricultural expansion of the early nineteenth century, or did migration and settlement force the government to follow the policy it did? Was it governmental promotion of the transcontinental railroads later in the century, and the Panama Canal early in this century, that linked the two coasts into an economic unit, or did the economic ties and links make the governmental public works enterprises necessary? Was it the massive public water system that made possible the settlement of so

[16] Reinsberg, pp. 18-19.

many people in and around New York, and the development and operation of the subway system that enabled them to focus such a concentration of economic activity in Manhattan, or were these great public enterprises produced rather haltingly to meet the necessities of the developing situation? No simple answer is possible to such chicken-and-egg priority questions, but recent searching economic studies of metropolitan regions suggest very strongly that, as Charles Adrian summarizes it:

> Both local and regional (metropolitan) governments tend to follow the economic pattern rather than to lead it. Governmental innovations that complement the decisions of the market place are likely to succeed; others are not.[17]

. . . [T]he evidence seems clear that . . . our farms and small towns are being abandoned in a great movement into an urban way of life. At the same time the city, in the sense of a tightly-knit corporate community with a clear distinction between its high-density living and the rural countryside, is fast becoming so blurred at the edges as to be incapable of operational definition. There seems little to block an endless expansion of urban or semi-urban ways of life over vast areas of the countryside outside our traditional city limits. Instead of distinct cities with distinguishable centers and edges somewhat like a fried egg, we seem likely to be approaching in large segments of our country a condition somewhat like that of a thin layer of scrambled eggs spread over much of the platter. The more urban we become, the more shaky become both the concept and the reality of the city.

[17] Charles R. Adrian, "Metropology: Folklore and Field Research," *Public Administration Review*, XXI (Summer, 1961), 155.

LEWIS MUMFORD

In Defense of the City

When I speak of the future of the city, I refer not to what is probable and therefore predictable, but to what is possible; and not merely to what is possible, but to what, out of the entire range of possibilities, is valuable and desirable.

No single future looms before us as inescapable — but rather a number of conceivable futures, depending upon the actual situation we confront from year to year, the way we read our statistical data, the way we evaluate our experience, the extent to which we collectively apply our intelligence and imagination to the problems before us, and the purposes which we value and seek to carry out.

Statistics often provide essential information, provided we treat them for what they are worth. But in attempting to envisage future alternatives in urban development, I take statistical predictions as road guides that indicate what will happen if we go further, at the same pace, on the same route: not as commands to continue on this road if we find by consulting the map that we are headed in the wrong direction.

When statistics reveal, as they do even in Europe, that the private motor car as a complete substitute for public transportation will soon destroy the city, I take that probability very seriously indeed. But as I observed recently to some friends in Oxford, who are facing this disastrous eruption of traffic and the disruption of their city, this information says to me: "On guard! The city, and all that uniquely belongs to the city, is in danger. This invasion of vehicles threatens

Reprinted from *University, A Princeton Quarterly,* No. 24 (Spring 1965), pp. 10-13, © Princeton University 1965, where it appeared under the title "On Guard! The City Is in Danger!," with the permission of the author and the publisher.

your very existence as a University. But thanks to our timely intelligence, we are still in command of the situation: Let us mount a counterattack!"

Too many people, unfortunately, regard statistical information as the implacable voice of the Inevitable. To them the same facts say: "The situation is hopeless. Prepare for unconditional surrender to the motor car. But let us continue to use it to flee from the city into an ever remoter exurban wilderness." That is a counsel of despair and a needless submission to barbarism.

Many of the plans before us for modernizing and rebuilding our cities take all the most negative and threatening features of our civilization and proclaim the new form of life: Progressive, avant garde, automatic, computer-directed life: the pseudo-life of the Space Age. In this lovely age only an infinitesimal minority will, it is true, be able to afford the multimillion dollar ride in a rocket to the moon, and only licensed lunatics would dream of mounting a mass colonization to another planet, but each of us will be able to afford at least a modest, static, substitute capsule: air-conditioned, hermetically sealed, equipped with teaching machines, feeding machines, fun machines, insulated against direct human contact of any sort, either with the natural environment or with other people. Only so much of the outside world will filter into this capsule as can be brought under central control.

Perhaps this sounds like the crudest sort of caricature of our age, or the one we are rapidly heading for; but it is quite impossible to caricature that coming age: what might even ten years ago have seemed fanciful Wellsian exaggerations are now accurate descriptions. How can one exaggerate the absurdity of a proposed skyscraper a mile high, a tedious technological stunt that has no relation to any serious human function except technology — even though this particular stunt was unhappily the last infirmity of the most creative mind in modern architecture? How can one exaggerate the emptiness of the most powerful model for a new city that captured the megalopolitan imagination all over the planet — Le Corbusier's Voisin plan for the renovation of Paris introduced more than forty years ago? That plan proposed to wipe out the historic center of Paris, leaving a few pathetic relics to serve as comfort stations for the spirit, in order to replace it with a grid of tall office buildings floating in a parking lot, misnamed a park. With no sense of the city's significant complexity, that plan proposed to extirpate all the multitu-

dinous details of real life and every historical association, for the
sake of enshrining in empty space an ever-emptier mode of bureaucratic life. Yet this particular image of the city has proved so thoroughly acceptable to the spirit of our time, its financial aims, its
bureaucratic procedures, its regimented daily routines, that glossy
replicas of Le Corbusier's original dream are now visible everywhere: too often disguised as urban renewal.

The city is an historic entity; an entity that arose originally, on my
interpretation, through the coalescence and fusion of certain archetypal political and religious institutions (the palace and temple)
which at an early date found expression in a characteristic nuclear
form that is still dimly visible.

Urbanization, on the other hand, is merely the process of creating
close human settlements, buildings and roads — any kind of building,
any kind of road — in an environment that thereby becomes increasingly unsuited to the pursuit of rural occupations like hunting, fish-
ing, farming, gardening. You have only to contrast Princeton, which
though small in size has many of the identifying marks of a city, with
the vast amorphous urbanoid wasteland that stretches between
Camden and Jersey City, to perceive this essential difference. Urbanization could go on coagulating indefinitely, as the sociologist, Jean
Gottmann, expects it to go on, without once creating a city; and even
though Dr. Gottmann has affixed a name to this sprawling urbanized
nonentity, calling it "megalopolis," it is still not a polis or a city in
even the loosest and most superficial sense of that term. To apply
the term city to such an unstructured mass is to increase the deplor-
able mental confusion we are now in. Whatever megalopolis may be,
it is not the new form of the city.

Cities, when considered with respect to their physical structure
alone, are different in shape and size and function more or less in the
way that a human being differs as he passes through the stages of
embryo, infant, child, adolescent, adult, and senescent — though by
far the greater number of communities have been arrested at some
point in this process, since until now four-fifths of the population of
the planet lived in villages. And though the words hamlet, village,
town and metropolis have some reference to this quantitative difference, the further qualitative stages in development and integration
have, for lack of attention, been left vague, as if Medicean Florence
and Trenton were comparable because they were about the same
size.

The fact is that one key characteristic of the city is variety: Variety of biological and cultural stocks, variety of wants, variety of opportunities, variety of institutions, variety of fulfillments. Where variety is absent, the city does not exist. Though it contain a million inhabitants it is still culturally and socially a village.

There is not in fact a *single* so-called urban function that has not been practiced successfully outside the city, in villages, manors, and monasteries. Many seemingly characteristic urban institutions, in fact, began like the theater in a purely rural environment. *The unique office of the city, the one thing that cannot be delegated to any other institution, is precisely the assemblage of the single parts into a new kind of structure.*

Togetherness, then, is the essence of the city's life: it concentrates, as no single other institution can do, the opportunities for human association and intercourse, multiplying challenges and encounters, widening the area of two-way communication and unspoken communion, making present and visible, in the transaction of daily affairs, the realities of human cooperation.

But our actual cities have forfeited many of these characteristics: our biggest cities have become, through congestion and disorganization and dispersion, the very negation of urban virtues: deserts of loneliness, thwarted humanity, social frustration and insensate violence; and much of this same empty disordered life has been handed on even to smaller centers. This grim spectacle only makes it the more necessary to understand what the historic role of the city has actually been and what we are rapidly forfeiting, perhaps forever.

By drawing different cultures, occupations, biological strains, and resources into a single center, the first cities performed a tremendous act of cultural hybridization, whose human consequences were comparable to the domestication of plants and animals. The unique, emergent function of the city, and increasingly now the main reason for its existence, is the continued enlargement, storage and transmission of an ever larger portion of the cultural heritage. Not merely the symbolic heritage of science and art, not merely what can be written or carved or painted or built, but likewise what must be transmitted directly, by word of mouth, from teacher to student, from craftsman to apprentice, from priest or prophet to disciple, or just from man to man.

The city is people, as the late Henry Churchill properly insisted: but people joined together in a special, intimate way: face-to-face in an environment that favors differences and stimulates a never-ending dialogue; people in what Martin Buber calls the I-and-Thou relationship: people who are no longer simply agents or servants or slaves, or specialists or experts, but who have become real persons, and who, to the extent that they are persons, can no longer be manipulated or controlled by purely external pressure or physical compulsions.

But if the forces that dominate our affluent society go on increasing at the present rate, the city will soon be extinct: extinct, that is, as a meeting place for minds, as the setting for a constant human dialogue, as a stage on which the drama of life, in both its private and its public forms, can be enacted, with a symbolic heightening and magnification of all its meanings and values.

Fortunately the very violence of the forces attacking the city may itself at last be enough to provoke a healthy reaction. The hope for a rebirth of the city rests mainly on a growing realization that there is no electronic substitute for the city; and that no mere flight from the city by either private families or corporate industries will in fact save anything.

Beneath this hope lies the perception that, though both villages and cities are being swallowed up and obliterated by megalopolis today, this cannot go on indefinitely without undermining the very forces that are working against the city. In the end even the most effective and heavily supported parts of our civilization, science and technics, will suffer from general human malnutrition.

Much that is vital to the humanization of man in society has already been lost in our time; and in another generation it will become evident that no culture so rich and complex as ours today can be run by insulated suburban minds, constrained to live, for lack of the resources only a city can offer, mainly on one-generation knowledge. Our huge cultural heritage cannot be transmitted through the dismembered fragments of the city that are being scattered about our vast conurbations (to use a deliberately ugly term coined by Patrick Geddes half a century ago) even though batteries of computers and tape recorders and two-way television transmitters attempt, in the costliest and most clumsy fashion possible, to assemble, fitfully and temporarily, the component parts.

Slowly, it is beginning to dawn on everyone that the prospect of living without the aid of the city is too dismal and unprofitable to be faced. Ideally the city remains man's best invention for overcoming both segregation in time and segregation in space. And at the same moment, it is becoming equally plain that the dehumanized forms of the city, expressed in the fashionable stereotypes of contemporary architecture, need no longer be tolerated as symbols of human progress, since they are in fact a regression to mechanical barbarism and human desolation.

The future of the city depends upon a general awakening to the importance of urban life, as essential if we are to rebuild any common life at all, and equally essential, for that matter, if we are to preserve the genuine values of the countryside. Without an intense revitalization of the essential functions of the city, without a reassemblage of its human and institutional parts, urbanization will lower the whole level of life. Such an awakening to urban probabilities and possibilities is, I believe, coming about. Let me conclude by giving three small but significant examples.

The fashionable academic word for what is now going on is "feedback": a word that has a mystical aura because it is derived from computer analysis; but in plain human terms it means a process, common to all organisms, of overcoming faulty behavior by becoming sufficiently aware of it to try something else. Feedback is taking place now because an increasing number of people, other than criminals or beatniks, are aware that life on the terms that it is now offered them — that is, a fake life, or half-life, expansive and expensive as conceived on Madison Avenue — is not sufficiently rewarding. Feedback is what makes any confident statistical extrapolation of the past into the future look foolish, almost before it has gotten into print. Even the dire population explosion already bears witness to feedback: first on a massive scale in Japan, but more astonishingly, when one considers how little preparation people have had for it, in the State of New York, where the rate of increase already has begun to go downward.

Now feedback was at work when the citizens of San Francisco brought a halt to the highway engineers' project for engirdling and choking off their whole waterfront with an expressway; and it went even more significantly into operation when the citizens of the Bay Region voted for the restoration of public rapid transit, because they had discovered that the daily crawl to work by private car had become too tedious and too unpleasant to be endured for a whole lifetime.

All over the country now there are signs of a genuine urban feedback: even the reclamation of Washington Square by the embattled Greenwich Villagers was a more significant triumph than people

generally realize, because the local community defied the whole
system of bureaucratic control by talking back and compelling the
authorities to listen and, despite Robert Moses, to give in. This talking back is precisely what the city exists to further. So, too, the citizens of New Jersey, who saved their own communities and the great
swamp area nearby from the presumptuous jetport plans of the Port
of New York Authority, likewise showed that at least in the older
suburbs of Northern New Jersey some of the residual forces that belong to the city still exist.

And finally, as signs of a new attitude toward the recognition of
the city's essential functions, and of the need to take positive steps
for overcoming the dynamic disintegration whose other name is
megalopolis, I would cite two planning reports that have come out
this past year. The more modest in scope, by Professors McHarg
and Wallace of the University of Pennsylvania, demonstrates bril-
liantly how an ecological balance between the rural environment
and an increasing urban population may be maintained by a reorganization of both public and private agencies. This report grap-
ples with the essential problem of our civilization: the control of
quantity by quality, of urbanization by community integration, of
process by purpose. The other report is that brought out by the
Office for Regional Development of the State of New York, a branch
of the executive. This report definitely turns its back upon continued
megalopolitan dispersion: it proposes, rather, to divide the State into
ten natural and cultural regions, each with its metropolitan center,
each with a network of smaller towns and villages grouped around
it; each seeking to maintain a permanent balance between city and
countryside, while enlarging the area of close urban intercourse. No
megalopolis there!

The State of California has taken an even greater potential step
toward the rebuilding of the city as the essential organ of human
culture and human continuity: though so far they have badly muffed
the opportunity they themselves have created. Many years ago the
University of California, threatened with overgrowth in Berkeley,
created a second university in Los Angeles. By now this process of
colonization has led to the foundation of eight other University Centers, each of which is potentially the center of either a new city or
an old small town that might, through the presence of the university,
take on all the functions of a great city. Despite San Francisco's
good example, California is still unfortunately largely in the hands

of arrogant highway engineers, who prefer cloverleaves to the natural landscape and vaster parking lots to smaller cities. But a great civic opportunity beckons there: the embryo of a new kind of city, which shall have the capacity to embrace and enhance all the potential goods of our civilization, has already been conceived.

All these I take to be good signs for the future of the city, but I would not minimize the huge difficulties that confront us. The forces making for the disintegration and destruction of the city are highly dynamic, while more constructive organic processes, because of their very complexity, operate more slowly, and require more conscious effort and more intelligent cooperation. But perhaps the most hopeful thing about the present situation is that we are at last, though all too belatedly and all too slowly, beginning to wake up: to realize that we *need* the city: that there is no mechanical or electronic substitute for it: Our task is not easy, for we must now rebuild the city from the bottom up, beginning with the neighborhood and its special needs, and proceeding thence to the ultimate organization of a great regional grid, whose units will be individual, and highly individualized, cities. At the same time, we must consciously resist the forces that are producing megalopolis, and we must challenge those who would turn the city into a disposable container, a kind of temporary auxiliary to the parking lot and the highway interchange.

When we once realize that what is probable has become humanly impossible, then all those changes which are possible and desirable will become probable.

RAYMOND VERNON

Urban Change and Public Opinion

As the 20th century opened, the number of people in America's urban areas who could afford to buy living space was growing at a tremendous pace. New streets and speculative subdivisions were opening up at the edges of every big city as fast as the curbing could be put into place. Electric trolley lines were appearing all over the country, complete with parks at the end of the run to generate the week-end traffic. America's cities were spreading out.

The new subdivisions, it is true, continued to shun the extravagant use of land. The automobile, after all, was still a novelty and most breadwinners had to assume that their daily trek to office, store, or factory would begin with a walk to the nearest public conveyance. So the style of the era continued to be the three- or four-story tenement, the triple decker, the row house, or the private dwelling on a handkerchief-sized lot.

As we follow this middle-income group through the decades of the 20th century, we see an almost continuous process of movement. By the 1920's, some of the more adventurous settlers at the edges of the urban mass were beginning to take the automobile into account as a fixed feature of their existence. By that time, some were willing to choose their living space on the assumption that they would ride, not walk, to a trolley or train; or, more daring still, that the trip to the office, plant, or store would be made regularly by car. As a result, building sites became much more plentiful — more plentiful in the sense that larger areas became accessible to the urban mass. Sub-

Reprinted from *The Myth and Reality of Our Urban Problems* (Cambridge: Joint Center for Urban Studies of the Massachusetts Institute of Technology and Harvard University, 1962), pp. 14-31, with the permission of the author and the publisher.

divisions began to break away from the public transportation lines and locate in open country. With the car becoming an indispensable part of the family's possessions, more households elected to live in private homes, even in areas where the prevailing style up to that time had been the multifamily dwelling.

The 1930's, though a period of depression, postponed marriages, and undersized families, still saw a continuation of the trend. The craving of most people for a place of their own in the suburbs was reflected in Federal programs, such as the FHA guaranteed-mortgage program, to meet the financing problems of home-buying. Hand in hand went the proliferation of consumer credit devices to ease the purchase of the ubiquitous family car and all the other hard goods of the home owner.

The period after World War II witnessed an even swifter acceleration of the trend. Now, single-family dwelling units were overwhelmingly important in the new construction undertaken each year within the big urban areas of the country. There were, of course, exceptions to the pattern — exceptions which make much more impact on the eye than on the cold and impersonal statistical totals. Each year, some tens of thousands of dwelling units in new low-cost public housing structures were built for operation under government subsidy. Each year, too, there were some hundreds of thousands more of private apartment units, though some involved land-acquisition subsidies or credit subsidies from one arm or another of government. But the overwhelming bulk of new housing in the post-war period was the ranch-house-in-the-suburb, in one variant or another, complete with one- or two-car garage.

America's middle-income group seems hungry for land — for quarter acres, half acres, or more, well removed from the crowded urban centers where their parents may have lived. And the nation has managed to provide them with the land they seem to want, by a process which can continue to go on for quite some time to come. The spreading national system of highways and superhighways has had two effects on the supply of land. First, of course, it has placed more land in reach of the urban mass — that is, within a radius of the thirty or forty minutes which most people seem prepared to spend in going from home to work. Thirty minutes, after all, was two miles to a swift and steady walker, and eight or ten miles on a speedy electric trolley; and it now represents 15 to 25 miles of distance on the road system of the 1960's.

At the same time, the highways have had a profound effect on the land-using propensities of the farmers who surround the big cities. As the roads drew the cities closer to the land, the farmers discovered that hired help was getting costly; either help could not be had at all in the periods of planting and harvest or else it was demanding a wage equivalent to that offered in the city nearby. So the farmers at the edges of most urban areas began to make adjustments to their new problems. Some gave up serious farming and lived on the sale of land parcels to the city folk. Others altered the lines of agriculture in which they were engaged; they abandoned their land-extensive pursuits such as raising grain and grass and began to feed their cooped-up cows and chickens with commercial feeds. Considerable acreage reverted to scrub pine and weedy pasture, awaiting the day when the suburban developer would appear.

As a result, though developers grouse about the mounting cost of land, no dearth of land has developed around the margins of the big urban masses. No dearth has developed, that is, if we take into account the fact that every urban area now can reach much further outward along its various spokes than was possible a decade or two ago. True, neighborhoods that were once potato fields are now covered with the spread of urban growth. But the land taken up each year with the new split-level, the Cape Cod, the Colonial, and the ranch house amounts to less acreage in most parts of the country than the added land made congruent to the urban mass by the improvement of the highway system.

And there is no reason to suppose that this process is at an end. Here and there, the edge of some urban area may merge with the spreading reaches of another, or may back up into some natural barrier such as a mountain range or seaside. But for a quarter century or more, the land around Boston, New York, Chicago, Washington, Philadelphia, St. Louis, and most of the other great urban clusters of the country will easily absorb their growing populations.

The process of spread which we have been at such pains to describe in the last few paragraphs has not merely affected the growing edges of the urban mass. It has also had its effects — profound effects — on the older neighborhoods left behind inside the mass. In simple terms, the children with middle-class incomes have chosen not to live where their parents lived; they have chosen not to refurbish their parents' homes, even if their parents enjoyed an income level not unlike their own in its relative position on the national income ladder. As a result, one can detect a cycle which appears again and again in many older middle-class neighborhoods. The new compact neighborhod of 1920, filled with its close-drawn homes of young families, has now become 30 or 40 years old. The children have grown up and departed, but the older folks have stayed on. The sidewalks have heaved and cracked over the roots of overgrown trees; the shrubbery has got out of hand; the lawns have been choked off by the heavy shade; the retail trade of the neighborhood, living off the declining purchases of the aging households, has begun to shrivel.

Why? Why have the children not stayed on, trimming the shrubbery, wielding the brush and paintpot, maintaining the walks, and providing themselves with decent shelter at half the price? The answers are not obscure. For one thing, the middle-income family today enjoys a real income which is close to double the absolute level of 30 or 40 years ago. It can afford two cars where its parents had one; a dozen electric appliances in lieu of a day worker; a television set instead of a neighborhood movie. Could the old house have been made to do for these needs? Sometimes, yes; more often, no. No, partly because the old houses were set up on plots so small that space for the second car — or the first one for that matter, as long as it sported the tailfins of the 1950's — could not have been provided on the site.

But another factor has discouraged the refurbishing of the older houses — the fact that the cost of skilled labor comes so high in the United States, as an unavoidable by-product of our high productivity and high living standards. This last point is worth a moment's more consideration. The cost of wiring a new home for the heavy electrical loads of modern living sometimes amounts to a good deal less than the cost of rewiring an old one to carry modern loads. The cost of installing the sleek, aseptic trim of the 1960's in a newly constructed house is less than the price of ripping out and replacing the dustcatcher moldings and Dutch shelves of the 1920's. To steam the ancient paper off crumbling plaster a third-of-a-century old, to patch, size, and repaint the walls, costs more than the pristine decoration of the newbuilt home. In short, in a nation whose economy places a heavy price on hand labor and a low price on materials, the cost of repairs and remodelling can easily outrun the cost of new construction. Like economic men, therefore, the children of the middle class have moved to the modernity of the split-level-in-the-suburbs, leaving many of the older middle-income neighborhoods to stagnate or decline.

This process of spread, to be sure, might not have gone on forever if the jobs of our metropolitan areas had not evidenced a similar tendency to spread outward. The reasons for this spread of jobs are not hard to find. Of every twenty jobs in urban areas, about four are in the consumer trade lines and another five or six in local governments, local utilities, local business or professional services, and local construction; these jobs, making up about half the urban labor force, more or less automatically follow the drift of the population as it spreads outward from the old city.

The other half of the job market is subject to a more complicated calculus of location. In a word, however, most of the labor force employed in manufacturing — the lighter manufacturing plants as well as the abattoirs and chemical plants — have joined the outward move. The kind of site required for the modern space-hungry plant simply cannot be found in the older portions of an urban area. The time-cost and money-cost involved in assembling an industrial site in some ossified district already encumbered by structures are extremely high — so high as to make that kind of operation simply out of the question, at least without summary public powers and extensive public subsidy. And even when public powers and the public subsidy are at hand, they are not swift enough or flexible enough or generous enough to match the offerings of private land on the outskirts.

Besides, with the advent of the truck, the erstwhile attraction of the railroads and rivers for industrial plants has grown weaker. With the ubiquitous use of the automobile, the labor force of the city no longer offers a unique attraction to the factory employer. Power, water, and sewage can now be had over much wider areas, a by-product of the spread of the homes. So industry has followed the trek to the suburbs, gobbling up land at the rate of about ten employees to the acre.

In fact only one major cluster of employment has resisted the outward move. This is the complex of frenetic economic activities . . . whose elite are overwhelmed with uncertainties, demanding face-to-face communication, and dependent for their effective operation upon swift access to various other enterprises. Most of these activities are in offices, some are in showrooms, and some are in manufacturing lofts. All told, they account for perhaps one-fifth of the urban areas' labor force and represent the critical nub of employment in the central business districts of most major cities.

Even in these activities, however, one can see a certain loosening of ties to the old city center. After all, the needs for swift and easy access and face-to-face communication do not apply to more than a tiny fraction of the office workers in the downtown area. In fact, the locational needs of the average stenographer or billing clerk can scarcely be said to differ very much from the locational needs of the mechanic or warehouseman. The unique requirements of many offices are confined to the office elite — to the vice president and treasurer, to the sales manager, the house counsel, and so on.

As offices have grown, therefore, and as the line of authority between the billing clerks and the treasurer has become more and more attenuated, one company after another has reconsidered whether the billing department and functions like it ought to remain in the central business district. Here and there, the decision has been made to peel off some of these functions and to locate them in the suburbs.

The trend to suburban locations for the billing clerks, if not the bosses, has been accelerated by two factors. One has been the appearance of the first generation of young women who drive cars more naturally than they walk; to recruit a workforce of young women office workers it is no longer necessary to sit astride a public transportation facility. The second factor has been the growing remoteness of the daughters of the middle class from the old city centers. In weighing the attractiveness of alternative job opportunities, a significant fraction of these young women have preferred a job in the suburbs near home to one in the more remote, albeit more ebullient, city centers.

As far as the middle class is concerned, therefore, there has been little to impede the outward movement of homes and jobs. Both have drifted outward, sometimes for independent reasons, sometimes as a mutually reinforcing phenomenon. Except for the minority — the declining minority — who work in the central business district, travel from home to office is probably no more difficult for the middle class than it was twenty years ago. There is nothing to suggest that the outward drift of the middle class will not continue. There is no rubber band being stretched to the breaking point, no growing pressure which cannot be contained.

For the poor of the urban areas, the story of the last fifty or sixty years has been rather different. Each urban area has had its own particular brand of poor, each stamped with some ill-fitting mass label. In the South and West, the cities have housed large numbers of Mexicans and Oakies; in the Southeast and Midwest, hillbillies and southern Negroes; on the Eastern Seaboard, Italians and Jews from Eastern Europe, then Puerto Ricans and more southern Negroes.

Each immigrant group has developed on a slightly different pattern from any other. Nonetheless, most immigrants have made a swift adjustment to their new urban life. When I say "swift," however, I am speaking in terms of decades, not of years. In the first decade or so, it has been enough for most newcomers to cling to the slim security of friends and relatives, and to take the hand-me-downs in jobs and living space that came along. Typically, therefore, these groups have settled on the edges of the neighborhoods where they first found shelter and have taken jobs that their friends have found for them.

By the first part of the 20th century, . . . the newcomers had little choice but to settle in the oldest parts of the older cities. Barred from shacktowns in the suburbs, they crowded such structures as had been already surrendered by the middle class in the older neighborhoods. Incredible living densities were recorded in some cities; in New York, where such densities were at their highest, some 300,000 people could be found living in one square mile of lower Manhattan.

But neighborhoods such as these did not retain their peak densities for many years. After a time, they began to show population declines. For if the parents could abide such brutal crowding, the children could not. So the children of the poor, like the children of the middle class, moved on, leaving their parents to luxuriate in the moldering space of the ancient neighborhoods. Some of the offspring acquired income sufficient to buy new housing, and became a part of the extensive middle-income group. Others used their growing knowledge of the city to ferret out less ancient structures, structures which in turn were at the stage of being surrendered by the middle class.

In many large cities, therefore, the location of the most notorious slum neighborhood of today is different from that of a generation ago. More likely than not, the current slum is in a "newer" portion of the city. The chances are very high, too, that it is rather less crowded. In addition, it is typically less compact and covers a good deal more acreage than the slums of a generation or two ago.

It is in this last characteristic — the extensive acreage covered by the modern slum — that we find one key to the heightened public interest in the slum phenomenon. As long as the slum was contained in a small congested mass within the old center of the city, most of the middle- and upper-income inhabitants of the urban area could live out their lives without being acutely aware of its existence. As the slum-dweller has taken to less dense living, however, the manifestations of his existence have not been quite so easy to suppress. In more recent decades, slum neighborhoods have come to ring the business districts of the city and have even begun to reach out into the less congested fringes of some urban areas. As they have reached out into the newer areas, their march has driven the middle-income groups before them, giving still more space to the poor. In some degree, therefore, the poor have created their own housing supply, simply by ostentatiously bidding for it.

The latest phase of this outward spread of low-income families is one which is especially calculated to draw attention to their existence. In this phase, low-income families have begun to discover that structures ripe for downgrading are to be found not only in the ancient central city of the urban mass but in nearby suburban towns as well. Sometimes these are suburban towns with an old industrial core of their own; but sometimes they are residential satellites, built for the rail- or trolley-riding commuters of 1900 or 1910, with a supply of obsolete housing just about ready for the low-income market. Discovering these caches of obsolescent structures, low-income families have begun to appear in little ghettoes in some of the most "exclusive" suburban communities of the country. The signs of their coming are evident from a close reading of the 1960 population census data, which show widespread population declines in the slum areas of the old cities and substantial increases among the identifiable low-income groups in many suburban cities. And this is only the beginning.

The spread of the low-income groups outward from the old city center has been sparked not only by the spread of obsolescent housing but also by the redistribution of low-income jobs. As a rule, the jobs of the low-income groups have consisted of common labor on streets and docks, stevedoring in warehouses, factories, or yards, and menial help in the consumer trades. Practically every sector of employment in which low-wage labor has predominated is to be found drifting outward away from the old slum neighborhoods. The warehouses, factories, and consumer trades have followed the trend; and while the docks have remained anchored to their waterside locations, they have been giving up their economic function to trucking terminals located further out from the center. The low-income groups, therefore, have been faced with a growing need to keep up with their peripatetic jobs.

It is evident, however, that many have not yet looked for newer living space or have not succeeded in their search. This grows apparent as one views the changes in the commuting streams that are beginning to appear in many cities. Outcommuting — the movement each morning of people from homes in the center portions of the urban area to jobs on the periphery — is growing fast. The spectacle of groups of blue-collar workers, travelling outward by car pool against the flow of incoming traffic, is now a common sight on the roads of many large cities. In fact, the spotty and fragmentary information of this phenomenon suggests that it may be one of the fastest-growing streams of traffic among the complex currents of our urban areas.

As far as the low-income groups are concerned, therefore, one sees a process of a constant turnover, a constant pushing outward to take possession of the housing hand-me-downs of the middle-income group. This is the trickle-down theory of progress in its most graphic form.

Distasteful as the trickle-down theory may be in the abstract, it seems to have worked in some measure to improve the housing of the poor in recent years. Between the 1950 housing census and the 1956 housing census, the number of so-called "substandard dwellings" in our major urban areas underwent a rather considerable decline. Of course, statistics which purport to measure any such abstraction as "substandard housing" are rarely invulnerable; and so it is with these. But there is no serious doubt that there has been a substantial upgrading in the housing stock available to the poor as the middle-income groups have fled to the suburbs from the advancing salients of the poor. In those urban areas where new home construction has been highest, the upgrading has been most apparent. As an added measure of the improving situation for the poor, the number of available vacancies in the major urban areas also seems to have gone up rather considerably between the two housing censuses.

In our concentration upon the *trend* in housing for the poor, however, we must never lose sight of the *level*. One needs only his eyes, his nose, and a willingness to walk through the slums of America's great cities to be aware that we are many leagues away from the goal of tolerable housing for all Americans. Besides, the disconcerting statistics of the 1956 housing census remind us that Negroes and other recognizable minority groups are suffering from a systematic economic discrimination in the housing market, paying more for comparable space than white families. On top of all this, the aspirations of the low-income groups may well be expanding faster than their actual living conditions.

Nonetheless, it is important to be aware that the trend is not clearly retrogressive. Once more there is no clear evidence of the taut stretching of a rubber band close to its breaking point, no indication of the building up of pressure to levels which the political vessel can no longer contain.

The medium-income group and the poor, according to our argument, have made some kind of adjustment to the changing urban structure. But the well-to-do — that small but critically important group which is in a position to pay whatever may be demanded for the living space it desires — seem not to have fared as well.

At the turn of the century, . . . the well-to-do urban dweller had a number of satisfactory living choices. One possibility was to take a mansion on Fifth Avenue, the Gold Coast, Nob Hill, or Rittenhouse Square. Here, one could have propinquity to the office and the theater, the easy use of the city streets in the evening or on weekends, and only a minimum of exposure to the relatively localized and compact slums. Alternatively — or in addition — one could maintain a home in an exclusive suburb, barely thirty or forty minutes from an office in the central city by way of the new suburban trains.

In the past fifty or sixty years, however, these comparatively idyllic arrangements have gradually been threatened. As the mansions of the downtown areas have grown obsolete, it has not been easy to replace them with equally adequate quarters in the same neighborhoods. Apartment houses, office buildings, parking lots, and slums have swallowed up the accessible land; and even if money was no object, in a country in which the Protestant ethic still prevails it would be unconscionable to pay $500,000 or so for a site on which to locate a private residence.

Besides, the city streets were no longer quite so easily used in off-hours. The middle class was gradually abandoning the use of mass transit as a means of off-hour travel in the central business district and was crowding the downtown streets with private cars and taxicabs. The slums were gradually ringing the central business district in neighborhoods many miles deep. The possibility of a mansion in town was no longer anywhere nearly as attractive as it had been in America's Age of Innocence.

At the same time, the exclusive suburban location was falling prey to another kind of outside pressure. The inexorable tide of the middle class was surrounding the elite suburb, infiltrating the empty land where it could, crowding the little shopping centers, undermining the air of exclusivity and remoteness which had once prevailed.

There were two escapes available to the well-to-do, and they availed themselves of both. One was to abandon the town house for the exclusive flat in an expensive apartment house. In many big cities, therefore, elaborate apartments began to appear in or very near the central business district — overlooking a park or a river, or dominating a hill. This compromise was not an altogether felicitous one, of course. Though it allowed the rich to remain close to offices and theaters, it did not deal with the problems of comfort and security on the public streets.

Another alternative — one especially attractive to families with children — has been to flee from the sound of the subdivision steamshovel into even more remote settlements in the country. Instead of spending 30 or 40 minutes on the daily suburban trains to downtown offices, the well-to-do have taken to spending an hour or more on their way to or from the office. To heap difficulty on difficulty, the services of the suburban trains . . . have deteriorated in quality and frequency.

These problems might have been mitigated in some degree if the jobs of the elite, like the jobs of the middle-income groups and the poor, had shown any tendency to move out rapidly toward the suburbs. Some, of course, did. A number of insurance companies and a few large central offices, responding to the pressures of their commuting executives, moved from their downtown locations to more felicitous surroundings in the suburbs. For the most part, however, the compulsion of executives to remain in the central business district has been very strong. The delicate problems of face-to-face communication to which we earlier referred have prevented them from moving very far from the tight-woven mass of which they are a part. Typically, therefore, the executive suites of the large manufacturing enterprises, the advertising agencies, the banks, and the law firms have remained firmly anchored to the central business district.

There is still another reason why the plight of the central city is calculated to draw more response from the elite of the urban area than from the rank and file of the middle-income groups or of the poor. In every major city, there is a group of substantial business interests which are immobilized in the city — prevented from sharing in the swifter rates of suburban growth. Under many state laws, the chartered banks of the central city are prohibited from opening branches freely in the suburbs. In other cases, the public utilities of the central city are prevented from extending their franchises into the suburbs. In still others, department stores with heavy investments sunk in their central city locations are eyeing with concern the need to make new investments in the growing suburban areas. And there are cases, as well, in which central city newspapers fear an irretrievable loss of circulation and advertising from the drift of homes and jobs to outside locations. One can safely predict, therefore, how the articulate and influential elite of the urban areas is likely to react to the problem of increasing remoteness between the central business district and the suburbs.

The attachment of the rich to the central city, however, is not based solely upon the need for shortening the journey-to-work or upon business interest. At least in equal measure, the attachment derives from sentiment, tradition, and avocational ties. These latter are made up of many strands. One, for instance, is the uniqueness of the institutions to which the rich tend to belong. Few urban areas can support more than one Harvard Club, one Council on Foreign Relations, one Union Club. Given only one such institution in the area, its location is bound to be at the center of the urban mass. In this respect, therefore, the rich who want both the exclusivity of the suburbs and propinquity to their clubs are less well-situated than the middle class who can find their bowling league, their VFW post, or their bridge club reproduced in any suburban area close to home.

Another strand in the tie to the central city is created by the role of the rich as supporters of the cultural activities of the city. No list of sponsors for the leading orchestra or the leading art museum of any urban area fails to include a generous sampling of the leading families. Often the sponsorship goes back in an uninterrupted chain over many generations. Once again, therefore, the rich are the victims of the urban area's spread, pulling them from the neighborhoods in which their absorbing interests lie.

To understand today's growing literature of protest against the metropolis, however, we have to take cognizance of the reactions of elite who do not derive their status from wealth. They are typified, perhaps caricatured, by the man who, when asked why he felt the need to settle in a metropolis of seven or eight million, said with all sincerity and accuracy, "I need seven or eight million from whom to select my 70 or 80 friends." They are people who find the mass media and the mass forms of amusement inadequate for their needs. Commonly, they include the individuals who are more than casual onlookers in their relation to the cultural institutions peculiar to the established city — the museum, the symphony orchestra, the art galleries, the foreign policy clubs, the social workers' organizations, the public hospitals. Sometimes they are not well-to-do. And when they are not, their bitterness against the spread of the urban areas is greatest of all. For they do not have the ability of the rich to maintain propinquity to their interests in the city by buying luxury downtown space.

Add to these groups the influential sectors of the opinion-forming elite of the community: the political organizations, built up on a carefully developed structure of city political clubs; the older church parishes, rich in tradition, yet reliant for their support on neighborhood parishioners; the director of the symphony orchestra, the curator of the public or private museum, the superintendent of the adult education program. The wonder of it is that the cry for the preservation of the old city or for improved access to its center is not even louder and more insistent than it is.

And yet, if my analysis has any validity at all, we may have an answer to the riddle of the curious passivity of America to its urban problems. To most Americans, the personal experience of urban living seems not one of personal retrogression but of continuous improvement. By moving out of the slag heaps of the worked-out city, they have improved their surroundings sufficient for a generation. The worries of a Riesman, the strivings of a Mumford, are inarticulate, scarce-comprehensible murmurings. Let the central city weep; let the sociologists fume; except for such intractable problems as death, war, and taxes, things are getting slightly better all the time.

JOHN H. STRANGE

Racial Segregation in the Metropolis

Despite the promise of the New Frontier and the Great Society, racial segregation is rapidly *increasing* in our largest metropolitan areas. This segregation is being institutionalized and legalized as the Negroes move to the central cities and the whites move to the suburbs. There is little indication that the political system of the metropolis will alter this pattern of growth; nor is it likely to provide solutions for the growing problems facing minority groups in our cities.

Population Growth:
The Emerging Racial Segregation

Between 1950 and 1960 the metropolitan population increased by 26.4 percent. Most of this increase occurred in the largest metropolitan areas. Twenty-four standard metropolitan statistical areas, each with more than a million population in 1960, accounted for 43 percent of the metropolitan population growth. This growth produced a significant change in the racial composition of the metropolis. In central cities the Negro population mounted rapidly, increasing by over 50 percent, while the growth in the white population was less than 5 percent. During this decade almost a million and a half whites left the central cities in the 24 largest metropolitan areas, while the Negro population *increased* by over two million persons (Table 1).

As a consequence, the Negro proportion of the population has increased in almost every central city in the country, and in the central cities of the 24 largest metropolitan areas many of the increases

This article was prepared for this volume.

TABLE 1

POPULATION CHANGE BETWEEN 1930 AND 1960 IN THE
24 LARGEST STANDARD METROPOLITAN STATISTICAL
AREAS IN 1960, BY RACE, YEAR AND RESIDENCE

CENTER CITY	1930-40	Percent of Increase Non-white	1940-50	Percent of Increase Non-white	1950-60	Percent of Increase Non-white
Whites	+ 884,000		+1,474,000		−1,459,000	
Negroes	+ 455,000		+1,457,000		+2,145,000	
Total*	+1,347,000	34%	+2,990,000	49%	+ 843,000	100%
OUTSIDE CENTER CITY						
Whites	+1,787,000		+5,264,000		+10,667,000	
Negroes	+ 75,000		+ 294,000		+ 343,000	
Total*	+1,867,000	04%	+5,556,000	05%	+11,092,000	03%
TOTAL METRO-POLITAN AREA						
INCREASE	+3,214,000	17%	+8,547,000	21%	+11,935,000	21%

Source: Derived from Table 1 in U.S. Bureau of the Census, *U.S. Census of Population: 1960, Selected Area Reports, Standard Metropolitan Statistical Areas,* Final Report PC(3)–1D, U.S. Government Printing Office, Washington, D.C., 1963.
* Totals include Negroes and other non-whites.

TABLE 2

NUMBER OF THE 24 LARGEST STANDARD METROPOLITAN
STATISTICAL AREAS IN 1960, BY PERCENTAGE
NON-WHITE IN 1940, 1950, AND 1960

Percentage Non-White	Number of Cities		
	1940	1950	1960
0-5%	8	3	1
5.1-10%	6	6	5
10.1-15%	5	5	2
15.1-20%	2	6	5
20.1-25%	1	2	3
25.1-30%	1		4
30.1-35%	1		2
35.1-40%		2	1
40.1-45%			
45.1-50%			
50.1-55%			1

Source: U.S. Bureau of the Census, *op. cit.*

have been dramatically large (Figure 1). In 1940, non-whites comprised less than 10 percent of the population in 14 out of these 24 cities. The number of these cities with non-white populations exceeding 15 percent grew from 5 in 1940 to 10 in 1950 and reached 16 in 1960. In four of these 24 cities, the 1960 census indicated that Negroes comprised over 30 percent of the city's population (Table 2).

This rapid increase in the Negro population of the central cities has outstripped all predictions. In 1950 only one of the cities in the 14 largest metropolitan areas had a Negro population greater than 25 percent of the total population. Using these data Morton Grodzins predicted in 1958 that "within 30 years Negroes will constitute from 25 to 50 percent of the total population in [the central cities of] at least 10 of the 14 largest [metropolitan areas]."[1] Only *two* years later Grodzins' prediction was almost fact. Seven central cities of the 14 largest metropolitan areas had a non-white population exceeding 25 per cent. One city, Washington, D. C., was 54.8 percent non-white.

There is every reason to believe that the Negro population in our central cities will continue to increase rapidly. As southern farms are mechanized, especially in the tobacco and cotton growing regions, Negro migration to the cities, in both the North and South, will continue to escalate. But the major factor which will contribute to the growing urban Negro population is the natural increase of the population. Between 1940 and 1950 migration was the most important source of increased Negro population, accounting for some 71 percent of the increase in standard metropolitan statistical areas. By 1960 the natural increase of the non-white population had become much more important than migration, which accounted for only 42 percent of the increase between 1950 and 1960.

Negro birth rates will continue to expand the Negro population relative to the white. The Negro population in the central cities is younger than the white. In Baltimore and Philadelphia, for example, the non-white median age is 24.7 and 27.5 years, respectively; the white median age in the two cities is considerably higher, 35.2 and 35.9 years.[2] Also, the Negro population has a higher fertility rate

[1] Morton Grodzins, *The Metropolitan Area as a Racial Problem.* Pittsburgh, University of Pittsburgh Press, 1958, p. 3.
[2] City of Baltimore — Planning Department, *Population and Housing,* Baltimore, 1964, figure 74, p. 48, and City of Philadelphia, Commission on Human Relations, *Philadelphia's Non-White Population 1960, Report No. 1, Demographic Data,* Philadelphia, 1961, table 9, p. 26.

FIGURE 1 • PERCENTAGE POPULATION NON-WHITE IN 1940, 1950, AND 1960 OF THE 24 LARGEST STANDARD METRO-POLITAN STATISTICAL AREAS IN 1960, BY CENTRAL CITY (———) AND SUBURBS (⋯⋯⋯)

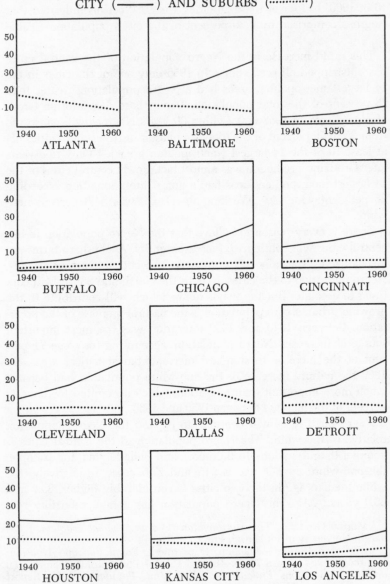

Source: U.S. Bureau of the Census, *op. cit.*

FIGURE 1 (CONTINUED)

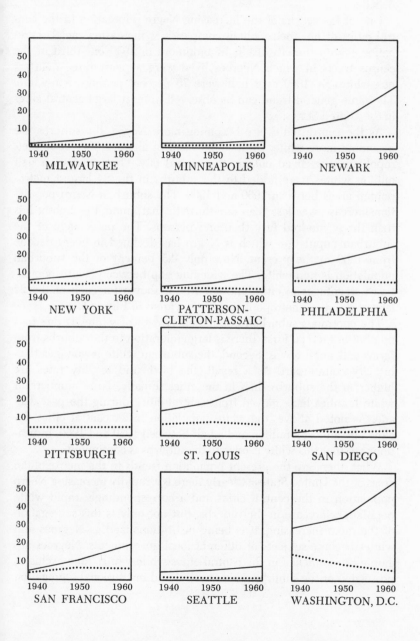

than the white population, and there are more Negroes than whites in the central city who will reach child bearing age during this decade.

One of the results of the increasing Negro population in the central cities of our metropolitan complexes is increasing racial segregation *within* the city itself. In Baltimore in 1950 one-third of the census tracts in which Negroes lived were at least three quarters non-white. By 1960 over half were 75 percent or more non-white. The same general trend can be observed in most large central cities in the United States.

As the central cities are becoming more Negro, the suburbs are becoming more white. By 1960 over half of all whites living in metropolitan areas lived outside the central city. Over ten and a half million whites were added to the suburbs in the 24 largest metropolitan areas between 1950 and 1960. The suburban Negro population increase was less than one-thirtieth that amount — slightly less than three hundred fifty thousand persons. The percentage of the suburban population which is Negro has declined in every decade from 1900 to the present. Now only 4.5 percent of the suburban population is non-white. The widening gap between Negro population percentages in cities and suburbs is shown for each of the 24 largest standard metropolitan statistical areas in Figure 1.

The enormous suburban population growth of whites is due to a number of factors. First, there is large migration to the suburbs from farms and small towns. Second, the suburban white is younger than his city counterpart. As a result, the birth and fertility rates are higher in the suburbs than in the cities. Finally, large numbers of white families have moved from central cities during the past decade. As noted above, the white population in 24 central cities declined by almost a million and a half between 1950 and 1960. Indications are that this white exodus to the suburbs is continuing.

What, then, are the present population trends in the metropolitan areas of the United States? Clearly there is a rapidly increasing Negro population in the central cities and a correspondingly rapid white population increase in the suburbs. But not only is this segregation of the races increasing, it is being institutionalized as Negroes and whites become subjects of different local governments. Negroes are gaining prominence in the central cities while whites take exclusive possession of the suburbs. This physical and institutional segregation has a number of political and social implications for our growing metropolitan areas. It is to these implications that we now turn.[3]

Political and Social Implications

There is every indication that the growing separation of the races in the metropolitan areas of the United States will continue unabated. Some of the demographic reasons for this conclusion have been noted above. But there are also other factors at work which are likely to increase the separation of whites and Negroes in metropolitan areas.

The segregation which is occurring is being institutionalized. The Negroes are being left to the central cities, while "lily" white suburbs are being built all around the city. Each of these suburbs has legal powers available by which it can severely limit the numbers of Negroes moving into the community or exclude them entirely. Although zoning laws are most often used to tighten what former Mayor Richardson Dilworth called the "white noose," some suburban communities have resorted to condemnation proceedings, to excessively rigid enforcement of building regulations against builders of interracial developments or, on occasion, to violence such as that which erupted in Folcroft, Pennsylvania, in September 1963.[4]

As Negroes become more prevalent and concentrated in the metropolitan areas, white opposition to desegregation of housing, schools, and other facilities is likely to increase. As a result there is likely to be a growing antagonism between the separated groups in the future.

A third factor likely to perpetuate the separation of the races is the ineffectiveness of fair housing legislation passed by a number of states. Most fair housing laws exempt owner occupied houses, and almost all rely on individual complaints for enforcement. Evasion of the law is common, especially by the real estate profession, which itself is segregated.

Finally, since many Negroes benefit from the present pattern, they

---

[3] For a somewhat different analysis of the implications of racial segregation in the metropolis see Grodzins, *op. cit.*, pp. 9-14.

[4] U. S. Commission on Civil Rights, *Housing*, Washington, D. C., 1961, pp. 119-138. See also *The Evening Bulletin* (Philadelphia) August 31-September 5, 1963 for details of the Folcroft riots.

are unwilling to give up the advantages which accrue to them as a result of the physical and governmental separation from whites. Like many Irishmen and Italians, numerous Negroes hope to translate the strength of their numbers in the central city into political power, thus gaining the offices and influence which to date have been denied Negroes. In addition, the livelihood of Negro politicians, lawyers, publishers, doctors, undertakers, and real estate brokers depends to a very great extent upon the continued existence of a separate Negro community. The conflicting desires of Negroes for complete integration and for a continuing Negro community can be seen in Negro reaction to those Negroes who leave the ghetto and make an attempt to integrate a neighborhood or a suburban community. On the one hand, the Negro community applauds and defends the escaping Negro as he seeks to battle white prejudice and gain acceptance in a white community. But on the other hand, Negroes resent those of their race who they think have sold out, who have become "black bourgeois" by leaving the ghetto behind them. Cecil Moore, militant president of the Philadelphia NAACP, calls them "so-called Negroes."

This increased segregation is likely to be accomplished by attempts of the white population to maintain control of the politics of the central city despite the growing Negro populations. In Washington, D. C., the only major city in which Negroes constitute a majority of the population, white control is maintained through the absence of home rule and the influence of the House and Senate District of Columbia Committees. In other cities, the bureaucratization and professionalization of the governmental machinery will tend to keep the government white even though the city's population might become more than half Negro. Civil service laws will prohibit any sudden change in the racial composition of employees, and Negroes are presently so under-represented in every city government that it would take a long time for them to gain their proportionate share of the jobs available.

In some instances legislatures will use their apportionment powers to maintain control by whites. Gerrymandering for racial and ethnic purposes is already practiced in many cities. Philadelphia provides a good example of the tactics employed to block the access of Negroes to public office. The Negro proportion of the population was reduced in all eight Senate districts in Philadelphia when the

Pennsylvania Senate was reapportioned in 1963.[5] The only district with a Negro majority was reduced from 81 percent to 69 percent Negro. And to prevent this district from electing a Negro State Senator, the Democratic minority leader of the Senate had his ward included in the district. Since legislative leaders rarely are challenged in primaries, the Pennsylvania Senate still does not have a single Negro member.

The 1963 legislative gerrymandering also successfully reduced the number of Assembly Districts in Philadelphia with a majority Negro population. The 1953 apportionment produced eleven Assembly Districts electing 13 Assemblymen which had Negro majorities in 1960. The 1963 apportionment created only six such districts electing eight Assemblymen.

As long as the white politicians control the party organization, they can effectively stifle Negro political activity. Even a Negro majority in a district does not guarantee that it will be controlled by Negroes. Sixteen out of Philadelphia's fifty-nine wards had a population in 1960 which was at least half Negro. Thirty-two ward leaders ran the Republican and Democratic party machines in these Negro wards, but only eleven of these thirty-two leaders were Negroes — six Democrats and five Republicans. In January 1965, the Democratic machine successfully defeated a Negro candidate for leader in a ward which is about 65 percent Negro. The strength of the City Committee was such that the Negro candidate was defeated 50-9 even though 41 out of the 78 committeemen in the ward were Negroes.

The political parties will continue to exercise controls over those Negroes who do get elected. In Pennsylvania, as well as in other urban states, the custom has been to allow Negroes to run for the state legislature — as long as they could be controlled through some damaging information known to the City Committee, or where the political party could remove the candidate from his regular job as well as from his political post. The Negro legislative delegation from Cook County, Illinois, includes a former Assistant State Attorney of Cook County, the Chicago Motor Vehicle Commissioner, the foreman of the Cutting Section of the Chicago Bureau of Sanitation, a

---

[5] This was accomplished by transferring white wards in white districts to districts with large proportions of Negroes.

minister who is also a city employee, a Corporation Counsel for the City of Chicago, and others bound to the party by their jobs.

Negroes will also be limited in their recognition by the party because of their overwhelming attachment to the Democratic party. In a situation where competition for the Negro vote is exceedingly slight, the Negroes will not be able to demand or receive their proportionate share of attention.

This does not mean, however, that there will be no Negro protests or demands. Nor does the growing population split indicate there will be a decrease in Negro militancy in the future. Rather all indications point to increasing militancy on the part of Negroes in the large central cities of our metropolitan areas. The activities of Chester's Stanley Branche, Philadelphia's Cecil Moore, and New York's Jesse Gray and Milton Galimison reflect the growing restlessness and militancy of Negro leadership. James Q. Wilson has argued that this growing militancy is due to better education for Negroes which is not producing proportionate increases in income.[6] Another explanation for the growing militancy is that expectations of Negroes are rising but benefits are limited or are slow in coming. Rewards which are won will have to be shared among more people and in many instances demands cannot or will not be met. One unobtainable demand is for integrated schools. The schools in Manhattan (81 percent Negro and Puerto Rican) or Washington, D. C. (88 percent Negro) cannot be integrated unless Negro students are bussed to the outlying neighborhoods of the city or the suburbs. This wide gap between expectations and achievements contributes to militancy and unrest.

As a result of a growing segregation in metropolitan areas, the racial problems of the metropolis often go unseen and unnoticed. In part this is because there is a widespread belief that there is no racial problem in the North. In 1963 the Philadelphia Board of Education stated that "The Board of Public Education cannot agree to file a plan of desegregation because the School District of Philadelphia is not operating an illegally segregated school system."[7] Yet

[6] See James Q. Wilson, "The Changing Political Position of the Negro," in *Assuring Freedom to the Free*, edited by Arnold M. Rose, pp. 165-167.

[7] Defendant's Answers, *Chisholm v. The Board of Public Education*, U.S. District Court, Eastern District of Pennsylvania, Civil Action no. 29706. The Board has since changed its position.

at that time 39 percent of all schools in Philadelphia were "Negro Schools."[8]

The problems of the Negro in the metropolis are also in a sense invisible. Superhighways and commuter trains bypass the slums. Urban renewal has moved the Negroes out of some downtown shopping areas. Many people no longer live, work, or shop in the central city and therefore do not see the Negro and his often utter destitution.

It is often argued that Negroes will assimilate as all other ethnic groups have in the past. But when this is shown not to be the case, it is argued that the Negro is living in better houses and earning more money than ever before.[9] Or it is argued that the civil rights legislation will bring about integration and equality. But the Negro's income relative to the income of whites has declined slightly since 1950, and cities and states have been relatively unsuccessful in bringing about changes in housing and employment discrimination.[10]

In addition suburbanites think of racial problems as the city's problems. They are unwilling to acknowledge that the zoning laws of the suburban communities effectively restrict the entry of Negroes. Nor do they worry about the integration of the city's schools. Their children are in school districts where there are no Negroes and consequently segregation "is not a problem." Furthermore, there rarely is a Negro constituency in the suburban community to remind the suburbanite and his political and community leaders that the racial problem is their problem.

As a result, the prospects for local solutions to the racial crisis in the metropolis are dim. The Negro population in the central cities will continue to expand as will the white population in the suburbs. The tax base of the cities will continue to erode as service businesses and many retail stores follow their employees and customers to the suburbs. Central city children will not be bussed to suburban

[8] Special Committee on nondiscrimination of the Board of Public Education of Philadelphia, *Report*, Philadelphia (mimeo.), 1964, p. 10.

[9] See Charles E. Silberman, *Crisis in Black and White*, New York, Random House, 1964, pp. 37-8 and *passim*.

[10] In 1950 non-white median family income was 56 percent that of the white median family income. In 1954 it was 53.5 percent; in 1961, 53.4 percent that of whites. By 1963 it was even lower — 52.9 percent of the median white family income. See U. S. Bureau of the Census, *Current Population Reports*, "Consumer Income," Series P 60.

schools, nor will suburban children integrate city schools. *De facto* segregation in central city schools will continue. Zoning laws are unlikely to be altered in order to allow for Negro diffusion into the suburban area. City welfare costs, housing rehabilitation costs, police protection costs will mount — but they will not be shared by suburbanites. The benefits which accrue and the costs which are avoided by living in the suburbs will continue the strong support for neighborhood governments as well as neighborhood schools. The problems of the metropolis will not be attacked on a metropolitan basis.

The inescapable conclusion is that solutions will have to come from Washington. The poverty program, medicare, equal employment legislation may have some effect — but these are federal solutions, not metropolitan solutions. What Morton Grodzins said in 1958 is true now: "Almost nothing is being done today to meet what is likely to be the nation's most pressing social problem tomorrow."[11] Because of increasing segregation and the fragmentation of government in the metropolitan areas, nothing is likely to be done tomorrow, either, within the metropolis to meet the problem.

[11] Grodzins, *op. cit.*, p. 1.

2

THE POLITICAL SYSTEM OF
THE METROPOLIS

Seventy years ago the political system of the metropolis
was the city, a legal entity whose boundaries enclosed
most urban development. As population increased and
transportation improvements moved residences outward
in the years between the Civil War and World War I,
most cities expanded to encompass the urban growth
which spilled over their borders, usually by annexing
adjacent unincorporated territory. Less frequent, but
more dramatic, was expansion by merger or consolidation. The most notable of these amalgamations was the
joining in 1898 of the nation's biggest city, New York,
with its fourth largest, Brooklyn. The politics of annexation often fostered bitter strife, especially when city
governments used their utility systems as a lever to force
annexation on reluctant suburbs. In arid Southern California, this strategy has been pursued with considerable
success by Los Angeles, which developed the area's major
water supply system.

With few exceptions, cities have failed to keep pace
with the spread of urban development in the twentieth
century. Natural barriers checked their growth in some
metropolitan areas. State and county boundaries also
halted the march of some cities. In addition, city adminis-
trations occasionally declined to annex because the costs

of servicing the new territory exceeded the anticipated benefits to the city. But the overriding reason for the containment of the central cities has been the drive for suburban autonomy. Independence through incorporation or the prevention of annexation provides the residents of the new neighborhoods of the metropolis with a degree of personal control over taxes, zoning, and the educational system not available to the city dweller. Autonomy divorces the Republican suburbanite from the political system of the Democratic city, a government usually perceived by the middle class as corrupt and unresponsive. By living in a separate political jurisdiction, the suburbanite tries to insulate himself from the social welfare burdens, racial problems and crime of the city. He may also evade responsibility for maintaining the city's educational, cultural, recreation, and transportation facilities, which serve a population broader than that of the city alone.

Like most conflicts in local politics, the struggle between the annexationists and the autonomists was resolved in the state capital. As usually occurs in the triangular city-suburban-state relationship, the state legislatures were responsive to the suburbs and the cities were thwarted. Annexation was made more difficult in most states, particularly when incorporated municipalities were the target. Regulations governing incorporation were eased in many states, stimulating the creation of municipalities by suburbanites seeking to avoid annexation. In the two decades before World War II, most of the larger cities, and many of the smaller ones, were ringed by independent suburban governments. With the great urban exodus of the postwar years came a vast proliferation in the number of suburban municipalities. Only in the newer metropolitan areas of the Southeast, Southwest, and Northern plains has annexation kept pace with urban growth. City-suburban disparities and antagonisms tend to be less significant in these younger and usually smaller areas. In the absence of strong pressures for autonomy, states in these sections of the nation have facilitated rather than blocked the expansion of cities. Texas, for instance, permits annexation without the consent of the residents of the territory to be acquired. Elsewhere, a few cities have stubbornly clung to their irredentist dreams. But as David Gladfelter indicates in his account of Milwaukee's attempts in the 1950's to induce incorporated suburbs to accept annexation in return for city water, the durability of the suburban-state house alliance probably forecloses a revival of imperialism in the cities.

The effects of the political separation of city and suburb are not immediately apparent to the casual observer of the metropolis. Rarely does the city line mark a sharp change in the pattern of urban development. Instead, as one moves outward from the urban core, there is a gradual transformation from the densely populated multi-family working class dwellings of the city's older neighborhoods to the low density single family housing typical of the suburban middle class. Since every city has some of the latter, city and suburb tend to blend together in the outer neighborhoods of the city. The amount of low density development within the city varies greatly. Old cities like Boston which were almost completely settled before the automobile revolution have relatively few "suburban" residents within their borders. Much of the development of newer cities like Miami and Los Angeles, on the other hand, was strongly influenced by the forces of dispersion. As a result, large areas of these cities are "suburban" in character.

Although the change in the pattern of development is gradual, political separation none the less produces important differences in the aggregate population of the city as compared with that of the suburbs. Regardless of when or where the city stopped growing, it encompasses far more of the older residential, commercial, and industrial development of the metropolis than suburbia. Especially in the larger and older metropolitan areas, a relatively high proportion of city residents are in the lower socio-economic ranks. The average city dweller occupies less living space, is older, has had fewer years of school, and earns a lower income than the suburbanite. In addition, he is more likely to be unemployed or impoverished, or to be a Negro, a Puerto Rican, or foreign born. Most residents of the suburbs are members of the broad strata we call the middle class. Compared to their neighbors in the city, they are more likely to be managers or professionals, to be married, to have school-age children, and to own a home and an automobile.

These socio-economic differences play a major role in shaping political behavior in the metropolis. The city dweller and the suburbanite bring different perceptions, attitudes, loyalties, and demands to their respective political systems. City government tends to be partisan and Democratic. Suburban politics usually is non-partisan or Republican. Party cleavages, and the ethnic, racial, and class distinctions underlying them, as Edward C. Banfield explains, undermine efforts to reunite the metropolis through the creation of an areawide government. Hence, the conflicts arising from the division of the metropolis into city and suburb help insure its continued separation.

Party is only one of the major differences between the political systems of the city and the suburbs. Since the city's share of the metropolitan population lives in a single juridiction while suburbanites reside in many small communities, the central city usually has the only big government in the metropolis. Its fiscal and professional resources exceed those of the remaining political units of the metropolis combined. Its mayor frequently commands a political machine, overwhelming electoral support, and widespread backing in the business community. Almost always, he is the most visible and influential political figure in the metropolis. Yet, as Scott Greer points out in his analysis of the political systems of the larger cities, the city's size and resources, its mayor and his machine, are no guarantee that the challenges of urban growth will be effectively met. Instead, Greer sees a disappearing economic elite, a sluggish bureaucracy, and a stagnant one party system combining to produce an inertial "machine of the incumbents" which increasingly is unable to check the flight of the middle class and industry, to halt the decay of neighborhoods, or to meet the demands of the burgeoning ghettos.

Suburbia's political system differs in most important respects from that of the central city. Instead of a single large government, there are many small ones, most with fewer than 25,000 residents. In place of political machines and professional politicians, there is nonpartisanship and amateur government. Rather than specialized bureaucracies and an elected mayor earning $20,000 or more a year, there is a city manager and a part time unpaid council. In comparison with the city, the fiscal, personnel, and political resources of the average suburb are meager. In fact, its most important political resource is its independent existence. Autonomy provides suburbanites with local control over the vital parameters of community life. It also protects them against absorption by the city or a larger suburb, or inclusion in a regional arrangement which threatens unequal costs and benefits. Political activity in these small communities tends to be focused almost entirely on local issues, particularly tax levels, the maintenance of property values, and the schools, which usually have their own independent political system, complete with nonpartisan school board, professional superintendent, and autonomous taxing power.

Autonomy also fosters differentiation among suburbs, which in turn encourages the proliferation of suburban governments and homogeneity within individual communities. Social, ethnic, and income differentiations among suburbs are as important an aspect of metropolitan politics as the social, racial, and economic disparities between the city and the suburbs. While the many sections of the city are amalgamated in a single heterogeneous political system, neighborhood differences in social status, income, and property values are institutionalized in suburbia through the creation of numerous independent municipalities. The key elements in the politics of differentiation are the zoning and building codes and the tax and service policies of the autonomous suburb. The larger the metropolitan area, the greater the splintering of suburbia, and the wider the range between the rich suburb and the poor one. Moreover, the spread of geographic autonomy through the creation of general purpose suburban governments breeds functional autonomy. Special districts, usually responsible for the provision of a single service such as water supply or sewage disposal, are created to supply services whose provision is beyond the capabilities of the multiplying suburban municipalities. These unifunctional devices also are employed within a suburb to insure that only those directly benefited, for instance, the residents of a housing development requiring the replacement of septic tanks with a community sewage disposal system, pay for public improvements.

A crucial factor in the fragmentation of the suburban political system is the property tax, the chief fiscal resource available to the governments of suburbia. Robert C. Wood's analysis reveals how the suburban dependence upon local property taxes encourages competitive neomercantilist policies based on maximizing high-value development and minimizing inexpensive residential development. Suburbia's tireless pursuit of a favorable balance between resources and demands produces considerable differences in the levels of public service, reinforces the social and ethnic homogeneity of individual suburbs through segregation by home value, and fosters the creation of new suburban units of government. While the system works to the advantage of the upper income community, Wood concludes that the average suburb cannot survive without outside assistance.

The processes of separation and differentiation have produced a fragmented metropolitan political system. It is a system which institutionalizes the diversity of the metropolis, separates numbers and wealth, and enhances the partisan, social, ethnic, and economic differences among the people of the metropolis. These divisions, in turn, insure that the differential impact of urban growth and change on the various sectors of the metropolis will continue to be reflected in the political system. In most metropolitan areas, fragmentation and differentiation have foreclosed the development of areawide government. General purpose governments with metropolitan constituencies exist only in Miami, Nashville, and Baton Rouge, and in the handful of cities, mostly in Texas, whose boundaries encompass the metropolis. The absence of central instrumentalities means that public policy for the metropolis is made either by the area's many jurisdictions acting unilaterally or by surrogates for metropolitan government such as special districts, the states, and the federal government.

As Norton E. Long indicates in his essay on metropolitan decision-making, the fragmented institutional base shapes the perceptions, attitudes, resources, and goals of all the participants in metropolitan politics. Aside from the central city business and civic leaders who seek to save the city through reunification, few contestants in the political arenas of the metropolis are oriented toward the problems or the interests of the metropolitan area as a whole. A similar picture of metropolitan decision-making emerges from studies recently undertaken in the Syracuse area. With a relatively cohesive business community and the Republican Party in control of both the city and county, politics in this medium-sized metropolis have been less fragmented than in most metropolitan areas. Yet Frank J. Munger finds little evidence in the Syracuse studies of an integrated system of political leadership. Instead, the growth of the metropolitan area and the spread of urban development has fostered the specialization of influence and an increase in the number of decisional foci of the metropolis.

DAVID D. GLADFELTER

The Political Separation of City and Suburb:
Water for Wauwatosa

I The Setting

In 1954, the city of Wauwatosa, Wisconsin, a suburb adjoining
Milwaukee to the west (see map), suddenly developed a serious
problem of water supply. The suburb had often experienced shortages during summer droughts and periods of heavy use, and it had
been warned for over ten years that its water table was steadily falling. Engineers, however, considered the independent Wauwatosa
water system, a utility which drew upon eight artesian wells, adequate to meet the needs of users within the suburb's original area of
4 square miles.

When the suburb annexed 8.5 square miles from the town of Wauwatosa in 1954, it was suddenly faced with the responsibility of supplying water to that rapidly growing residential and industrial area
which already contained some 12,000 inhabitants. The suburb had
made no provision for new sources of water before carrying out the
annexation.

Wauwatosa officials took this problem to a firm of consulting engineers for study and recommendations. In December, 1954, Samuel
J. Gates, one of the firm's executives, recommended that Wauwatosa
purchase water from Milwaukee to supplement its supply of well
water. Unless the suburb could obtain Milwaukee water, Gates said,
it would be forced either to sink additional wells or to join in form-
ing a suburban utility with other suburbs. Gates did not consider the

Reprinted from *Cases in State and Local Government*, Richard T. Frost,
Editor. © 1961, by permission of Prentice-Hall, Inc., Englewood Cliffs,
New Jersey.

THE AREA INVOLVED IN THE WAUWATOSA WATER CASE

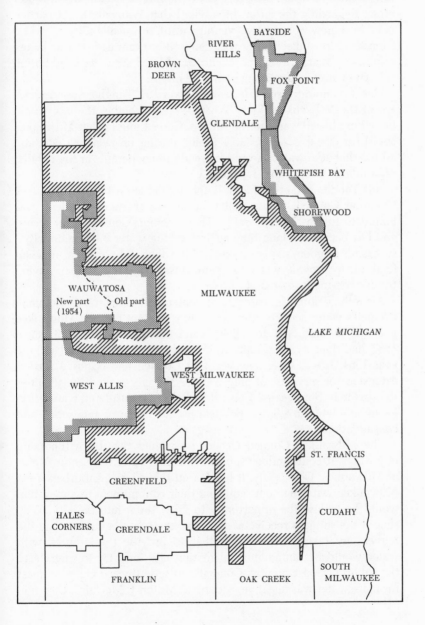

former alternative to be good engineering. To drill additional wells in Wauwatosa would only accelerate the rate of decline of the water table. Regarding the latter, he advised that Wauwatosa not participate in a new cooperative venture until the availability of water from the Milwaukee utility was thoroughly examined. It was Gates' impression that Milwaukee would be able to serve its neighboring suburb by means of existing plant and mains.

Gates then addressed a letter to Edward F. Tanghe, Superintendent of the Milwaukee Water Works, asking whether the city would be willing to sell water to the suburb. Gates thought that Milwaukee could furnish this water "at a profit" during off-peak periods, and added that Wauwatosa would be ready to cooperate "in the details" of building storage tanks for the city water.

But Tanghe had other ideas. Referring the letter to the Milwaukee Common Council, whose policy he, as water superintendent, was bound to follow, Tanghe said, "The Common Council is on record and has been for a long time against selling water outside the city." It was his opinion, moreover, that Milwaukee did not have sufficient facilities to provide water to Wauwatosa, since it was then having trouble serving its own users adequately.

Actually, Tanghe's categorical statement concerning Common Council's water service extension policy was not correct. Milwaukee had had the authority to sell its water outside the city limits since 1887, had done so since 1902, and was doing so to six suburbs in the year 1954. It was true, however, that Council had opposed *further* extensions of service, not only because the city lacked the facilities to provide it, but because Council had always considered water service to be related to a larger political problem, that of annexation and consolidation.

The Milwaukee Council has long assumed that by withholding city water, it could induce suburbs needing water to become a part of Milwaukee. Conversely, it has feared that to give suburban users Milwaukee water without requiring their commitment to annexation would be to lose the opportunity to draw them into the city. Why should the suburbs receive a vital city service without incurring the higher city taxes? Council felt that to provide the suburbs with water would be tantamount to inviting city industry to migrate to the suburbs. Consequently, Council's attitude toward Gates' request for more water was negative. Alderman Milton J. McGuire, Common

Council president in 1954, suggested that suburbs desiring city water "join the city, and then they'll get it."

After receiving Gates' letter via Tanghe, the Common Council did what was expected. Early in January, 1955, after the Council's utilities committee had voted 3-2 to reject, Milwaukee killed the proposal. This ended Wauwatosa's first attempt to secure a supply of Milwaukee water.

II Interim Measures

For the year and a half following the Milwaukee Council's decision, Wauwatosa relied on stopgap measures to meet its water problem. During that time, further engineering studies were made, and the two alternative plans suggested by Gates — well drilling and membership in a suburban utility — were investigated further. During that time also, the water problem became more and more acute, affecting homeowners and to a lesser extent industry. When the suburb again turned to the city, in May of 1956, it was prepared to do serious battle; for the problem had reached the point where residents were aroused and were "behind their government one hundred percent." This is the way the Wauwatosa City Attorney phrased it.

Water needs were greatest in the newly annexed areas on Wauwatosa's west side. The suburb had not yet provided these areas with piped water; existing homes located there relied upon relatively shallow private wells for water. The development of the area had led to an increase in the number of wells being sunk, which had lowered the water table and had caused some wells to fail or become polluted. On one occasion when a "cooperative well" serving the neighborhood went dry, the suburb had to haul water by tank truck to supply an entire subdivision on an emergency basis for a week. The well had been constructed thirty years earlier to supply a much smaller number of families.

And, on another occasion, about a dozen homeowners protested to the Wauwatosa Board of Public Works that their wells were polluted and that action must be taken at once. As a stopgap, Wauwatosa considered drilling a ninth public well in an area of particular hardship, the Park Ridge area, and supplying the homes directly; but later developments made this project, which would have cost an estimated $175,000, unnecessary.

Other interim measures taken by the suburb included a requirement that subdividers, before receiving approval of proposed plats,
sink cooperative wells to serve the homes until a public supply were
available. New industries also, specifically Harley-Davidson, Briggs
and Stratton, and the Mayfair shopping center, were assigned the
responsibility of providing their own water until such time as the
suburb could furnish it.

Three months after the Milwaukee rejection, Gates' firm "reluc-
tantly" recommended that Wauwatosa drill two deep wells immediately to meet supply problems. The cost of the wells and necessary
mains and storage facilities was estimated at $2 million. The firm
also recommended that efforts to obtain water either from Milwaukee or from a suburban utility be renewed, and that unless such a
supply could be obtained, the suburb would need three additional
new wells. This second Gates report was critical of the water policy
of the Milwaukee Common Council; saying:

> It would seem to us that public convenience and necessity, plus the
> opportunity to profit, would determine utility policy, but they [Mil-
> waukee officials] are concerned about annexation and other con-
> siderations which in our opinion are not relevant. Under the present
> circumstances we are forced to look elsewhere for water.

Meanwhile, other suburbs of Milwaukee were considering increasing their own water supply by creating independent water districts.
But none of these suburbs (Oak Creek to the south and Whitefish
Bay, Fox Point, and Glendale, to the north) was contiguous in
boundaries to Wauwatosa. This discouraged the Wauwatosa government from participating, because expensive easements would be required at substantial costs in money and time. The suburbs decided
not to join in these efforts.

III   Back to the City

In May, 1956, Wauwatosa directed its attention once again to
Milwaukee as a source of water. Wauwatosa Mayor William B.
Knuese, in a letter to his common council, urged that the suburb
start a proceeding "in the proper state commission (the Public Service Commission — PSC) or in the courts" to force Milwaukee to supply water to Wauwatosa. His position was simply this — since the

Milwaukee water department was a public utility already selling water outside the Milwaukee city limits, it could not legally refuse to sell water to Wauwatosa. Knuese's letter said in part:

> With the single exception of the City of Wauwatosa, the water department of the City of Milwaukee now furnishes water to every incorporated city or village immediately adjacent to its boundaries. It also furnishes water to other communities and people. It has been in the public utility business beyond its own corporate limits for a long period of time.

The mayor further recommended that, should action through the PSC or the courts be unsuccessful, Wauwatosa should seek state legislation establishing a metropolitan water district. "If Milwaukee won't sell water," he said, "it should step aside and permit creation of an authority that will."

The Wauwatosa council did not dally. It referred Knuese's letter to its Board of Public Works, which reported back a week later with recommendations for a council resolution. Before another ten days were past, the council had unanimously passed the resolution, its first formal action taken in its quest for Milwaukee water.

The resolution, addressed to the Milwaukee Council, requested permission to connect Wauwatosa mains with those of the city, and further authorized the Wauwatosa attorney to start proceedings with the State or in the courts if Milwaukee continued to refuse. On May 29 the resolution was delivered to the Milwaukee Common Council.

Milwaukee's reaction was unsympathetic. Alderman Matt Schimenz, chairman of the Council's utilities committee, emphatically stated:

> The City's water will go to Wauwatosa over my dead body unless there is a political consolidation of Milwaukee and Wauwatosa.

Mayor Frank P. Zeidler added:

> Wauwatosa wants city services without paying city taxes. When a city like Wauwatosa holds itself out as a city, it takes on the obligation of supplying all services from its own sources. . . . If we extend our water to everyone outside the city, we will lose industry itself just as we have lost the captains of industry.

The utilities committee referred Wauwatosa's resolution to a special nine-member study committe composed of aldermen and administrative officials. Toward the end of June the committee recommended that Milwaukee not serve any new municipal customers until it could take adequate care of its present customers in the City and in six suburbs. On July 10 the Common Council again rejected Wauwatosa's demand.

This action brought a prompt decision by Wauwatosa to appeal to the State PSC. Herbert L. Mount, special counsel for Wauwatosa, said that even if the city did not have the plant capacity to begin service to the suburb, the PSC could fix a schedule of expansion to meet Wauwatosa's needs. He announced that he would ask the PSC for such an order. In the months ahead, Wauwatosa prepared its testimony and briefs with the aid of engineering consultants and special counsel, and on November 14, 1956 the suburb filed its petition with the state agency.

IV   The State Agency

The Public Service Commission's authority to require public utilities to extend service was explicit in the 1931 statute that created it. The temper of that regulatory body, up to the time of Wauwatosa's petition, had been opposed to Milwaukee's policy of using water to attain other ends. Earlier, for example, in a 1937 test case, the Commission had gone on record as favoring water service extension with a minimum of hardship and delay wherever needed in metropolitan areas.

In this first test case, Milwaukee protested an order of the Commission requiring it to extend service to an adjacent unincorporated town. The city claimed it was not a water utility for the metropolitan area, but sold only by contract; thus it had no obligation to serve outside the city limits and the PSC had no jurisdiction over it. After a rehearing, the Commission had ruled:

> The contracts indicate that the city has voluntarily taken upon itself a public utility obligation of supplying water to various municipalities. Once undertaken the public utility may not arbitrarily discontinue it. . . . Nor may the public utility arbitrarily select its customers. The city of Milwaukee holds itself out as a public utility in a metropolitan area to render service by sundry methods to all contiguous municipalities or to individuals; the position of the city that it is under no obligation to serve another potential customer outside its limits creates an intolerably discriminatory situation.

The circuit court to which Milwaukee appealed dismissed the case on stipulation agreeable to both parties, so the PSC's finding was not actually reviewed by a court of law.

The outcome of a similar case, decided by the PSC in 1940 and by the Wisconsin Supreme Court in 1942, modified somewhat the PSC's 1937 opinion. In this case, the Commission ruled that Milwaukee, having contracted to serve a few areas in an unincorporated town, had incurred an obligation to serve the entire town. In its order, the Commission reasserted its authority to require extension of service by the city within the metropolitan area. But the Supreme Court held that the question at issue was much narrower than the PSC had assumed, and refused to comment as to whether Milwaukee could be obligated to serve the entire metropolitan area. The Court did rule that the city had not "held itself out" to serve the whole unincorporated town by agreeing to serve a part of it, since in its contracts, the city had made express limitation upon the extent of its service. The court disallowed the Commission's order.

The upshot of the Supreme Court's ruling was this: The PSC's statutory power to require extensions of service had not been actually denied, nor had the Court defined the area which the Milwaukee utility could be required to serve. The court *had* ruled that the city was not obligated to extend water service within *un*incorporated areas, thereby leaving the city free to continue to use water as a club to promote annexation of such areas. It had *not* ruled upon Milwaukee's obligation toward incorporated suburbs already possessing water utilities.

V   The Current Controversy

Hearings before the PSC on Wauwatosa's new application for service were held throughout 1957 and early 1958.

Wauwatosa's counsel, City Attorney Milton F. Burmaster and Special Attorneys Herbert L. Mount and Maxwell Herriott, concentrated their efforts on proving that Milwaukee had an obligation to provide water service. They used two lines of argument: first, that since Milwaukee supplied water to six suburbs, its refusal to serve another was "unjustly discriminatory and in violation of the statutory obligation of the Milwaukee water utility"; and second, that Milwaukee had obligated itself to serve because of a contract made in 1908 to supply water to several Milwaukee County institutions in Wauwatosa.

The 1908 contract did not enter into the PSC's findings of fact, but it did present a technicality. The city of Milwaukee had contracted with the county to supply its hospitals, homes, and asylums via a main through Wauwatosa. In the contract the city had agreed to permit the county to sell water to persons along the pipeline. The county then had obtained an easement from Wauwatosa, upon which Wauwatosa had imposed the condition that in the future "the city of Wauwatosa and the citizens thereof may and shall be eventually supplied with water" from the main. The city of Milwaukee never protested this provision in the contract between Wauwatosa and the county, and by 1956, 236 inhabitants of the suburb were being served by the county from its main. Wauwatosa's lawyers claimed that although the suburb had made no contract directly with the city, the city was nevertheless obligated to the suburb by virtue of both Milwaukee's and Wauwatosa's contracts with the county.

Milwaukee's counsel, First Asst. City Attorney Harry G. Slater, replied to both of Wauwatosa's arguments with a motion to dismiss the petition. Regarding the first argument, Slater contended that the city had not held itself out to serve Wauwatosa and could not be compelled to enter a contract against its will. As for the second, he asserted that the PSC had no jurisdiction in determining the existence of a contract; such a finding was a matter for the courts. The city lost the motion, however, and the PSC ordered hearings to proceed on the merits of the case.

In presenting Milwaukee's petition, Slater reiterated the city Council's viewpoint that Milwaukee would be unable to serve a new customer because it was having trouble serving its present users. To compel Milwaukee to serve additional outside areas "would result in aggravated service deficiencies, substantial engineering difficulties, hardship to our present customers and inequitable burdens to rate payers," he said.

To this, Wauwatosa replied that Milwauke could supply Wauwatosa reservoirs during off-peak periods without having to add more than a "comparatively small capital outlay" to that already contemplated by Milwaukee. Wauwatosa would pay for needed improvements in its own system, its counsel said.

Slater emphasized the point that Wauwatosa's troubles stemmed directly from its own previous annexations. He said:

> Milwaukee should not be required . . . to meet the problems which the city of Wauwatosa has created for itself . . . through annexations. . . . If Wauwatosa has problems as a result of its annexation policies, the city of Milwaukee offers its sympathy. But Milwaukee should not be expected to take over Wauwatosa's responsibilities.

Slater argued that all of the areas in which Wauwatosa had pressing water needs were in the newly annexed part of the suburb, and that Wauwatosa's well system had been quite adequate to serve the older part. As Slater put it, Wauwatosa officials "bit off more than they could supply with water."

The suburb's attorney, Herriott, replied, "This is a case of the pot calling the kettle black." By this he meant that Milwaukee's difficulties in serving its present customers had resulted from its own recent annexations.

Even during the most bitter moments, the hearings yielded occasional humor. In the stormy final session, Wauwatosa Attorney Mount emphasized the inadequacy of his suburb's water facilities and again doubted the feasibility of Wauwatosa's joining an independent suburban water system. "It would be a duplication of Milwaukee's facilities," he said. Attorney Slater rejoined that the whole network of suburbs surrounding Milwaukee was a "duplication of Milwaukee's facilities." He said he was amazed that Wauwatosa officials would admit, after operating a water utility for 50 years, that they had bad tasting, polluted water, insufficient pressure, and that only Milwaukee could solve these problems.

VI The PSC Decides

The Commission handed down its order on April 2, 1958. It was in two parts. The first part ordered Milwaukee within 60 days to provide temporary service of up to 2 million gallons a day to Wauwatosa "on an off-peak basis." The second part ordered Milwaukee to "proceed with due diligence" to provide additional plant and facilities as are necessary to supply Wauwatosa permanently.

The Commission, after recapitulating the history of Milwaukee's extension of water service to its suburbs, concluded that the city had held itself out as a water utility by supplying six suburban municipal customers. Because of this, it continued, Milwaukee "thereby assumed an obligation as a water public utility to provide such a service to any municipal water utility" located in Milwaukee County and contiguous to the city. Therefore, Milwaukee could be required to supply Wauwatosa. The PSC's findings as to the capacity and needs of both Milwaukee and Wauwatosa were that Milwaukee would be able to furnish Wauwatosa with 2 million gallons a day with its present plant, such service being "necessary as a temporary measure."

The gist of the case was summarized in the printed abstract:

> A municipal utility's obligation to furnish . . . service to adjacent municipal utilities, while not inherent in its public utility status, may be assumed by legislative authority or by voluntary acts of the utility. Having acquired such obligation to serve, refusal to serve a contiguous municipal utility is discriminatory between it and other similarly situated utilities now served.

Wauwatosa officials were elated by the news. Mayor Knuese praised the decision as "of the greatest importance and benefit to the entire metropolitan area, including the city of Milwaukee . . ."

To Milwaukee the decision was no surprise, but neither was it welcome. Mayor Zeidler said that if Milwaukee's water works were to take on all applicants, as the PSC had hinted it might require, an extra cost of $50 million for expansion, over and above the $54 million already budgeted, would be needed over the next 20 years.

The Commission's ruling confronted the Milwaukee Common Council with a dilemma. If it accepted the ruling it would be no longer able to use water service extension as a bargaining tool with which to negotiate adjustment of city-suburb controversies. If the city succesfully challenged the ruling in court, then the state legislature might act to force Milwaukee to serve Wauwatosa and other suburbs or might create a metropolitan water district for the area. Council met on April 14 to decide which course to follow. A resolution calling for a court appeal was presented and passed.

But Mayor Zeidler vetoed this resolution four days later, explaining that he had concluded that acceptance of the order would be the "least injurious course" for the city "however unjust and contrary to our original defense it may seem." He warned that if the city should continue the battle further, it might lose control of its water works. The Council sustained the mayor's veto, and on April 30, in a tradition-breaking vote, it was decided to sell water to Wauwatosa without a further legal fight. A chastened Alderman Schimenz, who had made the "dead body" statement two years earlier, now remarked:

> Isn't it better for some of us to eat a little crow around here, rather than go into the courts? The water works will be taken away from us.

Postscript 1. The friction between Wauwatosa and Milwaukee did not end with the PSC order. Sixty days came and went, and not a drop of water crossed the Milwaukee-Wauwatosa border. Each side accused the other of delaying; the city charged that the suburb's storage tanks were not ready, and the suburb claimed that the city's connections were not in order. When Milwaukee water tardily began to flow to Wauwatosa, the suburb alleged that the city was not providing the full two million gallons a day. Milwaukee Attorney Slater replied that he construed the order to mean that Wauwatosa could draw water from Milwaukee "if we have any water left after meeting our own needs."

2. Early in 1959, Wisconsin Governor Gaylord Nelson submitted the name of Alderman Matt Schimenz to the State Senate for confirmation as Chairman of the Public Service Commission of Wisconsin.

An immediate protest was sent to the Governor by the Municipal League of Milwaukee County (an organization of the suburban governments). State Senator Allen Busby (R-West Milwaukee, one of the suburbs) announced that he would vote against confirmation of Schimenz because the Milwaukee Alderman was "an advocate of the suburbs' adversary — the city."

Other state legislators indicated no particular interest in blocking the nomination at first, but one of the suburban representatives was reported in the *Milwaukee Journal* to have said, "Our only hope of blocking the appointment is to make it a Republican Party issue, one of party loyalty." The vote on the confirmation showed the success of the suburban effort. The Governor's candidate was rejected, 14 to 18. Republicans voted 18-2 against, while Democrats voted 12-0 for confirmation. Another rural legislature had done its work.

EDWARD C. BANFIELD

Party Cleavages in the Metropolis

. . . For many years to come it will be difficult or impossible to
integrate local governments where the two-party system operates.
Even if the proportion of Republicans declines sharply in the suburbs, metropolitan area government north of the Mason-Dixon line
would almost everywhere be Republican government. In effect, advocates of consolidation schemes are asking the Democrats to give
up their control of the central cities or, at least, to place it in
jeopardy.

It may be that in time Democratic politicians will become so persuaded of the necessity of metropolitan government by the propaganda of the good government movement that they will support it
against their own interest and that of their party. (Certainly many
politicians are convinced of the merits of the merit system, although
it has gone far toward undermining the party system.) Or it may be
that the Democrats will be forced to accept metropolitan government by a public opinion which will have come to share the general
bias of the experts in favor of symmetry and simplicity. These even-
tualities are not unlikely, but it will probably be a good many years
before they are realized.

Three-quarters of the metropolitan areas lie entirely within a single county. From the standpoint of administration there is much to
be said for city-county consolidation: it would make sense to endow
county governments with the powers of cities and to organize them
to exercise those powers efficiently. Schemes like this are being
worked out in Miami, Atlanta, and Nashville, but it is highly unlikely

Reprinted from "The Politics of Metropolitan Organization," *Midwest
Journal of Political Science,* Vol. 1, No. 1 (May 1957) by Edward C.
Banfield by permission of the author and the Wayne State University
Press, Copyright, 1957, Wayne State University Press, Detroit 2, Michigan.

that they will be tried where there is a two-party system. If Buffalo, for example, were to be consolidated with Erie County, control over it would pass from the Democratic party to the Republican. If Chicago were consolidated with Cook County, the Democrats would have a fighting chance of capturing it. But as matters now stand control of Chicago is a sure thing for the Democrats. Why should they change?

City-county separation will be unacceptable for the same reason. If Chicago — to take a typical case — were made a county by itself, apart from the rest of Cook County, the Democrats, although their control of the city would not be jeopardized, would no longer have a chance in Cook County. That would be safely Republican.

For the same reason that they will refuse to turn all of their powers over to a Republican county government, the Democrats of the central cities will refuse to turn over some of them to special function districts. Recently Sheriff Joseph Lohman of Cook County, a good government and planning-minded Democrat (he was formerly chairman of the Washington, D. C. Planning Commission), observed that law enforcement in the Chicago metropolitan area is "hamstrung" by limited jurisdictions and resources. He proposed putting the 11,000 policemen who now serve more than two hundred governmental units within the county under nine elected commissioners and suggested that a police commissioner be elected from each of nine wedge-shaped districts extending from the center of Chicago to the county line. The plan attracted no support from either Lohman's fellow-Democrats or from the Republicans. Obviously the Democrats are not going to give the Republicans the chance — the very good chance — of controlling the police of the central city. Nor are the Republicans going to run the risk of letting control of their suburban police fall into the hands of the central city Democrats.

There will probably be some instances — Detroit and Wayne County appear to be one and Pittsburgh and Allegheny County another — where the number of suburban Republicans is too small to make much difference. Consolidation may be possible in these cases. They will be few, however.

The Republicans outside of the central cities will of course want to remain apart: they are as well satisfied with a one-party system as are the Democrats of the central cities.

It would be a mistake to suppose that the conflict lies altogether or even mainly between the two party organizations or among the

professional politicians who have a stake in them. The party differences are important in themselves, but they reflect deeper and still
more important differences. Metropolitan government would mean
the transfer of power over the central cities from the largely lower-
class Negro and Catholic elements who live in them to the largely
middle-class white and Protestant elements who live in the suburbs.

It should be remembered that between the central city resident
and the suburbanite there are also differences of interest which have
no necessary connection with race or class. If overnight all of the
people of the central cities were transformed into middle-class white
Protestants, there would still be the basis for conflict between them
and the suburbanites. It would still have to be decided, for example,
whether thousands of central city residents should be relocated to
build expressways to give suburbanites quicker access to the city as
well as how taxes to pay for such improvements should be levied. In
St. Louis a metropolitan transit scheme failed of adoption recently
apparently because of fears that improved service for suburbanites
would be paid for by the fares of central city residents. Such instances abound.

The situation will not be altogether different where the city is
non-partisan. The major parties are alive and watching for their
chances even in non-partisan cities. But even if they were not alive,
the fundamental differences of interest and of status which separate
the central city and the suburban populations would nevertheless be
expressed at the polls and elsewhere. In non-partisan Milwaukee
Mayor Frank P. Zeidler recently complained that influential suburbanites — leaders of industry, of business and real estate, and of
the press; presidents of utilities; attorneys; and trained technical persons — "working through their suburban governments and especially
through the county government and state legislature . . . can exercise an almost compulsory power on the city." Through the process
of functional consolidation, Mayor Zeidler said, "the city is being
stripped of more and more of its desirable functions, but it is being
left with its problems — especially the social problems."

The few Republicans of the central cities and, in general, the good
government forces — in short, all those who want to weaken the
Democratic machines — will favor adding the suburban vote to the
central city vote wherever the suburbs are predominantly middle or
upper class. It is not surprising that in Kansas City, Mo., City Manager Cookingham annexed some fringe areas over their violent oppo-

sition. He knew that, bitter as they might be at forced annexation, in the long run they would have to side with him against the remains of the Pendergast machine.

As the Negro tide rises in the central cities, many white Democrats will begin to think of annexation and consolidation as ways to maintain a white (but, alas, Republican!) majority. Unless there is consolidation, some cities will probably have Negro mayors within the next twenty years. Negroes can be expected to oppose annexation and consolidation under these circumstances, of course, and if the issue were to be decided on the metropolitan scene they could probably prevent gerrymandering along racial lines. Rural — and therefore white — dominated legislatures will have the decisive say in these matters, however, and they will be almost immune from Negro influence.

There are fast-growing lower class, and even Negro, suburbs close to some central cities. Democratic politicians will not ordinarily have much incentive to annex these because the Democratic majorities in the central cities will be large enough without them. But where lower class suburbs are large enough to insure Democratic county government, one stumbling block in the way of city-county consolidation will not exist. There will be another in such cases, however: Republican legislatures will be reluctant to pass enabling legislation.

SCOTT GREER

The Machine of the Incumbents:
The Governance of the Central City

Continual increase in scale has had four major consequences for the problems of urban government and their solution. It has produced an increasing bureaucratization of governmental and other functions: it has led to rapid organizational mergers in private enterprise; it has radically changed the general character of the urban population; and it has resulted in a massive multiplication of the population and therefore of the size of the organizational tools of urban government. Let us consider each of these in relation to its implications for the classic big city machine.

The bureaucratization of governmental services affected the machine in two separate ways. First, with the Great Depression of the 1930's it became apparent that all Americans were part of a nationwide economic system, and when that system failed the problem of unemployment and poverty was a nationwide problem. As a consequence, what had been charity became the work of the Department of Health, Education, and Welfare, and vast programs were administered through the nationwide bureaucracies of government. Second, the management of local governmental enterprises became increasingly professionalized; the reformers were successful in convincing the people (and later the politicians) that such services as the city provided were better handled by civil servants, selected and trained through nonpolitical methods to do their jobs without favoritism or political counsel. These two changes struck deep at the roots of politics as a simple exchange system. The goods which the precinct captain once traded for votes were disbursed by a federal

Reprinted from *Governing the Metropolis* (New York: Wiley, 1962), pp. 65-81, by permission of the author and John Wiley & Sons, Inc.

76

agency staffed by civil servants. The decisions about street layouts, hospital construction, zoning, and planning, once so profitably controlled by politicians, were increasingly made by professional public personnel — planners, hospital administrators, traffic engineers. At the same time voting became better organized, and mechanized, with a bureaucracy (subject to review) in charge of the tallies. Quality control made fraud difficult and dangerous. Both at the lowest and highest levels the exchange system of the machine was mortally damaged.

The rapid and continuous process of organizational merger had other effects upon the urban polity. The drawing of major enterprise into national organizations and the further bureaucratization of the corporation, as it separated ownership from management, resulted in a class of professional managers whose first duty was to the nationwide, or international, corporate network. The most powerful economic figure in town was no longer the owner of the major industry; he was a manager. Consequently, the economic dominants (as they are sometimes called in the literature on the power elite) became increasingly withdrawn from concern with the local community. Schulze has documented the steps by which Ypsilanti, Michigan, moved from a classical power elite structure to one in which the branch plant managers were interested in the local community only on rare occasions. Rather than wishing to run the show, they only wanted a veto on certain kinds of governmental act. Otherwise, they did not wish to be involved.[1]

The result of corporate merger has been the freeing of economic organizations from dependence upon, and hence interest in, particular cities. This has combined with the increasing geographical mobility of the managerial elite; as they move upward in the corporate hierarchy they move around the country. They become identified with one community only when they have ceased to be occupationally mobile. (One longitudinal study indicated that, even in Red Wing, Minnesota, a town of ten thousand, the personnel change among those nominated as civic leaders was more than 60 per cent in the relatively short period of six years.)[2] Turnover of leadership

[1] Robert O. Schulze, "The Bifurcation of Power in a Satellite City," in Morris Janowitz, editor, *Community Political Systems,* Glencoe, Ill.: The Free Press of Glencoe, Inc., 1961.

[2] "Organizational Leadership and Social Structure in a Small City," Donald W. Olmstead, *American Sociological Review,* Vol. 19, pp. 273-281.

makes effective organization (the compromising of interests, the assignment of tasks, the integrating of action) extremely difficult. Furthermore, we must remember that the business leadership in a city of any size is apt to be divisible on more issues than those on which it is unitable. (A recent study by Scoble, for example, shows a very low rate of consensus among the dominant leaders in a New England town of less than fifteen thousand persons.)[3] It requires *more* work to achieve coordination when there is high turnover, yet there are fewer people committed to achieving it. In short, the changing nature of exclusive, membership organizations has greatly weakened their machinery for controlling the political decisions of the city. And such change is of particular importance in the metropolis, the headquarters city of the corporation.

Meanwhile, the population of the metropolis has been changing . . . Social rank has on the average moved upwards; the illiterate, unskilled workman of foreign birth is a vanishing breed. Even in the central city education, occupation, and real income have risen to once-unimaginable levels in the past sixty years. At the same time, the children and grandchildren of the foreign born are socialized from the beginning to the American urban milieu. As a result of these changes in combination the definition of the vote has changed; it is no longer simply an expression of ethnic solidarity, but rather a more complex decision, based on a variety of interests. The children of the immigrants live in a different city from that of their parents and have different techniques for managing their urban environment. Their toleration for fraud shrinks as they become more informed and committed to American civic virtues. Their vote is not for sale.

An indirect effect of increasing size, but an important one, is the suburban-central city dichotomy. With increasing population and static boundary lines, the population of the metropolis is almost equally divided between central city and suburbs. . . . [T]hose who remain in the central city are predominantly ethnic and working class social types. In 1950, according to Philip Hauser, "Los Angeles was the only city among the five largest in the United States in which the native white population of native parentage was greater

[3] "Leadership Hierarchies and Political Issues in a New England Town," by Harry Scoble, in *Community Political Systems,* Morris Janowitz, editor, Glencoe, Ill.: The Free Press of Glencoe, Inc., 1961.

than half, and even there it was only 55 per cent.[4] These populations are the ones most likely to prefer the Democratic party in national elections; when there is a partisan organization of local elections (and this is true of all but one of our very large cities) the working class and the ethnic voters go Democratic. A direct consequence is the collapse of the Republican Party in the political arena of the central city. One by one, Republican strongholds are giving way to Democratic majorities, as the nordic white Protestant middle class makes its way to the suburbs. Today, in many of our great cities, two or three Republican councilmen represent the "two party system" among a host of Democratic officials. As the process of segregation by polity continues, the central city will become, in fact if not in theory, a one-party state.

Finally, we have to consider the increase in the size of urban concentrations. In 1900 two American metropolitan areas had a population of a million or more; in 1960, there were nineteen complexes this large. The sheer aggregation of population had two major effects upon the control system of the central city. First, and not to be overlooked, was the sheer increase in the size of the problems that had to be handled within the rounds of urban housekeeping, and the consequent size of the organizations which handled them. The City of New York, for example, employs 50,000 persons in its educational system, 26,000 in its police department, and 13,000 in its fire department.[5] The sheer aggregation of numbers and budget results in the proliferation of organizational centers with a degree of autonomy and, hence, power. The number and strength of leadership groups is multiplied with increasing population.

The total effect of these changes has been the destruction of the old-time political machine, and with it the power elite. Increase in scale has destroyed the basis for the political machine *as an exchange system;* in the urban wards of Stackton it is as hard to recruit precinct workers as in the small-town Republican strongholds of Illinois. Whyte reports the visible attrition of the Democratic machine in Boston during the 1930's, while Reichley discusses the steady weakening of Republican power in Philadelphia during the

---

[4] Hauser, *Population Perspectives,* New Brunswick, N.J.: Rutgers University Press, 1960, p. 125.
[5] Wallace S. Sayre and Herbert Kaufman, *Governing New York,* New York: The Russell Sage Foundation, 1960.

same period.[6] The ability of the political boss to control his "Hes-sians" and through them the vote of the people, may have been over-rated in the past: it is very easy to over-rate it today.

The collapse of the exchange system has, in turn, destroyed the ability of the power elite to call the tune. Businessmen have never had a preponderant influence, at the polls, on the city population as a whole. They have relied upon the machine as a mechanism for translating money into political power. By bribing the politicians and by contributing to campaign chests, business interests assured themselves a strong voice in the political decisions of the central city. Even with the Republican Party's power fading away they could still exert leverage upon the Democratic machine, for the machine was primarily a nonideological exchange system. With its weakening, however, the businessman had literally no way of reaching the voters.

The result is a drastic separation of numbers and wealth in the contemporary metropolis. Businessmen, resident in the suburbs, have great stakes in the central city polity. That polity, however, is con-trolled by a set of politicians who have a declining need for the busi-nessman, and who are elected by the votes of the ethnic and work-ing class constituencies of the center. Such a separation of numbers and wealth is not, of course, contrary to the democratic dogma. It is, however, an anomaly to those who still consider the businessman as the first class citizen and his interests as paramount for the com-munity.

It is also anomalous to those who explain American government through the theory of the two-party system, with its assumptions of organized control and competition for power. The anomaly leads us to ask: How, then, does the government of today's central city oper-ate? How is it that order is maintained and essential tasks are per-formed?

The disappearance of party competition in the general elections of the central city does not destroy party organization. Instead it changes the basis of organization: the old-style exchange system is

[6] The political machine in Stackton is described and analyzed by Peter H. Rossi and Phillips Cutright in "The Impact of Party Organization in an Industrial Setting," in Morris Janowitz, editor, *Community Political Systems*, Glencoe, Ill.: The Free Press of Glencoe, Inc., 1961. For the Philadelphia case see James Reichley, *The Art of Government*, New York: The Fund for the Republic, 1959. William Foote Whyte presents a study, in depth, of the changing relations of the machine to the ethnic neighbor-hood he studied in Boston, in *Streetcorner Society*, Chicago: University of Chicago Press, 1943.

replaced by a new order. Before discussing the new state of things, however, it is important to note the cause and consequences of one-party government for the dominant Democratic organization.

The central city electorate, with its predisposition to vote Democratic, is (like the Southern Democrats) basically a captive electorate. Whoever is designated Democrat on the ballot will usually get a majority of the votes. One might jump to the conclusion that such one-party government could mean only a sort of totalitarianism. Instead, it seems to result in a general loosening of the control mechanism; as V. O. Key demonstrates for the one-party system in the South, the very basis for much of the party's control is weakened by the disappearance of the opposition party.[7] The reduction of threat in the general election eliminates the need for party discipline and ferocious *esprit de corps* for, no matter what happens, the Democratic Party will take most of the elective offices.

Under these circumstances, however, the Republican minority is rapidly demoralized. Political organization is postulated upon occasional victory; moral victories are sustaining only when there is some eventual possibility of non-moral, tangible victory. In the central city, however, Republican votes continue to decline despite all efforts made by the Republican Parties. As this occurs, the Republican Party's leadership and its elected local officials in cities like St. Louis and Chicago begin to resemble Republicans of the South. They are either lonely idealists, whose words are purely symbolic since they lack power to implement them, or else a sort of auxiliary of the dominant Democrats. (Chicago's delegation to the State legislature in Springfield includes the "sanitary Republicans," Republican legislators whose chief source of income is office in the Democratic-controlled Chicago Sanitary District.) Such officials may even vote with the Democrats and against their fellow Republicans on crucial issues. Thus even if the Republicans had a powerful issue, it is doubtful that the existing leadership could mobilize a campaign to exploit it. They stand not so much for an alternative governance as for the existing distribution of electoral strength in the central city; in fact, they depend upon it for their working conditions.

The Democratic monopoly of victory in the general election, however, means that the primary election becomes the major arena for gaining office. And at the primary level the party organization is considerably weakened, for nomination to office (tantamount to elec-

[7] V. O. Key, *Southern Politics*, New York: Alfred A. Knopf, 1949.

tion) becomes an apple of discord thrown among the Democratic ranks. In some cities the party cannot officially designate a slate in the primary; even when it can, its decisions are basically divisive. There are many deserving party men, and little to prevent one from running from his district. If he has been an effective leader at the block and precinct level, he may very well win, for the mobilization of friends and neighbors can easily produce strong opposition to the organization's designated candidate. Since the candidates do not need actual logistic support in the general election (the simple party designation will usually suffice), the field is clear for "mavericks" to compete.

Yet the party organization can usually control most of the offices in the primary election. The reason for this is clear enough; the ordinary voter usually does not know or care enough about the primary to vote. Thus the organization, though it may control only a small percentage of the potential vote, can nevertheless swing the margin of victory to its candidate. This organizational level is considerably augmented in many cities by the organization's control of the electoral machinery. Efforts range from differential requirements for certification as a candidate, to the ignoring of irregularities in the campaign and the voting (though the latter practices are becoming increasingly dangerous . . .). We may surmise also that much of the power of the organization results from a simple misapprehension of its effective force by potential dissidents. The machine *was* all-powerful for many years in some of our cities; those interested in politics are differentially exposed to the organization. They may fear official disapproval, not just in the immediate election, but in the future. Even if the party machine's power is now a myth, myths may long outlive their factual base and have consequences.

Thus the organization maintains a continuing control, though not an ironclad one, over the distribution of offices. However, with the disappearance of effective opposition it no longer needs the money of the businessman to win its campaigns. Being able to win the general election in any event, the power relations between politician and business leader have shifted radically. The politician is clearly in the more advantageous position: he has the trading cards.

There have also been radical changes within the dominant party's organization. With the weakening of the machine, the power relation between the nonelective party Boss and the elected officials reverses. First the elected mayor develops a considerable autonomy from the machine; standing above all other elected figures in the metropolis, his role is visible and his words are news. From the rostrum of office he tends to dominate the mass media, and through the media develops a powerful electoral attraction of his own. Then party ceases to be a differentiating label in the one-party central city; the major differentiator becomes incumbency. Those who are in office become *de facto* rulers of the party, for the party needs them more than they need its cohorts. They dispense the patronage and make the decisions.

Thus the central city mayor assumes a major if not dominating role in the *dramatis personae* of local politics. Other stellar roles include the head of the county government and perhaps the president of the council or board of aldermen. They also are familiar figures in the news, for they are elected officials with city-wide constituencies in image if not in fact. Along with them rise the managers of the great governmental bureaucracies, school superintendents, engineers, police commissioners, and the like. Such men, elected or appointed, stand for the expertise of their office, the legitimacy of the tasks which their bureaucracy performs, and the logistics of money and men. The dominant figures in central city politics tend to be the dominant officials of government; they constitute a "machine of the incumbents." No matter how they reached office in the first place, once there they are formidable forces.

The central city mayor can, indeed, become an enemy of his party's organization. Concerned with the entire city, he is sensitive to opinion in the middle class, familistic, outer wards of the city; his political score in the general elections depends upon his ability to carry these "good government" and "newspaper" wards. He responds to the criticism of the daily press and the statements of public leaders representing various interests: welfare, hospital, education, and the like. Though these interests cannot defeat him at the polls, he nevertheless engages in implicit bargaining with them, anticipating the effects of his words and actions on the newspapers, civic leaders, and hence, the outer wards. At the same time the central city mayor is the dominant public official for the entire metropolitan area. Insofar as there is a metropolitan community, he is its highest elected official. (In St. Louis, suburbanites and central city voters alike accorded the Mayor of the City more trust and confidence than all other leaders combined, and their reasons rested upon his office, his expertise, and his character as a civic notable.) As representative of more than the laundry list of special interests in the area, he stands for the general welfare. Businessmen, no longer his employers, return as influentials insofar as they are virtual representatives of many values and aspects of the metropolis.

In fact, the central city mayor tends to believe that good government is good politics. But in the process of pursuing good government he may destroy much of the effectiveness of the Democratic organization.[8] The separation of the offices of precinct captain for the party and precinct captain of police may be good governmental administration: it may also be very demoralizing for the political actors who had counted upon the promotion to police captain as a possible reward. Nevertheless, the metropolitan mayor is free to continue his swing towards good government, for the machine cannot control him. And he may look beyond the central city, to position in the state government, or the federal government in Washington, where his "good government" policies may count heavily. Furthermore, he is, ironically, strengthened at home by his symbolic separation from the machine. He can have his cake and eat it too. Meanwhile the old-style political machine is further weakened; the rewards of political work disappear right and left. As one consequence, the persons who can be recruited for the hard and tedious work at the block level change in character; the ranks of party workers become disproportionately composed of those who have few alternatives for social distinction and mobility. The over-all picture is one in which old-style machine politics fades away before the new order, the machine of the incumbents.

To repeat the argument: The continual segregation of population by governmental boundaries means an increasing domination of the central city vote by the poor, the ethnics, and therefore the Democratic party label. This, in turn, relaxes the tensions of conflict at a party level, leading to a one-party state. To be sure, the process has gone further in some cities than others; it is still possible for the Republicans to win a battle occasionally if their wards are numerous and the Democrats make a series of catastrophic mistakes.

This will become rarer as the proportion of working class ethnics increases. It is also true that, in West Coast cities like Los Angeles, Republicans may rule under the guise of nonpartisanship. It is likely, however, that such cities, never having known a machine, have sim-

---

[8] Banfield discusses the destructive effect of the "good government mayor" at some length in *Political Influence,* New York: The Free Press of Glencoe, Inc., 1961.

ply skipped a stage and landed directly in the future — the one party or non-party polity ruled by the machine of the incumbents.

One-party government, in fact, approaches very closely the condition of non-partisan government. The weakening of the party organization's hold on the incumbents softens the impact of those who wish to translate wealth and social power garnered in other fields into pressure on the policy of the city. The incumbents are freed from many pressures; however, it is a "freedom from," rather than a freedom to accomplish new and radical enterprises. This is because power becomes basically fractionated and dispersed. The elected officials, the heads of the great bureaucracies, state and federal levels of government, private capital, and the party organization, each hold certain resources necessary for massive action. To these must be added the governmental divisions of the metropolis. Multiple municipalities, counties, and special districts are vested with the legitimate power to perform certain tasks and to refuse to cooperate in others.

Banfield's description of Chicago emphasizes the continual deadlocking of these forces. In *Political Influence* he notes that the political head (usually the mayor) will ratify almost any proposal on which principal parties can agree. He thus escapes criticism from newspapers, civic leaders, and the like. However, he hesitates to force compromise because of the cost in goodwill, support, public image, or other intangibles of influence. He can usually afford to wait indefinitely for decisions to emerge: what usually emerges is stalemate. Of the six major issues Banfield studied (all of the major public issues for a two year period), two were resolved, one was abandoned by its protagonists, and the remainder were simply tabled. Thus half the major public issues remained in limbo. This is hardly evidence of a tightly knit ruling clique. Instead, Banfield sees the power elite as essentially part of "The Mythology of Influence."

> The notion that "top leaders" run the city is certainly not supported by the facts of the controversies described in this book. On the contrary, in these cases the richest men of Chicago are conspicuous by their absence. Lesser business figures appear, but they do not act concertedly: some of them are on every side of every issue. The most influential people are the managers of large organizations the maintenance of which is at stake, a few "civic leaders" whose judgment, negotiating skill, and distinterestedness are unusual and, above all, the chief elected officials. Businessmen exert influence (to the extent that they exercise it at all) not so

much because they are rich or in a position to make threats and promises as, in the words of one of them, "by main force of being right."[9]

To be sure, Banfield thinks that if all the wealth were organized in a permanent organization, it could exert great influence on the polity. This is not likely to come about, however, for three reasons: (1) there are fundamental conflicts of interest among private organizations, (2) the required communication would be great enough to cut seriously into the time necessary for private interest, and (3) any formal organization would rapidly become immobilized by its own commitments and organizational structure.

The overriding power of the mayor is also a logical possibility in Banfield's interpretation. He dismisses it in these words.

> To be sure, his power is great enough, thanks to the machine and to his ability to make the trades the planners deplore, so that he can exercise wide discretion in almost any matter. But being able to exercise wide discretion in almost any matter does not mean that he can exercise it in *all* matters. With respect to any one or two, or any few, moves, he is free. But if he wishes to stay in the game and to win, most of his moves, like most of the moves of the "civic leaders" and the businessmen in *their* games, must be determined by the exigencies of the game itself. Like them, he must act as the game requires or else get out of it.[10]

Thus Banfield's picture of Chicago is one that underlines the stability of the order, its underlying resistance to change, and the recalcitrant nature of government as a tool for major control and planning.

Sayre and Kaufman come to similar conclusions with respect to the greatest city in the country, New York City. Much as they love it, they report that its government is essentially static and conservative. The council is hamstrung, the mayor has responsibilities far beyond his power, and the Board of Estimate (made up of borough presidents and some central city officials) has usurped effective power. The result is a city government which has no legislative process, no strong executive, no party division visible to the public: one which is, in short, neither democratically responsible nor capable of a strong polity. Neither innovation nor planning can come about except in piecemeal response to the maintenance needs of the great city bureaucracies whose managers are as important in New York

[9] *Ibid.*, p. 288.
[10] *Ibid.*, pp. 302-303.

as in Banfield's Chicago.[11] For the Mayor of New York to function as leader and responsible head of the government he must be a political genius. When any social role requires such a rare person to operate it, we can judge it poorly designed for a world dominated by the "fairly bright."

The mayors of our great cities, symbols and symbolic leaders of the metropolitan community, reign but do not rule. They are brokers, conciliators, who reconcile the people to what they get from their government. They legitimatize the *fait accompli* on the rare occasions when the necessary resources for action result from transitory coalitions among the major contending organizations. For the rest, they preside over routine caretaker governments. And from one point of view, this is what the situation may seem to demand. The pioneer work of building the plant and establishing an order for the central city is long since complete: the population explosion will not rock its foundations, for a vast apparatus is in existence, and new growth will largely settle outside the center, in suburbia. The great bureaucracies which provide necessary governmental goods and services are already in being: they pursue the organizational destiny of expansion, increasing professionalization and multiplying the career opportunities for civil servants. All this they can do within the precedents established in the past and legitimatized through use.

There is, however, no organization capable of mounting a major offensive for innovation. The central city's polity is passive and adaptive before the continuing results of increase in scale; only catastrophe seems capable of creating the opportunity for new development. Meanwhile, the trends continue; the suburban move of industry is added to the differentiation of central city and suburban populations, the increasingly obsolete neighborhoods, and the increasing proportion of colored populations who suffer most from economic depression and expect the most action from their city government. Taken all together these trends result in a rapid drift of the city away from its older status of centrality and totality. Faced with such changes, most people who consider the central city's destiny agree that massive counteraction, planning and construction, and governmental change are necessary. Such counteraction is difficult to imagine within the governmental structure of our great cities as they operate today.

[11] Sayre and Kaufman, *op. cit.*, Chapter XVII.

ROBERT C. WOOD

Suburbia: The Fiscal Roots of
Political Fragmentation and Differentiation

For the suburbs as a whole, the problem involved in their tax system is less the evils of the property tax as such than the inflexibility of their general tax structure implied by the heavy reliance on property taxes. While other local governments, particularly large cities and independent cities with a rural hinterland, have been able to broaden their tax base considerably, suburbs, with notable exceptions, have not. Municipal income taxes, sales and gross taxes, tobacco and admission taxes, levies on earnings, are not well suited to suburban governments. For one thing, they are difficult to administer, requiring a bureaucratic sophistication, an array of financial power, an assurance that their residents cannot shop elsewhere, and a variety of land uses that few suburbs possess. For another, they often place a suburb at a competitive disadvantage with its neighbors so far as the attraction of presumably desirable business and commercial activity is concerned. Although, as we will see later, suburbs have shown great ingenuity in discovering and inventing new sources of revenue, by and large they are excluded from the big money earners. While nonproperty taxes accounted for 27 per cent of all local revenues in the 481 cities over 25,000 population in 1956, and multiplied six times in the years between 1950 and 1955, it is doubtful that suburban governments — municipalities, school districts, and towns — figured prominently in the increase.

The heavy reliance on property taxation is the first fiscal liability of the suburbs. The second is the fact that, contrary to popular opin-

Reprinted from *Suburbia: Its People and Their Politics* (Boston: Houghton Mifflin Company, 1958), pp. 208-225, with the permission of the author and the publisher.

88

ion, the property to be taxed is becoming less lucrative. The comfortable assumption that residential property values are almost always higher in outlying districts of the metropolitan areas — and, therefore, the suburban tax base is proportionately larger than that of the core city — justified many family migrations to the metropolitan fringe. In prewar years this was to a considerable degree correct, but for the last fifteen years suburban real estate has lost a great deal of its comparative advantage over that in the central city.

Almost 50 per cent of the dwelling units constructed between 1940 and 1950 were in the suburbs, and, typically, the values of the new residences were higher than the values of residences built before 1940. But the differences between old and new values are not nearly as great as they were fifteen years ago, and so far as the more expensive residential construction is concerned — houses costing over $15,000 — two important developments have taken place. First, in this category there is no significant difference between old and new suburban houses, and second, median values for new housing in the central cities are almost 30 per cent higher than in the suburbs. Moreover, the faster a metropolitan area grows, the lower the median value of residential housing constructed. In short, when housing values new or old are compared, there is a persistent tendency for the central city to have higher residential values and to retain them, and the faster the suburb grows, the lower is the average residential value. Suburbs are not attracting the high value development of our decade.

Even more important, general averages are likely to be misleading in suburbia, where land uses tend to cluster in the same way different occupations bunch together. Unlike the median values of a large city that encompasses all types of property, the limited jurisdiction of each suburb means that usually only one type of property value predominates. The search for homogeneity carries its inevitable corollary in property values, and suburbs differentiate themselves sharply in their financial resources when they segregate themselves by social status. For the suburbs taken collectively, this range has great significance, for it means that the cheaper construction now underway, especially in rapidly growing areas, is not spread throughout each suburb. Instead, it is concentrated in particular suburbs, heightening their fiscal crises while others take the lion's share of the more expensive residential property to provide the base for their public services.

The continuing dispersion of industrial and service activity may

well tend to supply additional resources for the suburbs as a class
and provide a welcome cushion to the tax base. But here again the
question of variations among suburbs arises. Despite the newly
favorable attitude many fringe communities are exhibiting toward
light industry, there is, as yet, little evidence that industry locates
where it is most needed in terms of tax resources. Most observers
believe a contrary pattern is at work, in which "industries tend to
locate in one suburban community and the workers locate in another community, with the result that the problem of financing services to the employees, and their families, of those industries, gets
very serious indeed."

Nor are shopping centers likely to relieve the plight of low housing value suburbs. They tend to locate where incomes are higher
and their aim is to draw together a number of businesses in a concentrated space. Thus their very success reduces the likelihood that
neighborhood stores will scatter themselves throughout the suburbs,
in physically unattractive but financially rewarding string developments along major streets. With the rich getting richer and the poor
poorer, those suburbs with lower value housing and probably a
greater need for services may have to depend more and more on residential property value to support their governments.

The continued shift in the labor force from agricultural and manufacturing occupations to "service" industries — and the consequent
spread of trade establishments — may well alleviate the tight fiscal
situation. And if the diffusion of industry accelerates in the next
generation as many expect, more suburbs will find additional revenue sources. Stern reassessments, bringing tax valuations more in
line with market price, may also increase the yield of present resources. But these trends are still in the making; at the present time,
suburbs in general and in particular seem to face an uphill fight.

Yet the critical factor is not the present difficulties of suburbs as a
class, the shortcomings of the property tax as such or the inability of
most suburbs to develop other resources. Even the relative decline
in suburban residential property value as compared to the central
city may not be serious. Rather, it is the haphazard pattern of distribution of property resources among political jurisdictions, and the
effect of the property tax upon that distribution, that spells real
trouble.

Specifically, financial trouble lies ahead for the metropolitan regions because the property tax system works to encourage a further
political fragmentation of the areas. It sets off a game of musical

chairs which coincides with social and political proclivities for exclusiveness, and although the process carries with it the seeds of self-destruction, the logic of maintaining the separate status of each such suburb is inescapably reinforced. This is the real significance of the present financial pattern which, in the face of snowballing new demands, works to keep the suburbs divided.

The internal workings of the property tax within suburbia are complicated, and it exists only because the region is already fragmented. But it is the policy induced by the financial system — not the tax itself, not the real wealth of the communities in relation to public expenditures — that is the key to understanding the so-called suburban financial crisis. George Duggar has provided the theoretical framework that explains the suburban maneuvers in their self-imposed battle for resources. He reasons that suburbanites tend to judge governmental expenditures according to whether or not the services they provide add to the land values, or, more specifically, whether their benefits for the individual land owner add to the total value of his property more than his taxes detract from it. Given this tendency, the logical tax policy for any local government is to maximize the benefits of public services and minimize their tax costs. Thus the objective it must seek is to entice high-value property within its borders and prevent the intrusion of low-value construction.

The rationale for this policy of "financial efficiency," so far as residential construction is concerned, is, of course, that expensive properties pay high taxes while they typically require the same level of public services as any other type of property of equal size. For high-value residences, the value of the land itself is proportionately higher and the share of private improvement value in the total value is lower than for low-value property. Thus the total taxable value is greater, compared to the services required, the higher a community climbs up the scale of residential quality. The suburban government of better-class neighborhoods finds itself in a happy position of being able to receive tax returns considerably in excess of the cost of services it must offer.

Moreover, because there is a monopolistic element involved in land prices, arising from the relative scarcity of good sites, the prestige value associated with exclusive neighborhoods, and the reduced importance of money for those who are able to live in them, the suburban government can exact higher prices for the services it provides. In actual practice, it can, of course, reduce the tax rate to the point where revenue equals expenditures, but in theory it behaves like a firm engaged in monopolistic competition — receiving revenues for each unit of service considerably higher than the cost of providing the service. By offering a special type of land advantages, it is able to extract taxes that are considerably larger than those received by other suburbs which do not have choice property but which have the same service needs.

On the other hand, suburbs in which very inexpensive development has taken place cannot hope to receive revenues commensurate with costs. In these municipalities, the value of a typical home is a much larger proportion of total real estate value — house and site taken together. Since the costs for government services are more closely related to the number of houses than the value of the land they are built upon, as construction becomes cheaper and cheaper, the captialized costs of services per house or square foot of land come to exceed the capitalized taxable value, or even the market value per house or foot of land. Without the cushion which high site values give, the suburban government is forced to increase the tax rate to as high a level as possible, or to cut services. Even then, if total residential values are very low, it may not be able to make ends meet. Its financial position becomes progressively worse, for the ratio between tax burdens and benefits is reduced, each additional unit of service costing more on a capitalized basis than the corresponding unit of revenues the property produces, with the inevitable result of a rising tax rate. In these municipalities property values are not enhanced by government services; instead, they are adversely affected.

Thus, the overall policy implication of the property tax, as Duggar points out, is that suburban governments are led inevitably into an effort to achieve "financial efficiency" by a policy of "value differentiation" — that is, using local governmental powers to attract expensive improvements or to repel lower-cost improvements. This drive for high values may take the form of exclusive residential development or it may induce suburbs into the now fashionable search for "light industry," breaking down earlier attitudes antagonistic to industrial development. As these financial problems increase, as the amount of undeveloped land dwindles, many municipalities become actively engaged in enticing industry, regardless of the intrinsic economic value of their particular sites. Unwilling to trust the operation of market forces, they engage in "a sort of mercantilist interplay between municipalities, each fighting to keep its taxes down and its notables up."

Whether residentially or industrially inclined, however, from the point of view of any suburban government the sensible aim is to attract and maintain as large a concentration of high values as possible. Such a policy not only assures an excess of revenues over normal local government expenditures; in the end, it enhances property values even more, since the individual owner finds indirect benefits accruing from the "monopolist" position his government has attained — the value of "exclusive" neighborhoods, the provision of services that add to site value.

These value differentiation policies have obvious injurious effects on particular individuals. For the property owner the implication is, of course, that total property values are increased among expensive properties and reduced for less costly properties. The owner of a $10,000 Cape Cod house on a quarter acre lot has little economic incentive to build an extra room or add a garage. These "improvements" not only reduce the value of his site in a theoretical sense by distorting it from its "best and most economically desirable purpose" but they increase his taxes more than they increase the benefits he receives from local public services. While, from the municipality's point of view, his total tax burden does not exceed the cost of services rendered, the additional taxes on his new improvements reduce the total value of his property, for in effect they impose expenses greater than benefits. In extreme cases, the after-tax value of low-value property can even be reduced below the level of value of the improvements on the land alone, the market prices of the cheaper houses will fall, and expenditures for proper maintenance and further improvements will be discouraged.

In short, value-differentiation policies, when in full swing in a metropolitan area, work against the provision of reasonably inexpensive homes for the majority of Americans, handicap national policies designed to further home ownership, and encourage high-value construction rather than low for prudent investors. The further down the income scale a family is located, the less likely it is that a suburban house is a good investment. The more improvements made, the less the portion of investment which goes into land alone, the harsher are the tax burdens.

Individual inequities aside, an even more significant effect of these policies from the governmental perspective is the reinforcement of suburban autonomy. Inevitably, the drive for value-differentiation sets in motion a continued process of segregation of high-value property and continued depression of low-value property prices below the market price. Suburban governments, by any doctrine of prudent fiscal management, are forced to prefer expensive construction; such property returns more than it costs in services. The owners of high-value property are then rationally inclined to encourage their governments to resist invasion by owners of lower-value property. Even though the latter pay more than their proportionate share, the presence of cheaper homes may depress prices of the older, more expensive residences, and certainly it will increase overall municipal costs. A process is triggered off by which the suburb initially seeks high value because of the financial advantages accruing to the government and then is led into restrictive practices because these appear to be the only way to preserve the initial investments in the area.

Some authorities find the scramble for resources that goes on in metropolitan areas ethically questionable. Henry Fagin, for example, complains that "the very cities that can most easily afford to carry the burdens of inexpensive homes are the ones which most vigorously resist such homes and are the most successful in avoiding them." Certainly the drive for high-value and only high-value property buttresses the social and ethnic exclusiveness which suburbanites display in their search for small town homogeneity.

Yet, given the nature of the property tax, it is difficult to criticize suburban officials who are fortunate enough to have desirable locations for exploiting their position. To do otherwise when government costs are rising steadily — to be liberal in their attitude toward lower-income newcomers, to strive for heterogeneous neighborhoods, to welcome citizens regardless of race, creed or color — is to invite financial disaster. If the town fathers are to be faithful to their economic trust, they must practice discrimination. Having forsworn association with the metropolis, which might possess the variety of land uses to hold the injurious effects of the property tax to a minimum, there is now no stopping point. Ethically, segregation may be intolerable, but from the individual perspective of any given suburb, the continued splintering of the metropolitan region is now a financial necessity.

The upshot of this inquiry into the implications of property taxation in suburbia is that, so far as the question of financial adequacy is concerned, the answer is, "It all depends." Some suburbs have ample resources to meet the demands of modern government; others are obviously inadequately equipped to stand on their own. As long as the property tax is the bulwark of their defense, the capacity of the suburbs to survive breaks down into at least two different issues, with a broad twilight zone in between. The answers to these questions require a study of the strategy of two types of suburbs as they go about resolving their quite different financial problems.

For the suburbs blessed with natural advantages, where big mansions are in existence and Levittowns have not appeared, the strategy of "high value" dictates a constant surveillance of the changing metropolitan scene to make sure no unwelcome intruders are admitted. A whole series of tactics are usually employed: the judicious use of regulatory powers, special requirements and restrictions demanded of builders, discrimination in taxation and in the quality of services extended to particular neighborhoods, selective annexations, imaginative employment of eminent domain, are all standard weapons in the battle. Collectively, they attest to the strength of will and stubbornness of suburban officials and citizens in preserving their land values and their communities.

The most spectacular weapon, of course, is the use of regulatory powers — zoning and subdivision control — for here the potency of the value-differentiation policy is most clearly seen. Henry Fagin has documented for the New York region the extent to which suburbs will go to preserve high values and exclude low ones. Among his investigations there appears the case of the New Jersey township which imposed an informal building permit moratorium "until 'the law' finally caught up with it"; the instance of the suburb which prevented mass development by requiring that each house differ in certain design characteristics from five of its neighbors; the town which set a five-acre minimum lot size; and the New Jersey borough which owns one third of the land in its jurisdiction and sells lots at the rate of a dozen a year to purchasers of its own choosing. Throughout the cases he studied, Fagin found a consistent policy, in towns which were financially able to support a growing population, to resist new residents and inexpensive construction. His extreme instance was the town which cheapened the existing school program while advocating, as an alternative, policies to encourage birth control.

In more detail, Charles Harr has reviewed the type of zoning program, popularized by the Wayne Township, New Jersey, case. Here, not only did the suburb establish a minimum house size, but it required a larger living space for those houses without an attached garage than for those with such an appendage, on the dubious rationale that the proper care of the automobile affected the health and safety of the family. Acting to halt suburban expansion, Wayne established stringent zoning regulations and set the minimum price of new residences above that of older comparable buildings. In the end, the New Jersey Supreme Court upheld the township, and neither Wayne nor New Jersey are unique. Around San Francisco, St. Louis, and Boston, and in almost every metropolitan area, zoning restrictions have come into effect which can only be designed to require high-cost construction or none at all.

Coincidentally with zoning regulations, communities frequently use a second tactic: they establish, as part of the building regulations or as prerequisite to construction permits, a series of requirements for builders — supplemental taxes, fees, land dedications for schools, parks, donations of facilities. These requirements often serve good purposes, but they also direct special discrimination against lower-value homes, for the charges are almost always passed on to the buyer, and sometimes they serve outright to prohibit development.

A third device — employed in low-value as well as high-value communities — is the creation of special districts within parts of a suburb to offset the financial drain of lower-value houses where they occur. The supplemental taxes which these districts impose result in a higher total tax burden than the suburb could otherwise legally levy and allow a discriminatory tax burden to be imposed on lower-income residents. So the consultants from the University of Pennsylvania could blandly assure the supervisors of Middletown Township that permitting a Levittown within their borders would not lead to financial difficulties; the "three expensive services" of street lighting, fire hydrants and refuse collection, the consultants suggested, "can be financed through special district taxes or assessments, paid for by residents of the Levittown area only." The greater the proliferation of districts, the greater the probability of taxing similar property values at different rates.

Discrimination may also take place in the provision of services, to help assure that tax returns cover costs and to penalize — if they cannot exclude — lower income residents in the more expensive parts of suburbia. Suburban governments commonly differentiate today in the type of fire-fighting facilities and police services required in certain areas, and, significantly enough, these differences do not correlate with need but rather with taxable value. In the words of one commentator, "Them what has taxable value gets," and exclusive residential streets are usually better cleaned and repaired, high-pressure fire systems first installed there, and the neighboring school newer and better staffed. It is only in the slum areas of the large cities, where high expenditures are required to maintain law and order and overcome the hazards of congestion, that per capita expenditures are likely to be higher than in the better parts of the better suburbs.

These weapons — zoning, building requirements, tax and service differentiation — are part of every planning kit, and, as tools, there is nothing reprehensible about them. It is also clearly legitimate for every community to shape its land-use pattern, to use foresight, to prevent blight, and to develop as its citizens desire. The ethical issue, if there is one, is not the propriety of these stratagems, but rather the extreme forms which they may take. Ethics aside, a factual evaluation of the policies of well-to-do municipalities in terms of their capacity to protect their own seems to lead to one conclusion: given the reluctance of the courts to intervene and the number of methods available to suburban officials for the practice of discrimination, the high-value suburbs can remain high-value if they wish. In their response to the welfare state, they can do more than survive; they can flourish.

While the exclusive residential suburb, and perhaps the well-planned industrial enclave, can take care of themselves, relatively few suburbs can succeed in enticing only expensive real estate inside their borders. The bleak fact remains that most new suburban construction is of an inexpensive character and that, despite unparalleled prosperity and all the innovations in residential financing, private or public, suburban property values are declining relative to the central city. Moreover, some suburbs incorporate only after the developers' bulldozers have come and gone, leaving a pent-up demand for municipal services that the property tax could not finance if every home in town were worth fifty thousand dollars. In other cases, the political bulwarks against invasion prove weak, and even in settled communities zoning standards crumble and hundred-foot frontages are authorized. Finally, there are limits, legal and moral, to the extent of segregation that is permissible. The courts may ultimately strike down the most outrageous regulations and restrictions. Here and there, community ethics forbid the self-imposition of a ghetto philosophy. The new migrants are settling somewhere in suburbia, and as they do, municipal costs rise, property values become depressed and financial adversity becomes the rule, not the exception.

For the unwanted, kept out of the exclusive suburbs, a policy of value differentiation will not help, for they cannot zone themselves away. New strategies and tactics are required, both within the local finance system and from outside. One common method is to dispense with all but the most rudimentary of public services, and sometimes even with those. John Scott reports on Whyte's suburban Park Forest that the salvation of its government is that its citizens are fortunately unaware of the array of services its big city neighbors offer. "It is an interesting fact," he writes, "that if you have an honest police department and one that takes good care of lost kids, you can get a lot of credit for giving a high level of police service when, in fact, you may actually not be giving as good police service as at least is potentially possible within the police force of a large city."

The taint of poorer services and amateurism, regardless of the financial effort the new suburbanite is willing to make, spreads beyond the maintenance of law and order. Sewer systems are frequently not available even when the density of population clearly requires them, and often there are neither storm sewers nor water distribution systems. Streets may not be paved, street signs and lights not available. Fire protection is almost always provided by volunteer departments, and though the firemen may be enthusiastic, they are not likely to be as competent or efficient as professionals.

Even for the schools, the public function suburbanites treasure most fondly and for which they will spend most willingly, compromises are made. The desire to escape big city schools, to secure for their children the advantages of better teachers, newer buildings, smaller classes and higher instructional standards, becomes ultimately self-defeating. Precisely because the school is the heart of the community and its independence consequently most jealously guarded, the pooling of its financial support among jurisdictions is generally a last, desperate resort. Suburbanites frequently prefer overcrowding, inexperienced teachers, double sessions, and the deterioration of standards rather than to relinquish their personal supervision, however ineffective, over their schools. So, while the *New*

York Times' survey of contemporary metropolitan problems could find public school systems in expensive suburbs that epitomized the suburban ideal, it found two other types as well: one in the mass development suburb in which the schools had been overwhelmed by the influx of new residents, and the other in the older suburb in which the new residents were not a majority and their demands for better education were ignored by the old-timers who wanted above all to keep the tax rate down.

Yet even the poorer suburbs cannot push the quality of public services below the minimum for urban life, and where the suburban government has municipal powers and effective representation in the state legislature, a second tactic for self-survival is frequently employed. Every effort is made to broaden the local tax base by whatever means are available. Rarely can the suburbs impose lucrative new levies on income or general sales, or establish municipal businesses. But they can, in company with rich suburbs, require subdividers to finance streets, curbs, gutters, sewers and street lights, and they can join other municipalities in imposing a whole series of clumsy and expensive nuisance taxes.

The discovery and exploitation of these new sources of revenue varies from state to state according to legislative authorization, but it does not, in the last analysis, bail the suburbs out. Despite increased yield from these revenues, the new funds come nowhere near to "replacing" the property tax; they merely slow down the rise in property tax rates which follows the increased demand for public services. The new revenues are, moreover, typically available only to municipalities. Suburban counties and school districts must rely far more on the property tax than do other units of local government, while financial pressures may be heaviest on them.

Given the limited jurisdictions suburbia imposes upon itself, no single municipality can go far in developing a balanced tax system. For all their valiant efforts — the rows and rows of parking meters installed, the special licenses invented, the hidden charges inserted in the sale prices of "immoral" luxuries — suburban governments do little more than add nuisance burdens to the total tax bill. If the array of special taxes they have devised in the last decade were applied vigorously and enforced rigorously, the whole system of local nonproperty taxation would fall of its own weight. And it would fall because, given the intense financial competition among metropolitan jurisdictions, any suburb moving too far out of line would experience

economic decline and abandonment. It would deserve to fall, for
when the crazy-quilt of extra levies came to replace the property
tax, it would be even more regressive than that tax has proven.

By striving to emulate the manners of the exclusive suburbs, then,
the poorer jurisdictions push their analogy to the grassroots image to
an extreme they may not desire: they recreate, for their governments
at any rate, the conditions of frontier scarcity and poverty, the struggle for community existence that characterized the new settlements
on a new continent. Left to themselves — as suburban municipalities
were in Florida after the boom and bust of the twenties, and
throughout the nation in the early years of the depression — these
suburbs move inexorably to bankruptcy. Fractured urban government can recreate social and political conditions of small town life,
but in a fundamental sense the reformers were right in emphasizing
the economic base for community existence. No government is an
island, if that island cannot have the means for its basic self-support.

NORTON E. LONG

Who Makes Decisions in Metropolitan Areas?

The peculiarity of "the metropolitan problem" is that it is characteristically felt to be a problem requiring a governmental solution
for which there is no readily available appropriate governmental
machinery. This means that there is no structured decision-making
process that has been developed for dealing with this order of problem. The lack of such a structured process means further that there
is little institutional support for decision-makers envisioning their
primary role as representing a "metropolitan public interest" rather

Reprinted from *The Polity* (Chicago: Rand McNally & Company, 1962),
pp. 156-164, with the permission of the author and the publisher.

than the interest of their particular group, organization or local government. The most likely role to be called into play in a territory without common political loyalty and institutions is that of the special interest ambassador.

The term, metropolitan problem, almost seems to assume that there is a metropolitan common interest, and the assumption that there is a metropolitan common interest leads easily to the notion that there is a metropolitan community. Many earnest souls have thought that the European problems should follow this same logic, to say nothing of the even more ambitious World Federalists. Common problems may create a community among those who share them. However, much history, especially where people have become accustomed to living under different governments, with different values and resources, underscores the painful fact that common problems may do little more than produce common quarrels.

What this adds up to is that the term decision in our title may be optimistic. One makes a decision in a business, a government, a conference of ambassadors, maybe even sometimes at the summit, but these are structured decision-making institutions. What is characteristic of metropolitan areas is the lack of overall decision-making institutions. This does not mean that there are not institutions with power in metropolitan areas. It does mean that there are not institutions with sufficient power and overall responsibility to make decisions settling metropolitan issues and solving metropolitan problems. As a consequence, it is rare that we can speak of who makes metropolitan decisions. What we can speak about is who make decisions that have a significant effect on metropolitan problems.

Characteristically, metropolitan issues do not relate to problems that are solved by decisions in the sense we would use that term in a business or governmental organization, and naturally so, since the metropolitan area is not organized so as to be capable of making decisions. What does happen is that issues and problems have a career and over time processes of interaction develop through which interested and powerful parties exercise influence over the outcome.

We might then concern ourselves with who makes decisions that influence the processes by which metropolitan problems and issues get handled. As in a business, one hates to admit that the concern just drifts along by guess and by god, so we are reluctant to admit that this is the way that a metropolitan area runs. This is especially true if one has little faith in an unseen hand guiding the selfish interests of the particular groups and local governments to an unintended but beneficent metropolitan result. Yet in large measure, the metropolitan area is a kind of natural governmental ecology in which institutions, groups and governments have developed a system of largely unintended cooperation through which things get done and the area considered as a system functions. The owls and the field mice, the oaks and the acorns, the flora and fauna of the woodlot have worked out over time a most effective system of unintended cooperation that, barring catastrophe, preserves and maintains a systemic balance, though one that evolves over time.

By and large, we accept a similar system of unintended cooperation for running our economy. The complex task of supplying the city of Philadelphia occurs without any central planning machinery. The fact is we are used to a largely unplanned economy producing functional results. It's a little difficult for us to accept this of an unplanned polity, but to a considerable degree this is just what happens in a metropolitan area. To be sure, the analogy to the economy may be closer to oligopoly than free market competition. What we have is a number of institutions, public and private, sharing a common territory, making demands on each other, cooperating, hindering, damaging and helping in an interdependent set of relations with no overall government exercising control.

The relationships among the governments, government departments, Federal, State and Local, businesses, associations, newspapers, and the myriad groups whose activities intersect and interact have grown up over time. They have a history, they have created habits and customs, use and want, ways that are accepted for handling problems that arise. The metropolitan area as a system for handling common problems is a going concern. The rather considerable problems of very large populations living under great diversity of governments have been managed.

If we look at the who, who make decisions in the metropolitan areas, we will be most interested in the actors, individual and institutional, that play the major roles in the process by which the metropolitan system handles the issues that confront it. We can best appreciate these actors if we see them as dealing with metropolitan problems from the limited point of view of a particular institutional base. This particular institutional base determines the point of view of the actor and how he scores his own success or failure. Much of the blame that is heaped on the heads of actors in the metropolitan scene for their lack of a sense of overall responsibility stems from the failure to recognize the constraints of their institutional reality. It is idle to blame a downtown store for behaving like a downtown store or the Port of New York Authority for behaving like the rubber based, toll fed, revenue bond undertaking that it is. There are very few actors whose particular institutionalized interests parallel in any complete way the metropolitan area. Just as there are almost no institutions, private or public, whose interests and organization cover the metropolitan territory, so there are few, if any, whose interests extend to any considerable number of the problems of the metropolitan area.

By and large, actors and institutions in the metropolitan area, civic ritual apart, are confined in their interests to particular areas and particular problems. Highways, schools, sewer and water, housing, parks and recreation, these problems have their peculiar clientele just as the diseases that afflict the human body have their special funds. Thus, in the highway area you may have a Port of New York Authority, a Bob Moses and the Triborough Bridge Authority, a New York City Transit Authority, Commuter Railways and Buses, two or more state governments and their assorted departments, a variety of political communities, businesses, trade associations, civic organizations, newspapers, all involved. Quite probably, the issues in the transportation field will be agitated with little effective concern for overall problems of coordination and none whatever for the implication of highway resource allocation for other claimants in the metropolitan area.

If we were to make a typology of the key actors in the typical metropolitan area, it might run as follows. First, we would have the metropolitan dailies. In almost all cases, they would exhibit a commitment to the preservation of downtown real estate, a consequent concern for mass transit, extending frequently to the advocacy of subsidy, a belief in planning and a disposition to favor some form of metropolitan integration. These newspapers are in a position to agitate the issues they favor, reward with publicity the politicians and civic leaders who agree with them and by appropriate news selection determine to a large extent what most people will be thinking are the hot issues. Rarely, except in a place like Miami, can the metropolitan press carry a general proposal for governmental change. On piecemeal bond issues and administrative matters, however, it can do much. Beginning to enter the field as a competitor in some areas are television and radio. Just how the structure of their interests will differ from that of the metropolitan press is not clear.

Frequently opposing the metropolitan dailies and following a particularist line is the community press. Usually, they support the interests of small business threatened by planning and the parochialism of suburban city governments.

Of equal importance with the media are, of course, the public officials concerned with the production of public services that cut across political boundaries or require resources that must be allocated among a number of claimants. These officials run the gamut from village to state and nation. They embrace such disparate undertakings as schools, watersheds, airports and a host of other things. Quite often it is the service departments of the governments badgered by their clientele that press the metropolitan issues with still other government officials in their budgetary capacity playing the role of reluctant Solomons.

Downtown stores, real estate interests concerned with central city property values, commuter railways, central city banks, central city and even other politicians concerned with the implications of the worsening of the central city tax base frequently make common cause with the press, university professors, the foundations and the civic leaders in a crusade to save downtown. A subsidy at the expense of the highway user for mass transit, a massive urban renewal program, a new layer of metropolitan government, at the very least, a metropolitan planning agency, all or some combination of these, comprise a set of symbolic and frequently more than symbolic acts by which a multitude of parties with the most varied concerns express their feeling about the dynamic changes that are transforming urban America.

However, these overall actions have all too often bogged down in the quagmire of divisive local interests and electoral conservatism. Given the circumstances of local public life it is usually easy to mount a campaign of metropolitan reform. The electoral consultation which our home rule tradition insists on forces such proposals to run the gauntlet of the antagonism of suburban voters to the central city, vested interests of all kinds in the status quo, central city ethnic and minority groups who fear any dilution of their achieved central city power and a host of public officials and employees who may fear the unsettling of their empires and jobs. Certainly, high among the list of the who that make metropolitan decisions, if no more than negatively, are the varied active electorates called into play by referenda and the officials who have a stake in the existing system.

The revolutionaries who wish to overturn the status quo are most often university professors, foundations, Leagues of Women Voters, Chambers of Commerce, civic leader businessmen especially those with a stake in downtown, those with a concern in the planning of major metropolitan highways and utilities, suburban residents, officials and real estate promoters needing sewer and water facilities, the media people seeking a cause and the intellectuals of local government who follow the thinking of *Fortune*, The National Municipal League and "the authorities."

The attempts at revolution have mobilized financial support from elements of the business community such as Civic Progress, Inc., in St. Louis, and the Cleveland Development Foundation. They have usually enjoyed the support of the metropolitan dailies, the League of Women Voters, the professors and most of the do-gooders. The opposition the campaigns have mobilized, especially where general metropolitan integration has been sought, has been sufficient to insure defeat at the polls. These defeats have usually been as much due to the political ineptitude and lack of energy of the proponents of change as to the power of the opposition.

It must be remembered that the existing metropolitan areas are going concerns — going systems — as systems we can expect them to react vigorously to attempts to seriously alter them. If the existing system of local government could be easily changed it would be intolerably unstable. If no powerful interests were vested in the status quo, the existing order would have so little allegiance it could scarcely run, much less endure. Some such situation obtained in Miami, the one successful case of metropolitan integration and a case where change won by an eyelash and the decision could have gone either way.

If we turn from overall decisions such as those that are embodied in researching county charters, studying metropolitan regions, writing new local constitutions and campaigning to the piecemeal decisions that are by their sheer cumulative weight determining the future of the metropolitan areas, a different order of actions emerged. Clearly among the most significant decisions affecting our metropolitan areas are those which determine the importation of cheap rural labor from the South, Puerto Rico and Mexico, without any provision for adequately housing it in standard housing. The demand for labor insures no equivalent demand for standard housing; it is in fact a demand for slums. Given the desire of the average low income rural immigrant to the city for television, the automobile

106 NORTON E. LONG

and the other gadgets of the affluent society, plus his habitation to a very low housing standard in his place of origin, it is not surprising that expensive standard housing should be low on his list of priorities.[1] Doubtless, we could force urban immigrants to buy housing rather than other consumer goods by outlawing substandard housing. We probably won't and this is a key decision in metropolitan areas. The central city has a vested interest in slums as do those employers of cheap labor and those sellers of consumer goods which compete with housing for the slum dwellers' dollar.

Another key decision made by real estate people, bankers, building and loans, suburban neighborhoods and the rest, is whether the new minorities, Negroes, Puerto Ricans and Mexicans, but especially Negroes, will be able to follow the earlier ethnics into the melting pot of middle-class America or whether the color bar will prevent assimilation. This decision which will be made by a myriad of individual decisions will determine whether or not we create our own version of Algeria in our larger cities with an alienated group of second-class citizens led by an unassimilated, rejected but educated elite.

The decisions by our businesses on the location of industry, of manufacturing, retail trade and office buildings will over time critically determine the fate of downtown, the relation of residence and place of work and the future of our system of metropolitan transportation. While we may talk bravely of a pattern of land use control and a massive rehabilitation of the central city, the odds are probably with Professor Raymond Vernon of Harvard that our public expenditures and our controls are unlikely to be sufficiently massive or powerful to offset the natural locational forces. This seems the more likely if dozens of communities scramble to beef up their tax base in a competition for industry to meet mounting municipal costs. With the property tax still a major reliance of central city and suburbs, the struggle for tax base will conflict with and in all probability override the efforts at a general plan of metropolitan land use.

While it is unpopular to say it, one of the crucial decisions in the metropolitan areas will relate to the preservation of the middle-class values of American culture. Despite all its clumsiness the separate but not watertight compartments of the suburban communities prevent the flooding of schools and neighborhoods by an undigestible mass of immigrants of a different culture. In all probability, despite

[1] I wish to credit Anthony Downs of the University of Chicago with the forceful development of this point.

an uneasy conscience, there will be efforts by middle-class neighbor-hoods to preserve the political dikes that protect their values. How-ever unsatisfactory, and it is clearly unsatisfactory, the present sys-tem of social absenteeism in the massive change in the central city has probably rendered impossible a desirable balance between the social classes. The recolonization of the central city by disenchanted suburbanites is probably little more than the utopia of the builders of luxury high rise apartments.

We can confidently expect that as the incomes of the mass of cen-tral city residents rise they will make the same key metropolitan decisions that the earlier middle-class ethnics made — to cross the tracks into suburbia.

Since the positions of power in our society can be expected to fight for survival, it can be expected that the vested interests in down-town should fight as hard for the preservation of outmoded central city land values as the embattled farmers have to preserve an out-grown pattern of agriculture. When one looks at the vested stake in central city real estate it is hard to imagine that the fight to achieve public subsidies to resist its obsolescence will be less than that put up by agriculture. Certainly, there might seem to be a greater appeal for spending the massive sums that now go into subsidizing an un-productive agriculture on the maintenance of our obsolescing central city plant. The sentimental appeal that persuades us to save the fam-ily farm can and has been raised to save "downtown." As yet the appeal goes no further than the appeal for urban renewal, and the subsidization of commuter railways and mass transit. If this does not work, we can expect the ante will be raised rather than the end abandoned.

An older generation accustomed to what Mumford has called the eotechnic city, the city of steam and mass transit can be frightened by a specter, the specter of the city of the automobile, Los Angeles. Lord Marple, the British Minister of Transport, said recently, "I saw Los Angeles, the city of the future, a fate we must avoid." Perhaps one day we will cease to regard Los Angeles as a monstrosity and accept the technological obsolescence of the older city. Our agricul-tural experience indicates the old will die hard.

One last decision, the greatest, I think, in our lifetime and the one nobody made but that has changed everything. In 1929 the shape of the American income was a pyramid with a broad base of the bulk of society close to the means of subsistence living at a family income of below $2,000. In the twenty-five years that *Business Week* once said remade America, 1929 to 1954, the income structure changed from a pyramid to a diamond — America had become a middle-class country. Even in 1929, the middle-class values led to a family centered suburban standard of life. This has been the dynamic. As the lower half of the present diamond of our income structure shrinks with the growth in its income we can expect the new middle classes to continue the trek and the pressure of their movement to continue to tax the public sector of our local economies.

Beyond the dynamic of the growth of the new middle class is the growing market orientation of industry and the new pattern of settlement of business in the metropolitan areas. How the community earns its living will, as always, be a vital determinant of the structure of metropolitan areas.

Ours, however, is an affluent society and the increasing desire to consume public goods will press constantly on our governments. Thus, the rush to the week-end especially with the four-day work week may mean that the peak loads for play will outweigh the peak loads for work on our highways.

The decisions than that may be most important in our metropolitan areas are economic, piecemeal, harmonized if at all by market forces. This is not to say we could not generate enough political power to make effective public metropolitan decision-making possible; it is to express a doubt that we will, in more than a piecemeal way, substitute government action for the forces of the economy. I suspect that as long as the existing system functions even tolerably well, we will tinker with it getting rid of the worst annoyances but putting up with what we know rather than venturing on untried seas. Should Miami and other areas provide an attractive imitable lesson, however, we can expect new civic fashions to spread. The unresolved problem of local government remains the desire for sharply increased amounts of public goods but at the same time stable or decreased taxes, the desire for the fruits of planning and control and the desire for the energy and enterprise of unregimented economic individualism.

Perhaps it is our successful capacity to live with and entertain these contradictory desires that is the genius of our tradition. As an Englishman once told an exasperated French colleague, "England is governed by parliament, not logic."

FRANK J. MUNGER

Community Power and Metropolitan
Decision-Making

The mythology of community power in Syracuse today is very clear. Any number of observers, including many knowledgeable in local affairs, will assert that a single man stands at the top (or, some might say, behind the top) of community affairs and runs things. This is Stewart F. Hancock, lawyer, banker, gentleman, spokesman for the old-line aristocracy, without whose consent, tacit or explicit, nothing of importance can be done. One writer refers to Hancock as "Mr. Syracuse." . . . Syracuse is commonly believed to have a slack, monolithic, pyramidal power structure with a businessman-attorney as its dominant figure. Many who hold this view concede that Hancock's power is now declining. The time spanned by this study, however, covers the period of his greatest reputed power, and the cases examined should demonstrate his leadership if in fact it possessed substance.

These anlyses of actual decisions taken with respect to public problems in the Syracuse metropolitan area do not support an interpretation based on the concept of monolithic power. What is clear from the cases is that the pattern of decision-making in Syracuse has changed markedly over the last 30 years. The cases suggest that at one time the current myth had a solid foundation in fact, for earlier there was a high concentration of community authority in the hands of a single man, simultaneously a political leader and a public official. Expanding the already substantial powers vested in his predecessor as Republican County Chairman, Rolland Marvin consolidated

Reprinted from *Decisions in Syracuse*, Roscoe C. Martin, *et al*, (Bloomington, Ind.: Indiana University Press, 1961), pp. 305-311, with the permission of the author and publisher.

those powers with his authority as Mayor to wield an unprecedented influence over public decisions. Moreover, he exercised his control with a minimum of public oversight. His ultimate rejection resulted partly from reaction against his autocratic methods, but more from the bitter opposition of Governor Thomas Dewey, still smarting over Marvin's support of Wendell Willkie at the 1940 Republican national convention.

After Marvin's defeat, a disintegration of political power took place. It was during this period that Stewart Hancock maximized his influence, and community leadership passed from a combined political boss and elective public official to a lawyer-businessman with no pronounced inclination for public notice. In the process, a change occurred in the process of leadership itself. Partly in reaction to the tight control exercised by Marvin, partly perhaps as a result of the example set by the Post-War Planning Council, the circle of participants in community affairs broadened. Such a change was no doubt inevitable in any case in view of the steady growth in the size of the metropolitan community and the complexity of its interests; nevertheless it accompanied, perhaps as both cause and effect, a significant change in the pattern of leadership. Since more persons were involved in community affairs and more individuals therefore had to be consulted, no successor's influence could be as unequivocally dominant as that of Marvin. Indeed, in the cases examined here Hancock appears only as one among several leaders. A notable consequence of Marvin's fall was the collapse of central control over the Republican party organization. Lacking this essential part of Marvin's arsenal, subsequent community figures have never been able to force through measures over town opposition with Marvin's abandon. Whether the power system can at present be regarded as polylithic or whether it is in transition to monolithic control by some new individual leader is clearly an open question, although the fact that the change in the type of community leadership has accompanied changes in social forces would seem to suggest the former.

Even during the period of monolithic control, the case studies demonstrate the point that broad areas of public policy were left undirected by the dominant leaders of the community. That fact does not necessarily destroy the monolithic concept. As noted before, some distinction between major and minor policy must necessarily be made. So long as the top leaders continued to exercise tight control over such focal concerns as city and county budgets they might properly be considered to be dominant even though they failed to assert control at all points of decision-making. The establishment of a children's court, for example, might be offered to interested citizens' groups as a minor concession which would not affect substantially the central financial concerns of local government.

Although this abdication of control over certain areas of policy-making may be accommodated to a monolithic interpretation of the exercise of community power, it nevertheless has important consequences which are particularly evident within the real estate field. . . . In this area especially many lesser decisions are continually being made without reference to the power structure at its top levels. These decisions may be minimized as affecting only minor policy, but the fact remains that their cumulative impact has tremendous effect in shaping the course of development of the metropolitan area. The only recognized tool that might give the community leaders effective control over the accumulation of these decisions would be area-wide planning of land use, and either through tradition or through their own laissez-faire inclinations the leaders have been slow to grasp this weapon.

With respect to local-state relations, the cases clearly reveal the legislative advantages enjoyed by Syracuse and Onondaga County. By reason of their Republican affiliation both city and county are accorded a friendly reception in the perennially Republican legislature. When they ask for a special law, the legislature is quick to oblige. The only law sought from the state that provided any difficulty involved passage of the Alternative County Government law, a statute of general application. Two measures were indeed blocked, but both by gubernatorial vetoes.

The cases also demonstrate the difficulty of obtaining popular approval of a proposal for governmental reorganization. Three referenda were held on variations of this proposal. The first, supported by Democrats and opposed by Republicans, failed in both city and towns. The next, supported by neither party but opposed by neither, suffered a like fate. And even the third proposal (the county director plan), which was supported by both newspapers, a banner list of city leaders, and numerous party officials, failed to receive a county majority though carrying the city. The uniform lack of success of these efforts attests the conservatism of the electorate, the influence of the county bureaucracy, and the strong opposition of the towns (and more particularly their supervisors) to change.

Of the 22 cases examined, 14 are found on examination to have involved decisions at the county level. Isolating these 14 in order to obtain greater comparability through greater uniformity, it is possible to make an analysis of the effectiveness of exercise of power from an examination of the decisions reached. Robert Dahl has suggested a possible formula for such a calculation in his definition of a community leader in terms of ability to (1) initiate proposals and carry them through, (2) override substantial opposition on behalf of a proposal, and (3) veto a proposal initiated by others. Making some rather arbitrary groupings of the interests involved in the cases at hand, the power demonstrated in these terms assumes the following pattern:

	Won	Lost	Did Not Participate
Republican Party	5	2	7
Democratic Party	1	3	10
Manufacturers Association	2	0	12
Chamber of Commerce – Governmental Research Bureau	2	2	10
CIO	0	1	13
Real estate interests	3	0	11
League of Women Voters	2	5	7
Community Chest/Council of Social Agencies/Onondaga County Health Association	2	2	10
Town government officials	5	2	7
Post-Standard	3	2	9
Herald-Journal	2	4	8
Village weekly newspapers	3	0	11

Such a listing, while of course not conclusive, nevertheless has high suggestive value. It demonstrates clearly that, in terms of community decision-making, the Democratic Party is not very important in Onondaga County; the lone Democratic victory represents the party's success in persuading Governor Lehman (Democrat) to veto a Republican county reorganization measure. The tabulation likewise shows that the League of Women Voters concerns itself with many problems, but is not very effective in winning acceptance for its proposals. The League's chief value obviously lies in the service it performs in calling problems up for consideration. The list also instances the ineffectiveness of organized labor in local decision-making. It indicates that labor does not lose: it simply fails to participate. Likewise less effective than might have been expected are the daily newspapers, which together lost oftener than they won.

The group with what appears to be the best record of effective action is the Republican Party. In only two cases, however, can the party be said to have initiated the action it supported, and both of those involved Rolland Marvin as leader. The party organization therefore was rather a vehicle through which other interests sought to attain their goals. Success in obtaining party support usually guaranteed victory; but the party's own role was passive or instrumental, consisting in most cases of embracing decisions made elsewhere and seeing that the county government carried them out. The town officials were equally successful with, perhaps because often indistinguishable from, the Republican Party. The industrialists and the realtors had a low rate of participation, but were uniformly successful where they elected to commit their resources.

The most striking feature of the tabulation is the low level of participation in the decision-making process. No group tested its strength in a majority of the decisions, and most were involved in only a few cases. This warrants the conclusion that separate clusters of decision areas exist, each with its own distinct group of participants. It effectively eliminates the notion of an all-sovereign wielder of community power, and it attacks (though it does not necessarily destroy) the concept of a monolithic power structures as applied to Syracuse. Under such circumstances it is meaningless to say that group A is more powerful than group B when A and B have never tested their strength against each other and because of their differing interests are not likely to.

The tabulation provides no clue concerning the problem of differential commitment, which as observed earlier is central to an appraisal of power and its exercise. The Chamber of Commerce, to illustrate, may take a mild interest in one measure and satisfy itself with a simple endorsement; in another case more tangibly related to the economic interest of its members, it may throw all its resources into a life-and-death struggle. It is manifestly unrealistic to regard the two commitments as being in any wise equal, for neither the rates nor the efficiencies of use of influence are comparable.

In summary, the decisions analyzed in this study afford no basis of easy generalizations about the structure and exercise of community power in the Syracuse metropolitan area. Only three overall conclusions seem warranted by the materials examined. First, the myth that significant decisions in Syracuse emanate from one source does not stand up under close scrutiny. Second, there tend to be as many decision centers as there are important decision areas, which means that the decision-making power is fragmented among the institutions, agencies, and individuals which cluster about these areas. Third, in reality there appear to be many kinds of community power, with one kind differing from another in so many fundamental ways as to make virtually impossible a meaningful comparison.

3

METROPOLITAN PROBLEMS AND THE ROLE OF GOVERNMENT

Snarled traffic, polluted water, overtaxed educational systems, spreading slums, these and numerous other problems are the inevitable concomitants of urban growth and change. More and more people living in rapidly expanding metropolitan areas generate seemingly insatiable demands for more water, schools, highways, parks, and a score of other public facilities and services. Problems like traffic congestion, water shortages, and overcrowded schools result primarily from the inability of hard-pressed local governments to keep up with burgeoning demand. The unwillingness or inability of local taxpayers to foot the bill underlies deficiencies such as non-existent or inadequate facilities for sewage treatment and for recreation. Another category of problems arises from the changing pattern of urban development; examples are the decline of public transportation and the deterioration of older neighborhoods. Every one of these problems requires public action — the selection of policy alternatives, the raising of funds, and the implementation of plans. And the ability of the governments of the metropolis to deal with most of them is affected by the fragmentation of the political system.

Prior to the past decade, metropolitan experts in the universities, planning groups, and civic associations were

practically unanimous in concluding that the decentralized political system was the basic cause of many urban
inadequacies and a critical hindrance to the solution of
all the problems associated with growth and change.
The metropolis, argued the metropolitan reformers, was
a socio-economic community lacking an inclusive set of
political institutions. Problems arising from the social and
economic interaction of the metropolis failed to respect
the political boundaries that artificially divided the metropolitan community. Thus, almost every urban problem
was a metropolitan problem which could not be effectively resolved by the fragmented political system, with
its fiscal inequities and lack of comprehensive planning.
The inadequacy of the structure of government, then,
was *the* metropolitan problem. In the pages of the local
government textbooks, the metropolitan surveys, and the
planning and civic bulletins, areawide government was
steadfastly promoted as the sure cure for the many ills of
the metropolis.

By focusing on the structure of government, the metropolitan reformers remained firmly in the tradition of municipal reform in the United States. Since their origins
during the heyday of the boss and the machine, the forces
of good government have sought to overcome the corruption, inefficiency, and excessive partisanship of city government through structural overhaul. In their quest for
a political system which would serve the public interest
— defined, of course, in terms of their own interests in
economic and efficient government — the middle class reformers promoted nonpartisanship, the city manager
plan, the merit system, and many other reforms in the
structure of local government. As urban development
spread over the boundaries of the city, professors, planners, and civic leaders shifted their frame of reference,
but not their basic approach. Economy, efficiency, and a
"rational" governmental structure responsive to the general interests of the entire community remained the fundamental goals of reform. In dealing with the metropolis
as in its efforts to improve the city, the good government
alliance has been convinced that its values are represent-

ative of the general community interest. Remove the impediments to the expression of the public interest through a reorganization of the fragmented political system, runs the reform argument, and the metropolis will be governed in the interest of the whole rather than in the conflicting interests of its many parts.

One of the most distinguished figures in the municipal and metropolitan reform movements is Luther H. Gulick. In an excerpt from his 1961 Cook lectures delivered at the University of Michigan, Gulick contends that the metropolitan problem arises from the breakdown of the traditional economic and political systems of the metropolis. "Once an indivisible problem is divided," argues Gulick, "nothing effective can be done about it." Thus, he concludes, a more inclusive system of local government is needed to handle problems such as traffic congestion, inadequate public transportation or water supply, air and water pollution, slums, crime, insufficient recreational or educational facilities, and a host of others. The thinking of Gulick and his confreres has been reflected in practically every survey of metropolitan problems and government undertaken in the United States. A typical example is the 1962 report of the Citizens Advisory Committee of the Washington legislature's Joint Committee on Urban Area Government. True to the reform tradition, the authors emphasize the interdependence of the metropolitan community, the inadequacies and inequities inherent in the fragmented political system, and the need for major structural changes to equip local government to meet the challenges of metropolitan development.

In recent years, political scientists have cast a skeptical eye on the assumptions and conclusions of metropolitan reform. By focusing on structure, according to Roscoe C. Martin and Douglas Price, the reformers tend to ignore the influence of scale and the processes of change on urban problems. To a considerable degree, the problems of providing adequate governmental services and a responsive political system are a result of the size and complexity of the modern urban community. Because metropolitan problems are manifestations of social and economic processes which are relatively autonomous from the political system, Martin and Price anticipate modest improvements at best from a restructuring of government in metropolitan areas.

Edward C. Banfield and Morton Grodzins also question the doctrines of the metropolitan reformers. They wonder how one devises a single "rational" unit of metropolitan government when almost every public function tends to have its own ideal service area. Why, they ask, shouldn't the residents of the metropolis have a wide choice in urban life styles, and a range of responsive local governments to provide them with variety through different land use, tax, and service policies? As Banfield and Grodzins point out, economy, efficiency, needs, and adequacy are relative rather than absolute concepts. Ultimately, the only metropolitan problems are those so perceived by the public officials and the electorates of the metropolis. Since the recognition of a problem as "metropolitan" implies regional action which threatens the political and fiscal integrity of the local community, the number of such area wide problems is small. Equally important in limiting the perception of "regional" problems is the ability of the decentralized political system to accommodate to the process of urban change through interlocal agreements, special districts, state and federal assistance, and other innovations. As Chapters Four and Five indicate, given the choice between revolution and accommodation, most metropolitan areas have adjusted to meet the demands of growth and change within the general framework of the decentralized political system.

———————————

LUTHER H. GULICK

The Rationale for Metropolitan Government

In the face of the radically changed requirements of metropolitan
areas, [the] traditional approach has now broken down. The proof
of this statement is everywhere. In every big city the slums are
spreading faster than they are being cleared up. Circulation of
people and goods is becoming less and less satisfactory and more
and more costly. Even the delightful expansion of suburban life is
beginning to run into difficulties as the suburbs "fill in"; and the
service and control jobs are so big that the local governmental units
involved are unequal to the tasks they face.

In spite of this accumulating evidence of failure on every hand,
some people talk as though the old approach can save us. It is my
contention that two of the chief props of the traditional approach
have collapsed. They are the "market mechanism" and traditional
"local municipal action."

At what points does the "unseen hand" fail to give us the kind of
city we demand in the modern day and age? A comprehensive answer for this embarrassing question would be a large order, but we
can list the easily recognizable factors to illustrate the point.

First comes the street layout. Private land owners and developers
have never, anywhere in the world, laid out their lot lines and their
building and development lines so that those of neighboring areas
would add up to form a convenient, adequate, and integrated pattern for posterity or even for themselves. Left to themselves, land
owners generally leave crooked, narrow, noncontinuous lanes which
may look "picturesque" to tourists from abroad but which are totally

unsatisfactory for any kind of sustained urban life, once industrialization has commenced.

Clearly the general street locations, widths, and specifications for
an entire urbanized region must be rationalized under the hand of
a single controlling governmental authority. No one will question
this. However, this admission leads us a good deal farther than we
have ever gone, now that the solidly built-up urban areas are so
extended and the traffic has become so heavy and complex.

Another implication of this statement as to streets is that there
must also be broad community control over land uses and densities
of occupancy. This necessity arises from the fact that the circulation
system, including the streets, and the related land uses are opposite
sides of the same coin. Without the streets there is no urban land
use; except for the land use, there is no need for streets. Each depends on and determines the other. Thus the seemingly simple
agreement as to the need of unified public control over contiguous
streets leads us far indeed in the modern urban setting.

Second, private enterprise will no longer give us any form of mass
transportation (except elevators!) in an urban area without requiring substantial governmental action and participation. This arises in
part because the public will not accept rates of fare adequate to attract the private investor — in an inflationary world — and will not
give to private groups "monopolies" to use the public streets, or the
public power of eminent domain.

As a result, government must be heavily involved in developing
and regulating mass transportation, if not also in owning, operating,
financing it, and conducting the developmental research required.
Even taxicabs have to be limited as to number, regulated as to their
service, and controlled as to their rates. The "unseen hand" will not
attend to these matters.

Third are water supplies, sewers, and sewerage. The time has
now passed when such community services can be supplied by private enterprise. Here and there, for a specific small operation, a
developer can put in a few pipes, drains, and utility connections,
and build private cesspools and septic tanks, but such arrangements
are temporizing makeshifts in any large developing urbanized area
and, in the long run, have to be tied into and controlled by a responsible governmental unit.

Electric power and telephones and occasionally gas are, however,
still extended to the developing metropolitan areas in the United

States by private utilities, under the general control of state public service commissions. In this we have been most fortunate. These private utilities have in fact a much better record of adjustment to increasing metropolitan demand than any other local urban services, in part because they are free to ignore existing small-government boundaries and because these services are the beneficiaries of extraordinary recent technological advances which have helped them to do a better job with very modest increases in costs and rates.

Fourth is the business of modernizing the older, obsolete, and no longer efficient neighborhoods and layout of the older urban community. The inability of private enterprise to act on this problem is not hard to explain. An obsolete neighborhood involves several or many blocks and scores or hundreds of individual properties. No one of these owners can reap a reward from individual efforts to improve his property unless all or most of his neighbors do so also *and at the same time*. One laggard can spoil the effort. Furthermore, even the street arrangement may need replanning and reconstruction, as where pedestrian malls, no-traffic sections, a revised ownership pattern, parking facilities, or large industrial or other plottages are called for. Urban renewal and modernization will, of course, be carried out primarily by private enterprise and with private investment, but only as part of a total scheme which establishes the new modern urban pattern, a thing which can be done only by governmental action. The "unseen hand" will not tear down existing obsolete buildings on a mass basis, but it will build individual new housing, new shops, new factories, new offices, *provided* a proper stage is first set by comprehensive public action.

Fifth is housing for the middle-income and low-income segments of the urban population. Private builders will build housing only for a profit. As a result, they will finance housing for the upper-middle and higher income brackets and for nobody else.

The major costs of housing, perhaps as much as 72 per cent, excluding the land, are for labor.[1] As a result, new housing is priced in large measure in relation to construction wages. Those who cannot afford existing rents, or capital charges for housing, are thus forever in a position where they cannot afford to meet the costs of new housing unless they have a wage rate on a par with or above the wage rates of the construction industry. While this relationship

[1] Charles Abrams: *The Future of Housing* (New York: Harper & Brothers; 1946), chap. xiii.

can be altered somewhat by free land, reductions in financing costs, increased economies in construction, and reduced taxes, the hard core of labor costs remains dominant. Thus, that part of the population with an annual earning rate below that of the construction industry, left to their own devices, will live overcrowded in various degrees of second-hand and substandard housing. The market mechanism cannot provide better housing than this.

This is in part due, of course, to changing standards of "decency." We now demand a kitchen and a flush toilet for each family, where once we were fighting only windowless rooms and the common backyard privy. It is also true that we now demand minimum provisions far in advance of "satisfactory" housing as seen in Asia. These observations are, however, beside the point of our people. We know more about health, and we know how the social costs rise when our people are submerged in crowded and hopeless indecency. And we know only too well that even our newest standards are still pitifully low.

Some social reformers have sought to meet this situation by reducing the cost of financing a home, by establishing a better "market," by making the construction of a home as efficient as assembling an automobile, by holding costs down, by encouraging the rise of wages of the tenants, by consumer education, and by more rigid local enforcement of housing standards. These efforts have accomplished a good deal. Incidentally, they also involve extensive governmental intervention in the economy.

Even the widespread increase of wage levels, which is frequently put forward as "the only real solution" of the bad housing problem, has its own built-in frustration — most of the labor cost of housing is paid at a rate higher than the general community wage average. General wage advances have not in fact been reflected in improved housing.[2] Apparently wage increases will solve the housing problem only when most people receive a wage above the average! Thus, when all is said and done in the most vigorous and dynamic cities, we still have more slums today than we had a generation ago.

The result is unacceptable in big urban areas. It produces expanding slums and all the social problems which gravitate to and are aggravated by substandard housing arrangements. If something is to be done about this situation, it can only be done by government. The "unseen hand" gives us no way out, and never can.

[2] Abrams: *The Future of Housing*, p. 165.

Sixth are health and welfare activities and all the standard community services. About these there is no argument now. Charitable people have undertaken part of the responsibility for very limited groups as a personal obligation, rather than for profit. But the main burden is now and will continue to be handled directly by government. No other arrangement is now possible. There is still an important job for private welfare activities, especially in experimental and demonstration work, but the major effort is now public.

Seventh are education and the many varied institutions which lift our life to new levels of achievement and enjoyment, such as schools, colleges, libraries, museums, adult education, parks, recreation, noncommercial leisure-time activities, and cultural and artistic enrichment. This is an area in which a few activities can always be organized for profit, such as some private trade schools and some recreations, like spectator sports and the commercial theaters. Fortunately there are still many avenues of service for generous and imaginative philanthropy, but any mass education or recreation or cultural enjoyment can be provided only through extensive public patronage and support of various kinds, running all the way from tax exemption to public construction of facilities and direct public tax support of certain activities. Modern society in the urban areas needs and demands a great deal that can never be developed without government backing and tax support. This will be increasingly the situation in the future.

These seven clearly identifiable points, at which *laissez faire* cannot produce the kind of urban structure and life we are willing to accept, amply justify the statement with which we started a few paragraphs ago: the market mechanism cannot save us.

If the market mechanism cannot save us, can the local governments? Here again, the answer is "no." The proof is the accumulating evidence of failure everywhere, in spite of many heroic efforts.

The reason for these failures is most instructive. Why have the great cities been unable to use their traditional governmental powers to deal with slums, traffic congestion, mass transportation, urban obsolescence, and the problems of migration, education, and crime, of water supply and air and water pollution, or recreation and cultural and other needs?

There are three interrelated reasons for this local inability to act: *First,* every one of these problems spreads out over an area broader than the boundaries of the local governments in question. It is clear that our big urban complexes are now so closely tied together economically, socially, and structurally by daily human movements and activities that every problem is a "spill-over" from the next jurisdiction. Little can be done about one piece of such a problem. *Once an indivisible problem is divided, nothing effective can be done about it.*

This is especially true as to the entire circulation and mass-transportation system, the water supply, air and water pollution, and land-use control. Once these jobs are split up into fractions, they are undoable, like trying to leap across a river in two jumps or mop up a part of a spilled bottle of milk on the kitchen floor.

Spreading area-wide problems cannot be handled, geographic piece by geographic piece. They must be tackled in their entirety, comprehensively, and are difficult enough even so.

Second is the problem of paying for the things that need doing. Almost everything we are talking about calls for increased governmental expenditures. Most big cities are already raising all the taxes they can legally. They are thus so "strapped" that there is little they can do about the new problems, especially such expensive projects as slum clearance, urban renewal, school expansion, recreation and cultural facilities, pollution controls, and mass transportation. Financing such activities is complicated further by the fact that many cities are losing taxable resources as the factories move or develop outside of town, and many of the city improvements are occasioned by, or are for the benefit of, the suburbs. Even among the suburbs, some are "have" and some "have-not" communities because of tax windfalls, a very serious matter when it comes to meeting school budgets, especially.

A few well-situated suburban enclaves can manage and finance their service and control needs, including a considerable part of the "spill-over" problems. But even with all the tax revenues they need, they are powerless to meet their pollution-control, commuter, advanced-education, and broader cultural requirements within their own boundaries.

Because of the nature of the new spread-out urban development, the needs, the taxable resources, and the benefits do not match up geographically. This makes it impossible for local governments to proceed with any chance of success, except with an occasional service which can be made self-supporting. These self-supporting operations are generally paid for by the users regardless of geography, as anyone can see by watching the many state and county license plates of the cars and trucks that use any major bridge, tunnel, or throughway.

Most of the needed urban improvements we are talking about, though costly today, will pay for themselves many times over in years to come. To tap this newly created wealth and ability to pay, and to use these resources to meet the costs of action, are obviously both desirable and fair. The existing local tax and revenue system, with its small geographic divisions, is precisely the wrong approach, because the costs will often fall in one jurisdiction and the benefits in another.

Matching up the costs of a governmental activity with the benefited persons or property is important also as a matter of economic justice. It is also indispensable as a political matter, because the decision to go ahead will hardly be made by those who have to pay but who receive little commensurate benefit or addition to their taxpaying capacity. . . .

Third, the final reason for the inability of local governments to solve problems arising from our current surge of metropolitan development is political. . . .

There are three kinds of governmental failures involved in the big, bursting urban regions. The *first shortage,* and the most obvious, is *service failure,* such as lack of water, inadequate sewers and drainage, rising crime, worsening traffic congestion, spreading slums, inordinate dirt, pollution, and noise, and the lack of educational, health, recreational, and cultural facilities and programs.

The *second shortage* is seldom recognized but is, in fact, far more serious. This is the failure in virtually every city, and in all metropolitan areas, to work out any *comprehensive community program for general development* and for tackling the major social and economic problems of the foreseeable future. For lack of such broad-scale community thinking and leadership, most urban areas are muddling along, wasting their constructive energies, trying to "solve" one problem at a time, but frequently making matters worse. Such urban areas cannot expect to guide their own fate. They will always be on the verge of chaos accompanied by galloping obsolescence and dominated by forces and developments beyond their knowledge, guidance, or control. Every city hoping or desiring to "go anywhere," in times like these, needs a great and practicable dream, a sense of purpose — something to guide each enterprise, public and private, in its forward expansion and something to inspire confidence and devotion. While such an imaginative program and plan is not solely the work of local government, it cannot be formulated or realized in the modern world except with the focused participation of local people and their local government. Without such a long-range community program, jointly developed and agreed to by local governments and by business, labor, and other leadership groups, there is little chance that anything really intelligent, efficient, or noble will happen anywhere, in spite of all the energy and promise wrapped up in each of our bursting metropolitan areas. The opportunity is there, but the ideas, the plans, the dreams are not pulled together.

The people who live and work in an urban area have a deep emotional need to have their city stand for something worthwhile in the world and to present to themselves and to mankind a strong physical image of this spiritual ambition in the structure of the city, in its vistas, in its major squares and monuments. Through these, men venerate the past, remember the achievements of those who have gone before, reach for the future, affirm their self-respect and idealism, capture the stranger within their gates, and commit the rising generation to the values and nobility of community life.

Fortunately, memories, beauty, power, imagination, and ordinary efficiency are all part of the same architectural tapestry in the hands of great artists. We are fortunate too in the natural beauty, friendliness, and power of even unplanned heterogeneous developments, provided they grow within the framework of a general design. For us, a beautiful and efficient city does not exclude little crooked lanes and modest shops in their place. In fact, nothing would be a poorer reflection of our pluralistic and individualistic society than the neat and completely uniform layouts we see programmed in the new communist world.

But there must be a general skeleton or design for each major urban area, a design which will afford our growing metropolises the same kind of sustaining structure that our political forefathers built into our governmental and economic life when they gave us a federal union with a federal constitutional framework. And similarly, this broad urban design must be the product of great genius, ratified, after debate, by democratic community decision. The feelings of local patriotism which will rise around such a noble structure are not only essential for the fulfillment of the individual human spirit; they are also a dynamic resource for the economy and for the effectiveness of political life as well.

The *third shortage* is the lack of *region-wide democratic machinery for teamwork*, for thinking about and dealing with the common problems of the metropolitan area. This is important because, without such machinery, the people who live in the metropolitan areas cannot rise up, develop plans for action, debate proposals, iron out acceptable compromises, and then agree to join hands and take action. Without such teamwork machinery, there is no constituency, no sense of common purpose, no "metropolitan community" in a political sense, and, what is all-important, no "metropolitan leadership."

CITIZENS ADVISORY COMMITTEE
JOINT COMMITTEE ON URBAN AREA GOVERNMENT
LEGISLATURE OF THE STATE OF WASHINGTON

Too Many Governments

Local government in Washington was designed for a simpler day when people were fewer and the line between city and country was clear. It has grown by patchwork additions of cities and special purpose districts and is now a crazy-quilt of overlapping jurisdictions, costly in higher taxes to the homeowner and businessman alike.

Most of the governmental units, like most of the people, are in the metropolitan areas. In King County there are now over 200 units, more than any other county in the United States except one. At

Reprinted by permission from *City and Suburb — Community or Chaos* (Report of Citizens Advisory Committee of the Joint Commitee on Urban Area Government), June 1962, pp. 4-9.

least fifteen local units have been added in the last three years, and proceedings are now pending for the creation of three more small cities and a special purpose district. Similarly, in 1959, Spokane County had 135 units; Yakima, 119; Pierce and Snohomish, each 93; and Clark County, 44.

The profusion of "little governments" is well illustrated by the Highline School District, south of Seattle, whose 100,000 residents are governed, taxed, or served by King County, the school district, the Port of Seattle, four small cities (Kent, Tukwila, Des Moines and Normandy Park), eight sewer districts, eleven water districts, six fire districts, a library district, a road district, a drainage district and the County Housing Authority — thirty-six local governments, with over one hundred elected officials.

The suburbs east of Lake Washington show a similar patchwork of cities and special districts, with, for example, two islands of unincorporated territory inside the city of Bellevue, and twenty-six units of local government having jurisdiction over part or all of the Bellevue School District.

The Tacoma metropolitan area is following the same pattern, with Pierce County, 11 cities, and 57 districts electing 299 officials in the urbanized area.

The Spokane area adds townships to county, cities and districts, and has special problems from the 43 domestic water suppliers of suburban Spokane.

A large urban area is more than the sum of its separate parts. It is a complex system for production, recreation, education, worship, play and rest. All its people share a common interest in the efficiency, order, and livability of the whole. A dust producing manufacturing plant can be located in an industrial zone of one city adjacent to residences in the next. Poor streets in one area can shift traffic to another community ill prepared or situated for the load. Wastes from one community can pollute the waters or air of another. Residents of a densely populated area without parks can overcrowd the playgrounds and picnic spots of neighboring communities. Small sewage treatment plants side by side can unnecessarily raise everyone's costs. There is in economic and social fact a metropolitan community, but in government there is none.

Such fragmentation is sapping the strength of local government. No citizen, no matter how civic minded, can inform himself of the affairs of a dozen or more local governments. No voter can keep track of the performance of 50 or more local elected officials. Citizens have lost control of their local affairs when they are unable to place responsibility for faulty decisions or inaction.

Nor is this divided government responsive, for it cannot respond to major problems which ignore its boundary lines. Time, energy, and money are being wasted in mounting traffic congestion; water and air pollution grow; downtowns are in trouble, older neighborhoods blighted, and social problems rise. Each of the hundreds of local officials of the metropolitan area is alert to see that no action to remedy these ills falls too heavily on his jurisdiction; none is responsible to see that there *is* action. Frustrated by local inertia and confusion, the citizen turns increasingly to state and federal programs for urban needs.

Fragmentation damages the financial as well as the political health of local government. Traditionally it was assumed that a family lived, worked, shopped, and sent its children to school within the boundaries of one unit of local government. But such is rarely the case today, when, for example, a man living in Lynnwood may drive through Seattle to and from work at a plant in south King County, while his family shops in Everett. Property taxes on the family's house are paid to the city of Lynnwood and to Snohomish County, while the street, police and other costs of rush hour traffic are borne by the city of Seattle. The plant, moreover, pays property taxes neither to the city, county, nor school district which serves the employee's family, nor to the city whose facilities bring its worker to his job. Fragmentation of the metropolitan areas separates benefits and burdens in ways which are often basically unfair.

In general, it is the central cities which suffer most to provide extra streets, police protection, parks, libraries and other facilities for expanded daytime populations of suburban residents they cannot tax. There is, moreover, in our local property tax system a built-in inequity between city and county residents. City residents tax their property to pay for their police, parks, garbage dumps, and other services; they are taxed again by the county partly to furnish some of these urban services for the residents of unincorporated areas. In King County, where property within the city of Seattle constitutes two-thirds of the county's assessed valuation, and property within all cities and towns constitutes four-fifths, city and town property owners are paying 80 cents of every dollar spent by the county on local urban services for tens of thousands of county residents. In 1962, this will amount to a subsidy of about $2,300,000 from Seattle property, about $2,775,000 from all the cities taken together. Ironically, elderly and low-income property owners struggling to rehabilitate their property in Seattle's Yesler-Atlantic urban renewal area are subsidizing residents of expensive suburban communities.

A similar inequity appears to exist in other populous counties where the county general fund supports police protection, local parks, garbage dumps and other urban services for densely settled unincorporated areas. In Pierce County, city of Tacoma property is 54% of the total assessed valuation, and property within all cities and towns represents 63.4%; in Spokane County, corresponding figures for the city of Spokane and all cities are 62.8% and 65%, respectively. In these counties, as in King, city property owners pay most of the cost of the local urban services received by county residents from the county general fund.

To function, an urban community must move people and goods quickly and economically between areas for work, recreation and rest. Transportation is everybody's problem — the downtown merchant wants easier movement for his shoppers and places for them to park; city residents are taxed to pay for wide arterials used to capacity only twice a day; the manufacturer suffers higher costs from late employees, delayed raw materials, slow deliveries, and valuable land tied up in parking lots; the distributor needs extra salesmen to serve the urban area. Suburban residents spend precious hours meant for children and gardens in autos and buses on congested highways and bridges, wasting the gain of shorter working hours on longer travel time For many, commuting is a twice daily ordeal through a miles-long alley of used car lots, junk yards, service stations, and billboards. To all of us, inadequate transportation means higher costs of what we buy.

For years transportation in our metropolitan areas has meant more and more automobiles, more and still more highways, fewer and still fewer riders on public buses, longer and longer commuting times. We have only to look at Los Angeles to see the futility of sole reliance on the automobile-highway answer. There, over two billion dollars have been spent on freeways, and the automobile has consumed two-thirds of the downtown land for highways, streets, and parking facilities — without ending congestion.

The peak hours are the critical times, the times which overtax facilities, pocketbooks, nerves and patience. There is growing agreement that we must supplement the automobile with improved mass transportation, growing recognition that capital facilities of such a system will require tax support from the whole "commuter shed," growing realization that other alternatives are still more costly.

It is now too late to design mass transit facilities into Seattle's 175 million dollar central freeway or the 30 million dollar Evergreen Point Bridge, but this lack of coordination should not be allowed to continue. We cannot afford more single purpose structures when multiple needs must be met. About half a billion dollars will be spent by the state, county, and cities in King County in the next decade on highways and bridges, many of which are presently being designed. They must be planned and coordinated for the requirements of a mass transit system as well as private automobiles. There is, however, no unit of government presently making such plans, none coordinating state and local activities into a balanced urban transportation system.

Of all the problems of the metropolitan area, none is more urgent than the acquisition of parks and recreation sites and the preservation of other open land. In the words of a recent editorial, we are witnessing a "voracious gulping of the land," an urban sprawl so rapid that if present suburban land use patterns continue, the more than one million additional people expected in King County by the end of this century could fill it from Puget Sound to the foothills of the Cascades.

Recreational use of land is growing even faster than population, for we have more leisure time each year, more opportunity to enjoy walking, boating, sports and family outings. For parks and waterfront, however, we are living largely on the generosity of our parents and grandparents. Seattle's 315,312 people of 1920 had 2209 acres of parks, about 144 persons per park acre; its 558,000 people of 1960 had only 2646 park acres, or 211 persons per acre. In the suburbs where population has boomed since World War II, local park acquisition has not kept pace with population growth. King County's recent purchase of Marymoor Farm adds its first new large park to serve the entire area in many years. Public support of this purchase shows the rising awareness of open space needs.

The Spokane and Tacoma urban areas must also act now to preserve parks, waterfront, and other accessible open land for the thousands of new residents coming each year. The city of Spokane has many large parks, almost all acquired half a century ago, but there are already few sites of ten acres or more left in the fast growing valley to the east. In the Tacoma suburbs, too, concern over parks is rising. But action is slow in coming, and action cannot be

132   CITIZENS ADVISORY COMMITTEE

delayed. Each piece of land is unique; once developed, it is lost to the general public. Indeed, experience shows that park land must be acquired beyond the developed areas, for land prices rise quickly once subdivision begins nearby.

Washington's large urban communities are peculiarly blessed with forests, lakes, and mountain views. But woodlands can be cut, lakes shut off from public access, views blocked. The first resident of a hillside may enjoy watching the construction of a house in the valley below, but he is shocked as woods and farms change to rooftops, wires, and television antennae. The fisherman is not concerned over the first summer house along his favorite stream, but is confused and angry when a solid row of houses blocks him from the banks. Our grandparents looked ahead to keep green space, beaches and beauty for us, but our vision has been short in recent times. We are taking our landscape for granted; its beauty is being mined, not tended.

Like transportation and open land, the provision of clean water, the disposal of wastes, and the preservation of clean air are tasks increasingly difficult for each local unit to perform. Seattle's water lines and Seattle Metro's sewage disposal plan demonstrate, however, the effectiveness and economy of metropolitan-wide systems. Both have anticipated the needs of an entire urban area; both demonstrate that metropolitan problems can be solved when attacked comprehensively, and with the courage to plan for decades ahead.

Seattle brings pure mountain water from the Cascades at low cost to about 735,000 people of the metropolitan area, serving not only its residents, but selling wholesale water to thirty water districts and municipalities as well. Present projects, when fully developed, will guarantee mountain water for a future metropolitan population of more than two million. In contrast, the city of Tacoma brings its water from the Green River watershed of the Cascades but does not supply the needs of its suburbs. The nearby community of University Place suffers from inadequate water supply and distribution. A metropolitan-wide system would benefit Tacoma and its suburbs alike.

There is a natural water supply under most of the Spokane metropolitan area which is easily reached by wells. As a result, there are forty-three domestic water distributors in suburban Spokane. Many of these districts, co-ops, and companies are doing an excellent job within their areas, but duplication of facilities, differing pipe sizes and pressures, and no means for systematic interconnection are shortcomings paid for by suburban residents in increased costs, sometimes inadequate service, and higher fire insurance rates.

Sewage disposal presents a still gloomier story in which the structural defects of fragmented local government are sharply exposed. In King County, before establishment of the Municipality of Metropolitan Seattle, raw sewage was being discharged into the Duwamish River, Elliott Bay and Puget Sound at about sixty places, and ten to fifteen million gallons of treated and untreated wastes went into Lake Washington every day. Effluent from thousands of malfunctioning septic tanks was rising to ground surface and, in some areas, flowing in open ditches. Health agencies necessarily stopped construction in some areas, while elsewhere citizens invested millions of dollars in septic tanks which became more inadequate each day.

Within the metropolitan area, not a single foot of salt water shoreline, and very little fresh water, was safe for recreational use. Lake Washington was degraded and rapidly approaching permanent impairment from algal growth. In brief, water resources were being ruined, health dangers created, orderly growth stunted, millions of dollars wasted, but even after years of discussion, the nineteen cities and twenty-two sewer districts of the Lake Washington watershed could not agree on any joint solution. Fragmented government could not act.

Only state enabling legislation for a metropolitan-wide unit and the voters' establishment of the Municipality of Metropolitan Seattle saved this appalling situation. Since its formation in 1958, Seattle Metro has planned and is now constructing a trunk sewer and treatment system for the entire Lake Washington watershed, a system which will end pollution in the watershed over the next ten years, most of it in the next five. The Metro trunk lines will also permit cities and districts throughout the area to develop orderly and economical sewer systems during the next 75 to 100 years.

Danger signals are growing now in the Spokane metropolitan area where more than 200,000 people literally live on top of their water supply. Blessed by nature with a giant underground river of clean water flowing slowly from the Idaho border beneath valley and city until it empties into the Spokane River, the metropolitan community may spoil this magnificent asset by pollution. The 181,-000 people of the city of Spokane discharge wastes through sewers and treatment plant to a spot downstream on the Spokane River. The 46,500 residents of the Valley, however, have only septic tanks draining through gravel and boulders toward the water below. New people arrive every day, new septic tanks are built, and the concentration of effluent in the earth increases. Health authorities have repeatedly warned citizens and local officials that action should begin now, for once pollution is discovered, it will be too late. The water, if contaminated, will not be pure again for years.

Here, also, fragmented government poses barriers to action. The city of Spokane has no jurisdiction in the Valley; neither county nor township has authority to build sewers; and a proper answer might require action by the entire metropolitan community. Everyone's water supply is threatened, but "everyone" has no government to act.

Tacoma has sewers and treatment plants adequate to handle its own problems of sewage disposal, but problems are accumulating in the suburbs. The drainage area around Lake Steilacoom and that of Clover Creek are reaching an acute state in which not even treated sewage can be safely added. The Lakewood area has problems ahead. There is a clear need for a comprehensive sewage system in the Tacoma area, but there is no unit of government authorized to construct or finance such a system.

Wastes of the urban community not buried in the earth or discharged into the waters are thrown into the air. Tons of material go up daily from thousands of smokestacks, chimneys, exhaust pipes and incinerators. Serious health, agricultural, economic and nuisance effects results — a heavy burden of respiratory ills, dirty buildings, expensive air purification systems, crop damage and cleaning bills.

Air pollution grows with population, and public patience is already growing short. In December 1961, 1,323 residents of Tacoma and Pierce County petitioned the Governor to put a stop to air pollution from a smelter in the city of Ruston, surrounded by Tacoma. Angry housewives of South Seattle forced an end to city burning of refuse at the South Park dump. On February 1, 1962, air pollution made front page headlines in Seattle, for air and sunlight conditions brought serious smog to the Puget Sound region and a new record of air pollution. Smog is rare in western Washington, but the stable air and abundant sunlight of the Spokane area lend themselves to its formation.

That a serious problem exists is clear. Equally clear is the inadequacy of present efforts to manage the problem. Seattle and Tacoma have modest pollution control ordinances, but air does not respect city boundaries. Pollution control districts were authorized by the Legislature some years ago, but none has been established to date. No authority exists, moreover, for applying controls within any jurisdiction which does not voluntarily agree.

Blight in cities, inadequate services in the suburbs, jammed highways, polluted water and air — these are warning signals of sickness in our urban communities. The cure for these ills lies, in the first instance, in major changes in the finances, structure, and powers of local government. Also essential are an informed and active citizenry and good men in office, but they are not enough, for the present structure defeats the efforts of citizens and officials alike. Good men with poor tools work hard to produce little; good men with good tools accomplish much for all.

ROSCOE C. MARTIN AND DOUGLAS PRICE

The Metropolis and Its Problems Reexamined

To speak of a "problem" is to indicate that an individual or group is experiencing difficulty in selecting a satisfactory course of action. Typically there is a desired goal, such as the clearing of slums; but there are major obstacles in the way of achieving this goal, such as cost in taxes or unfavorable political repercussions. If means were readily available for achieving the desired end without sacrificing other goals, then there would be no problem, for the line of action would be obvious. But a multiciplicity of goals, many of

Reprinted from *The Metropolis and Its Problems* (Syracuse, N.Y.: Maxwell Graduate School of Citizenship and Public Affairs, Syracuse University, 1959), pp. 11-18, by permission of the authors and the Dean of the Maxwell School.

which are at least partially conflicting, coupled with a scarcity of resources to use in pursuing them, is likely to generate a wide range of problems. These problems may be of importance only to an individual (for example, the New Yorker who wants easy access to Manhattan but also the spacious living of exurbia), or they may involve the formal institutions of government. Given the nature of American politics, when a problem becomes serious for a large number of individuals, they are likely to make it a problem for government.

From this point of view the metropolitan problem is not a particular substantive issue, whether of housing or transit or administration or segregation, but rather is the discontent of millions of metropolitan residents over these and other aspects of their common life. For research purposes, these might well be approached as dependent variables, with the metropolis as the independent variable. Professor Philip Hauser has urged that such research, treating the city or metropolis as an *independent* variable, needs to be more sharply differentiated from the study of the city or metropolis as a *dependent* variable. This is an important distinction, all to often ignored in current research.

What aspects of the metropolitan environment might be identified as important variables contributing to urban discontents? Fragmented local government is a standard answer; but it might be useful to consider additional variables, such as the relative complexity of the urban environment. Professors March and Simon have invited us to

> Consider a world that is mainly "empty" — in which most events are unrelated to most other events, causal connections are exceptional and not common. . . .[1]

Would this be typical of a modern metropolis? Certainly not in regard to most governmental functions; it is more nearly descriptive of the opposite extreme of a rural environment.[2] For example, consider the consequences resulting from an ordinary act, such as drill-

---

[1] James G. March and Herbert A. Simon, *Organizations* (New York: John Wiley & Son), 176.

[2] Obviously, this may not hold for every type of causal relation. Thus the network of informal social control is doubtless tighter in a rural community than in most cities, but this may mean that in the city there are fewer such restraints on personal acts which are likely to have more widespread consequences.

ing a hole in the ground. This simple act, which might not even be noticed by a farmer's nearest neighbor, would in mid-town Boston be likely to have immediate and drastic consequences. If done without careful regard to these possible consequences, such an act might plunge much of the city into darkness, interrupt subway service, paralyze elevators, break telephone connections, or disrupt sewers and water mains. These would be just the immediate consequences — the more indirect results would also be substantial.

This extreme complexity of the environment is typical of the metropolis in both physical and human aspects. Our hypothetical farmer might build a house on his lower forty acres without substantial consequences for his neighbors. But consider the problems involved in clearing a city slum and erecting new high-rise buildings. There are not only the vastly increased physical complications, which engineers can handle — at substantial added cost — but there are also profound human ramifications. Dwellings are razed and their occupants dispossessed, marginal business establishments are destroyed or deprived of their clientele, substantial demand is generated for various new services, and even the political complexion of the area is likely to be changed. For example, in New York City Mr. De Sapio may survive the ideological assaults of Mr. Finletter and Mrs. Roosevelt, but be unseated in his own district because of the rapid replacement of tenements (formerly housing low-income Italian-immigrant workers) by luxury apartment buildings.

It is, then, hardly surprising that slum clearance and urban renewal are exhausting, time-consuming, controversial affairs, even where funds are available. (Money is not the only scarce resource!). In addition to the normal hazards, the unscrupulous real estate dealer may deliberately make use of the tight causal network of the city, as when he moves a Negro family into a formerly all-white area in such a manner as to encourage panic sales. Such "block-busting" frequently sets off rapid and drastic reactions ranging from emergency sales (the intended consequence) to outright riot and violence (unintended by-products).

The concept of degree of causal consequences is, admittedly, highly abstract. It does not describe raw experience — or raw sewage — with the loving care for detail found in some empirical studies, but it does encourage the development of a body of theory which should be useful for analyzing what is involved. As Professor Hauser [indicates], efforts to nail down general-purpose boundaries for a given "metropolitan area" have repeatedly met with failure. The network of causal consequences around a metropolis extends different distances for different purposes. Hence, what is part of the metropolis with respect to, say, air pollution may not be part of the area with regard to water supply. It may be that Cape Cod and Miami Beach are functioning parts of the New York metropolis in regard to the network of recreation facilities, but they have no significance for the area's milk shed!

Under the heading of "external effects" economists have long concerned themselves with the causal ramifications of an action which extend beyond the immediate participants. These may be favorable effects, as when a resident receives pleasure from his neighbor's lovely front yard; or unfavorable, as when he is kept awake at night by his neighbor's yowling cat. The existence of external effects within a metropolitan area is endemic, as regards both individuals and communities. Raymond Vernon has made extensive use of the external economies concept in his analysis of the role of the central business district in the New York area.[3] But to date little attention has been paid to the other side of the coin, the external *diseconomies* created by extreme congestion and interdependence. This may be due to the tendency of economic studies to concentrate on the private sector of a region, whereas most of the "problems" (i.e., external diseconomies) affect primarily the public sector.

From an analytic point of view the existence of major external effects is one of the basic reasons for a wide range of governmental activities. At the national level it is citing the obvious to point to the recognition of the interrelatedness of modern industrial society and its consequences for the scope of government activity and regulation. At the more mundane local level such things as building permits, zoning regulations, auto safety and liability insurance requirements, public health laws, fire prevention, and smog and water pollution abatement are further examples. Significantly, most of these have been pioneered by, and are most highly developed in, our large metropolitan centers.

A causal network may be analyzed in terms of the density of the causal connections, the distance over which significant effects ramify, and the extent to which consequences endure over time. Mrs. O'Leary's cow, which supposedly started the great Chicago fire,

[3] Edgar M. Hoover and Raymond Vernon, *Anatomy of a Metropolis* (Cambridge: Harvard University Press, 1959), 62-73 and 88-105.

demonstrated conclusively both the density and the wide extent of a metropolitan causal network. Rural cows may burn down an occasional barn, but they seldom make history. Much of the concern for having a master plan turns on the temporal dimension — experience has indicated that early street patterns and systems of land use set almost unalterable constraints on what can be done by the next generation, thus emphasizing causal connections over time.

The resulting demand for planning and for more public regulation of activities in metropolitan areas doubtless reflects a variety of factors. Kenneth Boulding has emphasized the factor of size, or what he terms "the Brontosaurus Principle": "up to a certain point, the bigger the better; beyond that point, the bigger the worse."[4] In a reply to Boulding's article Harlan Cleveland has emphasized the point that one of the results of modern technology and organization "is to reduce the margins for error in a thousand ways."[5] This is particularly important, Dean Cleveland notes, in regard to the repercussions of actions in an urban setting:

> A hundred years ago most of the inhabitants of this continent were scattered about on farms or in rural towns with plenty of room to spare. But now that two-thirds of us live in urban areas, our accountability to each other is greatly enhanced. Childhood activities which used to be tolerated in rural societies are now regarded in cities as "deviant behavior"; one suspects it is not high-spirited youth that has changed, but the norms of delinquency against which juvenile conduct is measured. Similarly, for adults, driving a Buick on a crowded speedway requires more continuous exercise of a sense of responsibility to others than driving a Model T on a rural byway. . . .[6]

There are, however, limits on the extent to which planning or government intervention can control such effects. Government may indeed be an important influence on the operation of society, but is itself subject to "feedback" from society. This is a point often overlooked by the more enthusiastic city planners, who desire control over city development almost as complete as that which an artist exercises over a personal project. Such control, of course, is

[4] Kenneth Boulding, "The Jungle of Hugeness," *The Saturday Review* (March 1, 1958), 11.

[5] Harlan Cleveland, "Dinosaurs and Personal Freedom," *The Saturday Review* (February 28, 1959), 14.

[6] *Ibid.*, 14 and 38.

generally impossible. In any democratic society the flow of influence from society to government is apt to be as significant as the impact of government policy on society. Even when a new policy is accepted it is likely to have to provide exemptions for existing developments which do not accord with the policy — an example is found in acceptance of prior nonconforming uses in zoning (as with New York's acceptance and continued use of "old-law" tenements built prior to the 1901 statute setting minimum requirements).

There are also limits on the extent to which we can speak at all securely about causal ramifications. To a considerable extent the problem of defining appropriate local government jurisdictions and functions might be said to revolve around the proper way of factoring the causal connections of a metropolitan area into manageable sub-parts. A highly decentralized form of local government would seem appropriate to relatively independent communities, but when more and more problems become of common concern and require common action there is need for closer coordination. The sewage from one area may, if untreated, pollute the beaches and water supply of a second area; or industrial and auto fumes from both may contribute to smog over both. More and more actions which might be acceptable "locally," that is, without regard to their external effects, are resulting in serious problems for the larger metropolitan area.[7]

Students of public administration — with understandable if still lamentable professional bias — have concluded that the growth of the metropolitan complex beyond old city boundaries is the basic problem, and that establishment of some sort of area-wide governmental institutions is the basic answer. For a variety of reasons, however, it seems likely that this is by no means the whole answer. The process of piling more and more people into larger and denser agglomerations involves substantial social and economic changes, some desirable and some undesirable, which a mere recasting of organization charts or redrawing of political boundaries are unlikely to "solve."

Metropolitan government, viewed as a practical matter of organizational behavior rather than as a matter of administrative the-

[7] The "locally rational" attitude of some suburbs is roughly analogous to the "amoral familialism" which Edward C. Banfield describes in *The Moral Basis of a Backward Society* (Glencoe, Illinois: The Free Press, 1958), Chapter 5.

ology, represents an attempt to provide for greater centralization in political decision-making within a metropolitan area. The area is operationally defined for various functions by the range of significant causal couplings. The great advantage of central control lies in its ability to deal with external effects where there is a significant "spillover effect" of either the advantages or disadvantages of action by local units of government. Centralization, however, is seldom an unmixed blessing, and in any event it can be overdone. As March and Simon point out:

> When we take external economies and diseconomies into consideration, then the net advantage of decentralized over centralized decision-making, or vice versa, must be assessed by weighing the losses in the former through failure to take into account indirect consequences of actions (external economies) against the losses in the latter through inability to obtain the necessary facts and to carry through the necessary computations (bounded rationality).[8]

Where some degree of centralized decision-making is achieved, as in the "metro government" plans of Miami and Toronto, the results are unlikely to provide an automatic cure for all metropolitan problems. The metropolis faces other problems in addition to those involving external effects. Even full-scale establishment of a "unified" super-government would probably result in something roughly comparable to the "unification" achieved by the establishment of the Department of Defense in 1947. The more likely if less impressive step of establishing some form of metropolitan region council would doubtless achieve even less spectacular results. One might reasonably expect such a council to serve functions roughly comparable with those performed by the United Nations in international politics, or by a joint committee of the Corps of Engineers and Bureau of Reclamation in planning for river basin development. These purposes are, of course, worth pursuing, but their achievement would represent essentially modest gains.

If we recognize that in dealing with metropolitan problems we are often involved in the familiar phenomenon of external effects, there is less need for strained efforts to prove the existence of a metropolitan "community" requiring coterminous administrative boundaries. Joint action in the face of joint problems makes sense, whether in terms of East-West cooperation to control radioactive

[8] March and Simon, *op. cit.*, 204.

fallout or of city-suburb cooperation to provide adequate transportation facilities. In neither case do we need evidence of a "real" community; nor in considering the network of causal consequences need we become overly involved in speculation about possible metropolitan "dominance" or two-way "interdependence." The causal arrows may run in one direction only or in both directions, with two-way arrows being symmetrical or asymetrical. Finally, we need not succumb to cartographic delusions that all adjacent counties with a city of 50,000 or more necessarily constitute a single "megalopolis." A traffic jam in Times Square might spread to Brooklyn, but it is hardly likely that it would immobilize traffic in Washington or Boston.

EDWARD C. BANFIELD AND MORTON GRODZINS

Some Flaws in the Logic of Metropolitan Reorganization

In much of the discussion of metropolitan reorganization it is difficult to tell precisely what the nature of the problem really is. Frequently it is not clear on what grounds reorganization is thought necessary. Usually no convincing reasons are given for fixing the bounds of the metropolitan area in one way rather than in another. And there is seldom much critical examination of the assumptions, arguments, and conclusions with respect to various schemes for reorganization. . . .

Often the assumption is implicit, if not explicit, that it must be extremely wasteful to have many — perhaps several hundred — independent governing bodies within a single metropolitan area. Recently, for example, an insurance company president told a national conference on metropolitan problems:

> The businessman finds himself in a crazy quilt of communities of all sizes, shapes and systems. These are growing without planning — without reasonable relationship one to the other. These illogical governmental boundaries in many respects are like tariff walls, and the effect has been to increase immeasurably the cost of doing business. Such a wonderland of waste, paid for by tax dollars, is offensive to the tax-paying businessman.[1]

It is not likely that the speaker considers the insurance business a "wonderland of waste" because it is carried on by hundreds of companies of all sizes, operating within boundaries which are, from any general standpoint, illogical. If such a charge were made against the insurance business, he would be quick to point out the advantages which arise from the specialization of certain companies in one or another type of highly technical business, the encouragement to enterprise and risk-taking that results from the independent operation of small companies, and the gain to the consumer from being able to choose from a wide variety of offerings. He might even add that the lack of cooperation within the insurance business is not as great as it may appear to the outsider: there are many informal devices — trade associations, for example — through which the companies regulate their relations when it is in their mutual interest to do so.

Not uncommonly, of course, genuine savings may be made by consolidation of enterprises, whether they be local governments or insurance companies, or by formal arrangements to bring about greater coordination. And it is certainly true that wasteful governments can proliferate in a way denied to insurance companies. Many factors may perpetuate an ineffective business; yet a business does have a balance sheet as a relatively harsh criterion of effectiveness.

[1] Powell B. McHaney, President, General American Life Insurance Company, speaking before the National Conference on Metropolitan Problems, East Lansing, Michigan, Apr. 30, 1956. Mr. McHaney's address appears in the conference proceedings published by the Government Affairs Foundation, Washington, 1957.

No similar yardstick exists for governments. Furthermore, large organizations — in both industry and government — may make possible through economies of scale new functions (including research) that would otherwise be impossible. In industry, consolidations also diffuse risk-bearing; the analogous consideration in governmental consolidation is the widening of the tax base, which frees the local community from dependence upon the decision of the few owners of industrial property who, by controlling a large tax source, may thereby control the community itself.

Despite these qualifications, the simple number of government units in a given locality, or their lack of uniformity, simplicity, and symmetry, is at best only a rough indicator of the need for reorganization.

Sometimes the necessary distinction is not made between "problems which exist in metropolitan areas" and "problems which exist by virtue of the inadequacies of governmental structures in the metropolitan areas." Recently, for example, the Conference on Metropolitan Area Problems sponsored by the governors of Massachusetts, Connecticut, New York, New Jersey, and Pennsylvania and the mayor of New York City listed a number of "problems confronted by the metropolitan areas." Along with recommendations on mass transit, air pollution, waste disposal, and water pollution was the following: "It is essential that some playgrounds and other facilities be located within easy reach of the mother with the baby-carriage and the child on roller-skates."[2] Lack of playgrounds within easy reach of mothers and children may indeed be a problem in metropolitan areas; it is not, however, a problem which requires for its solution any reorganization of governments.

Some writers have sought to find the optimum scale for the organization of each public function in the nature of its technology and to infer from this an optimum size for the city government as a whole. Aside from the fact that technology is always changing, the main difficulty of this approach is that it does not take into account the nonmonetary advantages and disadvantages which are associated with a given scale of organization. Suppose, for example, that without any loss of services a suburb could reduce its tax rate by $1 per $100 of assessed valuation by becoming part of the central city. Presumably this would be a measure of the economies of scale that would result from consolidation. The suburbanites, how-

[2] *The New York Times,* Sept. 24, 1957, p. 29.

ever, might judge that the satisfaction of remaining apart from the city and controlling their own affairs in their own way was worth all it cost and more. If they made this judgment, consolidation would represent less rather than more efficiency, for in judging efficiency *all* valued outputs, not merely those measured in the market, must be taken into account.

The discussion of these matters by some advocates of metropolitan consolidation seems to assume that the suburbanite is wrong in valuing nonmonetary satisfactions as highly as he often does; that the pleasure of being identified with an autonomous suburb is illusory or socially irresponsible. Actually, the concern of the ordinary citizen for social status, and for housing and community surroundings as a symbol of status, is one of the driving forces of American life. If the upward mobile masses — the "new immigrants" in Samuel Lubell's term — want to buy the status advantages that go with residence in a town which has a name and an identity apart from the central city, and if they are willing to pay the added costs that this entails, it is hard to see why they should be discouraged. From a policy standpoint, only two questions are relevant: are they actually bearing all of the extra costs and are they aware of them? If the answer to these questions is "yes," there is little basis for public concern.

Even if intangibles like status are left out of account, and the calculation is made solely in terms of quantities which can be measured and priced, it is not clear that widespread consolidation of local governments would yield much of a saving. Posed in this oversimplified way, the problem of discovering the optimum scale of a single function, to say nothing of all functions together, would still be very difficult. Police protection may best be organized on one scale, sewage disposal on another, and recreation on still another. What, then, is the optimum size for a city which performs all three functions and many more besides?

Increases in the volume of work, in government as in industry, decrease the unit cost of work output. But in both cases there is a point of diminishing returns. The situation for government is complicated because the larger the population aggregate, the more extensive and more expensive the services required and demanded. Per capita expenditures for governmental services in cities generally increase with size of city. If costs, not services, were the criterion, this fact would argue for smaller, not larger, governments.

Per capita expenditures, of course, must be distinguished from *costs of a given service at a given standard.* And here there seems to be little doubt that the latter grow less expensive with increases in size of city, up to a population of about 50,000. Costs per unit of service do not seem to decrease much in still larger cities.[3]

Moreover, even if it could be proved that larger work units lead to lower costs, it would not follow that consolidation of local governments would be desirable from an economic standpoint: the city which is too small to provide certain services efficiently may arrange to buy them from a nearby city which can produce them efficiently. In other words, absorption of one government by another is not the only way of securing adequate scale.

It is often assumed that if sentimental and political obstacles ("irrationalities," they are often called) did not stand in the way, it would be possible to delineate a metropolitan area which would form the "logical" basis for an all-purpose local governmental jurisdiction.

Sometimes it is taken for granted that political boundaries ought to correspond to some features of the natural environment.[4] This thinking has led many geographers to delineate "natural regions" (e.g., drainage basins) and to recommend them as the "logical" units on which to base political and administrative jurisdictions. In

[3] See William Anderson, *The Units of Government in the United States,* Public Administration Service, Chicago, 1942; also the literature cited in *State-Local Relations,* Report of the Committee on State-Local Relations, The Council of State Governments, Chicago, 1946, pp. 183ff. But the optimum scale of governmental functions — and therefore the optimum scale of municipal organization — has never been established. It could be done only if some very important simplifying assumptions were made and then only by a major research effort.

[4] An early theorist on this topic was H. G. Wells. In "A Paper on Administrative Areas Read before the Fabian Society" (reprinted as an appendix to *Mankind in the Making,* Charles Scribner's Sons, New York, 1904, pp. 389-390) he spoke of the "new urban region." "I would suggest that watersheds make excellent boundaries. Let me remind you that railways, tramways, drain-pipes, water-pipes, and high-roads have this in common — they will not climb over a watershed if they can possibly avoid doing so, and that population and schools and poor tend to distribute themselves in accordance with these other things. You get the minimum of possible overlap — such overlap as the spreading out of the great midland city to meet London must some day cause — in this way. I would suggest that for the regulation of sanitation, education, communications, industrial control, and poor relief, and for the taxation for these purposes, this area should be one, governed by one body, elected by local constituencies that would make its activities independent of imperial politics."

the case of the metropolitan area, however, the physical feature usually fixed upon is not "natural" at all: it is the perimeter of contiguous urban settlement. This standard is usually highly ambiguous in application, since one hardly ever finds a sharp, sudden break in the continuity of settlement; usually the urban and rural places run together on the fringes of the cities in such a way that even a rather broad line must be arbitrary. One might, by taking one view of contiguity, regard the area from Portland, Maine, to Richmond, Virginia, as a single metropolitan area, although surely no governmental problem requires this particular jurisdiction for its solution.

If it were possible to delineate clear-cut population areas, it would not necessarily follow that these would be appropriate bases for local governmental jurisdictions. A large population occupying a single contiguous area might very well comprise two or more virtually distinct economic, social, or political communities. The difficulties in defining a "community" are as great as those in defining a "natural population block,"[5] and a single "community," even if defined, would not necessarily provide an appropriate base on which to organize all, or even any, local governmental services. If the community were large enough for one function (according to criteria of economy), it might be too large — or not large enough — for others.

It is often argued that as a matter of justice the level of services — education, police, fire, public health, and so on — should be equal throughout the metropolitan area, or at least that uniformity of service levels cannot be attained unless there is an authority with jurisdiction over the whole area.

[5] The notion of "community" as the basis of local government jurisdiction is itself full of ambiguities. Some geographers suppose that the trade area has some claim to be taken as the "logical" basis of political and administrative jurisdictions. In his book on *Human Ecology* (Ronald Press, New York, 1950), Amos Hawley defines the community as ". . . that area, the resident population of which is interrelated and integrated with reference to its daily requirements, whether contacts be direct or indirect." On the basis of this definition, it is hard to tell whether the people of the New York metropolian area are any more or less a community than are the people of the whole United States. But, apart from this lack of operational value, there is no special reason to believe that integration with regard to daily needs should be the basis of political and administrative jurisdictions.

For a recent discussion by a sociologist of the problem of defining the metropolitan community, see Albert J. Reiss, Jr., "The Community and the Corporate Area," *University of Pennsylvania Law Review*, vol. 105, February, 1957, pp. 443-463.

There are, obviously, certain minimum standards — especially those connected with health and education — below which it is intolerable that any community should fall. If these minima are met, there is no good reason to demand that all service levels be everywhere precisely, or even approximately, the same. Moreover, even if uniformity is desired, it is hard to see why it should be uniformity within the metropolitan area rather than within some larger area. If, for example, uniformity is desirable within the New York–New Jersey area, why is it not also desirable within the Richmond–Boston area, of which the former is a part? And if it is desirable within the Richmond–Boston area, why not throughout the United States? The argument leads to the conclusion that standards of local service should be defined and enforced for the whole country by the Federal government.

Provided minimum standards are everywhere met, there is much to be said for encouraging differentials in service levels. Many people do not wish to buy more of the services supplied by local government than absolutely necessary. Some are able to enjoy the satisfactions of homeownership because they are willing to forego — and because the market allows them to forego — other satisfactions, including those which would come from higher levels of local governmental service. Certainly freedom to make choices of this kind should be encouraged, not discouraged.

Apart from this, differentials in service levels may serve the useful function of discouraging settlement in places where it is not desirable. Herbert A. Simon has observed:

> To the extent that the higher cost of service, or the poorer quality of service provided to such an area, acts as a deterrent to its development until the more central portions of the city have been completely settled, differentials stemming from this particular cause must be considered beneficial — they are a penalty, so to speak, which reflect the higher cost of servicing the urban population when scattered over a large area, than when compactly distributed.[6]

Inequality of service levels does not constitute a problem of metropolitan area organization. Failure to maintain minimum service levels is a problem, although, as the later discussion will show, not one that requires drastic metropolitan reorganization.

The metropolitan-area problem is sometimes said to arise from

[6] Herbert A. Simon, *Fiscal Aspects of Metropolitan Consolidation*, Bureau of Public Administration, University of California, Berkeley, 1943, p. 20.

the lack of an all-purpose (or at least multipurpose) government able to plan and carry on functions which are best conducted on an area-wide basis. When these functions are listed, they often include most of what local government does.[7]

The claim that a certain function should be administered on a metropolitan basis may rest on one or the other of two grounds: that it is more economical to perform it on an area-wide basis, or that there are important needs which cannot adequately be met except by area-wide organization.

The issue of economy has already been discussed. The issue of adequacy must be distinguished from it. "Economical" action is action that minimizes waste: "adequate" action results in the attainment of purpose. Some functions can be performed on a less-than-metropolitan basis in an "economical" fashion (without waste), and others can be performed on this basis even though they are "uneconomical," i.e., involve waste. But the claim now under examina-

---

[7] For example, in the Chicago region, according to F. T. Aschman, at least nine major services "present problems for study on an area-wide basis." These are transportation, water distribution, drainage and sewage disposal, garbage and refuse disposal, fire protection, recreational services, health and welfare services, law enforcement, and schools. ["Chicago Metropolitan Area Problems," in Leverett S. Lyon (ed.), *Governmental Problems in the Chicago Metropolitan Area*, University of Chicago Press, Chicago, 1957, pp. 50-51.]

In the San Francisco Bay Region, according to John C. Bollens, the important regional problems are transportation, sewage, and recreation. Others, which he says deserve "brief mention," are water supply, public health, and fire and police protection. (*The Problems of Government in the San Francisco Bay Region*, Bureau of Public Administration, University of California, Berkeley ,1948, pp. 33-53.)

Luther Gulick takes a more discriminating view of what constitutes a metropolitan problem. In the New York–New Jersey region, according to Gulick, the four important needed regional services are a unified water supply; transportaion policy and structure; waste disposal and pollution control, both of water and of air; and development of the port as a world trade center. ("The Next Twenty-five Years in Government in the New York Metropolitan Region," *Metropolis in the Making*, Regional Plan Association, Inc., New York, 1955, p. 65.)

Background for Action (St. Louis Metropolitan Survey, 1957) lists six "weaknesses that stem from the complex governmental pattern of the St. Louis City–St. Louis County area." These are (1) disparity in number and extent of governmental services; (2) variation in ability of communities to finance essential services; (3) inadequacy of some services essential to the development of the area due to absence of single governmental jurisdiction (e.g., transit facilities and traffic control); (4) creation of sanitary problems in some communities by irresponsible action of others; (5) competition for tax resources that impedes land use planning; and (6) inequitable distribution of service costs.

tion goes beyond the issue of economy. It holds that some governmental needs cannot be adequately fulfilled at all, whatever the cost or waste, on anything less than an entire metropolitan basis.

What are the needs that demand metropolitan organization to be "adequately" fulfilled?

What is a "need," as well as what is an "adequate" performance in meeting the need, is in the last analysis a matter of opinion. Air-pollution control, for example, is a need only as someone — a professional group or the whole public — defines it as one. And it is a need which requires area-wide action only if the definition is such that nothing less than area-wide action will meet it.

If the "needs" and levels of "adequacy" as defined by the professional groups are accepted at face value, a few functions seem generally to require metropolitan-wide organization in order to be performed adequately. Circulation control (the whole problem of transport within the area) probably does. Civil defense probably does. So does air-pollution control, particularly as it involves control of the automobile. (The need to control the moving automobile requires area-wide administration for each of these functions.) It is impossible to be sure about these functions, however, since those who claim that they are metropolitan-area problems do not specify in a clear and unambiguous way what they mean by "adequate" performance.

It will be seen that definition itself can make any function one which can be "adequately" performed only on a metropolitan basis. Dogcatching, for example, could be done "adequately" only through a metropolitan-wide government if the following arguments were accepted: dogs are no respecters of municipal boundaries; the control of stray dogs is essential to the health and safety of urban populations; there must be quick and complete circulation of information regarding stray dogs throughout the metropolitan area; dogcatching services must be of the same quality throughout the area; dog pounds must be located so as to be within easy access of all population groups within the area; the need for dog control is so great and the professionalization of personnel so difficult that it would be dangerous to rely upon any cooperative dog-control arrangements among the separate local governments concerned; and "Balkanization" of local government prevents leaders in dogcatching from operating within the central cities where their services are most needed.

Other functions may be defined so as to make area-wide jurisdiction requisite for their "adequate" performance. Land-use planning, tax assessment, recreation, police (here the analogy with dogcatching is particularly close) are often so defined. Whether or not such functions are actually administered on an area-wide basis is often a matter of political persuasion rather than of technology.

Like all who think about these matters, the authors of this study must fall back upon their own notions of what is "needed" and what is "adequate" fulfillment of needs. By their standards, some aspects of circulation, civil defense, and air-pollution control are almost everywhere metropolitan-area problems in the sense that they are needs which cannot adequately be met without area-wide organization.

To the extent that circulation, civil defense, and air pollution are being dealt with today, it is by the action of many governments, including the Federal. The Federal government plays a leading part in transportation. Although sluggish about fully recognizing the fact, it undoubtedly has the leading role in civilian defense. As the experience of Los Angeles indicates, air-pollution control will sooner or later get Federal action. The Federal government's position in all these fields does not relieve the metropolitan areas of their responsibility. (This is true even with respect to civilian defense, where the national military primacy must be complete.) Nevertheless, it is clear that the relatively few essentially area-wide problems tend also to be nationwide problems, or at least national urban ones. Their solution, therefore, demands not merely a higher degree of metropolitan integration, but also the most intimate linkage of metropolitan areas with other levels of government.

A good number of the so-called metropolitan-area organization problems turn out on examination to involve something less than the whole metropolitan area. Generally speaking, in the nonarid parts of the country there is enough water so that supplies can be organized on a less-than-metropolitan basis. (Where control is needed, it is generally on a larger-than-metropolitan basis.) If newer technologies are employed, waste disposal may be highly decentralized. With regard to most aspects of public health, recreation, police and fire protection, adequate performance (still distinguished from economical performance) does not require metropolitan-area organization. These are usually subarea problems and imply for their solution subarea governments.

What are area problems in some places are, of course, subarea ones in others. If one looks at the differences among areas, one sees at once that the number and kind of problems requiring area-wide treatment vary from place to place, and that in general the number of such matters decreases as the size of the area increases. It is possible, for example, that Nashville, a metropolitan area of 300,000 population, ought to operate its hospitals on an area-wide basis, but it is hardly likely that the same type of operation will serve the New York–New Jersey area, which contains almost one-tenth of the population of the United States. Size aside, topographical or resource limitations will bring some areas, but not others, to area-wide programs. Water supply may be important in one place as an area-wide function; sewage disposal in another. But adequacy (and economy, too) in the performance of these same functions may be readily achievable in other areas on a less-than-metropolitan-area basis.

Most of the arguments for metropolitan government turn out to be, on inspection, something less than compelling, and the total case for metropolitan integration of local governments is a shaky one.[8] This is not to say, however, that the governments of metropolitan areas as they exist today should not be altered. If they do not make a case for wholesale integration, the arguments examined in this chapter nevertheless indicate both points of weakness and perspectives for future action.

Not all functions need to be organized on a metropolitan basis to achieve economic scale; most functions, however, cannot be economically operated (leaving intangibles out of consideration for the moment) in very small jurisdictions. Ordinarily there will be waste unless jurisdictions of at least 50,000 population are achieved by cooperative arrangements or other means, including consolidation. Subarea arrangement (as distinguished from metropolitan-wide arrangements) are indicated on grounds of both economy and adequacy for some functions in almost every metropolitan area. Given the prevailing notions of "adequacy," a few functions probably need area-wide jurisdictions in most places. Finally, what constitutes a metropolitan-wide "need" is in the long run what the relevant publics decide. As they change their definitions of area-wide needs, what is appropriate governmental structure will also change.

[8] A careful inspection of the arguments *against* metropolitan integration would reveal that they, too, are not always persuasive.

4

METROPOLITAN GOVERNMENT:
THE POLITICS OF REVOLUTION

Campaigns for areawide government are the "spec-
taculars" of metropolitan politics. Most issues contested
in the metropolis concern particular functions of government, such as highways, water supply, or land-use control. Rarely does the average issue involve a wide range
of metropolitan actors. Proposals for regional government, on the other hand, crosscut the many functional
arenas of the decentralized political system. No other
event in the political history of a metropolitan area offers
a better opportunity to observe the panorama of regional
interests in action. In no other contest are the potential
stakes as high, since metropolitan government threatens
to redistribute influence and alter the existing system of
public control over the vital parameters of community
life.

Attempts to revolutionize the political system of the
metropolis have been a natural outgrowth of the research
and preachings of the metropolitan reformers. In the hun-
dred-odd metropolitan areas where campaigns for area-
wide government have been launched, the civic associations, planning agencies, and universities have provided
most of the shock troops. Widespread support usually has
been forthcoming from the "big mules" of the central city:
the bankers, merchants, downtown property owners, util-

153

ity operators, and newspaper publishers, who embrace metropolitan reform as a means of saving the central business district. Completing the cast of characters in the revolutionary camp are various metropolitan have-nots — such as central city Republicans, suburban liberals, and ambitious young lawyers seeking publicity and political opportunities.

Upon the initiative of this alliance, the ritual of the campaign for metropolitan government commences. Like Kabuki dancers performing their timeless movements, the metropolitan specialists, frequently imported from the citadels of the reform movement and often supported by one or more of the foundations, solemnly catalog the units of government, evaluate services, compare costs and benefits, unearth inequities, and pinpoint a long list of deficiencies which can be corrected only by comprehensive planning and coordinated action. To no one's surprise, the expert survey produces a blueprint for the future featuring some sort of areawide government. Most common have been proposals for the transformation of the county into a metropolitan government as in Miami (Dade County), Nashville (Davidson County), and Cleveland (Cuyahoga County). Alternatives are the creation of a metropolitan federation with delegated powers following the Toronto prototype or the establishment of a multipurpose metropolitan district as proposed in St. Louis and Seattle. After the survey comes the constitutional convention, a body whose name, composition, selection, and powers vary from state to state. The task of this constituent assembly is to give birth to the official plan for metropolitan government. More often than not, the plan bears close resemblance to the fruit of the labors of the survey experts. Now the pace of the campaign quickens. Those somewhat incongruous revolutionaries, the middle class reformers and the downtown businessmen, go forth to convince the metropolis of the need for fundamental change in the political system. And, almost always, the campaign ends on election day in a shattering defeat for the plans and dreams of the metropolitan reformers.

The readings in this chapter provide some answers to the inevitable questions that arise from the sad history of metropolitan government. Why have more than a hundred attempts to overhaul the governmental structure of the metropolis produced so few successes that they can be counted on the fingers of one hand? Given the dismal record of metropolitan reform, how does one account for the creation of areawide government in two major metropolitan areas — Miami and Nashville — during the past decade?

After examining the campaigns for regional government in St. Louis, Cleveland, and Miami, Scott Greer concludes that the reformers' problems arise in part from the difficulty they experience in applying the traditional themes of municipal reform to the metropolis. Most proposals either add a new layer of government as in the St. Louis District Plan or expand existing units, as was the case with Cuyahoga and Dade Counties. Rarely are any units of government, elected positions, or political jobs eliminated. As a result, the municipal reformers have sallied forth onto the treacherous terrain of metropolitan politics without their most effective weapon — the cry of "throw the rascals out." Other good government themes such as economy and efficiency and the need for "streamlined modern" government to insure a bigger and better future metropolis lack the political sex appeal of what Greer calls the "purification rites," particularly when the issues are complex, the savings to the local taxpayer are obscure, and the benefits of change are dimly perceived.

Suburbia has been notoriously inhospitable to proposals for metropolitan government, and with good reason, argues Charles R. Adrian. As he indicates, the tenets of "metropology" are an expression of the interests of the downtown business leaders and the urban professionals —the planners, administrators, engineers, and other functional specialists. The "folklore," he contends, is largely irrelevant to the values and interests of the average urban dweller, particularly in the suburbs. Adrian sees the suburbanite as far more concerned with his access to local government and its representativeness than with efficiency and economy. Instead of comprehensive planning and coordinated programs, he wants to maintain his control over the local environment. Fearing unequal costs and benefits and a dilution of his influence in a larger polity, he rejects the notion of a metropolitan community and proposals to provide it with an area-wide government.

The fact that suburbia usually casts negative majorities in metropolitan government referenda does not mean that the politics of revolution can be explained in terms of a simple city-suburban dichotomy. The metropolitan status quo has a powerful appeal for many of the participants in the pluralist politics of the central city. Politicians have no desire to see their constituencies altered or their jobs disappear. Ward, labor, and minority group leaders are understandably reluctant to see their influence diluted by the creation of an areawide government dominated by middle class voters. Civil servants fear for their seniority, pensions, and bureaucratic folkways. Even the pro-metro façade among the city's economic interests proves to be fragile as businessmen with city contracts, favored positions, and other ties to the status quo enlist in the growing ranks of the opposition. In a fictional case study which reflects the experience of a number of metropolitan areas, Paul Ylvisaker portrays a city in the throes of a campaign for areawide government.

Most of the factors cited by Greer, Adrian, and Ylvisaker helped defeat metropolitan government in St. Louis in 1959. With over two million inhabitants, the St. Louis area is the nation's ninth metropolis, and the largest to be the scene of a campaign for areawide government in the postwar years. In many respects, the bistate St. Louis region is typical of the larger metropolitan areas. Growth is concentrated in the suburbs, with the principal suburban jurisdiction, St. Louis County, tripling its population between 1930 and 1960. The city of St. Louis lost more than ten per cent of its residents in the past decade as its population dropped precipitously from 850,000 to 750,000. Almost all the region's Negroes live in the city, where they account for approximately thirty per cent of the population. With almost a hundred municipalities, numerous special districts, and close to 200,000 county residents in unincorporated areas, the political system is highly fragmented. However, unlike the political situation in most metropolitan areas, the Democratic Party controls both the city and the county, although its hold on the former is considerably more secure than its position in the latter.

Numerous attempts have been made over the past thirty years to create regional institutions to deal with the many problems of urban growth and change in the St. Louis area. Although city voters approved them, proposals for areawide government were rebuffed by suburbanites in 1926 and 1930. A regional sewerage authority, the Metropolitan St. Louis Sewer District, was created in 1954; but the following year voters turned down a proposed metropolitan transit authority. In 1955, an ambitious young St. Louis alderman, A. J. Cervantes, set in motion a chain of events which produced: (1) the year-long $300,000 Metropolitan St. Louis Survey (financed by the Ford Foundation and the local McDonnell Aircraft Corporation Charitable Trust), which recommended creation of a multi-purpose metropolitan district for the city and county responsible for the highway system, mass transit, industrial development, sewerage, civil defense, property assessments, and regional planning; (2) a nineteen member metropolitan charter commission, known in Missouri as a board of freeholders, which divided sharply over the alternatives of merger of the city and county or a multi-purpose district along the lines recommended by the Metropolitan St. Louis Survey before selecting the latter by a ten to nine vote; and (3) an unsuccessful campaign for adoption of the district proposal in the autumn of 1959.

In their description and analysis of the St. Louis campaign, Henry J. Schmandt, Paul G. Steinbicker, who was co-director of the Metropolitan St. Louis Survey, and George D. Wendel show how the political parties, organized labor, St. Louis' Mayor Raymond Tucker, and practically everyone in suburbia united against the outmanned

and poorly organized supporters of the district plan.
Caught in a crossfire between those who wanted no
change and those who sought a complete merger of the
city and county, the businessmen and civic leaders waged
a tepid campaign which failed to overcome the apathy or
hostility of the residents of the metropolis. On November
3, 1959, about thirty per cent of the regional electorate
turned out to kill the district plan by a two to one majority in the city and a three to one margin in the county.
The only beneficiary of the time, effort, and money expended in St. Louis was the campaign's initiator, Alderman Cervantes, who moved on to less quixotic political
endeavors in 1965 when he ended the long reign of Mayor
Tucker by defeating him in the Democratic primary, after
which he won an easy victory in the general election.

After so many defeats, no one could blame the metropolitan reformers if they decided to give up, consoling
themselves with thoughts like "we were ahead of our time"
or "it's still a good idea, but you can't beat the system."
But like the New York Met fan, the metropolitan reformer retains boundless faith in what almost everyone
else perceives as a lost cause. The lessons that he learns
from the monotonous string of setbacks are not that most
people are reasonably satisfied with the status quo, that
the decentralized political system creates an almost un-
beatable coalition of interests dedicated to its preservation,
or that the fragmented metropolis accommodates to urban change sufficiently to keep discontent well below the
revolutionary level. Instead, surveying the wreckage of
the latest unsuccessful effort to achieve areawide government, he concludes that better metro plans are needed,
that efforts to educate the public must be improved, and
that more effective campaign techniques have to be developed and implemented. And to clinch his argument,
the reformer points to Miami and Nashville and asks
"why not here?"

Hard work no doubt contributed to metropolitan reform's only two successes in the past decade. Some of the
lessons that Edward Sofen and Daniel R. Grant draw

from the Miami and Nashville experiences certainly may be applied with profit elsewhere. Yet it is clear from their analyses that these victories resulted more from the nature of the two political systems than from the efforts and techniques of the metropolitan revolutionaries. Miami, as Sofen makes clear, is atypical in its politics, its economy, its pattern of development, and in many other ways. In the unorganized no-party politics of Miami, few of the countervailing forces that normally check the metropolitan reformers existed. Local political leaders were weak, political organizations non-existent. Rapid population growth and turnover left few citizens with strong attachments to their communities. Elements which normally oppose metropolitan government such as organized labor and minority groups are politically ineffectual in Miami. Operating in this power vacuum, the standard alliance of downtown businessmen, civic leaders, central city newspapers, and public administration specialists carried the day. But even in Miami they barely mustered a majority, as only 51 per cent of the 87,000 voters (about one-quarter of the Dade County electorate) who went to the polls on May 21, 1957 voted for the metropolitan charter.

Conflict between politicians rather than their absence as in Miami was the critical factor, according to Grant, in the creation of the Nashville-Davidson County metropolitan government in 1962. Four years earlier an areawide government proposal had been defeated in a lackluster campaign despite the support of both the central city mayor and the leading county politician. Things were different in 1962 when the mayor and the county leader, long-time factional rivals, took contrary positions on a new metro proposal. With the mayor and his faction leading the opposition and the county organization supporting metro, far more political activity on the part of professional politicians resulted than normally is found in campaigns for metropolitan government. Equally important, smoldering resentment in the suburbs over a series of aggressive annexations by Nashville brought the reformer's best weapon — the "purification rites" — into play as the cry was heard that a vote for metro was a vote against Mayor Ben West and his city hall machine.

Against formidable odds, then, the forces of metropolitan reform were able to take advantage of special circumstances and win footholds in Miami and Nashville. No one can say with certainty that other sets of conditions will not set the stage for more victories for the middle class revolutionaries of the metropolis. Yet both the evidence and the odds point in the other direction. Two out of a hundred is a poor batting average indeed. The Miamis and the Nashvilles are likely to be few and far between.

SCOTT GREER

The Morality Plays of Metropolitan Reform

. . . [M]ovements aimed at achieving overall metropolitan government . . . are efforts to make revolutions, bloodless to be sure, but far from pacific and rational. Each plan proposes a radical change in the division of power, rewards, and labor in the governance of the metropolis. Each proposes basic changes in the structure of control and in the process by which controllers are recruited. They are minor in the sense that they are proposed within the broad framework of constitutional, democratic, local government. (Each of them assumes a referendum.) Furthermore, they are minor insofar as they are local and segmental, referring only to a

Reprinted from *Metropolitics* (New York: John Wiley, 1963), pp. 1-4, 6-10, 13-18, by permission of the author and John Wiley & Sons, Inc.

part of a local polity, which is, in turn, extremely dependent on the state and federal government levels.

Some people, however, take them very seriously indeed and have elaborate arguments supporting their involvement as well as the particular positions they take upon the issues. We wish, first, to look at these arguments in terms of certain broad norms of government, understandable to a wide array of political actors in the society. We have called these complexes "morality plays," for they are typically dramatic in tone, self-contained in aims, and archetypal in form; they represent vocabularies with which men may converse about common interests or disputes. . . .

The morality plays of American civic life . . . seldom transcend the formally governmental. Their emphasis is, again and again, upon the structure of government: the integration of different municipalities, the structural change of country governments, improved public personnel policies, and so forth. Rarely do we see a morality play that attempts to unite the enormous engines of private corporate enterprise (and *their* policies) to those of the public enterprise. Urban renewal is such a play. In short, the common culture of metropolitan reform, the morality plays that allow the actors to organize and speak to the citizens, can be seen as a set of blinders. They reveal certain aspects of the metropolitan area at the cost of suppressing many others.

. . . The inherited morality plays of American civic life may be seen as a conservative tradition of radical reform, conservative in the procedures used in change but radical in the consequences expected. In these dramas, innovators struggle to apply new definitions of broad norms to the specific machinations and actions of their local governments. Out of the conflict between their notions of what should be, derived from these sacred rubrics, they criticize what is. Struggling to change the cities, these innovators emphasize the form of the charters—the constitutions of the cities. (As Adrian has remarked of the National Municipal League: "In its 'model' charters and laws, its booklets and pamphlets, it made available to local groups ammunition that included all of the most recently developed reform favorites.")[1] They frequently go to the voters with their innovations, because of the broader norms of the democratic system.

[1] Charles R. Adrian, *Governing Urban America*. New York: The McGraw-Hill Book Company, 1955, page 60.

The movement to improve local government in America has typically dealt with administration and representation. It has aimed at the exclusion of ordinary business interests from the motivations of political officials, at the broadening of the electorate so that the public interest may be represented, at the increased coordination and efficiency possible with professionalism and centralization of local government. Urban home rule, the city manager system, the nonpartisan election (or proportional representation), election at large, the "strong executive," have been some of the specific aims of the movement.

To be sure, not all of these formulas are now in favor with all urban reformers. The general approach has permeated downwards, however, through many strata of the opinionated. We may imagine the public for local government to be a pyramid, with the technical innovators at the top, then the congeries of educated, middle-class men of good will (and ladies, particularly those in The League of Women Voters), the lawyers with vested interests in the subject, and finally the interested citizens. In general, change at the peak of the pyramid does not affect the lower echelons for many years. Thus the technical innovators are bound to the inherited vocabulary because of its utility in communicating with their publics. . . .

Anselm Strauss has recently documented the ideological resistance of Americans to their urbanization. He shows us clearly the resistance of many kinds of people to the living conditions of a great city.[2] Americans have not easily accepted the concentration of poverty and blight typical of the center city as their ecological home. The "city beautiful" movement of the past, the urban renewal program today, indicate support for a movement to transform the earthly city into the Heavenly City. Equally long-standing and just as impressive has been the struggle to reform the politics of the central city — to take government away from those who regard it as a business, a hunting license for a peculiar kind of game, and turn it into a process as responsible as our idealized memory of the New England townships, as efficient as our stereotypes of the corporate headquarters.[3]

The key arena has been government. The earlier battles for civic reform concentrated on the problems of the central city, for the

[2] Anselm Strauss, *Images of the American City*. Glencoe: The Free Press, 1961.
[3] Adrian, *op. cit.*

city's boundaries included reformers and reformees, just as its powers were the key powers for corruption, achievement, change, or stasis. However, the governmental boundaries have shifted greatly with the continuous growth of the city and the outward move of the middle class. Those who care about urban reform are usually suburban in their residence. Robert Wood has noted the congruence of the socially homogeneous, small-scale suburban community with the dream of the "republic in minature."[4] Though Americans have, willy-nilly, become a preponderantly urban people, they have refused to accept an image of the megalopolis as their true home. Instead, they have endeavored to transform the conditions of the great city into "garden towns" — and have, in the suburbs, come close to achieving their aims. The American middle class, in trying to make itself at home in the urban area, has solved many problems by developing suburban neighborhoods separated from the central city by governmental walls.

But other problems have been created in the process. We need not review the consequences of the suburban *hegira* for the polity of the urban area as a whole; they have been discussed many times by knowledgeable observers.[5] Let us say in summary that the consequence of governmental proliferation at the municipal level has been to aggravate problems of providing public services, determining equity, and planning for the future. Furthermore, the proliferation of municipalities has prevented development of a polity that might face these problems in any systematic or effective way. These considerations are at the roots of what has been called, in a phrase, "the metropolitan problem." Middle-class persons who were usually those most concerned with governmental reform in the older city solved their personal problems by removing to suburbia. In the process they were also achieving the political dismemberment of the social city. The ghosts of old pieties return to haunt some consciences in suburbia.

These ghosts all speak for an image of the city as a unity. And indeed, there is a plausibility in the notion that our contemporary metropolitan areas, despite their hundreds of governments, are still

[4] Robert C. Wood, *Suburbia, Its People and Their Politics.* Boston: Houghton-Mifflin, 1959.
[5] For a recent example see *Exploring the Metropolitan Community*, John Bollens (Editor). Berkeley and Los Angeles: University of California Press, 1961.

unitary. They represent one local labor market, one housing market, one transport and communication system: they are interdependent in many ways. But in one major way they are different from the city of the past: their governmental boundaries do not include all of the interdependent, problem-generating population. Thus the morality plays that defined the civic problems of the past are still usable: they are simply shifted to a larger stage — the sprawling urban complex which crosses political boundaries of many cities and counties. But now a first condition for resolving the older conflicts in old ways becomes the integration of local government. Seen not as an end in itself, but as a means to older ends, metropolitan government comes to represent a "one best way" to solve many traditional urban problems.

Definitions of these traditional urban problems may be usefully grouped around three kinds of morality plays. Each is as old as urban reform and as American as apple pie. The first is the Purification Ritual, or "Throw the rascals out!" The second might be called the drama of "Capitalist Realism," in which rational men strive to modernize "horse-and-buggy" government. The third is that of fertility and the future: "Progress or Decay! Our City Must Choose!" Each of these plays has a basic cast — heroes, villains, and innocent bystanders. Each has an end in view and a demon in view. Each script assumes the sacrosanctness of the reform and the efficacy of the means to achieve it: all imply that political validation is the one key for opening the way to the Heavenly City.

Purification Rites. In his study of the history of British town planning, William Ashworth attributes public concern for slum clearance, civic beautification, and planning to one major source: middle-class anxiety over disease and crime in the slums.[6] A great deal of the American middle class's concern for local government has been connected with anxieties aroused by evils that threaten their person and pocketbook: the corruption of political office holders, the judges who "sell their eyes," the working relationship between police and criminals known as "the fix."

A typical morality play of Purification begins with indictment of the villains, politicians who have used politics as a business. *The Shame of the Cities* was written by Lincoln Steffens in 1904, but in

[6] William Ashworth, *The Genesis of Modern British Town Planning.* London: Routledge and Kegan Paul, 1954.

the late 1950's a national magazine devoted an issue to "The Shame of New York"; the villains remain the same: party politicians, elected officials, policemen, judges. The heroes are typically reform candidates (or officials) playing the role of "Mr. District Attorney." The demon in view is the threat that "the gangsters will take over the city," that public morality will collapse, that safety of person and property will go by the board. The end in view is the elimination of the corrupt from public office — "surgery" — and their replacement with the upright. These themes recur *ad infinitum* in American civic dramatics. Through time, the major change has been the belief that the political system as a whole is evil, and thus we have the efforts to invent a bureaucracy which will be self-correcting and which will eliminate the corrupt, even as it rewards the just.

Capitalist Realism. The effort to create a self-correcting system is closely allied to the effort to modernize local government. Here the civic demons appear as statistics. The statistics show waste and inefficiency. They show overlapping jurisdictions, confusion of responsibility, and lack of responsibility. They show incompetent men in important offices, competent men bypassed in the decision-making process. The drama has its roots in the speed of change in American society at large, contrasted with the slow pace of governmental change. It is a theme from Dickens or Galsworthy: government remains in chancery, while great problems wait outside the courtroom.

The villains are those who oppose progress, for whatever reason. Their commitment to the *status quo* gives rise to various imputations of dishonesty, malfeasance, or simple stupidity. And the heroes are technicians who are experts in government, businessmen who want to see government run at least as well as the business corporation. From the early efforts to get rid of bicameral legislatures in the cities to the most recent efforts to introduce performance budgets and "scientific personnel management," the drama has been that of mechanical revision, resisted tooth and nail by those who benefit from the *status quo*. It is the attack of the twentieth century on ox-cart government.

The beast in view is the possibility of astronomical costs for little gain, increasingly inadequate services, or breakdowns in such important jobs as police protection and sewerage. The increasing tax bill and the declining service payoff are the bogeys. The aim seems to be to "take garbage collection out of politics" and to turn government into the large-scale public business it should be.) Triumph is the achievement of rationality: a perfected bureaucracy operated by professionally trained managers and judged as a business concern.

Fertility and the Future. There is a civic patriotism as old as the planting of new cities, a commitment to hallowed ground. In America, where cities sprang up from the prairie and proliferated with the spread of the railroad, every crossroad hamlet has aspired to be the "Chicago of Wyoming," the "Metropolis of the Permian basin." The great plains and the deserts are littered with the bones of would-be metropolitan communities.[7]

Such cities were efforts to get rich quick. Their pioneers were entrepreneurs, and their slogan was "Boost, don't knock!" Their fortunes were measured by the increase in population, carloadings, and bank accounts. New building, any new building, was a sign of prosperity for all. This civic drama has always assumed a biological metaphor with growth as the good and decay as the horrible alternative. And growth is a result of massing what exists so that more may exist in the future. (Witness the outcry in Chicago when the Bureau of the Census decided to treat the Indiana portion of that metropolitan area as a separate unit.) "Boosterism" reflects a synthesis of the economic man's wish to improve his market and the civic patriot's identification with his city as home.

The heroes of such a drama are the "forward-looking, aggressive civic leaders," who want to make this city "the greatest center of paper-box manufacturing in the country." They act by organizing, building, advertising, allowing more room for growth (and hence, presumably, room at the top). The villains are those who have an unassailable position in the *status quo*, who resist change. Like the politician who prefers to lose an election rather than to lose control of his party, they would rather see the city remain stable. Every large city has its mythology about the "five families who own this town and don't want to see it change." But the beast in view is the spectacle of the town declining, losing ground in national rank orders. The fear is that of a shrinking market and a backward, physically unpleasant scene for living. . . .

These morality plays each influenced the definition of the metropolitan government as it was presented to the citizens in St. Louis,

[7] For a fascinating local history of such a would-be city see Wallace Stegner's *Wolf Willow*.

Cleveland, and Miami. The conservative tradition of reform in local affairs set the limits within which the plans were drafted, and within which their salient characteristics were defended.

In these three cities those who drafted the new charters envisaged a federal system in which existing units of government would be preserved. The new metropolitan government was seen as a vehicle to achieve what could not be done with the existing fragmented system. The radical nature of the departure was minimized, for the new plans did not attack *existing* governments so much as the existing "metropolitan system" of government. The morality of Purification was, in general, ignored. Nobody fighting for the plans could exploit the old slogan "Throw the rascals out!" The drafters of the plans seemed to assume that all were victims of the historical lag between government and the growing urban area.

The reasons for omitting the Purification Ritual have been as follows. First, in St. Louis and Cuyahoga, there was genuine belief in the integrity of existing governments *within their limits.* The long-term effort to tame municipal politics through professional management and civil service had been relatively successful in these cities. In Dade County there had been some extreme dissatisfaction with the government of Miami.[8] The belief in the integrity of existing government combined, in St. Louis and Cleveland, with a desire to neutralize the political parties, since it was thought that they might defeat any charter that threatened their organization and patronage systems. The campaigns deliberately avoided antagonizing the party chieftains. At most the supporters of the plans said "we will give you administration by experts, under elected officials responsible to the voters."

The metropolitan movement is, then, squarely in the tradition of capitalist realism. The organizational merging of the multifarious local governments for areawide services, the emphasis on metropolitan area planning and zoning, the predominance of appointed rather than elected heads for the great bureaucracies, all point to the image of technical efficiency as a goal. The Dade County plan

---

[8] "People really believed the hair-raising stories that you heard about the police sitting around with their feet on the tables, reading the scratch sheets with direct wires to the books." (*Interview Protocol* with a major executive in the mass media.) The Kefauver Committee supplied some evidence for such beliefs.

168   SCOTT GREER

even went so far as to specify an appointed county manager for the
metropolitan area, and in both St. Louis and Cuyahoga County the
issue of an elected versus an appointed head was the source of ideological conflict from study commission to voter. The vision of a
new, bright, freshly painted and efficient government was presented
to the voters. As a minor theme, in each area the increased "home
rule" which would accrue to the metropolitan county or district was
noted. This was most important in Dade County, which had been
largely dominated from the state capital in Tallahassee. In St. Louis
and Cleveland a large degree of home rule already existed and the
theme was not very important in these campaigns.

The Fertility Ritual was a major element in each city. In St. Louis
particularly, the consciousness of "decay" and the desire to continue
a supposed "renaissance" was a crucial part of the campaign. In
Miami, the dependence upon tourism and retirement and the assumed relationship between these economic assets and local services
is given credit by one observer for almost all of the interest manifested in Metro by the business community and the civic leaders.[9]
In one of the major pieces of campaign literature distributed by
supporters of the St. Louis District Plan, economic development
occupies the center of the stage.

> All surveys . . . show that our area is losing out to Kansas City,
> Chicago, Memphis, Dallas, and other places in attracting wealth-
> producing industry and commerce . . . By voting for the District
> Plan, we can start to return to our rightful place — as the major
> Mid-American district between the Alantic and the Pacific.[10]

And how was this to be achieved? We quote from the same leaflet:

> The District Plan will give us a chance to plan for the entire city-
> country area — not just one part at a time — so that industry, com-
> merce, and residential developments can be located where they be-
> long without destroying property values. It will set up a means for
> private and public groups to work together — to plan and assemble
> industrial parks — away from residential areas — to offer new indus-
> try at cost. And by eliminating some of our other problems, such as

[9] Reinhold P. Wolff, *Miami Metro.* Coral Gables, Florida: Bureau of
Business and Economic Research, 1960.
[10] "Some Plain Answers to Questions about the Greater St. Louis City-
County District Plan." St. Louis: City-County Partnership Committee,
1959.

the traffic mess, we'll have a chance to compete successfully for new business, and thousands of new jobs, which helps *everyone*.[11]

In short, the metropolitan government was a new means to old ends — economic prosperity, a better market for the individual, and a better city for the average resident.

These movements for metropolitan government relied heavily on two of the traditional morality plays of American civic life. Each emphasized the need to modernize local government through job analysis, coordination, and realignment of boundaries. Each offered improved services to the citizens as a reason for doing so. Each promised improvement in the local economy and, therefore, the value of the city as a place in which to work and to live.

If the public is accustomed to a given morality in the rhetoric of reform, that morality's absence will be quickly noted. The decision *not* to attack incumbent officials and existing governments for their incompetence and inability weakened the hands of the crusaders. Mounting an offensive which did in fact threaten many alignments and jobs (each plan took important powers away from municipal officials, and the Cuyahoga plan even dispensed with Civil Service safeguards), the plans provoked hostility from key members of the establishment without providing any ammunition to return their fire.

The head of a major department in the city of Cleveland gleefully related the advantage he had in fighting against the Cuyahoga County Charter.

> I'd say to them, "Say — what's wrong with the present situation? You got a good government. What's wrong? Show me?" I'd get right down to specifics — "what's been done wrong?"

Bypassing the elected representatives of the *status quo* thus pulled a key member out of the morality plays' structure. It left the elected officials blameless and free to attack the new plan from the rostrum of public office. (This made logical sense, however, if it was only the lack of a *single* system that was at fault.) As we shall see, this decision had important consequences for the campaigns in St. Louis and Cleveland.

The elimination of the Purification Ritual also affected the plausibility of the efficiency engineering approach. The decision to leave

[11] *Ibid.*

all municipalities in existence made the plans extremely vulnerable to those who felt that the existence of a multitude of governments was a handicap in attaining good governance. The first reason given by Mayor Tucker in his first speech opposing the District Plan hinged on this belief.

> *The proposed metropolitan District Plan does not eliminate one existing area government — with the exception of its absorption of the metropolitan sewer district.*
>
> The 99 country municipalities, the 21 fire districts, the separate City and County, and all the rest remain. Each of them is unimpaired in its present tax-levying authority.[12]

In St. Louis, the District Plan suffered from this further debility — it really added an additional government to the ones in existence. Though the other two plans escaped this through using existing county governments as bases for the metropolitan district, each was vulnerable to the attacks of purists who wished to see radical surgery on the governmental proliferation in the area.

The morality of "capitalist realism" suffered also from the tendency of the pro-Metro leaders to tell the truth. Instead of promising savings through increased efficiency, many of them tended to emphasize the *increase in services* possible through a Metro government. Again, this was less true of Dade County. There the leaders of the revolution were prone to hold out the carrot of lower taxes (though privately they believed Metro could only attack the area-wide service problems through increased taxation). In St. Louis, the protagonists tried to counter the "higher taxes" argument by showing that the plan would increase the fertility of the region and therefore its tax yield at existing rates.

The Fertility Ritual was not in basic conflict with the efficiency engineering and did not suffer from the absence of the Purificatory Rites. It did suffer, however, from its abstract and novel nature. While citizens are accustomed to hortatory slogans to "buy local," to "boost St. Louis," and the like, they are not used to the rather intricate arguments supporting metropolitan government as a source of future fertility. First, the argument moves from unknown to unknown — from land-use planning to plant location — and finally to

[12] Mayor Raymond F. Tucker, St. Louis: for release 7:00 p.m. Saturday, October 3, 1959.

greater local prosperity, lower taxes, and better services. Second, and perhaps more important, the possibility of land-use planning depends on the *time element*. Comprehensive land-use planning has never been popular or popularly understood, for it requires a knowledge of the effects of present political acts upon consequences many years in the future. This is the dilemma of those who see most present problems as produced by past planning failures: to change present planning requires that they use, as evidence, the very complex chain of events from lack of past planning to the contretemps of today. Metropolitan government, in the context of the Fertility Rites, presents a complex *answer* to people who have never understood the *questions* — much less asked them.

In summary: the metropolitan morality play leaned heavily on two earlier plots. It omitted the most familiar of all and the one with the greatest "box office" appeal — "throw the rascals out." Omission of this theme greatly weakened the most clearly understood argument that was used — "Get rid of ox-cart government" — for it left the *status quo* standing. While the efficiency engineering approach and the Fertility Ritual were mutually reinforcing, the latter was largely outside the conventional realm of discourse. The chief argument shared by the rebels and the general public was that of mechanical progress aimed at greater service benefits. It was weakened by a "live and let live" philosophy with respect to the existing municipalities. It was strengthened by demand for better services. It used the older drama of boosterism, though many did not understand the plot.

Within this metropolitan morality play the protagonists of reform organized themselves and made sense of their proposal to create a revolution in urban government. They defined their roles as crusaders for a new "one best way" to achieve the Heavenly City. They defined their enemies as the protectors of separatism, in bond to the *status quo* (leaving, however, the "dark man" of professional politics as an ambiguous character). The cadres were developed, the struggle was joined, and eventually the voters were approached, in this vocabulary.

CHARLES R. ADRIAN

Suburbia and the Folklore of Metropology

Metropology, as the minions of Henry Luce should by now have dubbed the study of metropolitan areas, is an infantile disorder among the social sciences. Its victims are deep in the agonies that were experienced by political science a generation ago when that field was torn between those who thought that students of government should be practitioners of reforms and those who took the word "science" seriously. Related to these agonies is the fact that academic municipal reformers of some years back drew their programs largely from the goals of a segment of the business community that wanted to apply "business principles" to local government. They did not seek to expand the horizons of knowledge by empirical examination of the assumptions of the business leaders. Similarly, much metropology since 1945 has dealt with efforts to propagandize on behalf of efficiency and economy goals. In neither period of urban history — before or after 1945 — has the problem of local democracy been the central focus of the participating academics. Significantly, the municipal reformers and the students of "metropolitan area problems" also have had in common a working relationship with businessmen who are "civic leaders." Although the urban planners — members of a profession — are accustomed to working with such persons, social scientists — members of academia — have not been. This has been especially true of political scientists. The others who study metropology — the economists perhaps excepted — have only a bit more experience and probably no more acceptance by the business community.

Reprinted from "Metropology: Folklore and Field Research" by Charles R. Adrian, *Public Administration Review*, the journal of the American Society for Public Administration, Vol. XXI, No. 2 (Summer 1961), pp. 148-153, by permission of the author and publisher.

So an alliance was formed between those who had money and believed they had problems — the business leaders — and those who craved social recognition and its pecuniary perquisites — the planners and professors. It is not surprising that this alliance produced in the years before and just after World War II "studies" and "reports" that for the most part emphasized the absence of long-range, metropolitan-wide planning, that counted the number of fire departments in an area, and deplored "unnecessary" duplications of services. A generation after Pearl Harbor had signalled the beginning of the nth urbanization movement in the United States, the shelves of city hall offices were groaning with motheaten and mildewed reports — reports that were not acceptable to the political decision makers because they were unacceptable to their constituents. It was not just that those who had financed and conducted the studies had sometimes mistakenly assumed that their truths were self-evident; a more serious cause of rejection centered in their almost total lack of concern with the political process and the probable ignorance of their authors of the fact that a democratic public is a "satisficing" public and not one concerned with optimum economy . . .

Many men who are regarded as "civic leaders" in America's larger cities began reaching for the panic button [in 1960]. They were joined by the municipal "pros" — city managers, chamber of commerce secretaries, mayors, and local civic-research directors. The alarm, of course, resulted from a good look at the 1960 census figures. These showed that an impressively large number of our metropolitan core cities had gained little or had actually lost population in the preceding decade. Former residents had retreated to the suburbs. Community newcomers of the middle classes — the now-famous "organization men" — had scarcely glanced at the central-city areas as they scurried to the suburbs looking for housing. The population losses in the huge core cities caught practically no one off guard. New York lost nearly one-quarter million people, Detroit took a 10 per cent cut, but no one was very surprised. It was in the smaller core cities — those under 200,000 population — where the shockers took place. Leaders in many of these areas thought their cities were gaining population nicely — they had local estimates to "prove" it. But dozens of Altoonas and Muskegons now find themselves in the same mold with the largest core cities — they have not gained; many have lost population. These findings need not have been unnerving to the local boosters. But they were.

The indignant cries of disbelief, the calls for immediate annexa-

tions, the demands for recounts, all stem from the fact that the 1960
census documents a trend that stomps underfoot in cruel fashion
some of the dearest values of civic boosters and of some students of
metropology. It is difficult for them to accept the trend as a normal
part of the growth of a mobile population based on an industrial
society. The folklore that many civic leaders have taken to be gospel
does not permit them to accept "the trend of social and economic
forces" as an explanation. Many of the leaders who formulate and
guide the policies of our larger communities hold to beliefs that are
based on a whole series of unrealistic assumptions about how metropolitan areas can and should be governed. Collectively, these assumptions represent the folklore that determines in large part the
policy statements found in the reports of Chamber of Commerce
committees, "citizens' committees" on metropolitan-area problems,
and local government research bureaus. There were a spate of
metropolitan-area studies after the results of the 1950 census became
known. Now 1960 should spur defenders of the community image
on to even greater efforts. They will be seeking "solutions" to the
"metropolitan problem." They will call for studies, as they did after
1950, and they will expect them to rest upon the following generally
accepted assumptions.

There is the belief that the core city of a metropolitan area must
"expand or die" — the notion is widespread that there is no such
thing as prosperous stability for a community. The idea is that central cities become socially and economically obsolescent faster if
they have no expansion space within their boundaries. It assumes
that the entire metropolitan area must grow and that the core city
must grow at a near-equal rate — growth being measured by population. The argument is a favorite of local persons who have a financial
stake in expansion — editors, chamber of commerce staff members,
downtown merchants, city managers — and also serves to placate
businessmen's anxieties concerning a tax base, or tax advantages
to businesses beyond the municipal limits. The policy demands of
this municipal application of the geo-politician's *lebensraum* theory
usually take the form of plans for annexation of all of the urbanized
hinterland, or of the creation of some kind of an "upper-tier" metropolitan-wide government.

The concept of growth is probably a product of our American
culture which developed from the frontier where population growth
was invariably associated with "progress" — progress against the

Suburbia and the Folklore of Metropology

175

Indians and forest, and in favor of Western civilization. It overlooks the fact that the real challenge in municipal policy today is to get away from the ringworm approach to urbanization — decay at the center and new growth at the periphery. It underestimates the need for finding socially useful functions for the older parts of town — as Europeans have done with considerable success in their much older cities. It represents an effort to flee social responsibility by taking over new lands rather than saving what we already have — a policy that was appropriate on the frontier, but not in a maturing America. It also represents a desire on the part of civic leaders and professionals to expand their policy controls as the area grows. These people are especially concerned about commercial development patterns. (A new suburban shopping center, particularly if it is financed from outside the area, can spell doom to central business district profits and to community fiscal control by local bankers.)

There is the belief that *efficiency and economy* are the highest political values held by the American homeowner. Leaders of metropolitan-area studies are likely to assume that efficiency of administration and economy in budgeting are the things that would be most preferred by residents — if only "politicians" didn't get in their way with selfish desires to preserve jobs and personal empires. Those who make this assumption sometimes exclaim in wonder and horror, "Why there are seventy-six different fire departments in the metropolitan area!" But to the suburbanite, who wants a voice in policies that affect his place of residence, this may spell "good" rather than "bad."

Those dedicated to efficiency and economy seem never to consider that the suburban merchant or homeowner may value other things higher — in particular, *access* to decision-making centers and *representativeness* of local government. . . . The suburban merchant wants local policies that will maximize his profits and minimize his competition. He probably sees his own suburban government as more likely to do this than would the core-city or some metropolitan government. To him, any supergovernment is likely to voice the values and business goals of the downtown merchants and large landowners. As a result of that feeling, the small fringe-area merchant, who frequently operates near the edge of financial disaster, is an advocate of grass-roots Jacksonianism. So is the suburban homeowner, who wants to have a hand in determining many things: service levels in the amenities provided by local government (according to what he thinks he can afford), land-use policies which he thinks will affect his property values, the kinds of neighbors he will have, and educational policies that will help determine the job and status opportunities of his children.

Efficiency and economy are probably among the suburbanites' lesser concerns — to him other things have a far higher priority. This attitude is in accord with a traditional view of Americans. We do not like to pay taxes and we do not associate taxes with services. Because this is the case, efficiency and economy arguments are nearly meaningless — the typical citizen probably does not see an important relationship between the way in which services are provided and the size of his own tax bill. He, rather cynically, *expects* government to be relatively inefficient. And since, to him, it is going to be inefficient come reformer or professional administrator, he wants a voice in local government. He wants to be able to reach the decision makers when he has a problem. He has a different concept of democracy from that of the advocate of efficiency and economy who seeks deemphasis of the popular decision-making process and who has always demonstrated an anti-grass-roots prejudice. . . .

There is the belief that the public is prepared to accept area-wide planning if a politically feasible way can be found to administer it. There is no question but that long-range, integrated planning of land-use and capital developments would offer certain advantages to the residents of today's metropolitan areas. No question, either, but that the ghettoization of suburbs costs heavily in terms of depriving many persons — of lower income or lower status ethnic categories — of housing of the kind our culture considers decent. Or that restrictive suburban land-use rules drive up the price of housing unnecessarily. Or that land is often used unsystematically and wastefully when its urban development is left to profit-motivated realtors. Or that people pay many times what they might have paid for municipal capital improvements by refusing to plan ahead. . . . Yet suburbanites do not support area-wide planning. Indeed, they are often hostile to it. They will cooperate with planners if there is a program — perhaps a new sewage disposal plant — that can most easily be financed by joint suburban-core city action. . . . But basically the suburbanite, in a strife-torn world, sees his home and its local government as a refuge from conflict, as Wood neatly pointed out in his . . . *Suburbia*. A place in Vertigo Heights represents a retreat to the womb. There, in secure isolation among those who live, work, believe, and act as he does, he seeks a school plant that symbolizes his status in society and a school curriculum that meets his style of life and the expectations he has for his children. He wants his friends and neighbors to make land-use policies for him, for only they, he believes, can be trusted to mold the suburb to fit the die he and his neighbors have cast. He wants the planners to prevent the development of ethnic, class, status, or value conflicts by keeping out those who do not fit the established pattern. Effective metropolitan land-use controls, potentially, would do violence to one of the main purposes — whether for good or evil — of independent suburbs.

There is the belief that professional administration — which the core city has and a metropolitan-area government would have — is preferable to amateur administration. Preferable to whom? To many, no doubt. But the typical citizen is ambivalent in his attitude. He wants a government of friends and neighbors, but he wants one that will deliver pure water to his tap. He often prefers amateurs to professionals — as in the case of the suburban volunteer fire department which he finds far cheaper than the core city professional system designed to protect (at considerable cost) warehouses, apartment buildings, and high-rise business structures. Amateur fire fighters provide enough service to meet his demands — and a little glamour rubs off on them in the process. He is not so sure, either, about professionals in welfare, health, and even sewage disposal.

Above all, the suburbanite appears to prefer doing business with the amateur or semipro rather than with an anonymous bureaucratic professional in a city hall miles from his home or business and dedicated to professional principles and goals which he does not share or even understand.

There is the belief that a metropolitan-area super-government would save the taxpayers some money. This idea probably stems from the notion that such a government would be more efficient. In fact, however, although we could undoubtedly get a better return on our tax dollars than we do, we could not save enough money by this method to make more than a slight dent in today's huge municipal budgets. And as for economy, the prospects are dim, and for good reason. Metropolitan governments would almost certainly seek — over the long pull — to raise service levels. They would demand bigger and better streets, street lights, public health services, school plants, engineering standards in subdivision development, and the like. Furthermore, they would probably be able to raise levels at a faster rate than would be the case in a balkanized metropolitan area. This is so because citizens would probably say, "All right, we voted this thing in — now let's see it solve my sewage-disposal (storm water, street surfacing, school finance, etc.) problem!" Also, metropolitan-area government would encourage a move toward the use of more genuinely professional administrators and these men would strive toward the optimum service levels established by their particular professions, whether in public health, highways, civil engineering, or whatever. These programs would almost certainly exceed in cost any savings the professionals could accumulate through greater "efficiency." Then, too, the service levels they would be raising would be chiefly in the relatively low-density suburban areas — and the large lots of suburbia run up the cost of many services — of curb and gutter, sewers, water supply, and fire protection, for example. These demands would also raise per capita costs for the core-city property owners (unless everything were done by special assessments), for the suburban areas in most cases not only have greater needs, but have lower assessed valuation per capita than does the core city.

There is the belief that a rational distinction can be made between functions that are strictly local (suburban and core city) and those that are appropriate for area-wide super-government. Plans which seek to divide responsibilities between "lower tier" and "upper tier" (metropolitan-wide) governments nearly always conclude by making virtually all significant functions metropolitan. When this happens, the efforts being made to secure change are dissipated before they are fairly under way, for they lose nearly all of their potential support in the suburbs. There is no method by which to distinguish local and metropolitan functions that would satisfy both professional administrators and suburban citizens. An arbitrary approach is necessary and the only one that is likely to be at all successful is one that transfers to the metropolitan government only those functions that involve problems of widespread urgency throughout the area, where consensus holds that no other workable solution can be found.

There is the belief that a metropolitan area is a monolithic interest — a single community — that stands, or should stand, against the world, as do the wheat farmers or the oil producers. Civic leaders talk of a need to present "the metro point-of-view" to the legislature or Congress. But is there a metropolitan point-of-view? A metropolis is a great collection of people who, for economic and other reasons, live in close geographic proximity. They are each active in the pursuit of a livelihood, of recreation, of social activities. Each wants to pay no more of the social cost of the metropolis than he must. To him, there is a water supply problem, or a school curriculum problem, no doubt. There is a Mad River interest. But is there a Dayton "metro" interest? There is a Westchester interest. But is there a New York "metro" interest? The answer is "yes" to professional urban planners, civil and sanitary engineers, social workers but not to the typical citizen. His own concerns make his views parochial. To him, the only realistic metropolitan-area policies will be those that recognize and accept — however unwillingly — that parochialism.

There is the closely related view that a metropolitan area, if "properly" organized in a "modern" fashion, would operate smoothly and with no more conflict than, say, that in an eighteenth century New England town. There seems to be a widespread idea among civic actionists that the procrastination, name-calling, and general confusion that characterizes decision making in metropolitan areas is a result of decentralized government and is in part artificially created by job-seeking politicians. A harmonic metropolitan "public interest" is often portrayed in study reports as a reality to be striven for. Actually, however, a metropolitan area is a maze of conflicting values, goals, activities, and ethnic subcultures. The governing body of a unified metropolitan area would contain as many different pressures and cross-pressures as are found in a state legislature, and its operations probably would be no more harmonious. A "metro" government would be strife-torn and its major decisions would be produced in agony. It might encourage better coordinated policies; it would not diminish conflict.

PAUL YLVISAKER

Why Mayors Oppose Metropolitan Government

If the Good Lord and His executive angels were to engineer the change, Mayor James of Central City would resolve his doubts and come out publicly in favor of establishing an over-all government for the metropolitan area — provided, of course, that when the system was installed, he would be left in charge as metro-mayor. As an idea, "Metro" made a lot of sense; government was about the only American enterprise these days that was not organized on at least a regional and more often a national basis; and if His Honor were to continue as mayor of anything, he'd have to find some way of catching up with the more affluent citizens and taxable industries which were constantly moving just out of reach beyond his municipal boundaries.

But the trouble was, as Madison long ago discerned, the Lord's work on earth has to be done by mere mortals; instead of angels, there are only angles. Keeping a close eye on these almost guarantees that public officials and the electorate won't see or think straight — certainly, the logic of metropolitan government, being straight, can't be followed by practicing politicians, at least not headlong. The safer way is the devious route which circumscribes all the angles.

But back to the good Mayor's predicament. The idea of metropolitan government is in the air. Two years ago, all the normally otherwise-occupied notables in the area — or as that new breed of academic interventionists has been calling them, the "decision makers" — begin signing petitions, holding forums, listening to experts fetched from a distance, and in other ways acting as their wives in

Reprinted from "Diversity and the Public Interest: Two Cases in Metropolitan Decision-Making" by Paul Ylvisaker, *AIP Journal*, Vol. XXVII, No. 2 (May 1961), pp. 109-113, by permission of the author and the American Institute of Planners.

the League of Women Voters would have them act. These early months had been quite a honeymoon. Mayor James's natural instinct of waiting out all reforms until he saw the self-interests showing through, had helped him keep his balance and be quoted only in the most rolling of generalities. But he had begun to wonder whether politics had indeed entered a new age when at a massive luncheon assembled representatives of every one of the community's warring and ignoring interest groups had signed a pledge of cooperation. This alliance had so impressed a prestigious foundation that it wrote a check for more money than any of the local factfinders dreamed would be theirs to play with, "to carry out the necessary research." Necessary? Well, yes — research was one of those rituals which sufficiently cleansed the political ground for those normally above politics to walk on it; and it added a mystique which confused the old pros long enough for some new voices and fresh ideas to be heard.

But that was two years ago; now the game was again being played for keeps. The armistice of research was over; in a month, the binding question of a new form of metropolitan government was coming to a referendum vote; and there was no avoiding it, the Mayor would have to say publicly whether he was for or against. The bliss of consensus had long since dissolved. All that had held it together was undefined apprehension and ambition, each group uneasily aware that the metropolitan community had grown beyond its understanding, yet vaguely hopeful that if a new order could be established, it would be theirs to inherit. Now the fears and the ambitions had been defined; and the only common element was the familiar one of mutual suspicion and jockeying for position. Labor had been among the first to disengage. It had joined the coalition mostly because it couldn't afford the public posture of not doing so — and to keep an eye on this new political animal that just might develop into something substantial. But when meeting after meeting produced nothing immediately of use at the bargaining table, when it became apparent the coalition was too divided to forge strength out of its diversity, and as more and more of the political iceberg of metropolitan government became visible, labor's representative attended less and less frequently until sufficiently dissociated to refer openly to "Metro" as dominated by the business interests.

But "business" as a dominating monolith had long ago proved a myth. In the first place, the usual distressing number of its magnates had again displayed their amateur status in politics and public affairs. Despite their heralded record of civic participation, the coalition was their first working contact with career politicians from the ward and city committee. They were out of their element; they didn't know the names and numbers; and their radar — sensitive enough to the signals of the market — was jammed by the shower of uncertain messages which emanated from a world where the laws of social abrasion and aspiration displaced the accepted canons of efficiency and economy.

Still, more than political naïveté had stymied the business community. The truth was, it wasn't a community except tenuously and occasionally so in opposition to labor and taxes. It was split between absentee and locally-owned enterprises; it was divided into big and small, into those socially registered and those not; it was bedevilled by old feuds and factions; and more relevant, it was torn between those committed to the core city and those who were accommodating very nicely to the suburban market. For example, the area's largest employment complex was entrenched in an industrial park which for a negligible cost to the companies concerned had traded local property taxes for the political hospitality of an outlying suburb; no siren call of metropolitan government could lure either the firms or the suburb from their protected enclave.

Mayor James was no stranger to this division in the business community; he had been embarrassed by it several times when "plugging the Chamber's line" only to find he had bought a factional plank — and he had exploited the same weakness on just as many occasions, dividing to conquer and even defying the local barons outright. For he knew what they and the ward politicians knew, that very few of the business leaders lived any longer in Central City; and since they no longer lived there, they couldn't vote there; and even if they could, there weren't enough of them to swing an election.

As a matter of fact, the Mayor often wondered whether the whole drive for metropolitan government wasn't basically a matter of ex-residents trying to have their cake and eat it — people who had moved to suburbia but still depended for their livelihood on white-collar jobs, businesses, and investment in central city, now trying to regain their vote and political influence by enlarging the city's boundaries. One of the Metro leaders had come dangerously close to letting the cat out of the bag by saying publicly he'd settle for a double vote for the commuter — one in the suburbs where he lived, and the other in central city where he worked. He hadn't added the reciprocal of double taxation, nor would he. Representation without taxation — what an ironic twist, mused the Mayor, of that earlier rallying cry of the American revolutionary.

Though he knew all this, Mayor James took care not to say it. On the one hand (though the reporting staff would quietly have loved him for it), he'd be clobbered by the editorial writers and publishers of Central City's newspapers who managed to be true to both halves of their schizoid selves by touting the virtues of downtown while living in the suburbs and using the press to endorse and plead what they no longer could vote for.

On the other hand, to have gone to the hustings with such candor and perhaps oversimplification would have invited extremism and demagogery. The city was tinderbox enough without touching a spark to it. Every year saw an accelerating turnover in population and a darkening of color. A decade ago he had been elected councilman from a ward with only a handful of Negroes in it; today, he was one of a handful of whites who still lived there. The rest had moved on, most of them beyond the Iron Ring of suburbia. They lunched with him to say thanks for staying to fight their battles, and to lay out the strategy and objectives for other campaigns they hoped he would lead; then they left him to forage for his votes among the other half who lived in the city at night.

He was, he felt more and more, a man between worlds — no longer a member of the society he had grown up with, nor yet and perhaps never completely at home among the newer constituency upon whose vote his political life increasingly depended. Each campaign, each budget, each bond issue found him swinging more and more into the orbit of the newcomers and the philosophy of government which responded to their needs. Why the shift? He still wasn't sure, even though he's spent most of his term defending this growing liberality to his economy-minded friends (now supporting council manager plans in their several suburbs — "a manager is for the homogeneous," he was fond of saying to the students who visited him in City Hall, "but it takes a mayor to preside over diversity") and to the cynics of precinct and city desk. Sure, he wanted to survive: what politician, or for that matter what industrial, labor, or other leader didn't? But it wasn't only that. Not out of preference but of necessity he had come to know the minority cultures of Central City — Negroes from the rural South, Puerto Ricans, hill folk from the Appalachians, and always the steady flow of immigrants from abroad. It had taken a long time to get rid of the stereotypes through which he and his generation of well-assimilated immigrants had regarded these newest recruits to the city. Even now, lingering resentment could flicker within him when he reviewed the lengthening lists of unmarried mothers, juvenile delinquents, and relief cases with color and speech so clearly marked. The historian's reminder that it was ever thus, wasn't much comfort. It would still be his wearying job to defend these untouchables among whom he didn't belong to the well-washed to whom he did; to explain again the need for understanding to a public which lived on stereotypes and through a press which gained readership by sensationalizing the deeds it condemned; to talk the language of civil liberties to a frightened citizenry and an underpaid constabulary who lived too close to acts of violence to see where noble sentiments fit in.

But these were his city's citizens; like them or not, their welfare was his responsibility and their votes were essential to his political program and future. And like them he did — the more so as he came to see the inner logic of their own codes of conduct (he had heard even the high rate of "illegitimacy" and A.D.C. payments explained in terms no less moral than the culture of affluence), and as he penetrated the veneer of exceptional and unfamiliar behavior to see beneath it an *élan* born of adversity which had long ago been dissipated in the wealthier climate of suburbia.

They were, thought the Mayor, more attractive than some of the leaders who rose to represent them. But politics were the life blood of these people. Collectively, it was their main legitimate means of redressing the social and economic imbalance between themselves and the Haves; for an individual, it was a way of achieving in one's own lifetime the social prominence and acceptance which by the route of other callings usually took three generations to attain. Not strange that their leaders should play Robin Hood, nor that they should seem at times to be intent on turning City Hall into Sherwood Forest — may the rich and the law beware.

Among this constituency of newcomers and their political chieftains, metropolitan government was making few converts. It seemed, or easily was made to seem, a gerrymandering tactic by the same suburban element which had abandoned the central city — and their instinct for the jugular told them that if these suburbanites now wanted to resume their political ties, it must be with the hope of gaining some undisclosed advantage. Suspicious, they were jealous as well; for as their constituency grew and the older population left, they were fast becoming the majority rather than the minority. The political prospects were obvious and appealing; certainly now was not the time to dissolve their growing identity in the larger metropolitan population, nor to be led by the propaganda of increased efficiency and economy into an alliance which would divert what little resources the central city could still command to the satisfaction of suburban needs.

And the Mayor — for all he disliked the demagogery of the argument — had to admit that the prospects of the central city's gaining financially from a metropolitan system of government were pretty dim. The suburbs had reached the point where they had population enough to outvote the mother city: and they would hardly play Alphonse and Gaston with the city at the door of the public treasury. For all their wealth — more likely because of it — they were now deeper in the quicksand of financial need than the core city. In a binge of expenditures, they had built their public plant from scratch, yet their outlays were just beginning. The cost of suburban development had been vastly underestimated; trouble was, everybody had assumed the advertised price of houses was the total cost to the suburban taxpayer of his new community. Now the full bill was becoming evident; public health people, finding up to forty per cent of the suburban water supply contaminated by septic tanks, were among those who could, if asked, tell what the final tab was likely to be.

Adding central city's present and imminent charges for maintenance and renewal directly to the suburban bill via the proposed route of metropolitan government would hardly help the Mayor in his campaign for more revenue. It was tough enough prying new tax money out of city, state, and Washington, when, as now, he was under no obligation to tell John Q. Taxpayer what all the costs of urban government amounted to.

No right-thinking man, the Mayor often thought, could avoid concluding from this combined balance-sheet that the United States had simply bought too much for its income — or if it managed to accumulate enough wealth to pay the bill, it would have a hard time internationally justifying its lavish way of life. For the country was discarding its central cities before they were fully used or paid for, and now was buying a new suburban plant on an instalment plan of staggering proportions.

That was where he began again to wonder whether metropolitan governments weren't the solution — not so much of the community's administrative problem of providing services more efficiently, but of its problem of public morals. For the metropolis as presently organized was a gigantic system of buckpassing, of avoiding difficult choices and unpleasant facts, of having your cake and eating it; a system of incomplete responsibilities which left everyone with an excuse for inaction or a justification of acting only to the convenient extent of self-interest; a system with opportune blinders, in which no one could be blamed for abjuring the role of Good Samaritan and Brother's Keeper, for the simple reason that one's neighbor or brother in need had been gerrymandered into the other fellow's jurisdiction; a system perfectly constructed for the Pharisee and the politician; a system he could play, as other mayors had done before him, to his own advantage — talking about problems, making token stabs at solving them, appointing study commissions, blaming other jurisdictions for neglecting "their" responsibilities, and coasting with prosperity and the taxpayers' love of postponed action to a re-election or two and then higher office, where the whole hypocrisy could be practiced again on the clear slate of a new set of problems and a new constituency.

The thought of higher office pulled him back to the realities of his choice. Next year — and not again — the gubernatorial nomination might be his if all went well, and "well" meant either a major coup of some sort or not rocking the boat. The odds against Metro's winning at the polls — judging from experience across the country — were more than 100 to 1; but since Sputnik, and the electorate's newly conditioned response in favor of experiment and invention, past history was no certain guide. Tote up the sides: For Metro — the League of Women Voters; central city newspapers, radio and TV; the college-educated, upper-income and commuting suburbanites; the managerial group, especially in the utilities; and a scattering of dissident, desperate, or aspiring politicians. Against Metro — the majority of Negroes in central city; suburban and central city office-holders, their families, friends and relatives; suburban newspapers; the working and middle class with jobs and homes on the same side of the city's boundaries; taxpayers' associations in the better-off suburbs; suburban industries; and most important, those of the party who controlled the nominations. Fill in the numbers, and it was pretty clear — the Noes had it, and only a gambling upstart would go for broke against such odds.

Damned if he supported Metro — would he be damned if he didn't? The newspapers and pundits would give him a hard time, but soon enough they'd be back in his corner — among central city candidates they had little or nothing else to turn to. There would also be disaffection and disillusion among the reform element. Many of these he'd shed no tears for — the self-interest of such do-gooders was hidden only from themselves. But he grieved genuinely when he thought of the few noble Romans he would cut the ground under by failing to endorse their campaign for Metro. These noble few were battling not for a disguised self-interest, nor for an unexamined panacea nor for the mere love of battling; they were out to stretch the mind and vision of the metropolitan community, and to give that community room and reason to grow to political maturity, finding in Metro a reform symbolic of their purpose and worthy of the effort. These people, too, had only a shallow well of opportunity to draw from; they, just as the Mayor, could risk their political equity only so many times before being pushed aside and their ideals discredited. They knew they were working against the odds, and they knew that the slim chance left to them depended on the Mayor's endorsement.

It would not be easy facing the disappointment of these noble few, less easy for the very fact they would be the most tolerant of his decision. More so than his own conscience, or whatever it was that kept echoing the categorical imperatives of his youth and his never-quieted expectancy that some day, if he were to prove his mettle and integrity, he would have to play the statesman on heroic scale even to the martyr's finish.

But was Metro this occasion? He had the courage; what came hard was the conviction.

And even if he were convinced that Metro was the public interest incarnate, and his martyrdom a way of speeding its birth, was this courage or presumption? Who was he to say that a rational order ought to be imposed on this imperfect thing called man or that a procrustean logic of the moment replace the disguised order of the evolutionary process? The present disorganization of the metropolity could hardly be blamed for the lack of solutions to all of man's problems or of resolutions of all his differences; it may, in fact, be a protection society instinctively erected against the disillusion that would follow if all institutional defects were to be corrected and man left naked to face his inherent political impotence.

And why should he feel conscience or suffer choice at all? Was "the public interest" only a theologian's invention which veiled the essential amorality of the political process – a process simply and purely of equilibrium, in which social forces out of balance strained toward equality? One could not say whether one resolution was better than another except in terms of his own interests, one could in selfishness then react, or in dispassion describe, or out of a projected abhorrence of violence help to secure an orderly and peaceful succession from one state of equilibrium to the next. Heroic acts proceeding from moral certainty were either irrelevent, or dangerous interventions inviting violent reactions.

When Mayor James lapsed that far into philosophy, he knew he had lost his way; and, by an instinct he long ago came to trust, he left off contemplating the universe and checked the specifics of the case before him, searching for the middle way out.

He found it where he should have looked at the outset, in the details of the proposal to be voted upon. It was, he saw, an attempt at compromise – a metropolitan authority for specified functions and with limited powers. As he took pen in hand, he wondered with as much amusement as he could muster what the reform element would say when they saw tomorrow's featured story.

MAYOR REJECTS METRO AS NOT ENOUGH. SAYS
NOTHING SHORT OF FULL CONSOLIDATION OF
AREA GOVERNMENT WILL PROVIDE
NEEDED SOLUTION

He knew, however, that the old hands among the politicians would smile and understand; and he turned to wondering whether Nancy, his wife, really meant it when she said she didn't want to move or whether she'd feel differently when ensconced in the Governor's mansion.

HENRY J. SCHMANDT, PAUL G. STEINBICKER,
AND GEORGE D. WENDEL

The Campaign for Metropolitan Government
in St. Louis

Almost three years of intensive study and deliberation had
elapsed since the institution of the survey in 1956. Six months now
remained before the voters of the city and county would be called
upon to signify their acceptance or rejection of the freeholders' work.
The metropolitan constituent assembly with the deep cleavage
among its members had left a legacy of uncertainty to the people
and had failed to provide them with a common rallying point or a
center of leadership. The issues that were to dominate the ensuing
campaign had already taken shape in its deliberations. Reflected
also in the position and attitudes of the freeholders were the likely
sources of support and opposition to the plan.

The proposed charter was necessarily complex, lengthy, and detailed. How could its contents, its meaning, and its intended purposes be communicated to a large electorate and the uncertainty
generated by the drafters dispelled within this relatively short period of time? And how and by what means could the area's leadership be effectively mobilized for the ensuing civic campaign? These
were troublesome questions that faced the proponents of metropolitan reorganization as the time of public decision approached.

All possible avenues for organizing the campaign were considered, including the use of the Board of Freeholders and the Citizens
Committee for City-County Coordination. The first was eliminated

because of the split in its membership which persisted even after the charter was presented for public consideration. The second group appeared the most logical agency for spearheading the campaign. It had been instrumental in creating the Board of Freeholders and had demonstrated its ability for organizing a large-scale movement in the face of discouraging setbacks. . . . However, the committee was politically suspect and lacking in influential community members. Leaders of the group, moreover, were by this time less than enthusiastic about the plan; several of them, in fact, had become convinced that merger was the proper solution.

Despite these reservations among some of its members, the citizens committee had invested too much effort, time, and hard work in the reorganization movement to see it collapse for lack of leadership. When no other group appeared willing to expend the time and resources necessary to organize the campaign, the committee stepped into the void. As one of its officials stated, "We were not 100 percent sold on the district plan, but experts recommend it, and someone had to carry the ball. When no one else stepped up to do it, we figured it was our responsibility."

Civic and business leaders who had previously remained aloof from the committee now seemed willing to accept it as the campaign vehicle. The only alternative was to organize and conduct the campaign themselves and this they were unwilling to do.

In order to broaden the base of support and remove the taint that had continually plagued it, the citizens committee was formally dissolved and a new organization known as the City-County Partnership Committee was formed. The first meeting on May 22, 1959 was attended by some 75 persons representing a wide variety of governmental, civic, and business interests. Over 400 invitations had been issued but only a minority of the invited groups sent representatives. Among the community leadership missing were the mayor of St. Louis, the county supervisor, and the political party chieftains. One official of the St. Louis Labor Council attended but remained silent.

At the time of the meeting the mayor had taken no public position on the plan, principally on the ground that he was actively engaged in a campaign to increase the city's earnings tax. The county supervisor had also refrained from any clear-cut stand, merely suggesting the need for more study. The Labor Council, whose president had been prominent in the earlier activities of the citizens committee, had indicated during the freeholders' sessions that it regarded merger of city and county as the most desirable remedy. At this time, the council had given no indication of its position on the district plan. The central committees of both political parties had likewise remained uncommitted.

Cervantes, the mainspring of the reorganization movement, presided at the meeting. The few speakers who expressed themselves agreed politely that the proposed plan had been carefully researched, that it was sound and practical, and that in any case the voters were now limited to a choice between the metropolitan district and continuance of the status quo. The group quickly agreed on the formal purpose of the new committee: "To promote the general welfare and orderly development and prosperity of St. Louis City and County by presenting to the people of this community for their favorable consideration the Greater St. Louis City-County District Plan."

Following this simple ritual, the chairman appointed an executive committee of fifteen members to formulate more specific plans for the campaign organization. In addition to Cervantes and his colleague on the old citizens committee, H. Jackson Daniel, the list included Edwin M. Clark, president of Southwestern Bell Telephone Company and a leading citizen; the presidents of the city and county chambers of commerce; the mayor of the largest suburban municipality who was currently serving as president of the County League of Municipalities; the former president of the League of Women Voters; and two members of the Board of Freeholders, Purteet, who had played a leading role in the development of the district plan, and Redmond, who had supported it. Missing from this array were the political and labor leaders of both city and county, those with the means and knowhow to mobilize the voters.

In the three months following its organizational meeting, the new committee evidenced few signs of life. St. Louis summers are hot and not conducive to active campaigning, but even the group's efforts to organize lagged. It was not until the end of August that campaign chairmen were announced. The general chairmanship went to William F. James, an automobile-firm executive and minor civic leader. James was best known for his work in connection with Boys Town of Missouri. His acceptance of the post was, by his own admission, his first venture into such matters as "politics and elections." He described himself as a "Republicrat," with no partisan leanings. James was surprised when the committee first approached him. As he stated, he had no knowledge of what the district plan "was all about"; but he took five days to study and discuss it with proponents and opponents. His decision to accept the appointment followed. "I was firmly convinced that here is what St. Louis needs because it is a step forward. . . . I felt it would be good for the County, which is where I live. I felt it would be good for my children."[1] These were noble sentiments but they gave no indication of capacity to assume the general direction of a major campaign.

The selection of James was as surprising to others as it was to himself. It was generally expected that some prominent civic leader would be given this assignment, but no one among the community elite could be persuaded to accept such an arduous role. By default, therefore, the appointment went to one in the lower ranks of leadership. City and county campaign chairmen were also named to complete the campaign organization: Cervantes in the city and Carroll J. Donohue in the county. The latter was a well-known attorney and former president of the local bar association. A Democrat, and a law partner of H. Jackson Daniel, he was active in county politics. Upon these three individuals fell the primary responsibility for arousing interest in a cause that up to this time had evoked little public response.

Formation of the Opposition

While proponents of metropolitan reform were preparing for action, organized opposition made its appearance in the form of three different groups: the Webster Groves Task Force for Self-government, the Citizens Committee for Self-government, and the Citizens Committee against the District Plan. The first originated in suburban Webster Groves, a high-income community of long standing. The least important of the three opposition organizations, it was led by Vernon Riehl, a former Republican alderman in St. Louis City who had moved to Webster Groves some years earlier and had found there "the ideal place to live." This largely Republican group remained local throughout the campaign.

The second organization, the Citizens Committee for Self-government, constituted a more important source of opposition. Almost entirely county based, it was heavily weighted with Republican party leaders and municipal officials. Its president was the mayor of a large suburban community; one of its two vice-presidents was an extremely vocal businessman who claimed credit for defeating

[1] *St. Louis Globe-Democrat*, August 28, 1959.

a recent attempt to consolidate three upper-income municipalities in the county; the other was editor of a suburban weekly. In addition to those with vested interests in retaining the existing governmental pattern, such as the Republican party stalwarts and local officeholders and employees, the organization attracted an agglomeration of chronic opposition groups including opponents of public housing, fluoridation, and federal income taxes.

The third opposing organization, the Citizens Committee against the District Plan, was created less than a month before the election. Bringing together the intransigent promergerites, the new group announced as its objectives: "To seek defeat of the Metropolitan District Plan because it does not go far enough"; and "to keep the way open for consolidation of City-County governments." Leaders of the organization stated that "it is not a question of the district or nothing. The question is rather whether the people of Greater St. Louis will have the vision to reject the timid and tragically inadequate district proposal in order to achieve the right solution to the real problem of government in our growing city-county community . . . a single, unified great city."[2]

The leadership of this third group was impressive. Of its three cochairmen, one was the Democratic National Committeeman from Missouri; another, the Republican gubernatorial candidate in 1956 and a member of a prominent St. Louis family; and the third, president of the St. Louis AFL-CIO Labor Council. The spark plug behind the organization was Lemoine Skinner, a public relations consultant, among whose clients were the Vatterott interests. Skinner, who had long been an advocate of complete consolidation, had little difficulty in convincing the three cochairmen that creation of a metropolitan district would delay if not destroy the chances for total merger. This group, in contrast to the Citizens Committee for Self-government, drew its support almost entirely from city residents. And in marked contrast also, its grounds for opposition were exactly the reverse of those of the county organization.

The Line-up For

As the campaign slowly progressed, efforts were made by both camps to enlist the various civic and interest groups and individual citizens in their respective causes. Expressions of support or opposition were secured from virtually every segment of the community.

[2] *St. Louis Post-Dispatch,* October 8, 1959.

In most instances, participation was limited to formal endorsement or condemnation of the proposed plan. Only a minority of these groups and individuals later took an active part in the campaign. For most of them, the issues were too far removed from their main interests to elicit active involvement and the commitment of scarce resources. Yet, as is generally believed, the endorsement technique can be highly useful when the matter to be decided at the polls is complex and difficult to clarify for the average voter — and certainly the district proposal was not simple. In such cases an appeal to "authority" — to the collective judgment of the organization as expressed by its leaders—often serves as a substitute for personal understanding.

Lined up on the side of the proponents were the major business organizations of the area, the churches, professional societies, civic groups, and the metropolitan dailies. Arrayed against them were organized labor, the politicians, the County League of Municipalities, the weekly press, and the diminishing farmers of the county. Each group needs further comment.

The business leadership of the community, with few exceptions, supported the district plan. Civic Progress, Incorporated early endorsed it as did both the city and county chambers of commerce and the heads of many leading St. Louis firms. The large business interests traditionally favored metropolitan reorganization, partly because they believe that the present fragmented system is not conducive to orderly and efficient administration, partly because they feel that reform will result in a better business and industrial climate, and partly because the development of their civic image requires them to promote such causes. The last motive appeared to be most prevalent among the businessmen supporting the district proposal. Many of the business leaders were only mildly interested in the proposed charter, viewing it neither as a desirable necessity nor as a threat. Yet, if for no other reason, their position in the community compelled them to voice approval of a civic proposal endowed with such respectable sponsorship.

A number of the religous groups also announced their support of the plan. Among those formally endorsing it were the Metropolitan Church Federation of Greater St. Louis and the Missionary Baptist Pastors and Ministers Union Conference, an organization of Negro clergymen. The Catholic hierarchy made no announcement, but the official Catholic weekly of the archdiocese editorially supported the proposal and expressed the wish that its readers would vote favorably on it. No Jewish association took an official stand, but a prominent rabbi gave personal endorsement. These expressions of support by religious groups were not surprising or particularly significant in the light of local tradition. It had long been common practice for the St. Louis churches to endorse movements for civic improvement, and the present campaign fell in that general category.

Although most of the trade and professional organizations remained neutral, a few such as the Realtors Association and the local chapters of the American Institute of Planners and the Institute of Architects publicly supported the proposal. Because of their concern with land use, each of these groups — realtors, planners, and architects — had something of a vocational or professional interest in the planning provisions of the charter.

The major civic organizations of the metropolitan area were also found in the ranks of the proponents. The ever-active League of Women Voters, including the suburban chapters, not only endorsed the charter but campaigned for its adoption. Other area-wide civic groups favoring the plan included the American Association of University Women, the Citizens Council on Housing and Community Planning, the General Council on Civic Needs, and the St. Louis Crime Commission. Local or sectional organizations such as improvement associations and neighborhood councils evidenced little public interest. Only three groups in this category took positions: two from the county in opposition and one from the city in favor.

The two metropolitan dailies, the *Post-Dispatch* and *Globe-Democrat*, gave full support to the district plan. Their news columns comprehensively covered all phases of the campaign while their editorial pages hammered away on the merits of the proposed charter. Starting in September the *Post-Dispatch* carried favorable editorials every four or five days. This pace was gradually stepped up until campaign editorials appeared daily during the two weeks prior to the election. Over this same period, Bill Mauldin's cartoon skills were utilized on eight different occasions. The *Globe-Democrat* followed a similar course but with less frequency. During the final week of the campaign both papers carried a huge banner headline in red ink across the top of the front page: VOTE YES ON METROPOLITAN DISTRICT PROPOSAL TUESDAY.

The Line-Up Against

Organized labor was preponderantly against the district plan. It has always felt that its local political strength would be better enhanced through governmental consolidation than other types of reorganization. Labor's opposition to the district plan apparently grew out of the conviction, nurtured by Ferris and its other freeholder delegates, that a federal-type system would only delay or prevent the attainment of consolidation. The position of the union members on the Board of Freeholders had presaged labor's later stand, but it is doubtful that these representatives had been committed to total opposition. In fact, some top union officials had previously indicated to the survey staff that they were not averse to the district approach although they considered merger the ideal solution.

The most significant unit of labor to declare its opposition was the St. Louis Labor Council, representing virtually all labor unions in the area. Other influential labor voices included the International Union of Electrical Workers, the Communications Workers of America, and the International Association of Machinists. However, some labor support, most of it from the old craft unions, such as the Building and Construction Trades Council, did go to the district proponents. This was not the first occasion on which the leadership of these unions had differed with the majority position of labor on civic issues.

The central committees of the political parties in both city and county refrained from taking any stand on the grounds that the issue was not a partisan one. Within the city ward organizations, the personal influence of Cervantes and others on the citizens committee produced endorsements by 3 of the 28 Democratic ward organizations. Two Republican wards also announced support. In the remainder of the wards no official position was taken by either party. All but a few of the ward leaders appeared indifferent to the election and those who announced their support made no great effort to deliver. In the county, despite official neutrality, the situation was quite different. Leaders of both parties were actively opposed to the plan. County Democrats wanted no part of any arrangement that would align them closer to their city counterparts in local governmental affairs. County Republicans, on the other hand, shuddered at the thought of an agency that might open the door to further Democratic encroachment on local offices. Numerous township officials of both parties quietly but effectively worked against the plan at the "grass roots" level while area political leaders contented themselves with formal denunciations of the proposal.

Opposition was also active among officials at the municipal level. While the mayors of several large suburban cities spoke in favor of the district plan, the overwhelming percentage of local office holders were against it. Most municipal officials who endorsed the plan were part-time officeholders who held executive positions or operated businesses in the central city. Despite the efforts of these individuals, the County League of Municipalities unanimously adopted a resolution of opposition with the supporters abstaining.

St. Louis County still has some agricultural land in its outer reaches although the total acreage is rapidly dwindling. Farmers in expanding metropolitan areas have always looked with suspicion upon attempts to change the local governmental structure, and those in the St. Louis environs have been no exception. It came as no surprise, therefore, when the St. Louis County Farm Bureau, with 200 members, voted unanimously to oppose the plan.

In contrast to the metropolitan dailies, the community or neighborhood weeklies took strong positions against the district proposal. Of the 29 such papers in the area (the majority of them in the suburbs), 22 expressed opposition and the others remained silent. Three of the neighborhood newspapers, strategically located in various sections of the area, took the unusual step of publishing a series of special Sunday editions attacking the plan and warning their readers of the "fallacious" arguments being used in its behalf by the metropolitan press. Typical of their observations is the following simplified reasoning in opposition to the district proposal:

> Whatever "metropolitan problems" exist or may arise as anyone well knows are of a peculiarly local nature. That holds true whether they are in the city, in the county or in any one of the county's incorporated areas. Local governments we strongly believe are best able to cope with them and we see no need whatever to set up a district layer of government to do the job.[3]

The community papers in suburban St. Louis have long been characterized by a strong anticentral-city bias and an equally strong antimetropolitan-press attitude. (In this latter respect they are

[3] *St. Louis County Observer,* September 9, 1959.

joined by their neighborhood counterparts in the central city.) The adamant and provincial stand of the suburban papers in matters of metropolitan concern is consistent with these two biases. It is also consistent in the minds of their publishers with good business practice. Protecting the virtues of the small community against the encroachment and evils of the big city provides them with a worthy, and at times dramatic, cause. And by fighting the "outsider," they are less likely to step on the toes of their local constituency. Metropolitan reorganization seems particularly worrisome to them probably because they feel that it may in some way pose a threat to their existence.

Governmental reorganization movements in other metropolitan areas have often run afoul of attacks by organized "hate" groups. For example, literature pinning the communist label on sponsors of metropolitan reform movements appeared during the Dade County, Knoxville, and Nashville campaigns of recent years. In St. Louis the only incident of this sort was a reprinting without comment in a county newspaper of the notorious "Terrible 1313" article that originally appeared in the *American Mercury*. This article was aimed at the professional public administration organizations headquartered at 1313 E. 60th Street, Chicago. It castigated them as "swift moving teams of social engineers . . . who operate through a radical political apparatus called Metro or Metropolitan Government."[4]

The Tucker Stand

The most crippling blow to the district plan was the "defection" of Mayor Raymond Tucker of St. Louis City. Tucker was by far the best-known political leader in the area. His stature and prestige were high in both city and county even though his close ties with the business community did not endear him to organized labor or the Negro. Tucker's position on the plan was not made known until shortly before the election, although his coolness toward it had been evident for some time. Shortly after publication of the survey report in August 1957, he had praised it in general terms, calling it an "excellent comprehensive study" that could serve as a guide in solving the area's problems. He made no mention, however, of the recommendation for a metropolitan district government. Later, during the hearings by the freeholders, he indicated that his ideal choice

[4] Jo Hindman, "Terrible 1313," *American Mercury*, January 7, 1959.

would be total merger, but since this was currently unattainable his practical choice was a return of the city into the county. Such a solution would be fiscally advantageous to the city because it would shift some welfare costs to the county and also abolish certain "county" offices that were saddled on the city by statute.[5]

In view of Tucker's prolonged silence and his evident lack of enthusiasm for the district approach, few observers expected him to endorse the plan. The question in their minds was whether he would publicly declare his opposition or take a neutral position. His most influential backers, the members of Civic Progress, Incorporated as well as other community elite and civic groups who had consistently supported him were on record as favoring the proposal. Heretofore they had always worked hand in hand with him on matters of civic concern, such as public-improvement bond issues, redevelopment projects, and charter revision. Now an obvious difference of opinion had arisen between them. Some key community leaders close to the mayor tried to persuade him to remain neutral at least. Others more politically minded endeavored to convince him that he would be the ideal choice for chief executive of the new government, but Tucker, already in his early sixties, apparently had no desire to embark on such a new and untried venture at this late stage in his public career.

On October 3, one month before the election, Tucker broke his silence with a carefully reasoned statement announcing his opposition to the plan. Calling it unsound and inefficient, he argued that it failed to reflect the economic, social, and cultural interdependence of the area. Among other criticisms, he objected to the omission of many metropolitan-type functions, the failure to reduce the number of governmental units, the increase in complexity of responsible area-wide government, and the continuance of "separateness of the City and County."[6] He contended that too much had been claimed for the plan, that it was too weak an instrument for carrying out the tasks assigned to it. "I fear," he said, "that adoption of the plan would be followed by widespread voter disillusionment and apathy toward further metropolitan area political reform." His statement concluded with a hopeful expression that should the voters reject the plan as he proposed, there were "a variety of fronts" on which to press for improvement. And with an ironic mention of the survey,

---

[5] The city as a county has certain statutory offices such as sheriff, coroner, and collector, which cannot be abolished by revision of the city charter.

[6] Statement issued by the mayor's office, October 3, 1959.

he added that the survey report would provide "valuable guidelines" for future planning.

Tucker's oposition was damaging to the plan even among county voters in the higher socioeconomic scales who were more influenced by his position than by the views of their own local officials. In attacking the proposal, the mayor chose to disagree with those most closely identified with him and his projects over the years and to place himself on the side of those groups — political and labor — who had not been particularly friendly toward him. A number of reasons prompted his choice, probably the most important of which was the conviction (held in common by large central-city mayors) that political merger is the only satisfactory solution to the metropolitan problem and that lesser remedies will only weaken the position of the core city and dilute its powers. Conceivably, too, he might have been influenced by the likelihood, feared by central-city mayors, that reorganization schemes based on local federalism will create a powerful rival for the area's top political honors in the person of a metropolitan executive.

Other factors also influenced the mayor. In 1954 he had vigorously supported the creation of the Metropolitan Sewer District but the early tribulations that befell this experience in district organization had caused some public disillusionment. In August 1957, several weeks prior to the referendum on a new city charter championed by Tucker and the civic elite, the sewer district officials announced a substantial increase in service rates. Opponents of charter revision had seized on this irrelevant issue in order to discredit supporters of the new document. The sewer rate increase was regarded by some, including the mayor, as a contributory factor in the charter's defeat, and from this time on, Tucker appeared to develop a more hostile attitude to metropolitan plans, especially to any district approach.

A third but less tangible factor in shaping the mayor's decision was his attitude toward the original leaders in the citizens committee. It was known at the time the movement was launched that Tucker was irked at Cervantes for trying to assume the role of a metropolitan statesman. Later in the mayoralty race of 1957, Tucker's Republican opponent, Richard Mehan, charged that the mayor had failed to furnish leadership in the most important task facing St. Louis, that of intergovernmental cooperation between city and county. "It was Alderman A. J. Cervantes," Mehan pointed out, "who started the movement for city-county coordination two years ago by circulating petitions for the creation of a board of freeholders to study the problem." Remarks of this kind were not calculated to increase the mayor's warmth for the present movement. Cervantes, moreover, continued to be a prominent force in the campaign for the district plan, and its adoption would bring much credit to him as the "father" of the new government.

Waging the Civic Battle

Despite the interest expressed by pressure groups and leaders and the exhortations of the press, the campaign was a curious phenomenon characterized more by inactivity and apathy than by vigor and action. As Cervantes remarked shortly before the election, "This damned campaign never got off the ground." It was as though the proponents were not seriously committed to winning while the opponents were confident that the plan did not have a chance. Yet here was an issue presented to the electorate that could radically change the future course of government in a major metropolis. Few citizens seemed aware of the implications.

The proponents of reform relied heavily on the services of a public relations firm and discussion forums. Raising over $70,000 through contributions largely from members of Civic Progress, Incorporated and other business leaders, the City-County Partnership Committee publicized the plan through various mass media and literature, secured and disseminated endorsements by groups and influential individuals, organized "information" meetings, and sent speakers throughout the area to debate the merits of the proposal. Handicapped by the lack of any existent ward and township organizations to assist in reaching the grass roots, the committee tried with little success to form teams of workers at the local level. Funds of $500 per ward were also offered to party committeemen to pay workers in those instances where the party organization endorsed the plan, but because only a few city wards and no county townships placed their official blessings on the proposal, this expenditure was minimal and had little impact.

Most of the influential people who endorsed the plan lent their names and financial support but then took no further part in the campaign. One of the key individuals in Civic Progress, Incorporated contributed $2,500 to the committee and then left on an extended vacation. Others in the organization of businessmen behaved similarly, none of them assuming an active role in the campaign. Apparently never fully sold on the plan or the need for it, they completely withdrew from all but nominal participation when they learned of Tucker's opposition.

The inactivity of the business elite in favor of the proposal left the burden of directing the campaign to a relatively small number of individuals of lesser stature, mainly those from the ranks of the original citizens movement. The freeholders, who might have been in the forefront of the battle, were so evenly divided that the two factions neutralized each other, to the bewilderment of the voter. A few of the freeholders, such as Purteet and Buder, made numerous public appearances in behalf of the plan while others, such as Shewmaker and Mrs. Deakin, spoke against it. Still others, including Vatterott and McClellan, remained conspicuously silent. The League of Women Voters did conduct a telephone campaign to get out the vote and the St. Louis Junior Chamber of Commerce stationed its members along major traffic arteries leading into the downtown area with large banners urging a favorable vote, but these efforts were the exception.

Opponents of the plan displayed no greater activity. The promergerite group — Citizens against the District Plan — expended $8,800, mostly contributed by organized labor, on the preparation and distribution of printed materials, and automobile stickers. The Webster Groves Task Force for Self-government spent less than $500, and the defenders of the status quo, the Citizens Committee for Self-government, functioned with virtually no expenditure. Each of these groups operated in isolation from the other and from individual opponents such as Tucker and the recently elected county supervisor, James McNary. No massive "conspiracy" to defeat the plan existed — and those opposed saw little necessity for such unity.

With several notable exceptions, personal involvement was minimal by the opponents. Mayor Tucker, after his announcement of opposition, made only two talks against the plan. McNary, after condemning the proposal as one that would "saddle our citizens with another layer of government," engaged in no further opposition activity. Even the leaders of the merger group, the Citizens Committee against the District Plan, were not active. None of the three cochairmen made more than one public pronouncement after their original statement. Labor leaders were likewise quiescent, giving no indication of intensive campaigning.

In the county, the Citizens Committee for Self-government showed greater concern. In early October it announced a series of 26 mass meetings in opposition to the plan. The extent of public apathy is illustrated by the attendance at the meetings; most of them had to be cancelled for lack of an audience. One was "well attended" — it drew 55 persons, and this was in suburban Brentwood where the mayor was a leader of the opposition group.

At the grass-roots level, the opposition functioned far more effectively than the proponents, principally because in the party organizations it had a ready mechanism for mobilizing voter action. Particular use was made of this machinery in the county, where the local politicians and officeholders viewed the plan as a threat to their interests. In many townships the party committeemen worked against the proposal. In the city, although the politicians were overwhelmingly opposed to the plan, few ward leaders thought it necessary to mount precinct campaigns. Some of them in the "delivery" wards simply let their opposition be known and then turned their attention to "more important" matters. . . .

Campaign Issues

The civic debate over the reorganization proposal generated numerous issues, some legitimate, others spurious; some important, others of petty concern. The proponents based their case on the common dogmas of metropolitan governmental reform: the inability of individual communities to cope with area-wide problems, such as traffic and transportation; the stifling effects of the existing system on the economic progress of the areas as demonstrated by "its failure to keep pace with comparable urban centers"; and the need for overall guidance and direction in planning the area's future. The opposition presented two different arguments. Promergerites admitted the problems but contended that the proposed remedy was wholly inadequate; the status quo faction denied most of the problems and asserted that only minor adjustments were necessary for those that did exist.

In addition to the dichotomous consolidation and home-rule arguments, two issues raised by the opposition had strong voter impact: taxes and a new level of government. Both recurred frequently during the campaign and both were used effectively in attacks on the plan. Any mention of new or increased taxes is a favorite theme of those opposing governmental innovation, a theme the average voter understands. Adoption of the reorganization proposal, opponents charged, would mean an increase in taxes. Pointing to the provision that would permit the new agency to levy a general property tax up to 50 cents on each $100 of assessed valuation, the impression was given that the homeowner's property tax would automatically be raised by that amount. Proponents countered by explaining that the net increase in property taxes would not be large because the district would reduce local governmental expenses and local taxes by relieving local units of certain responsibilities. Supporters also cited the improved services that would accrue, noting that "We get what we pay for." Taxpayers, however, are strangely immune to such arguments, and many voters were convinced that adoption of the district would mean a substantial tax increase.

The second issue was equally difficult to dispute. Opponents kept reiterating the idea that the plan would impose "a new layer of government while eliminating none now in existence." Proponents rejoined that no new layer was being created because a metropolitan district government already existed in the form of the sewer district, and that the plan did no more than expand and improve a government already in being. This argument, however, proved less than convincing to the voters, probably because many of them were unfavorably impressed by the sewer district.

A third, but spurious, issue was also raised in the county. The impression was given by some opponents that adoption of the plan would also alter or in some way affect the county school districts. Because the integrity of local school districts is a matter close to the hearts of many St. Louis Countians, even the erroneous intimation that the proposed reorganization scheme might somehow affect their school system was persuasive.

EDWARD SOFEN

Reflections on the Creation of Miami's Metro

To explain the success of the campaign for metropolitan government in Greater Miami, it is necessary to examine the relationship of
the central city to the remainder of Dade County, the socio-economic environment of Greater Miami, the people and forces who
worked for the charter, and the methods that were used.

The Miami Milieu

The difference between the central city and the suburbs in Greater
Miami is probably not as great as in other metropolitan areas in the
nation. Dade County, because of its youth, its many homeowners,
its relatively few apartment dwellers, and its unusual physical and
geographical setting, is in many respects one big suburbia. Suburbanites of Dade County are not an "overspill" from the core city
seeking greener pastures, but are primarily *émigrés* from many different sections of the United States. These newcomers have not had
sufficient time to develop deep roots or, often, even firm friendships,
and thus have few emotional ties to the Miami area. (It would seem
that the longer the residency the greater the emotional attachment
to a community.) [1]

[1] A September, 1958, poll (Beiler Survey No. 12) indicated that the
attitude of 433 registered voters towards the autonomy amendment, a
pro-city amendment to the home rule charter, varied with the length of
residence.
The statistics were as follows:

	7 months to 5 years (88 persons)	5 years to 13 years (144 persons)	13 years and longer (201 persons)
For	22.5%	23.0%	30.5%
Against	60.0%	53.5%	50.0%
Uncertain	17.0%	23.5%	19.5%

Reprinted from *The Miami Metropolitan Experiment* (Bloomington: Indiana University Press, 1963), pp. 71-81, 83-84, 86, with the permission
of the author and the publisher.

Nevertheless, these characteristics do not vitiate the reality of the struggle between the core city and its satellites. City of Miami officials, as well as spokesmen for the city's organized business groups, have consistently maintained that central city residents have to bear the financial burden of county-wide facilities. These sentiments were dramatically asserted at a 1957 Congressional subcommittee hearing in Dade County. Robert M. Morgan, civic leader, certified public accountant, and a member of the executive board of the Miami-Dade Chamber of Commerce, blasted the various "parasite communities," which, he said, owed their very existence to the central City of Miami. Replying to a denunciation of Metro by the mayor of Miami Beach, Mr. Morgan declared that Miami Beach was about the least self-sufficient city in the nation. "We Miamians furnish them with water, we burn their garbage, we house their servants, we furnish them with roads leading to Miami Beach . . . we even carry it to the ultimate extreme, we bury their dead."[2]

Some observers contend that the charter, from its inception to its adoption, was a conspiracy of the "downtown Miami merchants." Undoubtedly, this group played one of the more important roles in the genesis of the consolidation movement, but its activities can hardly be classified as a conspiracy. Nor can the general dissatisfaction of a large number of the residents of the City of Miami be traced to the influence of the merchants. The political difficulties that plagued the city for many years might well have disillusioned even the most stouthearted. Despite — or because of — a council-manager form of government, with many nonprofessional managers over the years, the City of Miami was in constant political turmoil. Charges of corruption filled the air, and the police force was under perpetual attack for its failure to enforce the laws against gambling and other forms of vice. It was to counteract this state of affairs that the Greater Miami Crime Commission, a citizens' group, was formed in 1948.[3] At about the same time the Dade County Research Foundation was created to serve as a "watchdog" over governmental ac-

---

[2] U. S. Congress, House, Subcommittee of the Committee on Government Operations, *Hearings, Federal-State-Local Relations, Dade County (Florida) Metropolitan Government,* 85th Cong. 1st. sess., Nov. 21 and 22, 1957, p. 114.

[3] The Crime Commission was founded on March 31, 1948. It was approved by 250 delegates representing some 90 Dade County civic, patriotic, and business organizations at a three-day law enforcement convention at the Mayfair Theater in the City of Miami (*The Crime Commission of Greater Miami,* undated pamphlet.)

tivities and to give assistance to the governments of the area whenever possible.[4]

At the very time that critics of the government of the City of Miami were strongly condemning the city council, these same critics had only the highest praise for the County Commission. The satisfaction with the County Commission can be attributed to its unanimity of outlook, its peace and harmony, and its fairly impressive handling, at least in the public mind, of the county parks, hospital, and Port Authority. The County Commissioners, who had had long experience in their elected offices, were acting as both administrators and policy makers under a commission form of government. The existence of this dichotomy of a "good" county government and an "evil" city government, together with the desire of the city's businessmen to have the county assume the financial burdens of metropolitan functions, helps to explain the transfer to the county of the City of Miami Port Authority and Jackson Memorial Hospital. The transfer of the hospital shifted the costs of support from the city to the county. The designation of the highly respected Board of County Commissioners as the governing board of the Port Authority was seen, by the supporters of the move, as a distinct advantage to the Port Authority in its negotiations with banks. The better credit standing of the county plus the high repute in which the County Commission was held may help to explain why the airlines and the businesses dealing with the airlines preferred county to city control of the airport. Moreover, since the spokesmen for most organized business groups in the central city see Greater Miami as a single unified area, it is to be expected that the central city businessmen would favor a governmental entity that had, in fact and in law, the power to deal with the problem of airports, harbors, and seaports.

From 1945 to 1953 all plans for geographical consolidation could be traced, in part, to the efforts of the powerful business elements within the City of Miami. The 1945 plan was abortive for a number of reasons. The members of the City of Miami Commission, at the time, were of high caliber, and there appeared to be no urgency to save the city. Moreover, the strong bond that was later forged between the Dade delegates to the state legislature and the City of Miami businessmen had not as yet materialized. Even the *Miami Herald* had not at this time realized its position of power.

[4] *Miami Herald*, Jan. 12, 1947, p. 1A. Businessmen were responsible for creating and financially supporting both the Crime Commission and the Research Foundation.

In the 1948 and 1953 elections,[5] a solid alliance was established between the Dade legislators and the proconsolidation elements in Dade County. Among the latter were the *Miami Herald,* the Dade County Research Foundation, the Miami Chamber of Commerce, the Junior Chamber of Commerce, and many members of the League of Women Voters. The near victory of the 1953 move to consolidate the City of Miami with the county led to the introduction, by the localists,[6] of a modified scheme of consolidation aimed at saving the cities from destruction. Even this proposal, however, was only a counteraction to the pressures from the consolidationists.[7]

The socio-political setting of Greater Miami also was conducive to the development of a metropolitan government because of a combination of characteristics peculiar to the area: the tremendous growth of population, the pervasive tourist atmosphere, the rapid population turnover, the existence of a no-party political system, the absence of relatively strong racial or religious minorities committed to the status quo, and the lack of a strong labor movement.

One student of politics has observed that for many years to come it will be difficult, if not impossible, to integrate local governments in areas where there is a two-party system.[8] Miami with its "every man for himself" type of politics has, in effect, a no-party system and, consequently, was spared the kind of struggle that might have occurred if the fate of political parties had hinged on the outcome of the move to create a new metropolitan government. By contrast, certain other metropolitan areas with more formalized party structures, such as Cuyahoga County in the Cleveland area, have reflected sharp divisions between the parties as well as within the parties on the issue of metropolitanization.[9] . . .

The opposition to recent movements to establish metropolitan governments in the United States stemmed not only from political parties but also from various pressure groups that considered themselves threatened. Minority groups which have found a *modus vivendi* in an existing government are particularly loath to change

[5] Regular elections are held in the Miami area in even-numbered years; special elections in odd-numbered years.
[6] The localists insisted upon maintaining the autonomy of the municipalities.
[7] The consolidationists espoused the abolition of the municipalities and the creation of a single government for the Greater Miami area.
[8] Edward C. Banfield, "The Politics of Metropolitan Area Organization," 1 *Midwest Journal of Political Science* 86 (May, 1957).
[9] Governmental Affairs Foundation, Inc., *Metropolitan Surveys: A Digest* (Chicago; Public Administrative Service, 1958), p. 163.

the political structure. Thus one finds that there were Negro leaders in both Cleveland and St. Louis who strongly opposed changing the existing governmental framework because of the fear that they would lose their personal influence in a larger, more rationalized government.

In Miami, Negroes constitute only 6.8 per cent of the registered voters.[10] Of those voting in the predominantly Negro precincts, an estimated 60 per cent have generally opposed the creation of a metropolitan government.[11] Although there may have been rare instances when the Negro vote on metropolitan or consolidation issues has been crucial to the outcome of certain municipal elections, this has not been the case in Dade's county elections. . . .

The powerful labor unions which are found in most metropolitan areas constitute yet another political force vitally concerned with any threat to its power status. Greater Miami, however, has a relatively small number of industrial workers,[12] and although there are some 50,000 union members in the area,[13] unions have played a relatively unimportant role in Dade County politics. By contrast again, in St. Louis there are 35,000 workers in the teamsters' union alone.[14] Also, the Teamsters Local 688 is a vitally significant force in St. Louis. Labor for the most part opposed the metropolitan-oriented District Plan in St. Louis.

In a number of industrial areas throughout the nation, the businessman, or at least an important segment of the business community, has been acutely conscious of the need for the establishment of county-wide metropolitan government. Although prometropolitan

[10] Interview with Dr. Thomas J. Wood, Department of Government, University of Miami.

[11] *Ibid.*

[12] In 1958 only 13 per cent of Greater Miami's nonagricultural labor force were employed by manufacturing concerns, while approximately 30 per cent of the national labor force were so employed. See University of Miami Bureau of Business and Economic Research, *Economic Almanac of Southeastern Florida, 1959* (Coral Gables: University of Miami, 1959), p. 25; United States Department of Commerce, *Statistical Abstract of the United States, 1959* (Washington, D. C.: U. S. Government Printing Office, 1959), p. 210.

[13] *Miami Herald*, Oct. 18, 1959, p. 1G.

[14] The city-wide distribution of its members and the aggressive leadership of its secretary-treasurer have made this union the most active and effective interest group in St. Louis. Once a month, assemblies of union stewards are held to discuss city problems and implement requests that have arisen at ward meetings. Their actions are confined primarily to endorsements of candidates and of issues in city, state, and national elections. See Gray, *Report on Politics*, Chapter V, pp. 7-12.

business organizations in such cities as Boston, Cleveland, and Dayton generally were ineffectual and ill designed for political action, large sums of money were raised by business groups in conjunction with Ford Foundation and other organizational grants, to advance the metropolitan cause. In Miami, on the other hand, the business leaders allowed the Dade County Research Foundation, a business-sponsored "good government" group, to expire for want of funds.

It may be that the "countervailing power theory" of big business begetting big unions also works in reverse. In the case of Miami, the lack of countervailing organizations, in the form of cohesive labor or minority groups, meant that the business community had no real competitors in the political arena. Moreover, since the cause of "good government" groups coincided with the desires of the more powerful Miami business organizations, the latter were quite content to allow the newspapers, professional groups, university professors, and the League of Women Voters to assume the positions of catalytic leadership in civic affairs.

To these variables revolving about the amorphous power setting of Miami one must add two other factors: the lack of a real crisis situation in Miami except, perhaps, in the minds of the more knowledgeable, and the deep political apathy of most Miami citizens. From what we know of other studies, these conditions are probably typical of most metropolitan areas. The extent of the existence of citizen apathy in Miami is made clear by the following observations:

> Any testing of levels of thought and feeling in the political substructure inevitably yields new evidence of abject apathy and gross ignorance in the citizen mass. This is particularly true in dealing with the subject of local government. To find, as we did in Survey #10, that only 15% of our registered citizens could think of anything good that the county commission had done in the preceding year, or that 24% could name something blameworthy that they had done (9% named a parks concession scandal) is routine.

> However, somehow one expects a thing as big as Metro to make an impression. When only 32% say they have heard or read about a new county charter and had a sliver of a correct idea about it, while 13% have a quite wrong idea about it, that sinking sensation returns. It was not only in the telephone poll that 64½% said they did not know of any big change in the county government in the last couple of years. The same question had produced the identical 64½% shrugging response when asked in Survey #10.[15]

[15] Ross C. Beiler and Thomas J. Wood, *Metropolitan Politics*, p. 13.

The authors of the above quotation concluded that those persons possessing little local political interest did not embrace a strong Metro position and, if low enough in interest, held a distinctly "neutral" position. There was also a definite correlation between high local political interest and a pro-Metro position. At first glance one might get the impression that apathy contributed to Metro's success by keeping the "neutral" and anti-Metro voter away from the polls. However, a statistical breakdown of voter turnout in the various precincts in Greater Miami refutes this. Surprisingly, it shows that there was no marked difference in voter turnout in the high socio-economic precincts, with a high degree of local political interest, and the lower socio-economic precincts with a low degree of local political interest.[16]

People, Forces, and Methods

Although the Miami environment and the political process as explained above may have created a setting conducive to the acceptance of metropolitan government, they scarcely account for the positive actions which were necessary to plan, promote, and push Metro to successful adoption. The political environment, in short, provided a favorable matrix; it did *not* provide the "catalytic action-spark." In the following pages the roles of the main actors involved in the formation of Metro will be examined and analyzed. The taxonomy of activists includes the newspapers, the business organizations, the civic groups, the Charter Board, and the professionals.

. . . The political vacuum in Miami was filled to a considerable extent by the *Miami Herald,* the influence of which in crystallizing public opinion has been recognized by friends and foes alike. The formulation of the *Herald* editorial policy is attributed by most civic leaders to Associate Editor John D. Pennekamp. Aspirants for political office eagerly seek the *Herald*'s endorsement, which is extremely important in this no-party area. Some of Miami's most important businessmen, elected officials, and administrative officers meet and consult with Mr. Pennekamp on important community problems. A few of the associate editor's close contacts are characterized by their enemies as "errand boys," with Mr. Pennekamp portrayed as a puppeteer pulling the strings. . . .

[16] The information was obtained from an interview with Dr. Thomas J. Wood, professor of Government, University of Miami, December 31, 1959.

A majority of the downtown City of Miami business elements constitute another faction that has consistently supported consolidation movements. The efforts of this group to win public support for Metro were centered around the activities of the Miami Chamber of Commerce. In 1955 the chamber changed its name to the Miami-Dade Chamber of Commerce and invited each of the chambers in the suburbs to appoint an associate director to the Miami-Dade board of directors.[17] The move was considered presumptuous and few chambers cooperated. It is significant that most of the local chambers of commerce, with the exception of the Miami-Dade chamber, have opposed geographical consolidation.

The Miami-Dade chamber, despite schisms within its membership, has played a significant role in all consolidation movements. The organization's support of the 1948 and 1953 drives lacked the fervor that was evident in later years, however. Despite the fact that chamber members were well represented on the [Metropolitan Miami Municipal] Board and the first and second Charter Boards, the movement for metropolitan government was never closely identified in the public mind with the Miami-Dade Chamber of Commerce.[18] The organization was considered by the public to be just another "civic" group supporting metropolitan government. This was probably fortunate, for if the Metro movement had been thought to be a chamber "conspiracy" aimed at shifting taxes from

[17] The information was obtained from an interview with Alfred Canel, executive vice-president of the Miami-Dade Chamber of Commerce.

[18] In a late 1957 and early 1958 poll (Beiler Survey No. 10) respondents were asked what individuals or groups they would name as most influential in the decisions shaping the new county government. Out of 723 persons questioned (422 registered, 301 unregistered), only 5.5 per cent alluded to a category that included the Chamber of Commerce, the Junior Chamber of Commerce, neighborhood groups, clubs and fraternal organizations. The other responses were as follows:

1. No group indicated   82.0 per cent
2. Municipal (city commissioners, city officials, Dade League of Municipalities, police, municipal employee groups)   3.5 per cent
3. County Commission and Port Authority   6.5 per cent
4. Newspapers   4.5 per cent
5. Television   1.0 per cent
6. Charter Board and other advisory boards   1.5 per cent

The response to the question on which individuals were most influential was practically nil. One would have to conclude that the "average" resident was unaware of the identity of the decision makers in the Greater Miami area.

the City of Miami to the county, it would undoubtedly have failed. This is not to suggest that the chamber was in reality the moving force behind Metro and that it managed successfully to disguise the fact. At most, the chamber was part of a loosely aligned group that, along with the *Miami Herald* and the Dade legislative delegation, was responsible, before appointment of the 3M Board, for initiating geographical consolidation movements — none of which succeeded. As already indicated, the initial step toward metropolitan government was a countermovement by the enemies of consolidation, who were concerned primarily with the preservation of the cities. The consolidationists joined the "localists" in support of a federal type of metropolitan government and, according to some observers, may have succeeded in leaving their consolidationist imprint on the charter.

The Dade County Research Foundation was created in 1947 primarily by business groups in the City of Miami to help bring about more economical and efficient government. The director and full-time staff of the organization was responsible for keeping its members informed of the foundation's findings and recommendations. The foundation enjoyed the respect of the community and the support of the newspapers. It reported on matters of integrity and efficiency in the operations of the City of Miami government and later of the Dade County government. John F. Willmott, first executive director of the foundation, met with opposition when he attempted to criticize the omnipotent County Commission, and in March, 1956, he thought it best to resign.[19] It was somewhat later that the *Herald* and the *News* also began to take the County Commissioners to task. . . .

Although the League of Women Voters, prior to 1957, took no official position on consolidation movements, its members individually gave strong support to such movements. The league, at the time of the charter referendum, however, officially supported the home rule charter.[20] League members were strong allies and formidable opponents. They centered their efforts on distributing pamphlets,

[19] The position of executive director remained vacant until filled by Harry T. Toulmin on August 19, 1956.

[20] There were actually four separate leagues at the time — City of Miami, Miami Beach, Hialeah and Coral Gables — with a total membership of 450. The information was obtained from an interview with Mrs. John Baker, former president of the League of Women Voters of (the City of) Miami.

ringing doorbells, making phone calls, holding parades, and carrying on other old-fashioned but effective means of "politicking." This group, which is most successful if it is provided with political leadership by a "nonpartisan, good government" organization, maintained such a symbiotic relationship with the Dade County Research Foundation.

The activities on behalf of consolidation by good government groups, as well as by newspapers and business groups would have come to naught without the introduction of appropriate bills by the Dade delegation in the Florida Legislature. Management of both the 1948 and 1953 consolidation bills was assumed by Dade Senator R. Bunn Gautier, who, because of his experience, his strong personality, and his political leadership might well be called the father of consolidation.[21]

Considering the role of Senator Gautier in the consolidation movement, a number of questions come to mind: Was the Senator a tool of the Miami Chamber of Commerce? Was he dictated to by the *Miami Herald?* Or was it purely fortuitous that the Senator's aims were compatible with those of the chamber and the *Herald?* The answers to all of these questions must be in the negative. It would seem that Senator Gautier at times had to rally the members of the chamber to support consolidation, rather than the reverse. Although a concord did exist between him and the *Herald,* it was hardly what one would describe as a case of follow the leader.[22] On the whole, the relationship between Senator Gautier and the consolidationist organizations evolved from interaction and a mutual concern; Senator Gautier's leadership was not merely an individual manifestation but rather a reflection of the group process at work.[23] . . .

To explain the importance of professionals in molding the charter and in gaining public support for its adoption, it is necessary to examine what might be called the "expert syndrome." Before inter-

[21] Mr. Gautier was a member of the Florida Legislature from 1947 through 1956. He served one term in the House and four in the Senate.

[22] The information was obtained from interviews with members of the Miami-Dade Chamber of Commerce, with representatives of the *Miami Herald,* and with R. Bunn Gautier.

[23] "It appears, then, that the group experiences and affiliations of an individual are the primary, though not the exclusive, means by which the individual knows, interprets, and reacts to the society in which he exists." David Bicknell Truman, *The Governmental Process* (New York: Alfred A. Knopf, 1951), p. 21.

preting this term, however, there should be some clarification of the different types of experts. [Public Administration Service consultant] Corcoran, in an interesting article,[24] makes a rather invidious comparison between the costs and results of the PAS studies on the one hand and the "probing research" of the foundation-endowed scholars on the other. Obviously, there is need for both types of research, but it would also seem fairly evident that the PAS study was far more productive of results than the work of the scholars. The "syndrome" developed, therefore, around the "practical" expert rather than the "theoretical" expert. The practical expert's laboratory is middle-class suburbia, which has its Book-of-the-Month, its Record-of-the-Month, even its Frozen-Food-of-the-Month, and may at any moment produce its Expert-of-the-Month. The typical suburbanite, with a better than average education and fairly high socio-economic status, has escaped from the unclean realm of politics to the antiseptic atmosphere of the expert. The appeal for good government, nonpartisanship, economy, and efficiency has found a favorable response in what might be characterized as "League of Women Voters" communities. Irrational loyalties to the old and established ways of doing things have not as yet taken root in suburbia.

In Miami the image of the PAS staff as nonpartisan experts provided the symbol of good government. Public Administration Service is not only a research group but a prestige organization as well. As expert consultants analyzing the Miami area, PAS staff members were able, through their recommendations, to keep a number of issues from becoming controversial. The authority of ideas emanating from PAS influenced both the newspapers and the Charter Boards, and PAS representatives worked closely with the Advisory Committee of the 3M Board and the Executive Committee of the first Charter Board. The PAS endorsement of the charter, a sort of *Good Housekeeping* "Seal of Approval," was repeatedly emphasized by the second Charter Board in its campaign for adoption of the home rule charter.

Still another important factor in the promotion of Metro was the symbol of nonpartisanship with which the public most closely identified the Charter Board. The members of the second Charter Board, appointed by the governor at the behest of the Dade delegation, were not representative of the Greater Miami community either geo-

[24] John D. Corcoran, "Seeking Better Government for Metropolitan Areas," 40 *Public Management* 82 (Apr., 1958).

graphically or economically. There were 7 members from Coral Gables, 4 from the City of Miami, 3 from Miami Beach, and 1 each from Miami Springs, Miami Shores, and the unincorporated area. The members, other than those from Coral Gables and the City of Miami, did not reflect the sentiments of the voters of their communities.

A significant number of Charter Board members were men of great wealth in agriculture, business, or finance; at least 6 of the 17 members were in this category. Among the members of the board were 6 experienced officeholders, 3 attorneys, 2 educators, 1 labor leader, and 1 housewife who was a civic leader. On the basis of economic status alone, the board appears to be representative of the people of Dade County. The board, however, was not intended to represent narrow geographic and economic interests. Nor were the board members conscious of strong identification with any specific area or group. For example, two board members — one a labor leader and the other a prominent agriculturist — were able to disregard the sharp anti-Metro feeling of their respective groups. Similarly, those members residing in Miami Beach, as well as a very intense partisan of local government from Coral Gables, joined wholeheartedly in the support of the home rule charter. . . .

Summary

Miami was able to create a metropolitan government with the very type of support that failed in other parts of the nation because of the ecological conditions earlier considered — particularly the absence of powerfully established political parties, labor organizations, and ethnic groups — and because Miamians have long been accustomed to depend on such non-party sources as the newspapers for political leadership. These factors, together with the astuteness of Dade's legislative delegation to the state legislature, the practical orientation of the 3M Board, the high caliber and independence of the Charter Board members, and the prestige of the Public Administration Service experts, were all responsible for the birth of Miami's metropolitan government.

DANIEL R. GRANT

Nashville's Politicians and Metro

In the search for scapegoats in the wake of unsuccessful "metro reform" efforts, eyes invariably turn to the professional politicians in the metropolitan area — the core-city boss and his "city hall crowd," the county boss and his "courthouse gang," and — or — the "parasitic suburban city officeholders." Many cases could be cited in which the professional politicians have been less than enthusiastic for metro reform proposals, and still others in which the public support of professional politicians amounted to a virtual kiss of death. The political boss is thus said to contribute to the defeat of metropolitan government reorganization proposals, *whatever* his stand on the issue.

While it is exceedingly difficult to pin the blame on any specific person or group for the rejection of metro reform, it should be helpful to look at the role of professional political leaders in the *adoption* of a major metro reform proposal. The newly adopted metropolitan government of Nashville and Davidson County provides such an opportunity. After rejecting in 1958 a city-county consolidation proposal supported by both the city and county political leaders, the electorate changed its mind and adopted a similar proposal in 1962 in spite of strong opposition from the mayor of the core city.

The role of profesional political leaders in "metropolitics" should be illuminated by investigating the case of Nashville in four respects: (1) what was the relationship of the local political leaders to the growth of the "metropolitan-type" problems which seemed to call for major structural reform, (2) what was their relationship to

Reprinted from "Metropolitics and Professional Political Leadership: The Case of Nashville," *Annals of the American Academy of Political and Science Social,* CCCLIII (May 1964), pp. 73-81, with the permission of the author and the American Academy of Political and Social Science.

early metropolitan reform strategy, (3) what was their role in the 1958 defeat and the 1962 victory for metro, and (4) what is the significance of having an *elective* metropolitan mayor (rather than an appointive professional manager) in the process and problems of transition to a single metropolitan government for Nashville and Davidson County?

Setting for Metro Reform

Before considering these four questions, a brief look at the political setting of Nashville and Davidson County is in order as well as at certain relevant demographic and geographic factors. Located in the upper middle portion of the state of Tennessee, Davidson County covers 533 square miles and contains the state's capital city, located on the Cumberland River. Its historic sites include the Hermitage, home of Andrew Jackson, and the replica of the Parthenon. While Nashville is an educational and religious center of considerable significance and claims the title "the Athens of the South," it may well be better known as the home of the "Grand Ole Opry" and as the country-music capital of the nation.

Metropolitan Nashville has a diversified economy with a moderate amount of manufacturing — such as DuPont, Ford Glass, Gates Rubber, and Genesco — supplemented strongly by an above-average quantity of religious printing, insurance and banking establishments, educational institutions, and state and federal payrolls. Prior to the adoption of metropolitan government, the city's governmental form was a fairly strong mayor-council type, and the county was governed by a fifty-five-member "quarterly county court" and a county judge whose role was more that of titular head than genuine chief executive. Factional politics, rather than party politics, is the dominant theme at the local level, with Nashville Mayor Ben West and County Judge Beverly Briley heading rival factions for the decade before metro's adoption. Of equal or greater importance in the factional picture, the two daily newspapers in Nashville, the *Tennessean* and the *Banner*, have played strong and active roles in supporting the opposing factions.

Although the proportion of Nashville's population which is Negro (37.9 per cent in 1960) is comparable to that in many cities of the deep South, Nashville has earned a reputation as a moderately progressive city for its desegregation activities. In spite of bombings and other inflammatory incidents, it was able to carry out gradual desegregation of schools as well as desegregation of buses and of downtown eating establishments. Negroes had served on the city council and school board for many years, though not on the county governing body or county school board.

Core-city and suburban population trends are quite similar to those in metropolitan areas of comparable size. In the decade of the 1950's, Davidson County's population grew from 321,758 to 399,743, while Nashville's population dropped from 174,307 to 170,874, even after counting 4,587 residents annexed in 1958. While the core city did not lose population between 1940 and 1950, its 4.1 per cent increase contrasted sharply with the 64.1 per cent increase outside the city. Failure to annex any appreciable amount of territory after 1929 had kept the city's area down to less than twenty-three square miles as late as 1957. The rural portions of the county in 1960 contained approximately 53,000 persons, but only 5,874 of these actually lived on farms; the remainder apparently were urban-oriented in their means of livelihood.

Political Leadership and "Metropolitan-Type" Problems

Nashville's "metropolitan-type" problems — those governmental problems uniquely related to the suburban spill-over beyond the city boundaries — were similar in many ways to those of most other medium-sized or smaller metropolitan areas in the United States. Beginning first as a trickle but ultimately assuming the proportions of a flood, old and new residents of Nashville settled in a massive fringe area outside the legal city and soon discovered that the urban service needs moved with them but urban government did not.

The "number-one problem" was generally conceded to be the absence of sanitary sewers in the suburbs with an uncertain dependence upon septic tanks in the limestone base of Davidson County and the resulting inhibitions on the attraction of new industries. Other service deficiencies were almost as serious, however, with suburban fire and police protection being provided in poor quality and quantity on a private subscription basis. Houses of nonsubscribers actually burned to the ground while firemen from a private department stood idly by, watching only to see that the house of the subscribing neighbor was safe. Some two hundred miles of suburban water lines of a size insufficient for fire hydrants were installed over a period of several decades. Thousands of acres of beautiful open space and woodland were cut up for residential subdivisions without reserving a single acre for public parks and playgrounds. County leaders declared they had no authority to operate suburban parks and city leaders declared they had no responsibility for such.

Suburban service deficiencies were not the only metropolitan problem. No area-wide authority existed for coping with many area-wide problems, and duplications existed between city and county agencies in a variety of ways. City-county financial inequities, some serious and some only minor irritants, provided steady fuel for a running feud between in-city and out-of-city taxpayers and their respective political leaders. Charges of "suburban free-loading" and counter charges of "city tax-grabbing" were common parlance and tended to make city and county buck-passing the expected thing. The dismay and even cynicism of the citizen seeking to fix responsibility for governmental action or inaction may well have been the most serious problem of all.

This brief and, necessarily, oversimplified view of Nashville's metropolitan governmental problem in the 1940's and 1950's leads one almost inevitably to such a question as "Who was keeping the store when the merchandise fell into such disarray?" What was the relationship of the two principal political leaders in the area, the mayor and the county judge, to the emergence of these problems? Quite obviously, their roles were not the only ones of importance — a whole host of interests, individuals, and influences were involved — but the following observations should make it clear that the roles of the elective political leaders were of critical importance:

(1) The Nashville mayor and the Davidson County judge were significantly involved in certain "nondecisional causes" of the growth of metropolitan problems; that is, it might be said that their inaction and failure to anticipate consequences of inaction helped start the problems on their way. For example, when suburban spill-over was only an initial trickle, the nontaxpaying suburbanites were permitted, primarily through inaction of city and county leaders, to initiate a financial inequity by receiving city water at the same rate as taxpaying city dwellers and to begin such suburban service deficiencies as laying water lines which were of inadequate size for fire

hydrants. It was only during these early years of the 1930's that preventive measures might have been adequate rather than the more drastic and expensive curative measures being undertaken today.

(2) For the thirty-year period of virtually no annexation by the city of Nashville, it is the mayor, the political leader of the core city, who must bear major responsibility for the failure to annex. Actually, all mayors during this time expressed an almost glib willingness to annex any area interested in becoming a part of the city, but, to even the most casual student of suburban politics, it would not be surprising that there were very few "takers." As the unserved area outside the city grew larger and larger, the political risks became formidable to any Nashville mayor who might push through large-scale annexation. Experts reported that the core city would lose money, at least in the short run, by annexing residential areas; city councilmen were apprehensive about a drop in services in their districts while new services were being installed in the annexed areas; any realistic estimate of the time required to serve — particularly to sewer — the suburbs involved a serious time lag, which could only mean to the mayor a new and hostile group of voters with which to reckon at election time.

(3) While the mayor's failure to push annexation during the early years of suburbanization must be termed a cause of the growth of metropolitan problems, metropolitan reformers may have to credit this do-nothingism with providing important assistance toward eventual consolidation of Nashville and Davidson County. It is quite probable that the absence of a vigorous push for annexation resulted in less antiannexation pressure in the suburbs for separate incorporation of "satellite cities." Prior to 1950, there was only one incorporated city in the county outside of Nashville. Five others were incorporated during the fifties, but even the total of six is small by comparison with other metropolitan areas. It is quite possible that a mayor might have triggered an epidemic of separate incorporations around Nashville if he had pushed more vigorously for annexation, with the resulting proliferation of separate governments making it considerably more difficult and perhaps impossible to achieve consolidation.

(4) Finally, the relative balance of power in the factional rivalry of the mayor and county judge probably had the effect of militating against any major change in the *status quo* and, thus, in favor of

continued growth and aggravation of the metropolitan problems.
Throughout most of the forties and fifties an uneasy stalemate existed in the power struggle between the mayor and the judge, each
having the support of one of the daily newspapers. Any major governmental change, such as annexation or city-county consolidation,
was likely to run counter to fears of an unfavorable disturbance of
this balance of power. It was only after it became obvious in the
late fifties that the suburbs *must* be sewered by one means or another that the log jam against governmental change began to break.
The mayor and the judge then began to scramble for position.

Early Strategy and Leadership

The first comprehensive study of the over-all metropolitan problem in Nashville and Davidson County was that conducted by the
Community Services Commission, created in 1951 by private act of
the Tennessee legislature. With the assistance of a small, full-time,
professional staff, the commission completed its study by June 1952
and recommended the extension of Nashville's boundaries to include
the bulk of the suburban fringe area, some sixty-nine square miles
and approximately 90,000 people. It further recommended that four
functions being performed by the city of Nashville (public health,
hospitals, schools, and welfare) be transferred to Davidson County
and performed on a county-wide basis. City-county consolidation
was not recommended at this time, primarily because it was felt that
a constitutional amendment permitting a tax differential between
urban and rural property would be required. In the absence of any
strong push for carrying out these recommendations, either by citizens' organizations or the heads of city and county government, no
annexation took place, and only a part of the recommended transfers
to the county were carried out. Mayor Ben West took the initiative
in abolishing the city's health department and letting the county assume responsibility in this field, with a city budgetary strain providing support for the move. In general, however, the role of the mayor
and of County Judge Beverly Briley with respect to the 1952 recommendations seemed to be one of inaction rather than of either
opposition or support in an active way.

Four years later, a second comprehensive study was made, this
time by the city and county planning commissions with professional
staff assistance from Vanderbilt University. This study was able to

utilize the detailed information of the earlier report and to concentrate primarily on the administrative, legal, and political feasibility of particular proposals for metropolitan reform. Most of the assumptions of this study were the same as those of the 1952 study: (1) that some kind of area-wide government was necessary in order to co-ordinate urban services and to spread the tax burden equitably, (2) that single-purpose approaches such as special districts or authorities would inhibit rather than facilitate co-ordination, (3) that either annexation or city-county consolidation would meet the need for area-wide jurisdiction, but (4) that *political* feasibility was the major hurdle in either case because it was becoming clear that Judge Briley favored city-county consolidation and Mayor West was leaning toward the annexation approach. This did not become apparent until after 1952, but both in 1952 and 1956 it was felt that a proposal could not survive the opposition of either the city or county political faction, led by the mayor and judge respectively, and that it would probably require the active support of both.

The 1956 "Plan of Metropolitan Government" which was the product of the planning commissions' study was carefully tailored to elicit the endorsement of both Mayor West and Judge Briley. The original strategy of the research staff was to recommend immediate annexation while working ultimately toward a single metropolitan government for the city and county. This would permit the mayor to emphasize "phase one" and the judge to emphasize "phase two," with each conceivably thinking privately that the other phase either would never be adopted or would be only temporary. During the period between March 1956, when the staff draft was first submitted to the planning commissions, and October 1956, when the finished report was released to the public, the proposal was subjected to painstaking analysis by both the mayor and the judge, serving as members of the commissions. As the report was released in final form, it gave much greater emphasis to phase two (city-county consolidation) than it did to phase one (annexation), and there was considerable speculation that Mayor West might have openly opposed the report had it not been for strong support for the plan from his newspaper ally, the Nashville *Banner*.

The report called for combining the functions and agencies of Nashville and Davidson County in a single metropolitan government, with provision for a higher level of services and taxes in an expandable "urban services district." The new government was to be neither a city nor a county but, rather, a new political entity. No more suburban incorporations could take place under the new government, but the existing cities outside of Nashville could retain their charters if they so desired. They must be a part of the "general services district," however, in the same manner as the unincorporated area. A recommended "plan of action" in the report called for the passage of general enabling legislation by the state legislature early in 1957, authorizing the creation of a "Metropolitan Government Charter Commission." Such an act was passed in March 1957, and, in view of the fact that opposition from either the mayor or judge could have killed it at that stage, its passage seems, in the light of hindsight, to be something of a political miracle. During this period and the months immediately following, the public position of Judge Briley was favorable to the idea of metropolitan government, while Mayor West maintained a kind of noncommittal "wait and see" policy. The charter commission consisted of five members appointed by the mayor and confirmed by the city council and five members appointed by the judge and confirmed by the county court. They completed their work in approximately one year, and a referendum was held in June 1958.

1958 Defeat and 1962 Victory

It is obviously not possible here to give a full account of the events leading up to the adoption of metro in 1962. A brief summary or chronology of events is necessary, however, as a background for generalizations about the role of professional political leaders in metropolitan reform in Nashville.

With the filing of the proposed charter on March 28, 1958, less than three months of campaigning were allowed before the June 17 referendum. The campaign for the charter was in large measure a newspaper campaign, with the *Banner* and the *Tennessean* laying aside their usual political differences and going "all out" with editorials, news stories, and special features in support of metro. In addition, the charter had the endorsement of Mayor West and Judge Briley, the Nashville Chamber of Commerce and the great majority of business leaders, the Nashville Trades and Labor Council, Tennessee Taxpayers Association, League of Women Voters, and several other civic and professional groups, as well as the ten members of the charter commission, including its two Negro members. A citizens' committee for metropolitan government was created, but its principal work was supplying speakers for civic clubs and distributing a pamphlet summarizing the provisions of the charter.

Active opposition to metro was hardly visible until the final week before the referendum, when a flood of antimetro handbills appeared at bus stops throughout the city and at suburban and rural mailboxes and front doors. Newspaper advertisements and singing jingles on radio and television hammered away on the theme that metro meant bigger government, higher taxes, and a "virtual mortgage on your home." Joining in the attack on metro were the suburban private fire and police companies, the constables, about one half of the members of the city council and the county court, most of the operators of the small suburban business establishments, and a few Nashville businessmen.

The scare campaign appeared to be most effective in the lower-income suburbs and least effective in the higher-income suburbs. A plausible explanation of this would be that it was a result of the proponents' excessive reliance on newspaper publicity and civic club speeches and failure to develop a precinct and block organization. The suburban and rural alarm was reflected in a fairly heavy negative vote, 19,234 to 13,794, while the vote inside the city of Nashville was light but favorable, 7,797 to 4,804.

Not long after the rejection of the metro charter, the city of Nashville began to use for the first time the strong annexation powers which had been authorized by the Tennessee legislature in 1955. Without a vote in the affected areas, the city council annexed first seven square miles of largely industrial property and then forty-three square miles of residential area containing some 82,000 persons. These actions had the effect of tripling the previous area of the city and of causing many unhappy suburbanites to re-examine their earlier opposition to metro. Mayor West supported the industrial annexation but vetoed the residential annexation bill because it did not provide for a referendum. His own majority faction in the city council overrode his veto, however, giving rise to the charge that he had actually given an informal "green light" to the residential annexation. County school officials and teachers were especially upset by the confused status of the annexed schools, and the *Tennessean* showed no mercy in reporting those annexation developments which tended to embarrass Mayor West.

While many factors were involved, including the levying of a "green sticker" tax for use of city streets, the second effort to secure metropolitan government received its main impetus from this massive annexation move by the city of Nashville. In brief outline, the events leading to the framing of a second proposed charter for metropolitan government were as follows: (1) passage of a resolution by the county quarterly court calling for the creation of a new charter commission, followed by an unsuccessful effort to secure passage by the city council; (2) election of a delegation to the state legislature pledged to give the people a second chance to vote on metro; (3) passage of state enabling legislation in 1961; (4) approval of the creation of the new charter commission in a referendum in August 1961 by a light but surprisingly favorable vote: 11,096 to 3,730 inside Nashville and 7,324 to 3,848 outside of Nashville; and (5) creation of a charter commission composed of identical membership to the 1958 group except for two vacancies filled by appointments by the mayor and the county judge.

The charter which was filed in April 1962 was not appreciably different from the 1958 charter, although some changes were made. The metropolitan council was enlarged from twenty-one to forty-one members in deference to the local tradition of large legislative bodies in both the city and county. Because of the new annexation, the urban services district would begin with an area of almost seventy-five square miles instead of the 1958 area of less than twenty-five square miles. The metropolitan mayor's salary was increased to $25,000 from $20,000, and the earlier two-term limit was changed to a three-term limit. Strong pressure for an independently elected school board was resisted by the charter commission in a narrow vote. A companion proposal was accepted, however, to permit the school board by a two-thirds vote to secure a public referendum on the school budget if it is cut by the metropolitan council.

Two major differences may be cited between the 1962 and 1958 metro campaigns. The first is the much more effective organization of the pro-metro forces in 1962 than in the earlier effort. As early as the summer of 1961, a fairly broad-based "Citizens' Committee for Better Government" was organized to support the creation of a charter commission. After the successful August referendum, it stayed in existence and built on this experience. A women's division enlisted more than 1,500 persons who worked zealously for metro with neighborhood coffees, telephoning, and doorbell ringing. Judge Briley and many of the same groups as before endorsed metropolitan government, and the *Tennessean* crusaded even more completely than in 1958, if such is possible. The county tax assessor and county trustee, whose elective jobs were protected in the charter, provided important support from some of the "organization politicians" in the county.

The second major difference in the 1962 campaign was the change-over of Mayor West, who campaigned publicly and vigorously against the charter. His reasons for the switch are disputed — he contended that the city's program of annexation should be given a fair chance before trying anything new, but his critics were unconvinced. They explained the cooling off on metro as a realization that his chances of becoming metropolitan mayor were not good in 1962, whereas they had been considerably better in 1958. Mayor West's opposition to metro permitted the *Tennessean* to adopt a "beat-the-city machine" theme in contrast to the more educational but less colorful approach in 1958. Joining in opposition to metro in 1962 were the *Banner,* most of the city councilmen, many of the county magistrates and constables, perhaps one third of the members of the chamber of commerce board of governors, the officials of the six incorporated suburban cities, and a few right-wing extremists such as racist agitator John Kasper and a leader of the John Birch Society.

In the referendum on June 28, 1962, the consolidation charter received the necessary separate majorities inside and outside Nashville. Even though Mayor West was able to carry the "old city" to a close vote against metro, this was more than outweighed by the overwhelmingly favorable vote in the newly annexed areas. The totals in Nashville were 21,064 in favor and 15,914 against. Outside Nashville, 15,591 voted in favor and 12,514 voted against. Following an early court test favorable to the metropolitan charter, Judge Briley was elected metropolitan mayor in November 1962, over Tax Assessor Clifford Allen — Mayor West did not run. The new government went into effect on April 1, 1963.

Mayor's and Judge's Roles in Defeat and Victory

With only this one case study to draw upon, what kinds of generalizations can be suggested about the role of professional political leaders in metropolitics? In addition to the broad assertion that

Nashville's experience with metropolitics offers no support for any inclination of metropolitan reformers elsewhere to leave the professional political leaders out of their plans, the following more specific conclusions may be drawn from the Nashville events.

(1) Plans for major structural change in local government in a metropolitan area *can* be devised in such a way as to achieve support of the primary political leaders. In the two campaigns in Nashville, the support of three of the four top politicians was achieved (two in the first and one in the second), and this should be considered a rather high batting average in the difficult arena of metropolitics.

(2) As in the case of city-manager reform campaigns, major metropolitan government reform *can* be used by one political faction as a device to oust an opposing faction from power. It would be difficult to say whether the Nashville *Tennessean* was more enthusiastic at the prospect of getting metro adopted or of getting Mayor West ousted. It would not be correct to conclude, however, that the 1962 metro campaign was entirely an anti-West struggle. The factional battle undoubtedly controlled many developments in the 1962 campaign but by no means all of them.

(3) The unanimous endorsement and even active support of the major political leaders for a metropolitan reorganization proposal is not sufficient to guarantee an affirmative vote of the electorate, even when an imposing array of the alleged "community elite" also support the proposal. The 1958 defeat of metro proved this and demonstrated the great depth of suburban and rural suspicion and distrust of the central city and of any "entangling alliances" with it. Also demonstrated was the ability of seemingly insignificant opinion leaders in the lower-income suburbs — barbers, filling station operators, cleaning and pressing shop operators — to remain virtually unaffected by the daily barrage of pro-metro newspaper publicity or by the endorsements of both the mayor and the judge.

(4) It is not always within the power of one of the chief political leaders to block a major metropolitan reorganization proposal. More specifically, the core city political organization *can* be beaten by metropolitan reform forces. But reformers in other metropolitan areas should not take too much hope or be misled by this statement, which is one of possibility rather than probability. The *probabilities* of winning over the opposition of the city machine are doubtless very poor. Mayor West's association with the controversial "green

sticker tax" and annexation program made his opposition to metro in 1962 an asset for the pro-metro forces rather than a liability, especially in the annexed area and the suburban and rural areas.

(5) In spite of appearances, it cannot be concluded from the Nashville experience that the prospects for a metro victory are greater if the major political factions are divided (as in 1962) than if they are united in favor of it (as in 1958). It is this writer's opinion that the victory in 1962 would not have been possible without the foundation laid in 1958 when *both* political factions endorsed metro. Proponents of metro in 1962 were able to make Mayor West's opposition seem more petty and personal because his statements seemed to contradict everything he said four years earlier. The unified, highly rational, "high road" campaign for metro in 1958, which was made possible by the endorsement of the mayor and the judge, did not result in victory, but it made significant contributions to the ultimate victory. While the margin of victory probably came from the vote-switchers who cast an emotional protest vote against annexation and the "green sticker," the greater part of the "yes" voters in 1962 were those who had been sold on metro in 1958 and had stayed with the cause.

5

THE ADAPTIVE METROPOLIS:
THE POLITICS OF ACCOMMODATION

Accommodation rather than revolution is the normal pattern of adjustment to urban growth and change. Instead of stimulating the creation of "rational" areawide governmental institutions, metropolitan development has produced a somewhat disorderly and pragmatic set of political responses to the steadily rising pressures for more public goods and services. Rather than anticipating problems through planning, the metropolitan political system usually responds to crisis. As a result, policies and programs are developed on an incremental ad hoc basis. Different governmental techniques, such as special districts, interlocal agreements, extension of county services, and state and federal aid, are used for different problems. Water supply, highways, parks, mosquito control, and almost every other function of government each tends to develop a unique set of institutional and jurisdictional arrangements. Each unit of general government finds itself participating in a variety of relationships, particularly in the suburbs where a mounting portion of the business of government is handled cooperatively, performed by special districts and county and state agencies, and financed in part by the higher levels of government.

One product of the development of this governmental crazy quilt is the growth of functional autonomy. The increased use of special districts, assistance programs, and other devices tends to shift control over broad areas of public policy from local officials and the electorate to relatively autonomous agencies responsible for particular functions of government. More and more key decisions affecting local and regional development are made by inter-municipal sewer agencies, county park districts, metropolitan water authorities, state highway departments, and a host of other independently financed agencies responsible for a single function and insulated from the local political process.

Diminished local control is an ironic development since the desire to maintain the political and fiscal integrity of the community underlies the system of accommodation. However, functional autonomy only partially affects local control, particularly since it rarely threatens directly the most critical of all local political concerns, the regulation of land use. In addition, the system of accommodation is highly flexible. The network of relationships is largely voluntary. Normally there is no way to compel a unit of government to participate in an interlocal agreement, a special district, or a county or state program. The individual units of the metropolis can avoid involvements which do not promise benefits commensurate with costs. Thus, communities can choose to accommodate by "going it alone" or failing to act. Unilateralism enhances local control, but usually at the price of higher taxes and sometimes lower levels of service as well. A policy of inaction almost always involves discomfort to the residents of the abnegating community, and sometimes also to their neighbors downstream or downwind who cannot escape the consequences of untreated sewage or polluted air.

The constant process of adjustment by which the political system of the metropolis accommodates to the presures generated by urban growth and change belies the central thesis of metropolitan reform. The experience of most metropolitan areas does not support Gulick's argument that "once an indivisible problem is divided, nothing effective can be done about it." While regional government might be more effective and more democratic,

a single set of areawide political institutions clearly is
not required for the amelioration or resolution of most of
the problems arising from metropolitan development.
By and large, these problems are not "indivisible"; something effective enough to satisfy most residents of the
metropolis can be done on a divided basis, either by individual units of general government or by functional
agencies encompassing some or all of the metropolitan
area. To be sure, as the readings in the chapter indicate,
there are many shortcomings in the system of accommodation. It encourages proliferation and differentiation,
diffuses responsibility, weakens the representative processes, handles some kinds of problems far more effectively than others, and lacks any commitment to the general welfare. None the less, it works sufficiently well to
foreclose more radical approaches to metropolitan prob-
lem-solving. As a result, the process of accommodation
might be said to reverse the maxim of metropolitan reform — the process of handling "indivisible" problems on
a divisible basis drastically reduces the probability of
developing indivisible approaches.

The proliferation of special districts and public authorities is one of the most important consequences of the
politics of accommodation. One reason for the widespread use of unifunctional metropolitan districts is their
acceptability to the many interests of the decentralized
political system. Unlike multipurpose regional government, special districts are not perceived as a threat to
local control. Because they usually are financed by user
feés, they do not raise the threat of unequal costs and
benefits implicit in proposals to create metropolitan institutions with general taxing powers. Other advantages are
manifest. The jurisdiction of the special district can be
tailored to fit a particular problem, the boundaries of the
participating communities, or the desires of the technicians involved. Districts and authorities are free from
the state-imposed tax and debt restraints which limit the
activities of local government practically everywhere in
the United States. Finally, the image of the "businesslike" special district which is "out of politics" with its

"pay as you go" revenue-financing strikes a responsive chord in the average resident of the metropolis who vaguely distrusts both politicians and the normal processes of local government.

To secure the advantages of the special district, however, the communities of the metropolis must pay a rather heavy price. The growth of functional autonomy, argues Victor Jones, erodes the key function of government — the allocation of limited resources to meet the many demands for public goods and services. As independently financed and politically insulated special districts and authorities acquire responsibility for an enlarging area of public policy, the range of choice available to the local elected official dwindles. The problem is further complicated because the self-supporting, revenue-financed special districts skim the cream off the top of the public economy of the metropolis. While the onerous task of raising taxes to finance those programs which incur deficits is left to the general purpose governments, special districts like the Port of New York Authority are free to pursue policies designed to maximize their revenues. Far from removing sectors of the public's business from politics, authorities create their own political worlds. Special district politics take place in functionally autonomous arenas which usually are shielded from public view and in which relations between the agency and its clientele frequently are cozy. To be sure, political and fiscal independence produces some magnificent public works, witness the George Washington Bridge or Kennedy International Airport. But as Jones indicates in his discussion of the Port of New York Authority, the proliferation of functionally autonomous special districts also cripples efforts to plan and implement comprehensive strategies for metropolitan development.

The great metropolitan districts — like the Port of New York Authority with its billion dollar empire of bridges, tunnels, airports, and terminals or the Metropolitan Water District of Southern California with its 250-mile aqueduct to carry water from the Colorado River to the Los Angeles area — are the glamorous well-publicized "stars"

among special districts. But far more numerous and
equally important elements in the process of accommodation are the small suburban service districts which provide water, sewerage, fire protection, and a variety of
other services, particularly in the unincorporated areas
along the urban frontier. Here there are no seventh won-
ders of the engineering world to match the Chicago Sanitary District's reversing of the flow of the Illinois River
or $60,000 a year officials like the Port of New York
Authority's executive director. But the essential features
remain the same. Like their giant cousins, the small special districts which dot the metropolitan landscape usually are unifunctional, revenue-financed, and politically
independent. And, as indicated in the account of the San
Francisco Bay Area's experience by Stanley Scott and
John Corzine, the use of small unifunctional districts
raises many of the same political, fiscal, and planning issues associated with the development of metropolitan
authorities.

Interlocal cooperation is an even more common response than special districts to the challenge of providing public goods and services in the decentralized metropolis. While there are approximately 18,000 special districts in the United States, Philadelphia, the nation's
fourth largest metropolitan area, alone has over 700
interlocal agreements. Accommodation through cooperation takes a variety of forms, ranging from ad hoc informal agreements to detailed contractual agreements.
Among the more common devices are sharing of facilities,
granting of extraterritorial jurisdiction, and contracting
for services supplied by another community. Since the
web of interjurisdictional relationships grows as a result
of responses to individual problems at particular points
in time, the agreements tend to be unifunctional rather
than multipurpose. For the same reason, their growth is
haphazard, following no general plan. However, as demonstrated by Thomas R. Dye and his colleagues, the pattern of interlocal cooperation is influenced by differences
among the units of the fragmented metropolis. Their findings indicate that intermunicipal agreements in the Phila-

delphia area are more likely to occur when communities resemble each other socially and economically. Thus, the politics of accommodation reflects the politics of differentiation.

Another vehicle for accommodation in the metropolis is the county. In the 130-odd single county metropolitan areas, county government is a natural candidate for tasks which are beyond the jurisdictional or fiscal capabilities of the municipalities. Even when they do not encompass the entire metropolitan area, counties retain jurisdictional advantages over the basic units of local government which lead to their increasing involvement in meeting the pressures generated by metropolitan development. And almost everywhere, the county provides urban services in the unincorporated areas where there is no other local government. County government, by and large, was not ready for the urban onslaught. In the wake of onrushing suburban development have come stresses and strains in the county courthouse. Under the pressures of urban change, the leaderless, part-time, decentralized, and rurally-oriented political and administrative machinery of the county gives way to elected or appointed executives and professional administrators and technicians. A political system emerges which is increasingly responsive to urban needs and which becomes a key element in the complex politics of accommodation.

Urban county government is more highly developed in California than anywhere else in the United States; and so is the role of the county in the process of accommodation. As Richard M. Cion shows, Los Angeles County's Lakewood Plan, an ingenious contracting scheme in which the county provides individual municipalities with almost every conceivable local service, from police protection to weed abatement, is a system of accommodation *par excellence.* By participating in the plan, the local community reaps the prime benefit of independence — control over land use — without having to pay the usual costs of autonomy, since the diseconomies of small size are avoided through the purchase of pre-packaged services from the large and relatively efficient government of

Los Angeles County. And because it successfully meets the service needs of the residents of a growing segment of the Los Angeles area, the Lakewood Plan, like other modes of accommodation, fosters continued proliferation and differentiation.

Two sharply contrasting views of the politics of accommodation and its implications for metropolitan development complete the chapter. Evaluating the decentralized political system largely in terms of its ability to provide public goods and services efficiently, Vincent Ostrom, Charles M. Tiebout, and Robert Warren view the "polycentric" metropolis and its processes of accommodation with equanimity. Underlying their analysis is the model of the competitive economic marketplace. They applaud the Lakewood Plan for developing "quasi-market" conditions and achieving an admirable degree of flexibility and responsiveness in the provision of public services. Ostrom and his colleagues conclude by arguing that the process of accommodation has provided most metropolitan areas with "a very rich and intricate 'framework' for negotiating, adjudicating, and deciding questions that affect their diverse interests."

Robert C. Wood grants that the process of accommodation can meet the service needs of most residents of the decentralized metropolis. By so doing, the many modes of adjustment create the essential conditions for the survival of the fragmented political system. But Wood deplores the system's exclusive concern with services; and doubts that the polycentric metropolis can thrive since a prolongation of the institutional status quo means more unplanned growth, widening social and economic disparities, and a continued lack of concern for the general welfare of the metropolitan area. The incomplete political system of the accommodating metropolis, he concludes, is both undemocratic and unequal to the challenges imposed by rapid social change and a complex economy.

VICTOR JONES

Metropolitan Authorities

There is no let-up in the pressure to shift responsibility for governmental activities from the general city or county government to special authorities and independent boards. Throughout the country parking authorities, traffic authorities, airport authorities, and redevelopment agencies are being added to the large number of existing police and fire commissions, sewerage commissions, soil conservation districts, school boards, water commissions, utility commissions, park boards, recreation boards, health boards, hospital boards, library boards, museum boards, housing agencies, public works boards, cemetery boards and other boards.[1]

It does not follow, however, that each function of government should be separately organized over a distinctive area. The logic can be carried further, of course, and appropriate areas designated for each of the activities that together are called a function and then

[1] See Victor Jones, "The Withering Away of the City," *Public Management*, XXXII (December, 1950), 270-74. The President's Water Resources Policy Commission recommends that "The States and Federal Government should encourage the formation of metropolitan water districts to develop and transmit necessary water to meet in the most economical way the requirements of a group of communities when those communities are dependent upon the same source of water supply or when existing water supplies prove inadequate" (*A Water Policy for the American People* [Washington, D.C., 1950], p. 184). This recommendation along with other excerpts from the report are reproduced and distributed by the Public Health Service.

The Governor's Committee on Community Readjustment in its *Report on Collateral Problems Likely to Result from Location of a Steel Mill in Connecticut* (Hartford, April 27, 1951) recommended special metropolitan districts for the Norwich-New London Area for water supply, for the collection and treatment of sanitary sewage, and for public health activities (pp. 6-8).

Reprinted from *The Future of Cities and Urban Redevelopment*, Coleman Woodbury, ed., by permission of The University of Chicago Press. © 1953 by The University of Chicago.

for subactivities. The same considerations when applied to a complex of activities, more or less related to each other, make up the case for a general metropolitan government.

This does not mean that it is necessary or desirable to centralize all or even most of the functions of local government in a single metropolitan government. Undoubtedly any satisfactory and feasible metropolitan government which may be developed will be a variant of what is known as the borough or federated type.[2] But the distribution of authority between the central and constituent units should not be based on "guild" autonomy.[3] Persistently in this country and in England as government has undertaken new activities or as crises have arisen in the administration of established functions, the professionalism of one group of specialists after another has shown itself in the demand for a preferential position. The most powerful group fighting for the autonomy of public schools is the professional educators. They now claim that educational administration should be considered as a fourth branch of government and accorded the constitutional protection of separation from the other three powers.

Tugwell and others have talked the same way about planning; Bauer and others about municipal utilities; Wier and others about parks and recreation. Some housing and redevelopment officials are using the same argument — their function is so important to the general welfare and the methods of carrying out their function are so technical that their objectives can be accomplished only if they are protected against interference by nonprofessionals.

There is nothing sinister about this attitude of specialists. Every person who is responsible for doing something should feel that the activity is important to the community. It only becomes dangerous when this professional attitude is tied up with a special interest pressure group powerful enough to take the activity out of reach of the periodic determination by the community of how its limited resources will be allocated.

This is a political judgment, not a scientific application of a formula. It is so complex and continuous that the so-called budgetary control (authority to vote appropriations) of a city council over

[2] See Report of the California Assembly Interim Committee on State and Local Taxation (January, 1951), Part III, "The Borough System of Government for Metropolitan Areas."

[3] Luther Gulick, "Politics, Administration, and the New Deal," *Annals*, Vol. 169 (September, 1933), p. 56.

boards and commissions is insufficient. Unless important questions of policy come up to the chief administrator and the council, or can be brought up by interested or aggrieved citizens, the raising or lowering of appropriation requests once a year will be little more than a formal act of ratification. And there is always the motive and the rationalization, from the point of view of special interest, for the clientèle and staff of a quasi-independent administrative board to urge financial as well as administrative autonomy.

All proponents of a new independent authority and defenders of existing boards and commissions claim the general city government cannot do the job. And it must be admitted that the actions, or lack of action, of many city governments give color to the charge.

The old battle cry, "Take our interest out of politics," either camouflages an attempt to substitute special politics for general politics or indicates a withdrawal from the everlasting struggle to change the political decisions being made in the community. Frequently both motives are involved. If "politics" refers to partisan or personal patronage and influence, the experience of special boards and commissions does not assure us that their independence of the city council or chief administrator will result in a merit system. Special boards and commissions, to paraphrase Anderson and Weidner, "have not been free from spoils politics but have developed methods of self-enrichment of their own."

Furthermore, the proliferation of autonomous agencies distracts the attention of important groups in the community from the general government. It encourages people with a strong interest in one aspect of community life and development to write off the general government and to feel that the community is sound if *only* it can have good schools, or if *only* it has adequate downtown parking facilities, or if *only* the slums are torn down. This is not only unfortunate because it diverts interest from securing or maintaining an active, effective, and efficient city government, but because it weakens the general government for its most important function of bringing the complementary and divergent interests of a locality together into a community.

If the proponents of administrative autonomy use the term "politics" to refer to the making of policies, then autonomy does not take the activity out of politics. It merely substitutes one kind of politics for another. It may be easier for a special interest group to play that kind of politics than to run the gauntlet of other interests. The observation has been frequently made that under an independent regulatory commission it is easy for the regulated to become the regulators. This happens easily enough in any government however organized, but it is much easier to bring about when the activity is given an organizational protection against "interference" by the chief administrator and council.

The political nature of the decisions of independent boards is well described by Luther Gulick:

> The vital political problems which arise in government are not the questions of patronage. They are the questions of basic social and economic policy which serve to give fundamental direction to social and economic forces. For example, a port authority has the power to determine whether a community as a whole will expand as a raw material center or as a manufacturing center by the priorities which it gives to port facilities, loading and unloading equipment, wharfage rates, and rail and road connections. Toll rates on bridges will determine the rapidity of suburban development and the rise of real-estate values as well as the time of obsolescence of prior investments in ferries and commuter rail services.
>
> The location of inland terminals, the creation of central bus facilities, the elimination of grade crossings, the arrangement of tunnel entrances and exits will determine the immediate and ultimate fate of entire neighborhoods, piling value increments here and destroying values there in spectacular fashion. Such a simple matter as the location of the express stops on the rapid transit system decides whether a street will be developed with high rental properties or with more modest shops and apartments. Similarly zone fares on city transit systems, and the system of water rates or electric power rates cannot fail to create their patterns of realty and housing developments and to influence the distribution of wealth and welfare for the people of the area.[4]

And Frederick L. Bird, who is certainly no enemy of independent authorities, says that:

> When you stop to think of it, an independent agency in charge of a basic service, that can fix its own rates, determine its own policies for supplying service and making extensions, and formulate and approve its long-range plans, holds an almost dictatorial control over how, and where, and how much a community is to develop residentially, commercially, and industrially.[5]

[4] "Authorities and How To Use Them," *The Tax Review* (November, 1947), pp. 50-51.
[5] Frederick L. Bird, "The Contribution of Authorities to Efficient Municipal Management," *The Authority* (December, 1949), p. 5.

It is often said that a metropolitan special district can be developed into a multipurpose metropolitan government. Nowhere has this occurred and after years of hopeful waiting, it appears to be an unlikely development. The two examples that have been frequently cited of special districts evolving into multipurpose metropolitan districts are the Port of New York Authority and the Metropolitan District Commission in the Boston area. The latter was organized in 1919 by consolidating three special metropolitan districts: sewage organized in 1889, parks in 1891, and water in 1895. In 1923, the Commission established a division of regional planning, but this function was transferred in 1941 to the State Planning Board.[6] Instead of giving the function of planning and financing rapid transit to the District Commission, another special district, the Boston Metropolitan District, was created for this purpose in 1929. And in 1947, when the facilities of the Boston Elevated Railway Company became public property, another special district, the Metropolitan Transit Authority, was created to operate them.[7]

The Port of New York Authority, established in 1921 by compact between New York and New Jersey, failed to accomplish the immediate purpose for which it was created — to secure the adoption by the railroads of a comprehensive plan of integrated freight terminals and switching arrangements in order to reduce the cost of terminal distribution and collection of freight, and to make all parts of the area accessible to any railroad.[8]

But in thirty years of its existence, it has helped to tie together the two parts of the metropolitan area cut by the Hudson River by constructing and operating six bridges and tunnels. After decades of controversy, planning at cross-purposes and recrimination by state and local agencies, the Port Authority, as Frederick L. Bird put it, has conquered the interstate water boundary. It has, furthermore, taken over the development and operation under long-term leases of Port Newark and of the three major airports of the region,

[6] The Metropolitan District Commission has ex-officio membership on the State Planning Board.

[7] Trustees of the Boston Metropolitan District, *Report* (June, 1950), pp. 3-4.

[8] It did establish in 1932 a Union Inland Freight Terminal in Manhattan where less-than-carload freight is handled for eight railroads. See E. W. Bard, *The Port of New York Authority* (New York: Columbia University Press, 1942), pp. 3-173, 313-19. Only passing attention is given to this phase of the Authority's activities by Frederick L. Bird, *A Study of the Port of New York Authority* (New York: Dun and Bradstreet, 1949).

Newark, LaGuardia, and Idlewild.[9] A central bus terminal has been built in Manhattan, a motor freight terminal is operated in lower Manhattan, and another has been constructed in Newark. It operates a grain terminal in Brooklyn.

None of its operations are financed by taxes. All of its revenues come from service charges, mostly vehicular tolls, which are pledged as security for the Authority's bonds. Since 1931, all surplus revenues have been pooled in a general reserve fund.[10]

In considering whether the Port of New York Authority is the kind of governmental organization we desire to handle metropolitan problems, the following observations are relevant:

1. The Authority has been a successful means of establishing jurisdiction for certain limited but important purposes over a metropolitan area bisected by state boundary lines. It has recently been imitated in the St. Louis–East St. Louis and in the Philadelphia–Camden areas.

2. It does not follow, however, that a metropolitan authority with jurisdiction in two or more states has to be organized as an agency of the state government. It is probably legally, administratively, and politically easier to so organize it. But we have to decide whether we want the metropolitan community to be governed by agencies responsible — however tenuously — to the state government or by agencies of local government. If we desire the latter, then however difficult it may be, we must devise a system of local selection and representation that can operate in two or more states.

3. Complete reliance upon service charges as a source of revenue will make it impossible for an authority to undertake nonrevenue-producing activities. It is unlikely to undertake projects or functions which have low-income producing value. The problems of a metropolitan community cannot be solved by giving to an area-wide authority those functions that are self-supporting and leaving all other governmental functions to existing units of local government. Frederick L. Bird recognized this when he wrote that

The Port Authority's limitations as an agency of regional govern-

[9] See Bird, *op. cit.*, for a description of the authority's operations, financing, and plans. The political negotiations among New York City, Robert Moses, the airlines, civic associations, and the Port Authority are discussed and analyzed in Herbert Kaufman's "Gotham in the Air Age," *Public Administration and Policy Development: A Case Book* (Harold Stein, ed., New York: Harcourt Brace and Co., 1952), pp. 143-97.

[10] For the financing of the Authority's operations, see Bird, *op. cit.*, pp. 41-82, and Bard, *op. cit.*, pp. 226-66.

ment are implicit in the absence of a taxing power. This is sometimes cited as a defect in the plans of the two States for the cooperative development of the Port district, in that self-support through
service charges is a too restrictive test of the public functions that
should be performed on a regional basis.[11]

4. Even in the field of highway traffic, the Authority has acted
apart from the other public agencies that are also responsible for
moving and parking vehicles in the metropolitan area. This is in
large part the result of the failure of other public agencies to work
with the Authority.[12] Certainly, the success of the Port Authority
and of [Robert] Moses in facilitating the vehicular movement of
passengers and goods into New York City has aggravated the problem of traffic congestion on the city streets. There is no official plan
for moving goods and people and for taking care of them when
they reach their destination. There are many plans, but they have
not been integrated.

By no means can the Port Authority alone be blamed for the failure to produce a metropolitan traffic-transit-transportation plan. But
E. W. Bard believes that its organization, its structural relation to
other agencies of government and its policies keep it from acting
effectively even in this relatively narrow field as a metropolitan
government.

> The Port Authority was conceived to function as a regional plan-
> ning agency, but was also clothed with power itself to make the
> plans effective in so far as appropriate through construction and
> operation. Other parts of the plans were premised upon action by
> the owners of private property or by the states or municipalities.
> Many aspects of these plans have been described in preceding chap-
> ters. In facing the problems of seeing them translated into reality
> the Port Authority has been structurally weak in certain respects.
> First, its proprietary powers were limited by ability to borrow upon
> the promise of charges to be collected. This weakness has been

---

[11] *Op. cit.*, pp. 186-87. He does not meet the argument, but makes the
counter-claim that no "political agency even partially dependent on tax
support" would have "been able to maintain the continuity of policy and
planning and to develop the special techniques that are essential to the
businesslike operation of public service enterprises."

[12] See the newspaper files for the last two years for conflicts between
the Port Authority and the governor of New York over the location of the
Hudson River bridge unit of the proposed New York State Thruway and
the conflict between the Authority on the one hand, and Robert Moses
and the New York City Planning Commission on the other, over a third
tube for the Lincoln Tunnel.

largely removed by the creation of a credit base or supplemental guarantee in the general reserve fund. Second, powers to regulate the use of private property in conformity with its plans were denied. Third, the autonomy of the Port Authority has so far removed it from the chief executive of either state, or for that matter of any city, as to deny it any real influence on executive policy.

On the other hand, this same autonomy does yield independence and continuity of which greater use might have been made. Actually the Port Authority's planning activities have followed narrowly in the wake of its first major effort, or else have been confined to the direct needs of its vehicular projects. An exception might be noted in the Port Authority's work with suburban transit. The techniques of coordinated study employed in that field might very well be applied to other fields, notably highway development. The greatest power possessed by the Port Authority, which it has not used to advantage, is the power of publicity. At no time since the campaign for the Comprehensive Plan has it done anything comparable to stir the public imagination. The Port Authority seems to have become frightened by the specter of controversy. Its policy has become totally receptive rather than aggressive.[13]

5. A corporate form of metropolitan government in which the selection of the authority or district commission members is once or more removed from the electoral controls may give us efficient and effective government but it cannot give us good government. It is not necessary, nor is it desirable, for all policy-making officials to be directly elected by popular vote. They should, however, be subject to the budgetary control of popularly elected legislators and their policies should be subject to debate and discussion.

Of course, any legislative body, whether it have jurisdiction over the matter or not, may debate anything it wishes. The object, however, is not futile and irresponsible talk. Our uneasiness should not be alloyed by saying that the ordinary municipal governments are frequently corrupt, irresponsible, ineffective, and inefficient. Our job is to make them responsible and efficient.[14] This cannot be done by slicing off the most important functions of local government and handing them over to one or several autonomous bodies.

[13] Bard, *op. cit.*, pp. 319-20.
[14] See Coleman Woodbury, "The Background and Prospects of Urban Redevelopment in the United States," *The Future of Cities and Urban Redevelopment* (Chicago: University of Chicago Press, 1953), pp. 671 ff.

STANLEY SCOTT AND JOHN CORZINE

Special Districts in the
San Francisco Bay Area

There are nearly five hundred special districts in the nine-county Bay Area, excluding school districts, multi-county districts, irrigation districts, and a number of others whose functions are not urban in character. Each of these districts normally performs only one municipal-type function in the area it serves. The few types of districts that are empowered to provide a range of services as the need arises, such as the community services districts, have not done so for the most part, but have remained de facto single-purpose districts.

Normally, two or more special districts are found in any unincorporated area having urban service needs. Fire protection districts, highway lighting districts, sanitary and county sanitation districts, county service areas, and sewer and sewer maintenance districts, are the most numerous types in the Bay Area. Hospital districts, fire protection districts, municipal water districts, county water districts, flood control and water conservation districts, and sanitary districts, in that order, reported the largest expenditure during fiscal year 1960-61.

Approximately half of the districts in the Bay Area are governed directly by the county boards of supervisors. These entities are, in effect, special taxing areas, through which the county government can raise funds to finance services within the districts. Such county-controlled districts are not a primary concern of this report. The other half of the districts are autonomous units, being governed by

Reprinted from *Special Districts in the San Francisco Bay Area: Some Problems and Issues*, pp. 1-11, 13-14, 16-18, with the permission of the authors and the Institute of Governmental Studies.

their own local boards. Most of these boards are directly elected (193). A minority of the districts (41) have appointed or ex-officio boards.

The special districts treated in this study have been established primarily to provide municipal-type services in urban communities that do not have a municipal government. Thus, one would expect districts to occur: (1) in areas with a moderate degree of urbanization, and (2) in areas outside the boundaries of existing cities. In fact, they are found most often on the fringes of incorporated areas, and within some of the newer and smaller cities.

There is a rough correlation between a county's unincorporated urban population and the number of special districts. San Francisco, consisting solely of incorporated territory has no special districts of the kinds considered here. Los Angeles County, which has the largest urban unincorporated population in the state also ranks first in the number of special districts. Sacramento County ranks second on both scores, and Contra Costa County fifth. Alameda County, with most of its urbanized area now incorporated, has comparatively few districts.

Superficially the chronicle of special districts in the Bay Area reads like a success story. Under district auspices many services are being supplied to important suburban communities that would otherwise have annexed to cities or incorporated separately. To be sure, the use of special districts in place of city government may be advantageous in some communities that are lightly urbanized, are growing slowly, and need only one or two services. But the proliferation of districts, and their retention even after the communities served have clearly matured into urban status, have raised many questions and resulted in a number of serious criticisms of autonomous local districts. These problems and issues are reviewed in the following sections.

Low Political Visibility

Special district elections are scheduled according to statute. The election date varies, depending on the type of district. Fire protection districts, for example, hold their elections annually on the first Tuesday of April; sanitary districts, biennially, on the second Tuesday in September in even numbered years; county water districts, biennially, on the fourth Tuesday in March every second year after the district's formation; and public utility districts on the first Tuesday in May every second year after formation. The elections are seldom given wide publicity; the local papers may or may not carry the returns. Unless a controversy has arisen in a district, the voters are not likely to be aware of the identity of either the incumbent directors or the opposing candidates, if any.

The result is very low voter participation. A recent sample revealed a median turnout at special district elections to be 27 percent, significantly lower than for either county elections (67 percent), or city elections (45 percent).[1] The turnout for special district elections is also normally much lower than the participation level in statewide primary or general elections. These averaged 63.8 percent and 80.7 percent, respectively, for the 1950-60 period. . . .

Low participation is, however, only part of the story of limited voter interest and awareness. District elections are often canceled because there are no contests, and the county board of supervisors simply re-appoints the unopposed incumbents. For example, 62 sanitary district and 121 fire protection district directors' elections were canceled during 1956-62, far more than were held. A survey of fire protection districts in Alameda County failed to find evidence that a single election had been held in any of the county's fire protection districts during the period 1955-62. The following comment by the secretary of the Tiburon Fire Protection District in Marin County dramatizes the infrequency of elections:

> In the last 13 years there have been only two elections in this district . . . only one commissioner is on this board because he was elected by the people. The remainder have been appointed or reappointed by the board of supervisors because nobody cared enough to contest their chairs.[2]

One reason for voter apathy and lack of concern is that citizens are not informed about or interested in district activities. Even if they were, the sheer number of districts and the frequency of elections make impossible demands upon the voters' time and attention. A sanitary district representative commented: "I know of two areas where there are five overlapping districts. They haven't had an election for eight or ten years because of the enormous trouble in-

[1] Don Koepp, "Nonpartisan Elections in the San Francisco Bay Area," *Public Affairs Report*, Vol. III No. 4, Bureau of Public Administration, University of California, Berkeley (August, 1962), p. 3.
[2] *San Rafael Independent Journal*, September 19, 1962.

volved.[3] Still other reasons for low voter interest have been suggested:

> The distribution of the range of turnout into two distinct groups, that of county governments, unified school districts, and city governments, and that of elementary, special, high school and junior college districts, suggests that turnout may be related to a sense of community identification or, at least, community visibility. In those elections where definite and familiar geographical boundaries exist, as in counties, cities, and school districts having boundaries coterminous with cities, turnout is higher than in elections for those units having boundaries which are diffuse, overlapping, or unknown to the voter, i.e., *the single-purpose districts,* the small elementary school districts, and the larger but overlapping high school and junior college districts. [Emphasis supplied] [4]

An extreme example of lack of district "visibility," or in this case, even of self-awareness, concerns the Brentwood Recreation and Park District in Contra Costa County. Under a recent law the three types of recreation districts were given until July 1, 1962 to reorganize according to new provisions of the Government Code, otherwise they would be dissolved automatically. The Brentwood district, whose only facility is a one square-block park in the City of Brentwood, failed to reorganize. As reported in a news story ". . . the district's five directors were stunned when it was accidentally discovered the district had ceased to exist seven months ago."[5] This raised some difficult problems regarding ownership and disposition of the park. It was necessary to pass emergency legislation at the 1963 session to permit recreation of the district, thus affording Brentwood a way out of its dilemma.

Low Fiscal Visibility

With few exceptions, the autonomous special districts have their taxes collected by the county. The districts submit a budget to the county government, which levies the necessary tax rate to raise the

[3] California. Assembly Interim Committee on Municipal and County Government, Hearings on Special Districts — Sewers, Sacramento, California, September 1958 (mimeo) Statement by Eugene K. Storgis, Counsel, Stege Sanitary District, p. 32.

[4] Koepp, *op. cit.,* p. 3.

[5] "Seen the Park District? Brentwood Can't Find it," *Oakland Tribune,* February 12, 1963.

amount required. The county's role is ministerial: The board of supervisors has no effective power to review and adjust tax requests submitted by the autonomous districts. Because the tax bill comes from the county, however, most voters assume that the county is in some way finally responsible for district tax levies. This partially explains the lack of awareness of the average taxpayer regarding the financial operations of districts. The phenomenon is analogous to the low political visibility just described. Since interest is minimal, special district budget deliberations are not observed. As with district elections, little or no publicity is given to the actions of the district boards. When citizens are upset over the activities of a district their normal response is to direct their complaints either to the county board of supervisors or to a municipal jurisdiction which they consider responsible.

Because of the large number of districts, all counties except San Francisco find it necessary to figure different tax rates for a huge array of tax code areas:

> San Mateo County, for example, has well over 400 different code areas for taxing purposes with approximately 75 special districts performing 8 to 12 different functions. The county taxpayer, when presented with his bill, often has very little realization that the Board of Supervisors is responsible for less than a third of his total tax rate and yet his ire and admonitions to do something about these growing tax bills are directed at the Board of Supervisors — not, it should be noted, against the various district boards about whom he knows very little, if anything.[6]

Most Bay Area counties publish a compilation of the tax rates assessed in the county, broken down by code areas. Sometimes this is sent out with the annual tax statement. Contra Costa County, in appreciation of the fact that many homeowners never see their tax bills — because they are handled by the financial institutions holding the mortgages — sends out a tax breakdown with veterans' exemption slips as well 'as with tax bills. Marin County includes this information in its final budget; San Mateo and Alameda send out single sheet charts; and San Mateo and Santa Clara counties compile separate books of tax rates and property valuations which they make

[6] California. Assembly Interim Committee on Municipal and County Government, Transcript of Hearing, Sacramento, California, January 17, 1962 (mimeo) Statement by E. Robert Stallings, County Manager, San Mateo County, p. 52.

available to taxpayers. Each of these efforts represents an attempt to inform the taxpayer of the maze of jurisdictions and tax rates that make up his total property tax bill.

The unincorporated community of Lafayette in Contra Costa County provides a good example of the variety of property tax rates levied on the average suburban home.

1963-64 PROPERTY TAX RATES, LAFAYETTE
(Unincorporated Area in Contra Costa County)

1. County tax rate	$2.345
2. Flood Control and Water Conservation District	.020
a. Flood control zone 3B	.180
3. County service area, library	.075
4. Contra Costa County Water Agency	no tax
5. Lafayette Fire Protection District	1.008
6. Mosquito Abatement District	.025
7. Central Contra Costra Costa Sanitary District	.570
8. Alamo-Lafayette Cemetery District	.028
9. East Bay Municipal Utility District	.200
10. San Francisco Bay Area Rapid Transit District	.084
11. Bay Area Air Pollution Control District	.010
12. Lafayette Elementary School District	3.177
13. Acalanes High School District	2.371
14. Contra Costa Junior College District	.416
15. County schools service fund for children who are severely retarded mentally	.003
16. Education of handicapped children	.001
Total	$10.513

County taxes amount to only $2.345 of the $10.513 total rate — or about 20 percent.

Adverse Effect on Local Governmental Structure

Districts have sometimes been employed strictly as transitional devices to provide essential services during the early states of urbanization. This appears to be an appropriate role for them, at least in situations where annexation is not feasible. Too often, however, districts have been created when they were not really needed, or have been retained as permanent entities in the face of continued growth and the resulting need for more effective local government.

Despite the need for general-purpose local government in urban areas, overly permissive special district legislation has made it possible for important portions of the metropolitan area to urbanize and develop without ever having to incorporate as a municipality or annex to an adjacent city. Districts have, in fact, sometimes been the primary *obstacle* to municipal incorporation or annexation. Sanitary districts and fire protection districts, especially, have sometimes prevented or hindered municipalities from extending their boundaries logically. Such districts, actively operating on the outskirts of a city, will often resist annexation or incorporation movements which threaten their existence. Once an area has its water, sewer and fire problems solved, it is likely to ignore the less obvious advantages of annexing to a nearby municipality. Thus a city may be faced with unplanned commercial and residential development on its borders which it can neither control nor annex. . . .

Sanitary districts, fire protection districts, water districts and park and recreation districts may hamper the efforts of local government to achieve coordinated planning. For example, independent special districts may be formed to provide sewers and water in an isolated area, making possible premature housing development inconsistent with county and city general planning. In Contra Costa County, fire districts have proven an effective obstacle to county plans for consolidation of fire protection facilities.[7] Other examples of districts which have in some manner or other resisted annexation and thus have probably affected adversely the development of a more rational governmental structure include the Agnew Sanitary District, now dissolved, which resisted absorption by the City of Santa Clara; the Tennyson Fire Protection District, whose original territory has been almost wholly absorbed by the City of Hayward, the East Vallejo Fire Protection District, which levies a $1.00 tax rate to contract with the City of Vallejo for fire protection, and the Cupertino Sanitary District in Santa Clara County. These are only a few examples; city and county officials in the Bay Area could name many more.

[7] This comment should not imply that fire district consolidation is necessarily more desirable than other organizational approaches. Some municipal officials in Contra Costa County believe the cities should assume fire protection as a municipal function, and should serve their unincorporated fringe areas under contract. In any event, the existing fire districts would probably oppose this suggestion as vigorously as they do district consolidation.

A specific case of the adverse effect of special districts on local governmental arrangements is provided by the complicated situation involving the City of Walnut Creek, the City of Pleasant Hill, and the Pleasant Hill Recreation and Park District, all in Contra Costa County. At one time certain groups in the then unincorporated community of Pleasant Hill — which is encompassed by the Pleasant Hill Recreation and Park District — wished to annex *in toto* to the nearby City of Walnut Creek. Step by step annexation was suggested by Walnut Creek officials, but was rejected by Pleasant Hill. Walnut Creek then agreed to annex the whole area, but the annexation election failed. Directors of the recreation and park district were active in the fight against annexation. If the annexation had succeeded, the district's functions would presumably have been taken over by the city recreation department.

The recreation and park district's directors then actively promoted the idea of incorporating Pleasant Hill. Subsequently Pleasant Hill was incorporated. The new city did not choose to attempt a withdrawal, although a study made before the incorporation of Pleasant Hill suggested that, after incorporation, the Pleasant Hill Recreation and Park District should be dissolved and its functions assumed by the city. The reasons advanced were that recreation and park maintenance is a normal city function, and that significant savings would accrue from consolidating of maintenance, administration and overhead.[8]

Potential resistance from the recreation and park district was an important reason why the City of Pleasant Hill did not attempt to take over the district's functions. There may have been another factor: Many municipalities, especially new or newly expanded cities, do not necessarily wish to dissolve the special districts serving them. By retaining several districts, a city can maintain a low property tax rate and pride itself on its thriftiness. Such frugality is usually an illusion, however, because the total tax rate includes the district levies.

The Pleasant Hill situation is further complicated by a small area lying within the Pleasant Hill Recreation and Park District, and containing some twenty or thirty householders, that has been annexed by Walnut Creek. The residents are faced with double taxation — by the district and by the city — for recreation services. (The dis-

---

[8] Public Affairs Research Inc., *Pleasant Hill Government Study*, (August, 1958), p. 28.

trict's rate is approximately $0.50). The people involved and the officials of Walnut Creek have appealed to the district's board, to no avail. The board states that withdrawal would work a financial hardship on the rest of the district.[9] The City of Walnut Creek argues the area is not a substantive portion of the district, and that the homeowners joined the city with the intention of taking advantage of the municipal recreation program.

Repeated attempts have been made to amend the law, which does not allow for automatic withdrawal upon annexation. It leaves to the district board the decision whether or not to allow an area to withdraw. Liberalizing amendments were defeated in both the 1961 and 1963 sessions of the legislature, primarily due to the influence of the recreation and park district's association lobby.

There is still another complicating factor. Walnut Creek and Pleasant Hill both have their eyes on unincorporated area lying between the two cities. The existence of the recreation and park district, and its policy against giving up territory even when annexed to a city, tends to favor Pleasant Hill by militating against annexation to Walnut Creek. This is because areas going into Walnut Creek would be exposing themselves to double taxation along with the troubled householders mentioned above. The situation has led Pleasant Hill city interests to oppose liberalization of the district law.

In a nearby area an aggressive sanitary district almost succeeded in stifling the growth of the City of Concord in 1954 by attempting to annex land all around the city. The district was already operating to the south and west of Concord, and it was proposing annexations to the east. This situation not only enabled developers outside the city to bargain with the city council about development standards in the additions by threatening to join the sanitary district, but also it threatened to stop the city's growth. The city won a major annexation election despite vigorous opposition by the sanitary district. If the city had not won the election, it is conceivable that Concord might now have little more than 12,000 residents, instead of the current 56,000. Walnut Creek is included in this same sanitary district, and had a 1962 population of only 10,000, although the surrounding unincorporated territory comprises an area and population hardly less than that of Concord. . . .

[9] "Recreation District Fights Annex Bill," *Oakland Tribune,* May 8, 1963.

Ease of Creation and Difficulty of Dissolution

Districts have a good deal of appeal as the "easy way out" for communities in need of a specific service. The creation of a district is often believed to be a less expensive way of obtaining service than incorporation as a municipality or annexation to an existing city. Thus there is a good deal less resistance to the creation of a special district than to municipal incorporation or annexation. Also, the legal provisions for district formation are often less strict and easier to comply with than are municipal incorporation or annexation requirements.

Furthermore, it is much simpler to create a new district than to dissolve an old one. The legal requirements for formation are often easily met — especially in the absence of significant community opposition. People interested in acquiring a service have only to hire an attorney or appeal to the county for help in setting up a special district.

Once a district is in existence, however, vested interest groups grow up around it, having a stake in its perpetuation. Employees and members of the board of directors often oppose district dissolution, consolidation, or annexation by a city. On a larger scale, many types of districts and/or district employees are organized into statewide associations. These groups usually oppose any state legislation that would curtail their members' activities. Further, extraordinary majorities are often required in dissolution elections, whereas formation is usually accomplished by a simple majority vote, or sometimes merely by a petition signed by a minority of landowners. And there are still a few instances of districts with no statutory provision for dissolution.

Following are a few examples of marginal districts that cling to life. The East Vallejo Fire Protection District, remnant of a much larger district that once almost surrounded the City of Vallejo, receives fire protection services from the city under contract. The district remains in existence for the sole purpose of levying a tax of approximately $1 per $100 of assessed valuation to pay for the contracted fire protection. A somewhat similar case is presented by the Tennyson Fire Protection District in Alameda County. Most of the area previously served by the district has been annexed to and is

served by the City of Hayward. The district continues to resist annexation, despite the logic of such action, as indicated by the fact
that the district's only remaining fire station is actually within the
city.

In Contra Costa County six county water districts were recently
dissolved whose functions had been taken over by East Bay MUD
years before. After these districts had the bonds retired there was
no reason for their continued existence. Yet it took a great deal of
encouragement and energy on the part of the county before the
districts were finally liquidated.

Use of Districts by Developers

Although municipal-type districts were originally intended to
provide the residents of an unincorporated urban community with
limited public services, in recent years they have sometimes been
employed in totally unpopulated areas. Thus a land developer may
utilize such districts to facilitate the creation of a new residential
community on a tract of raw land. The result is a public agency
that is, in fact, an individual or a private company "wearing another hat" and thereby assuming the privileges and advantages of
governmental status. Unquestionably this practice has facilitated
development, but it has also often left the public interest without
adequate protection. . . .

The Estero Municipal Improvement District in San Mateo County,
and the Embarcadero Improvement District in Santa Barbara
County were created in 1960 by special legislative acts. Each law
established an independent special district in a designated area for
the purpose of financing utility installation, other public improvements, and municipal-type services in connection with land development.

Each district was to be governed by a three-man board elected
by owners of land in the district, who were given one vote per $1.00
of assessed valuation of land owned. These provisions made certain
that the owners (developers) would select the districts' governing
bodies during the period of development. The districts were also
empowered to issue tax-exempt general obligation bonds on a two-
thirds vote by land owners, who were again given one vote per
$1.00 assessed valuation owned. Again, this provision meant that the

developers could approve the issuance of governmental general obligation bonds.

Ninety-five percent of the property within the Estero district is owned by T. Jack Foster and Sons. The real estate development firm is reputed to have paid $12.9 million for its property, which consists of 2,606 acres of marshy land in San Francisco Bay. Shortly after the Estero district was created, it authorized $55 million in general obligation bonds. These funds will be used to fill and reclaim land, lay streets and provide utilities. Plans call for a community of some 35,000 people when "Foster City" is fully developed.

> Seated in offices shared by the Foster firm and the Estero District, the developers and district officers predict Foster City will be worth $550 million when completed about eight years from now. As the district's land-filling operations proceed, the Foster firm intends to sell most of the lots to builders who, in turn, will put up and sell houses. The bonded debt of the district will be a first lien on the home owners' properties.[10]

The Estero project has the approval of the San Mateo County manager and the board of supervisors. Up to this point it appears to be a well-run enterprise. However, the Assembly interim committee pointed out that nothing in its organization, except the integrity of the developer, and safeguards which he has voluntarily employed, prevent an occurrence similar to that which took place in the Embarcadero project.

The aim of the Embarcadero Municipal Improvement District was to transform 1,320 acres of ranch land into a community. The two developers and their private secretary comprised the board of directors. Operating through the district, the developers authorized the issuance of $8,874,000 of general obligation bonds, and in January, 1961 sold $1,207,000 as a first issue.

Later, when a Los Angeles mortgage firm that had helped finance the enterprise failed, the state investigated, and a Los Angeles County grand jury indicted the developers on 35 counts of grand theft, misuse of public funds, and conspiracy. As it turned out, the developers had misappropriated private development funds and

[10] Norman C. Miller, "Tax-Free Enterprise: Land Developers Form Districts with Right to Sell Bonds," *Wall Street Journal*, (Pacific Coast Edition) March 14, 1962, p. 1, 9. See also Sidney P. Allen, "A New Kingdom for San Mateo," *San Francisco Chronicle*, Nov. 6, 1962, p. 44.

258   STANLEY SCOTT AND JOHN CORZINE

had also obtained district bond money through a false statement
when improvements were purchased by the district. The developers
were convicted of over 30 counts of grand theft and violations of
the corporation code.[11]

The following statement was made by Marshall S. Mayer of the
investment frauds unit in the Attorney General's Office:

> The Embarcadero District illustrates the major weaknesses of spe-
> cial laws which are designed to permit land promoters to create
> public agencies to aid in the development of subdivision land. When
> laws are tailormade for this purpose, when they omit basic govern-
> mental safeguards, such as prohibition against self-dealing, separa-
> tion of governmental powers, and when they provide no audit con-
> trols by independent bodies, the likelihood of abuse corresponds
> directly to the opportunity for abuse. The Embarcadero District
> sadly reflects this truism.[12]

District Diseconomies and Financial Problems

Because of their relatively small scale, the operations of many
special districts are subject to unavoidable diseconomies. One example is the sewer or water systems sometimes constructed by small
districts in rapidly growing areas. These limited facilities may soon
be outmoded or out-grown, whereupon costly replacements may be
necessary. Or several different jurisdictions, each attempting to deal
with portions of a larger watershed, may build separate sewer and
collector systems that are not only inadequate, but are in the long
run more expensive than a unified system would have been.

Fire districts provide one of the best examples of built-in diseconomies in district operations. The following comment refers to conditions in Sacramento County, but it can also be applied to many
situations in the Bay Area:

> Arbitrary political boundaries and limited size and assessment valu-
> ation militate against efficient and effective provision of services.
> An example of this can be seen in the fact that in the unincorporated
> area there are 26 fire districts. Location of fire stations, for instance,
> is often determined on the basis of service within the political

[11] California. Assembly Interim Committee on Municipal and County
Government, *Committee Report on the Uses of Special Assessment Procedures and Independent Special Districts to Aid Land Development.*
(1963), p. 34.
[12] *Ibid.*

boundaries of the district, with little or no attention given to service to other areas adjacent to the district, but located in other fire districts. No possibility for automatic distribution of equipment between districts exists so that in districts where rapid urbanization is taking place rural-type equipment becomes surplus, rather than being shifted to the rural areas of another district. Such logical distribution would be possible if there were a countrywide fire department.[13]

A Contra Costa County official recently commented in similar fashion on fire district diseconomies in the central Contra Costa area. There are surplus fire stations, he contended, in several of the county's fire districts, a condition that is caused by the multiplicity of fire-fighting jurisdictions.[14] Many of these problems could be remedied, of course, by fire district consolidation or by their annexation, where appropriate, to cities providing fire protection. This possibility has been explored and is currently being pressed by the Contra Costa Taxpayers Association. At least one example of successful consolidation has taken place in Marin County, where the Homestead Valley Fire District and the Tamalpais Valley Fire District joined in 1962 and reduced the tax rate for the 1962-63 fiscal year, besides providing better service.

An entirely different problem is posed by the heavy reliance of most districts on the property tax. This limitation on revenue sources is compounded by the fact that many districts are located in suburban areas with little or no industry and only modest commercial development. In such areas the district property tax burden may fall rather heavily on the homeowner.

Municipal governments have a more diversified tax structure than special districts, being able to obtain revenues from a variety of sources. The sales and use tax alone amounted to nearly 19 percent of total city revenues (statewide) in 1961-62. The sales tax, together with such other non-property tax sources as licenses and permits (6.3 percent), fines and penalties (3.6 percent), and franchise taxes (1.1 percent), yielded nearly 30 percent of all California municipal revenue in 1961-62. The property tax provided only a little over 37 percent of total city revenues. As the State Controller has pointed out, 1961-62 municipal sales and use tax receipts alone represented a property tax rate equivalent of $0.91 per $100 of as-

[13] Letter from Mr. Fred Christensen, Information Officer, Sacramento County, September 19, 1962.
[14] *Lafayette Sun,* July 12, 1963.

sessed valuation. The combination of sales tax receipts and the other non-property sources mentioned above produced revenue equivalent to a property tax rate of approximately $1.60 per $100 assessed valuation. Considering that the statewide average municipal property tax rate is less than $2.00 and the median only $1.35, the importance of non-property tax sources to city government is clear. In addition to the non-property tax revenues, city governments also obtain 14.51 percent of their revenue from subventions from other governments, a source that is not normally available to special districts. These figures illustrate quite effectively the weaknesses of the special district as a means of raising revenue to support municipal-type services in unincorporated areas.

The question of *balancing* service costs is an unsolved problem in areas served by special districts. Cities can weigh the costs of their different services against one another. They cannot afford to let the cost of one service, such as fire protection, throw the whole city budget out of line, leading to neglect of other city functions. But, relying on special districts, an area may have highly developed fire protection and primitive police protection in the same community. There is also likely to be little or no coordination or communication among the local governmental agencies serving the same area. In fact, the district apparatus, by its nature, leads to competition for the tax dollar, and this fragmented government can be expensive.

Another question, that of the efficiency and public responsibility of independent special districts, has never been thoroughly investigated. Charges of inefficiency and irresponsibility are sometimes heard.[15] This is not to imply that all or even a sizable fraction of special districts are not well run. But the very lack of public knowledge about districts makes it difficult to assess the quality of their operations.

[15] Cf. Tiburon Fire Commission, Open Letter to the Grand Jury, (Jan. 4, 1962). This regards the condition of the Tiburon Fire Protection District as of May 1959 when a new board of commissioners took over. A record of poor management existed for the previous two years, including inflated prices paid for land, unaccounted for expenditures by the fire chief, and district debts exceeding the budget. A county water district in Contra Costa County — now dissolved — had enough money left over after its bonds were retired to pay the secretary of the district $15 a month from bank interest, without touching the capital. The other members of the district's board did not realize this — thinking the district had been dissolved automatically years before.

THOMAS R. DYE, CHARLES S. LIEBMAN,
OLIVER P. WILLIAMS, AND HAROLD HERMAN

Differentiation and Cooperation in a
Metropolitan Area

A distinguishing characteristic of metropolitan areas is areal specialization, or differentiation among spatially defined subpopulations
with respect to class or status, life style, and economic function.
To sociologists the relationship between specialization and urbanization is a commonplace. Their analysis has commonly centered
on isolating the types of specialization and their discrete effects.
Ecologists have described functionally differentiated zones and sectors and have even identified specific behavioral patterns associated
with the residents of particular areas. To the political scientist, one
of the most interesting attributes of metropolitan areas is the fact
that urban specialization very often coincides with political boundaries. Not only has the familiar bedroom community become incorporated as a political entity, but within metropolitan regions one
can also find industrial enclaves, recreational resorts, commercial
centers, intellectual retreats, racial and ethnic ghettoes, company
towns, and religious colonies which correspond roughly with local
political units.

A central hypothesis of this paper . . . is that social and economic differentiation among communities in a metropolitan area is
associated with differing local governmental policies. Local governmental decisions in a metropolitan area are made at hundreds of

"Differentiation and Cooperation in a Metropolitan Area" by Thomas R.
Dye, Charles S. Liebman, Oliver P. Williams and Harold Herman, reprinted from *Midwest Journal of Political Science,* Vol. 7, No. 2 (May
1963), by permission of the Wayne State University Press. Copyright
1963 by Wayne State University Press.

decision centers, each set in a separate social and economic environment, each responding to different types of interests, and each struggling to maintain a separate existence. As a result of these differing conditions, local governments can be expected to select differing policy alternatives designed to cope with specific interests within their constituencies.

Yet because of the interdependency of urban communities, some interests express themselves through demands for integrative or cooperative actions among local governments. Frequently it is suggested that certain services can be administered more economically and planned more intelligently when handled on an area-wide basis, or at least on a multi-jurisdictional basis. These arguments are often encountered with regard to schools, water supply, police protection, waste disposal, libraries, and street maintenance. Cooperative responses of local communities to jointly felt pressures of urbanization are not uncommon. The popular forms of cooperative responses among urban communities include the interjurisdictional agreement and joint authorities.

Students of political integration at the international level have suggested that policy concensus is the basis of viable political integration. If this same proposition is operative at the intermunicipal level and if the pattern of local policy choices is associated with social and economic differences among municipalities, then one should be able to observe the effect of urban differentiation on integrative arrangements in a metropolitan area. In short, it is our hypothesis that intermunicipal cooperation in a metropolitan area is a function of social and economic distance. Intermunicipal cooperation will tend to occur more frequently among communities which are similar in character and less frequently among highly differentiated communities. In this paper we shall attempt to set forth this hypothesis about the effect of urban differentiation on patterns of intermunicipal cooperation in an operational manner and to test it with reference to characteristics of local governments within the Philadelphia metropolitan area.

There are 238 municipalities covering the Pennsylvania sector of the Philadelphia metropolitan area. Although they range in size and density from the core city of Philadelphia with nearly two million persons to sparsely populated rural townships with less than 300 inhabitants, each of these local governments has substantially the same legal powers with which to structure its internal life and to cope with social and economic diversity. Recognizing that specialization and differentiation increases with urbanization, a distinction was made between the urban and semi-rural portions of the metropolitan area. The definition of urban as opposed to semi-rural was established at 500 persons per square mile, a figure chosen to approximate the state of urbanization of an area when urban services are generally initiated by the local government. According to this classification there were 90 urban and 135 semi-rural municipalities composing the study's sample; 12 communities were dropped from analysis because of large institutional populations which interfered with social and economic measurement.

In addition to the development of satisfactory measures of social, life style, and economic diversities, several other conditions were required for the hypothesis to be tested: (1) To have a cooperative arrangement, the potential cooperators must have or want to have the same service. (If one community has a police force and another neither has nor wants one, there is no basis for a cooperative operation of a police radio transmitter); (2) For a particular service, some municipalities must have selected a cooperative approach and others rejected it. (There must be a basis for comparing cooperating and non-cooperating communities); (3) While not absolutely essential, local governments must generally be contiguous for cooperation to be feasible. Thus in the analysis which follows, only the relationships between contiguous municipalities are subject to examination.

For the purposes of this paper, urban differentiation was operationally defined by three indices; these indices were selected for their relevance to decisions involving one or more of the most common types of interjurisdictional agreements. They are "social rank," market value per capita, and party voting.

1. *"Social rank."* This is an adaptation of an objective measure of community social status developed by sociologists Eshref Shevky and Wendell Bell which gives equivalent weight to occupational and educational attributes of a community's population. The occupational factor is the percent of employed males in professional, managerial and sales occupations. The educational factor is the percent of persons over 25 years old with one or more years of college education. The percentages for each factor are first standardized in a range from 0 to 100 which assigns a zero score to the community with the lowest percent in the college age or status occupational

class and 100 to the highest community. Once the two standard scores are computed, they can be averaged. Thus every local unit is assigned a social rank score.

2. *Market value per capita.* A measure of community wealth which indicates the kind of financial resources which a municipality would bring to a cooperative enterprise.

3. *Party vote.* Partisan officials are the negotiators of cooperative arrangements. The percent Republican of the total vote for Governor in 1950 was used to identify the general partisan orientation of each community.

Cooperation is defined here as the joint financing of a service facility which is operated administratively as a single system. A cooperative arrangement may take the form of a contract, a joint authority, or a joint board. Non-cooperation is defined as the lack of any cooperative arrangement between contiguous municipalities which provide similar services. In the study area there are numerous cooperative arrangements for particular services. These arrangements represent local choices and are not imposed by higher legal authorities. The principal functional areas of cooperation are schools, sewers, police radio, libraries, water and solid waste disposal. Only in the first three areas is there a large enough number of cases to accommodate statistical analysis. Fortunately, these three functional areas represent three distinctly different kinds of local policies. Schools are an expression of the life style of a community but sewers and police radio systems are not. Both schools and sewers represent large financial commitments but police radio systems do not.

With 238 municipalities in the study area, there are 28,203 possible pairs of municipalities and therefore that same number of possible intermunicipal relationships. But if our analysis of intermunicipal relationships is limited to geographically contiguous municipalities, this figure is reduced to 534, the total number of pairs of contiguous municipalities.[1] This reduction was accomplished by inspecting a map of the area. Using the density classification, there were 198 pairs in the urban area, 294 in the rural and 42 pairs comprised of one urban and one rural municipality.

Since each of the 534 pairs consists of two municipalities and each municipality is described by three measures of urban differentiation,

[1] There were 66 pairs of contiguous municipalities which were eliminated because each involved at least one of the 12 municipalities with high institutional populations.

it was possible to identify quantitatively the social and economic distance involved in each pair of municipalities along three separate indices. The absolute difference in index scores between paired municipalities constituted the measures of social and economic distance; three measures of social and economic distance were available for each pair, namely, social rank, per capita market value, and party voting. The smaller the difference in any index for a pair of communities, the more similar the communities in that pair are to each other, and the less social and economic distance exists between them. The larger the differences in index scores between two municipalities in a pair, the more dissimilar these municipalities are said to be. The central hypothesis of this paper can now be stated in operational terms. *If intermunicipal cooperation in a metropolitan area is a function of social and economic distance between communities, the mean of the differences in index values will be smaller for cooperating than for non-cooperating pairs of municipalities.*

TABLE I. SCHOOLS

MEAN DIFFERENCES AMONG PAIRS OF COOPERATING AND
NON-COOPERATING MUNICIPALITIES

		Urban			Rural-Urban			Semi-Rural	
	Cooperating	Non-Cooperating	Total	Cooperating	Non-Cooperating	Total	Cooperating	Non-Cooperating	Total
1 Social Rank	10.4	16.9	16.0‡	8.6	14.1	12.8†	7.3	7.8	7.5
2 Market Value Per Capita	$1,131	$1,467	$1,424	$1,685	$1,437	$1,515	$957	$994	$974
3 Percent Republican	9.0	11.5	11.2*	7.1	10.2	9.2*	8.0	8.8	8.4
Number of Pairs	26	172	198	13	29	42	162	132	294

* Differences between cooperating and non-cooperating pairs of municipalities are significant at the .10 level of significance.
† Differences between cooperating and non-cooperating pairs of muncipalities are significant at the .05 level of significance.
‡ Differences between cooperating and non-cooperating pairs of municipalities are significant at the .01 level of significance.

❊   ❊   ❊   ❊

Table I presents the data on school arrangements. For the hypothesis to be borne out, the mean of the differences for cooperating pairs must always be less than for non-cooperating ones. Table I indicates that this is the case to the greatest extent in the urban area, is barely corroborated in the semi-rural one, and only partially so in the rural-urban — the area comprised of those mixed pairs of rural and urban municipalities.

The major incentive for cooperative school arrangements is the pooling of resources in constructing high schools. Both from a capital financing and a curricular standpoint, small municipalities have greater difficulty building high schools independently. As the number of pairs in the various categories of Table I indicate, the total incidence of agreement is greater in the semi-rural than the urban areas (urban 26 and semi-rural 162). This difference however, cannot be explained merely by the differences in size of urban and semi-rural municipalities. According to current Pennsylvania state policy, school districts should have at least 5,000 pupils. This means that ideally most municipalities with under 25,000 persons should be parties to joint arrangements. According to this standard only 12 urban and one semi-rural municipality are large enough to have independent systems. In fact there are many more than twelve urban municipalities with independent systems, but none in the semi-rural area. Indeed many urban municipalities which are quite small maintain their independence through *ad hoc* tuition arrangements with various neighboring governmental units.

Our hypothesis suggests that the more extensive use of cooperative school arrangements in the semi-rural area is a function, in part, of the lesser social distance among pairs there than is found in the urban area. Note that in the "Total" column the mean of the differences is larger for each index value for the urban area. Urban specialization tends to create sharp social breaks which follow municipal boundaries. Thus the intermunicipal social distances influence not only the pattern of cooperation, but also its extent. Only 26 out of 198 urban pairs had agreements, while, 162 out of 294 rural ones did. The urban-rural pairs lie in between with 13 out of 29 cooperating. The 26 urban pairs which did cooperate were atypical for the sample area. The mean differences in social rank for the entire urban area is 16.0, but only 10.4 for the cooperating communities. A similar pattern holds for the other three variables although not always at a high level of significance.

In the urban-rural area the mean differences in market value-per-capita between cooperating and non-cooperating pairs is in the opposite direction of that expected. Since none of the differences in market value-per-capita in any of the three sample areas are at a .10

level of significance, the difference in the urban-rural area might have arisen solely due to chance. It may also be a function of the market value index which does not always coincide with the year in which an agreement took place; variances of as much as ten years between index and agreement year are included.[2] Most communities do not experience rapid demographic changes. However, along the fringes of the urban area the most rapid shifts take place. Fringe area industrialization and large housing developments are the most common form which these changes take. It is likely that some disparities in market value per capita have taken place subsequent to the development of joint school systems. The hypothesis is supported even in this changing area with regard to social rank and the related variable, party voting. Either populations channeling into fringe areas are not upsetting the social balance of agreeing pairs, or changes in social composition occur at a slower rate than any of our other indexes. Our observation is that both these propositions are true.

TABLE II. SEWER AGREEMENTS

MEAN DIFFERENCES AMONG PAIRS OF COOPERATING AND
NON-COOPERATING MUNICIPALITIES*

	Total			Delaware River Outlet			Other Outlets		
	Cooperating	Non-Cooperating	Total	Cooperating	Non-Cooperating	Total	Cooperating	Non-Cooperating	Total
1 Social Rank	15.9	15.3	15.6	17.4	11.9	16.1	11.2	18.0	15.0
2 Market Value Per Capita	$1,223	$1,829	$1,440†	$1,278	$2,194	$1,506†	$1,057	$1,537	$1,324
3 Percent Republican	10.5	11.4	10.8	11.2	10.3	10.8	8.5	12.3	10.6
Number of Pairs	113	63	176	85	28	113	28	35	63

* Differences between cooperating and non-cooperating pairs of municipalities are significant at the .01 level of significance.
† Differences between cooperating and non-cooperating pairs of muncipalities are significant at the .05 level of significance.

[2] Methodologically, data for indices of agreeing pairs should be gathered at the time agreements occur. Aside from nonavailability of data in all years, there is a problem of selecting the proper year for an index of non-cooperating pairs.

In the semi-rural area the differences in means are all in the expected direction but at less than a .10 level of significance. Additional applications of the social rank concept to the Philadelphia metropolitan area suggest an explanation for this apparent difference between urban and semi-rural behavior. We suspect that social rank is not as determinative an influence in the public policies of semi-rural areas as in urban areas, where the closeness, size and more frequent interactions of populations evoke greater consciousness of differences in community social status.

Education is one of the more vital policy areas through which local communities may express particular cultural and social styles of living. Another service, which is essential for urban living, but which has very little to do with life style, is the disposal of sewage. The analysis was repeated for sewage disposal agreements. One of the conditions for analysis was that both potential parties to an agreement must provide the service in question; thus only sewered communities are included in the sample. The condition confined the sample to the contiguously urbanized area around the core city. A review of the first portion of Table II under the heading "TOTAL" indicates that there is little difference between agreeing and non-agreeing pairs with respect to social rank and party vote. There are significant differences with respect to community wealth. The conclusion might be drawn that municipalities do not mind negotiating with neighbors of differing social rank and party over matters of as little social significance as sewage, but are concerned about their neighbors wealth because the maintenance and future expansion of the joint system will be influenced by the tax situation of the members. However, as the remaining portions of the Table show, this is only partially true.

The municipalities along the Delaware River are old industrial locations. They frequently have substantial tax bases, but low social ranking populations. As one goes up the tributary streams from the River, the social rank rises. Since sewage "runs down hill," the low status communities have had a monopoly of the access points for sewer trunks to the river. For the higher status upstream communities to solve their problems, they must deal with the lower status downstream communities. Table II lists all sewered communities with systems emptying directly into the Delaware River from the Delaware-Pennsylvania state boundary to Bensalem Township, which represents the strip of prewar river front development. These are labeled "DELAWARE RIVER OUTLET."

These pairs of municipalities with sewer agreements have higher mean social rank difference (though not significantly higher) than the pairs of municipalities without sewer agreements. However, with regard to taxable wealth (market value per capita) the agreeing municipalities in the Delaware River Outlet sample have a significantly smaller mean difference than the pairs of municipalities without sewer agreements. Joint sewer systems are rarely financed by uniform tax rates applying to all participating municipalities. Rather the shares to be paid by each municipality are worked out at the time of the agreement. Nevertheless, as was indicated above, the economic well-being of cooperating municipalities is a matter of vital concern to the partners. High status municipalities in the Delaware River Outlet sample had no choice but to negotiate agreements with low status communities, but it would appear that they sought to cooperate with those low status communities that were high in taxable resources.

The differences in party voting between agreeing and non-agreeing pairs in the Delaware River Outlet sample is similar to the social rank pattern. This is not surprising since there is a .703 coefficient of correlation between social rank of each municipality and the percent Republican in the election used for the party affiliation index.

The remainder of the sewered communities not in the Delaware River Outlet sample are shown in Table II under the heading "OTHER OUTLETS." These municipalities are located further up the streams from the Delaware River and along the Schuylkill and its tributaries. In these areas, municipalities frequently have a range of choice in deciding which other communities, if any, they will join in building sewerage systems. Here there is no solidly built-up riparian industrial strip monopolizing river access.

Agreements among these communities occur between those of similar status (social rank). It is interesting that although the agreeing communities also resemble each other more closely than do the non-agreeing communities with respect to taxable wealth, the difference between agreeing and non-agreeing communities is not statistically significant, even at the .10 level. It would appear that where a range of choice does exist, status is a more important determinant of agreement than is taxable resources.

Party voting again shows the same pattern as social rank. The question may be raised whether it is social rank or the party affiliation of the negotiators which influences the pattern of cooperative arrangements. The data indicates that social rank is the more important variable. In both school and sewer agreements, whenever there are significant differences between agreeing and non-agreeing municipalities with respect to social rank, there are also significant differences (up to the .10 level) with respect to party voting. But in each instance, differences in social rank are greater (they are at a higher level of statistical significance) than are differences in party voting.

School and sewerage systems have entirely differing social and cultural connotations, but both involve expensive capital facilities. Thus in each case the formation of cooperative systems means at least protracted negotiations among the leadership representing the communities, though perhaps little general public involvement in the case of sewer systems. The formation of a cooperative police radio network involves very modest financial contributions from participating municipalities, is of concern primarily to police technicians, and is a subject which generally should involve the general public very little.

TABLE III. POLICE RADIO AGREEMENTS

MEAN DIFFERENCES AMONG COOPERATING AND NON-COOPERATING MUNICIPALITIES*

	Cooperating	Non-Cooperating	Total
1 Social Rank	14.2	17.1	15.9
2 Market Value Per Capita	$1,645	$1,304	$1,445
3 Percent Republican	11.3	11.5	11.4
Number of Pairs	80	114	194

* None of the differences were significant at the .10 level.

Here the pattern of cooperation indicates no preference for similar municipalities among cooperating pairs. Table III gives the results for all pairs which have police radios. Only pairs from the urban area are thereby included. For this rather minor service, social and economic distances apparently do not control the pattern of cooperation.

The interjurisdictional agreement and the joint authority are the most popular forms of metropolitan political integration at the present time. Operations performed with data on these forms of integration in the Philadelphia Metropolitan Area tend to support the hypothesis that intermunicipal cooperation is a function of social and economic distance. Areal specialization appears to be an important obstacle to cooperative relations among urban communities. It was observed that cooperative arrangements are more frequent in the relatively undifferentiated semirural sectors of the metropolitan area and less frequent in the highly differentiated urban sectors. It was also observed that what cooperation did occur among the urbanized communities of the metropolitan area tended to occur among communities which were socially and economically similar rather than dissimilar. In addition, our findings indicate that social distance is a more important determinant of cooperation than is economic distance.[3]

These findings suggest that social and economic differentiation among urban communities may be fundamental to the whole question of metropolitan government. The highly differentiated character of metropolitan communities may operate to maintain our present "fragmented" structure of local government and to inhibit the growth of intergovernmental cooperation. Of course social science at least since Durkheim has been acutely aware that interdependence is a concomitant of specialization and that our interdependent system must be organized in some manner. The demand for effective organization of metropolitan areas is likely to continue. But because of the highly differentiated character of urban communities, integrative demands are likely to be accommodated through patterns of cooperation which least conflict with the divisive effects of differentiation.

[3] For a discussion of changes in social and economic variables affecting interjurisdictional cooperation, see the authors' "Social Status, Tax Resources and Metropolitan Cooperation," *National Tax Journal*, XVI (March 1963) 56-62.

RICHARD M. CION

Accommodation Par Excellence:
The Lakewood Plan

The City of Lakewood, California, presents a perfect example of instant suburbia. In 1950, what is now Lakewood was primarily bean fields. During the next four years, developers transformed the land into a community of 50,000. Its growth was typical of postwar expansion throughout the country. In a pattern repeated over and over, suburbia moved outward, turning farmland into development tracts and crossroads into shopping centers. In Lakewood the bean fields disappeared, on Long Island the potato fields, and outside of Chicago the corn fields; but everywhere the result was the same: new homes appeared to house a predominantly young population. In this sense, Lakewood was a typical community. However, the political conditions in Los Angeles County stimulated a unique response: the contract plan.

Under the plan, cities contract with the County of Los Angeles for a wide range of municipal services (see Figure 1). For example, a city may purchase police protection by reimbursing the County for its costs in providing a patrol car on continuous duty with attendent backup services; or the city may purchase the services of more than one car if it so desires. Thus, the city is given some control over service quality through its power to determine how many units of a given service it will buy. The plan is distinguished from other systems of interlocal agreements by its comprehensiveness; participating cities enter the arrangement with the intention of securing all or most of their municipal services through contracting. The County acts as a clearing house, supplying specified services as they are demanded in the quantities requested by the cities.

This article was prepared for this volume.

SERVICES PROVIDED TO CITIES BY THE COUNTY OF LOS ANGELES / JULY 1, 1964

CONTRACTS AND RESOLUTIONS

Department / Service	Total of each service
GENERAL SERVICES AGREEMENT	57
AGRICULTURAL COMMISSIONER	
Noxious Weed Abatement	2
ASSESSOR AND TAX COLLECTOR	
Assessment and Collection of Taxes	74
CHARITIES DEPARTMENT	
Emergency Ambulance Service	62
Hospitalization of City Prisoners	32
CIVIL SERVICE COMMISSION	
Personnel Staff Services*	15
DISTRICT ATTORNEY	
City Prosecution Services*	43
ENGINEER	
Co. Eng. Appt. City Engineer	29
Building Inspection Services	31
Engineering Staff Services*	32
Industrial Waste Regulation	31
Master House No. Map Service*	25
Sewer Maintenance	2
Subdivision Final Map Check	71
FORESTER AND FIRE WARDEN	
Forester and Fire Warden Appt. Fire Chief	29
School Fire Safety Officer	1
Weed Abatement	2
HEALTH DEPARTMENT	
State Health Law Enforcement	73
City Health Ordinance Enforcement	73
Mobil Home and Trailer Park Inspection	45
Rodent Control	31
LIBRARY	
Reciprocal Library Services	9
MENTAL HEALTH DEPARTMENT	
Mental Health Services	1
PARKS AND RECREATION DEPARTMENT	
Park Maintenance	2
Recreation Services	7
Tree Trimming Services*	20
POUND DEPARTMENT	
Pound Services	38
REGIONAL PLANNING COMMISSION	
Planning and Zoning Services*	21
REGISTRAR OF VOTERS	
Election Services	76
ROAD DEPARTMENT	
Road Comm. Appt. City Superintendent of Streets	24
Street Maintenance and Construction	29
Bridge Maintenance	26
Street Light Maintenance	24
Street Signing	28
Street Sweeping	20
Subdivision Engineering	26
Traffic Signal Maintenance	38
Traffic Striping and Marking	31
SHERIFF	
Sheriff Appt. Chief of Police	28
Law Enforcement Services	29
Business License Enforcement	19
Maintenance of City Prisoners in County Jail	72
Crossing Guard Service	13
Disaster Law Enforcement	27
Microfilm Storage	7
Motorcycle Patrol	8
School Safety	6
Traffic Law Enforcement	25
TAX COLLECTOR	
Business License Issuance Service	11
SPECIAL DISTRICTS	
Fire Protection	27
Library	41
Lighting and Lighting Maintenance Districts	27
Recreation and Park	3
Sewer Maintenance Districts	29

City	TOTAL
ALHAMBRA	9
ARCADIA	10
ARTESIA	38
AVALON	15
AZUSA	19
BALDWIN PARK	18
BELL	11
BELLFLOWER	41
BELL GARDENS	43
BEVERLY HILLS	7
BRADBURY	17
BURBANK	11
CLAREMONT	12
COMMERCE	38
COMPTON	13
COVINA	14
CUDAHY	39
CULVER CITY	10
DAIRY VALLEY	32
DOWNEY	22
DUARTE	32
EL MONTE	14
EL SEGUNDO	11
GARDENA	16
GLENDALE	11
GLENDORA	13
HAWAIIAN GARDENS	29
HAWTHORNE	11
HERMOSA BEACH	11
HIDDEN HILLS	22
HUNTINGTON PARK	14
INDUSTRY	30
INGLEWOOD	8
IRWINDALE	31
LAKEWOOD	42
LA MIRADA	37
LA PUENTE	35
LA VERNE	17
LAWNDALE	41
LOMITA	30
LONG BEACH	4
LOS ANGELES	7
LYNWOOD	14
MANHATTAN BEACH	11
MAYWOOD	15
MONROVIA	10
MONTEBELLO	15
MONTEREY PARK	13
NORWALK	27
PALMDALE	42
PALOS VERDES ESTATES	13
PARAMOUNT	38
PASADENA	3
PICO RIVERA	37
POMONA	11
REDONDO BEACH	11
ROLLING HILLS	22
ROLLING HILLS ESTATES	35
ROSEMEAD	41
SAN DIMAS	38
SAN FERNANDO	12
SAN GABRIEL	10
SAN MARINO	7
SANTA FE SPRINGS	27
SANTA MONICA	9
SIERRA MADRE	10
SIGNAL HILL	13
SOUTH EL MONTE	37
SOUTH GATE	10
SOUTH PASADENA	10
TEMPLE CITY	39
TORRANCE	12
VERNON	8
WALNUT	36
WEST COVINA	16
WHITTIER	10

Source: Los Angeles County, Tabulation of Services Provided by the County of Los Angeles to Cities: July 1, 1964.

At its inception, the Lakewood Plan represented the convergence of three conflicting forces. On the one hand, the older cities in Los Angeles County opposed what they called subsidization of the built-up unincorporated areas by the County's board of supervisors. As in most areas, the Board had been paying for the services rendered to unincorporated areas out of the County's general fund. Simultaneously, the board of supervisors and the County bureaucrats were anxious lest incorporation of large segments of unincorporated territory reduce the size and quality of the County's service establishment. And finally, the unincorporated communities themselves desired control over their own territory. They sought the ability to guarantee the character of their population and the directions growth would take within their boundaries. The Lakewood Plan accommodated all of these various interests. Through incorporation, it gave the unincorporated communities the control they desired. At the same time, it removed the threat that incorporation posed to the County bureaucracy by retaining County services in the areas already using them. And by providing for the incorporation of built-up unincorporated communities, the plan cut the substance out of the older communities' complaints about subsidization; no longer could the League of California Cities complain that its members were bearing the financial burden of rendering services to people living in those communities.

In terms of popular acceptance, the Lakewood Plan is a success. Its clientele regard it with a euphoric mixture of contentment and admiration. One County official says the plan "is a partnership of cities and the County to provide joint services at the least cost while both agencies retain the power of self-determination and home rule."[1] This attitude is echoed by officials and citizens of the twenty-nine cities which depend on contracting for provision of virtually all of their municipal services. Yet, satisfied though its subscribers may be, the Lakewood Plan raises a number of troublesome issues. Plan communities must pay a high price for control over their own destinies. While contracting does provide them with decent services, it also restricts their freedom of action, severely limits the alternatives open to their leaders in many fields, forces them to bargain with the County for changes in policy, and compels them to operate within the rather narrow constraints of the contract plan.

[1] Arthur G. Will. *Lakewood Revisited: Six Years of Contract Services.* A paper presented to the First Annual Municipal Seminar of the California Contract Cities. Palm Springs, California. April 29, 1960, p. 1.

Under the contract arrangement, no unit is capable of acting independently for long; each is tied to the others by the workings of the plan. All of the relevant interests give up a significant measure of independence in return for what they perceive as the values to be. derived from participation. Ultimately, the only considerations of importance in the policy making process become those connected with preservation of the system. System-maintenance criteria replace other, more appropriate standards in determining governmental action.

Because the system satisfies their major goals, metropolitan actors do not perceive the sacrifices which they make in order to obtain the benefits of participation. And these sacrifices are real and considerable. Contract cities give up control over their service functions. Consider the case of a County sewer maintenance district coextensive with three newly incorporated contract cities. Unless the three city councils agree on policy matters, one or more of them will be frustrated. In practice, the governing body of the district will tend to ignore the councils and set policy for itself. Or consider the case of the sheriff's department. Every contract relevant to law enforcement contains a "sheriff supreme" clause. In essence, the clause provides that in the event of conflict between a city's views on law enforcement policy and the sheriff's, the sheriff has the final word. The plan is replete with such instances in which cities have no formal opportunity to achieve control over their services while remaining within its framework. And because withdrawal is always expensive and often impossible the cities are forced to remain within that framework.

In some cases, the system does not even let a city find out what its problems are, or permit it to do anything about them if it knows what they are. For example, there is uniform dissatisfaction with the sheriff's system of reporting on police activities to cities. Several city managers have noted that they are unable to determine the extent of their juvenile problem. Moreover, as the contracts are presently drawn, a city could not hire additional juvenile officers if it wanted to. Under the contract plan, a city is unable to initiate or pursue a program directed at some particular problem in which it is especially interested. In part this is an administrative failure and in part it is a flaw inherent in the system. Communications could be improved; indeed steps are being taken to make the sheriff's reporting system more satisfactory. However, as long as law enforcement services are sold on a patrol-car-package basis, there will be no way for a city to attack specific problems—it will be able to hire only the prescribed package of services and will not be able to obtain greater numbers of specialized officers.

Finally, while contract cities have nominal control over service levels, they are unable to establish independent service policy. Only the willingness of the County departments to negotiate disputes and to alter established policy has preserved a measure of local control. As a case in point, in 1958 the sheriff's department agreed to abandon a long-standing prohibition against the use of one-man cars. Until that time it had been the sheriff's practice never to send a man out alone in a patrol car. Several contract cities felt that the sheriff was being unnecessarily conservative and that his policy was increasing the cost of police protection unreasonably. There followed a lengthy debate which ended in a compromise. The sheriff adopted the use of one-man cars during the day shift; the cities were satisfied. Thus a workable settlement was reached after each side had a chance to present its own position and to assess the importance of the issue to the other. The whole incident illustrates the willingness of County departments to negotiate when necessary.

But the statement that County departments are willing to negotiate, and if possible to accommodate the demands of the cities is not identical with the statement that the cities have control over service policies. Quite the contrary, the long and tortuous bargaining behind the sheriff's acceptance of one-man cars did not constitute an exercise of home rule. The city councils involved did not change service policy, rather they used political pressure to induce the sheriff to change policy. There is a vast difference between a city council adopting a resolution to the effect that procedures will be altered in the future and the same council voting to engage in negotiations with the County over future policy.

Cities are willing to give up immediate control over policy because they have to; for most plan cities, the economy of participation was a necessary prerequisite of incorporation. The contract city subscribes to the plan in order to preserve its independent existence and to protect itself from outside encroachment by undesirable groups. Through application of the land-use controls which become available to it upon incorporation, the contract city is able to insure the continuing homogeneity of its residents. Complete control over service policy is the price it must pay for the benefit of incorporation.

When asked about the shortcomings of the plan, contract-city officials observe that they can cancel any agreement upon sixty days' notice. This right, they assert, insures the city's ultimate control. As long as the County's commitment to the arrangement remains strong, and there is no reason why it should not, then the city's right of withdrawal will guarantee its strong position in the bargaining process. However, experience has shown that it is not always easy for a city to cancel a contract when it wishes. In 1958, the newly formed City of Norwalk revised its police service policy. The city administrator, E. Frederick Bien, felt that the sheriff's services were expensive and unresponsive. A resolution to form a municipal police department was proposed and eventually defeated by a three-two vote of the Norwalk council. Interestingly, the decisive vote was cast by the measure's author. According to one councilman, the sheriff applied strong pressure to the group to reject the resolution, a view supported by other knowledgeable observers. In this case, the sheriff used his powerful position in County politics to prevent a city from exercising its formal right of withdrawal from the plan.

One point emerges clearly — a city cannot always withdraw from the contract system if it wants to. Its actions are not internally controlled; rather they are subject to outside political influence, particularly from actors in the County government whose interests lie in the continuation of the status quo. The city's great power in the negotiation process is largely a myth. Moreover, the myth is preserved by County officials for purposes of public relations. As one high-ranking County official observed, if the cities felt they had no control, new cities would fail to subscribe to the plan and the County's interest in its expansion would not be served.

Thus, the cities' drive for independence paradoxically results in a gross restriction of their freedom of action in all fields save one. While left with the ability to control their own land-use patterns, Lakewood Plan communities are unable to set independent policy in other areas. This is the price they pay for the ability to retain their particular character in the face of the rapid growth of the metropolitan area.

City interests are not the only ones subordinated to the maintenance values surrounding the plan. The County's commitment to the arrangement derives from the fact that contracting assures the continued growth of its service departments. However, by supporting the Lakewood Plan, County officials place serious limits on their freedom of action. While the County does have a position of strength relative to contract cities, it would be impractical to use pressure every time a city made a request. Frequent use of pressure would arouse city resistance and would discourage new cities from employing the arrangement. Therefore, County policy is to work whenever possible within the framework of the plan.

This decision implies that the County is ever ready to negotiate its differences with a city and, if necessary, to yield ground in the face of determined requests. It further implies that the County will make all of its resource allocation decisions with contract services in mind. For example, when establishing a new district library, the board of supervisors is likely to put it in a contract city if possible. When constructing a fire station or other facility, it must consider the stability of its contracts with cities in the area. Hence, the County must work under a certain amount of uncertainty; there is always the possibility, however remote, that contracts will be cancelled. In order to minimize the possibility, the board of supervisors tends to be very solicitous of contract cities.

Government in Los Angeles is then carried out by means of a dialogue between the cities and the County. Neither is free to pursue its own interest, yet neither is explicitly aware of the limitations placed upon it. The result is what Roscoe Martin calls a "fluid federalism."[2] All participants work to further their own interests within the rather rigorously defined constraints of the contract plan. The fluid quality derives from the fact that the constitution is continually subject to change by negotiation. But by subscribing to the system, the participants agree to work within its limitations; each must curb its own potential in order that the system as a whole will work, and each does so.

In the process, limits are placed not only on city and County interests, but also on the interests of the metropolitan area as a whole. A significant result of the Lakewood Plan has been to stimulate the creation of thirty-one new cities in Los Angeles County. That in itself would be enough to discourage any hope of voluntary cooperation for the solution of regional problems. Moreover, if the character of these new communities is considered, it is immediately apparent that voluntary regional consent on any significant matter is most unlikely. For example, the City of Industry is a bizarrely shaped industrial center. Following the outline of the Union Pacific and Southern Pacific Railroad yards, Industry is a tax shelter for factories

[2] Roscoe C. Martin. *Metropolis in Transition: Local Government Adaptation to Changing Urban Needs.* Washington: Housing and Home Finance Agency, 1963, p. 23.

and warehouses. In order to meet the minimum population requirement for incorporation (500), the city counted the inmates of an
insane asylum. A court challenge to the legality of this procedure
was halted before a decision was reached when the plaintiff declared
himself no longer interested by virtue of the fact that he had moved
out of the area (and into a house somewhat more luxurious than the
one which he had occupied at the beginning of the suit). Obviously,
Industry is not interested in any scheme which would mean sharing
its huge tax potential with the rest of the County.

Industry is neither an extreme nor an unusual case. The cities of
Commerce and Santa Fe Springs are similarly composed. Dairy
Valley is an agricultural enclave whose population is composed principally of cows. Other cities have their own peculiarities. Rolling
Hills is a city without public streets; they are all owned by a private
corporation. Hidden Hills is literally a walled city; its residents can
close the gates and refuse to let anyone in.

But the proliferation of special interest cities, each an additional
veto in the unit-veto system of regional government, is not the only
result of the plan. A desperate need in the metropolis is planning
for the future — planning for orderly development, for judicious use
of resources, and for regional facilities. Each time a new city is
launched, the ability of the County's planning organ, the Regional
Planning Commission, to meet the challenges or urbanization effectively is further vitiated. Instead, the County, through the Lakewood
Plan is forced to implement a variety of local land-use plans, each a
design which stresses protectivism, preservation of particularistic
values, and ignorance of regional needs. Although the Regional Planning Commission continues to construct master plans for the entire
County, it is increasingly powerless to implement them.

Another of the plan's significant products is the subtle alteration
it works on the role of County bureaucrats and officials. In most
metropolitan areas, if there is a strong central government like a
county, the officers of that unit generally have good reason to support area-wide government. Big government is in their interest; they
are likely to be the recipients of whatever new powers arise out of
metropolitan reform. But the Lakewood Plan has rechannelled
County imperialism. Instead of supporting the formation of regional
government, the County is committed to the status quo. Because the
plan provides a means of insuring the County's position, the bureaucrats' natural tendency to seek widening of their power through a

more general government is aborted. They live contentedly within the framework of the Lakewood Plan, their power already secure, their reason for seeking metro gone.

Far from strengthening the impetus toward regionalism, the Lakewood Plan actually vitiates it. By creating new and more aggressive enclaves of particularism in the County, each one protected by the home rule provisions of the state constitution, by strengthening the desire for status quo on the part of county officials, and by making the Regional Planning Commission totally ineffective, the plan builds the first line of resistance against metropolitan approaches to metropolitan problems. Moreover, the plan itself does not attempt to solve these problems. Planning, water supply, transportation, sewage, education, segregation — they are all beyond its scope. In so far as it eliminates the need for more local departments, the plan alleviates some of the duplication of functions which typically wastes metropolitan resources. But it avoids the hard problems. As a system of interlocal agreements, it cannot extend itself to regionalism; it is limited by the extent of consensual patterns among its subscribers.

It is interesting to note that the political system which emerges in Los Angeles County resembles politics in New York City as pictured by Sayre and Kaufman: "a loose-knit and multicentered network in which decisions are reached by ceaseless bargaining among the major categories of participants in each center, and in which the centers are partially but strikingly isolated from one another."[3] Thus, the nation's largest city, New York, and its most diffuse metropolis, Los Angeles, have developed curiously similar distributions of influence out of vastly different environments and institutional arrangements. In both areas, and indeed in all polycentric systems, three characteristics are consistently exhibited: First, by definition, there are many relevant actors, each invested with an independent base of power. Second, government is conducted by negotiation; no one actor is powerful enough to control policy alone, and no group of actors is motivated to unite on a large range of issues. And third, no actor is able to freely and completely pursue his own interest. The only interest which is fully served is that of the system itself; all others are subordinated to it.

[3] Wallace S. Sayre and Herbert Kaufman. *Governing New York City: Politics in the Metropolis.* New York: Russell Sage Foundation, 1960, p. 716.

VINCENT OSTROM, CHARLES M. TIEBOUT,
AND ROBERT WARREN

In Defense of the Polycentric Metropolis

Allusions to the "problem of metropolitan government" are often made in characterizing the difficulties supposed to arise because a metropolitan region is a legal non-entity. From this point of view, the people of a metropolitan region have no general instrumentality of government available to deal directly with the range of problems which they share in common. Rather there is a multiplicity of federal and state governmental agencies, counties, cities, and special districts that govern within a metropolitan region.

This view assumes that the multiplicity of political units in a metropolitan area is essentially a pathological phenomenon. The diagnosis asserts that there are too many governments and not enough government. The symptoms are described as "duplication of functions" and "overlapping jurisdictions." Autonomous units of government, acting in their own behalf, are considered incapable of resolving the diverse problems of the wider metropolitan community. The political topography of the metropolis is called a "crazy-quilt pattern" and its organization is said to be an "organized chaos." The prescription is reorganization into larger units — to provide "a general metropolitan framework" for gathering up the various functions of government. A political system with a single dominant center for making decisions is viewed as the ideal model for the or-

Reprinted by permission of the authors and The American Political Science Association from *The American Political Science Review*, Vol. LV (December 1961), pp. 831-842.

ganization of metropolitan government. "Gargantua" is one name for it.[1]

The assumption that each unit of local government acts independently without regard for other public interests in the metropolitan community has only a limited validity. The traditional pattern of government in a metropolitan area with its multiplicity of political jurisdictions may more appropriately be conceived as a "polycentric political system."[2] "Polycentric" connotes many centers of decision-making which are formally independent of each other. Whether they actually function independently, or instead constitute an interdependent system of relations, is an empirical question in particular cases. To the extent that they take each other into account in competitive relationships, enter into various contractual and cooperative undertakings or have recourse to central mechanisms to resolve conflicts, the various political jurisdictions in a metropolitan area may function in a coherent manner with consistent and predictable patterns of interacting behavior. To the extent that this is so, they may be said to function as a "system" . . .

No *a priori* judgment can be made about the adequacy of a polycentric system of government as against the single jurisdiction. The multiplicity of interests in various public goods sought by people in a metropolitan region can only be handled in the context of many different levels of organization. The polycentric system is confronted with the problem of realizing the needs of wider community interests or publics beyond the functional or territorial bounds of each of the formal entities within the broader metropolitan region. The single jurisdiction, in turn, confronts the problem of recognizing and

[1] The term is taken from Robert C. Wood, "The New Metropolis: Green Belts, Grass Roots or Gargantua," this REVIEW, Vol. 52 (March, 1958), pp. 108-122. Wood defines gargantua as "the invention of a single metropolitan government or at least the establishment of a regional superstructure which points in that direction." We do not argue the case for big units *vs.* small units as Wood does in his discussion of gargantua *vs.* grass roots. Rather, we argue that various scales of organization may be appropriate for different public services in a metropolitan area.

[2] We use this term for want of a better one. An alternative term might be "multinucleated political system." We do not use "pluralism" because it has been preempted as a broader term referring to society generally and not to a political system in particular.

Polycentric political systems are not limited to the field of metropolitan government. The concept is equally applicable to regional administration of water resources, regional administration of international affairs, and to a variety of other situations.

organizing the various subsidiary sets of interests within the big system. It is doubtful that sub-optimization in gargantua is any easier to accomplish than supra-optimazation in a polycentric political system.

The performance of a polycentric political system can only be understood and evaluated by reference to the patterns of cooperation, competition and conflict that may exist among its various units. Cooperative arrangements pose no difficulty when joint activities produce a greater return to all parties concerned, if the appropriate set of public interests are adequately represented among the negotiators. A contractual arrangement will suffice. As a result, this discussion of the behavior of a polycentric political system will focus upon the more difficult problems of competition, of conflict and its resolution. If a polycentric political system can resolve conflict and maintain competition within appropriate bounds it can be a viable arrangement for dealing with a variety of public problems in a metropolitan area.

Competition[3]

Where the provision of public goods and services has been successfully internalized within a public jurisdiction, there are no substantial spill-over effects, by definition. In such circumstances there need be no detrimental consequences from competition in the municipal services economy. Patterns of competition among producers of public services in a metropolitan area, just as among firms in the market, may produce substantial benefits by inducing self-regulating tendencies with pressure for the more efficient solution in the operation of the whole system.

Variety in service levels among various independent local government agencies within a larger metropolitan community may give rise to a quasi-market choice for local residents in permitting them to select the particular community in the metropolitan area that most closely approximates the public service levels they desire. Public service agencies then may be forced to compete over the service levels offered in relation to the taxes charged. Such competition,

[3] This analysis is confined to competition between units of government and makes no reference to competitive forces within a unit of government. Competition among pressure groups, factions and political parties is a fundamental feature of the democratic political process, but is not within the primary focus of this paper and its concern with the polycentric system.

however, would only be appropriate for those public goods which are adequately internalized within the boundaries of a given political jurisdiction.

Conditions amenable to competition normally exist among local units of government where a number of units are located in close proximity to each other and where information about each other's performance is publicly available. Information can lead to comparison and comparison can lead to pressure for performances to approximate the operations of the more efficient units. Where more than one public jurisdiction is capable of rendering service in a single area, further competitive tendencies may develop. Contractual arrangements among public jurisdictions for the provision of specific public services have long provided a competitive alternative to each jurisdiction which might otherwise produce its own services.

The separation of the *provision* of public goods and services from their *production* opens up the greatest possibility of redefining economic functions in a public service economy. Public control can be maintained in relation to performance criteria in the provision of services, while allowing an increasing amount of competition to develop among the agencies that produce them.

With the incorporation of the City of Lakewood in 1954, Los Angeles County, for example, expanded its system of contracting for the production of municipal services to a point approaching quasi-market conditions. Newly incorporated cities, operating under the so-called Lakewood Plan, contract with the county or other appropriate agencies to produce the general range of municipal services needed in the local community.

Each city contracts for municipal services for the city as a whole. Services beyond the general level of performance by county administration in unincorporated areas are subject to negotiation for most service functions. Each city also has the option of producing municipal services for itself. Private contractors too have undertaken such services as street sweeping, engineering, street maintenance and repair, and related public works. Some contracts have been negotiated with neighboring cities. As the number of vendors increases, competition brings pressures toward greater responsiveness and efficiency.

By separating the production from the provision of public goods it may be possible to differentiate, unitize and measure the production while continuing to provide undifferentiated public goods to the citizen-consumer. Thus Los Angeles County has, under the Lakewood Plan, unitized the production of police services into packages, each consisting of a police-car-on-continuous-patrol with associated auxiliary services. A price is placed on this police-car-on-continuous-patrol package, and a municipality may contract for police service on that basis. Within the local community, police service is still provided as a public good for the community as a whole.

Problems of scale arising from possible conflicts between criteria of production and criteria of political representation may be effectively resolved in this way. Efficient scales or organization for the production of different public goods may be quite independent of the scales required to recognize appropriate publics for their consumption of public goods and services. But competition among vendors may allow the most efficient organization to be utilized in the production, while an entirely different community of interest and scale of organization controls the provision of services in a local community.

The separation of production from provision may also have the consequence of turning local governments into the equivalents of associations of consumers. While Sidney and Beatrice Webb viewed local governments as associations of consumers, the dominance of production criteria in American municipal administration has largely led to the subordination of consumer interests.[4] However, cities organized to provide the local citizenry with public services produced by other agencies may be expected to give stronger representation to consumer interests. Among the so-called Lakewood Plan cities in Los Angeles County, for example, the local chief administrative officer has increasingly become a spokesman or bargainer for local consumer interests.

In this role, the chief administrative-officer is similar to a buyer in a large corporation. Recognizing that the greater the number of vendors of public services, the greater the competition, the local chief administrative officer may seek to expand the number of his potential suppliers. As competition increases, vendors become more sensitive to the consumer demands he negotiates.

The production of public goods under the contract system in Los Angeles County has also placed considerable pressure upon the

[4] Sidney and Beatrice Webb, *English Local Government: Statutory Authorities for Special Purposes* (London: Longmans, Green and Co., 1922), p. 437 ff.

county administration to become more responsive to demands of the public service clientele organized through their local cities. Important changes in operating procedures and organizational arrangements have been introduced into the county's administration of police protection, fire protection, library services, street maintenance, building inspection and engineering services in order to increase efficiency and responsiveness.

Under these circumstances, a polycentric political system can be viable in supplying a variety of public goods with many different scales of organization and in providing optimal arrangements for the production and consumption of public goods. With the development of quasi-market conditions in production, much of the flexibility and responsiveness of market organization can be realized in the public service economy.

Several difficulties in the regulation of a competitive public service economy can be anticipated. Economic pricing and cost allocation are dependent upon the development of effective measurement of municipal services. Since the preferred states of affairs in a community cannot be converted to a single scale of values such as dollar profits in a private enterprise, it may be more difficult to sustain an objective competitive relationship in a public service economy. Although costs of contract services from different vendors of a public good may be the same, objective standards for determining the value of the benefits are needed, and may be hard to come by; otherwise the latitude of discretion available to the negotiators may limit the competitive vitality of the system and shift the competition to side-payoffs.

Without careful control of cost allocations and pricing arrangements, funds from non-competitive welfare functions might be used to subsidize the more competitive service areas. In Los Angeles County, close scrutiny of cost accounting practices and pricing policies by the grand jury has helped to prevent funds from being so transferred.

Any long-term reliance upon quasi-market mechanisms in the production of public goods and services no doubt will require more of such careful scrutiny, control and regulation than has been applied toward maintaining the competitive structure of the private market economy. The measurement of cost and output performance may become an essential public function of the state in the administration of metropolitan affairs if continued reliance is placed primarily upon a polycentric system in the government of metropolitan areas.

Reliance upon outside vendors to produce public services may also reduce the degree of local political control exercised. The employee is subject to the control of the vendor and not directly to the control of the municipality. In contrast to the more immediate lines of responsibility and communication between local municipal employees and city officials, reliance upon vendors to provide municipal services may also restrict the quality and quantity of information about community affairs that are provided to the city's decision-makers. This constraint on information might reduce the degree of their control over public affairs.

This discussion merely indicates some of the considerations to be examined in an analysis of the effects of competitive arrangements in providing public services. As long as the particular contracting agencies encompass the appropriate set of public interests no absolute impediment to their use need exist. With appropriate public control, competitive arrangements may afford great flexibility in taking advantage of some of the economies of scale for the production of public services in a metropolitan area, while, at the same time, allowing substantial diversity in their provision for the more immediate communities, based upon political responsibility within local patterns of community identification.

Conflict and Conflict Resolution

More difficult problems for a polycentric political system are created when the provision of public goods cannot be confined to the boundaries of the existing units of government. These situations involving serious spill-over effects are apt to provoke conflict between the various units in the system. Arrangements must be available for the resolution of such conflicts if a polycentric political system is to solve its problems. Otherwise, competition and conflict are apt to become acute.

No community, on its own initiative, has much incentive to assume the full costs of controlling adverse consequences which are shared by a wider public. The competitive disadvantage of enforcing pollution abatement regulations, for example, against individuals and firms within a single community, when competitors in neighboring communities are not required to bear such costs, leads each community to excuse its failure to act by the failure of other similarly situated communities to act. In a polycentric system this is especially serious where many of the public "goods" involve the costly abatement of public nuisances.

Concerted action by the various units of government in a metropolitan area is easier to organize when costs and benefits are fairly uniformly distributed throughout the area. By way of example, this has been done under contractual agreements for mutual aid to assure the mobilization of greater fire-fighting capability in case of serious conflagrations. The random and unpredictable nature of such fires causes them to be treated as a uniform risk that might occur to any community in the larger metropolitan area.

Similar considerations apply to efforts to control mosquito infestations or air pollution. Leagues of cities, chambers of commerce and other civic associations have frequently become the agencies for negotiating legislative proposals for the creation of mosquito abatement districts, air pollution control districts and the like.

More difficult problems for the polycentric political system arise when the benefits and the costs are not uniformly distributed. Communities may differ in their perception of the benefits they receive from the provision of a common public good. In turn, a community may be unwilling to "pay its fair share" for providing that good simply because its demands for provision are less than in neighboring communities. These situations call for effective governmental mechanisms which can internalize the problem. If necessary, sanctions must be available for the enforcement of decisions.

The conflicting claims of municipal water supply systems pumping water from the same underground basins in Southern California, for example, have uniformly been resolved by recourse to legal actions in the state courts. The courts have thereby become the primary authorities for resolving conflicts among water supply agencies in Southern California; and their decisions have come to provide many of the basic policies of water administration in the Southern California metropolitan region. The state's judiciary has played a comparable role in conflicts among other local government agencies in such diverse fields as public health, incorporation and annexation proceedings, law enforcement, and urban planning.

The heavy reliance upon courts for the resolution of conflicts among local units of government unquestionably reflects an effort to minimize the risks of external control by a superior decision-maker. Court decisions are taken on a case-by-case basis. The adversaries usually define the issues and consequently limit the areas of judicial discretion. This method also minimizes the degree of control exercised following a judgment. California courts, in particular, have accepted the basic doctrines of home rule and are thus favorably disposed to the interests of local units of government in dealing with problems of municipal affairs.

The example of municipal water administration may be pursued further to illustrate other decision-making arrangements and their consequences which bear upon the resolution of conflict in a polycentric political system.[5]

While litigation may be an appropriate means for resolving conflicts over a given supply of water, local water administrators in Southern California have long recognized that law suits never produced any additional water. Organization for the importation of new water supplies was recognized as the only means for solving the long-term problem.

Los Angeles built the first major aqueduct to import water into the area on its own initiative. This water supply was used to force adjoining areas to annex or consolidate to the City of Los Angeles if they wished to gain access to the new supply. The condition for the provision of water required adjoining areas to sacrifice their identities as separate political communities. To get that one public good they were forced to give up other public goods. This provoked sufficient opposition to block any new developments which were not based upon consent and cooperation. The mechanisms for the resolution of subsequent conflicts were required to take on new forms.

The importation of Colorado River water was later undertaken by a coalition of communities in Southern California formed through the agency of the southern section of the League of California Cities. The League afforded a neutral ground for the negotiation of the common interests of the City of Los Angeles and the other cities in the metropolitan area which shared common water problems. After satisfactory arrangements had been negotiated, including provision for the formation of a new metropolitan water district and endorsement of the Boulder Canyon project, a Boulder Dam Asso-

[5] For further detail see: Vincent Ostrom, *Water and Politics* (Los Angeles, Haynes Foundation, 1953), esp. chs. 3, 6 and 7.

ciation was formed to realize these objectives. In due course a new agency, the Metropolitan Water District of Southern California was formed; and the Colorado River aqueduct was constructed and put into operation by this new district.

More recently, the Southern California Water Coordinating Conference, meeting under the auspices of the Los Angeles Chamber of Commerce, has been the agency for negotiating regional interests in the development of the California Water Program. The Metropolitan Water District was not able to represent areas in Southern California which did not belong to that district; and the rise of a variety of special municipal water districts precluded the League of California Cities, which represents cities only, from again serving as the agency for the negotiation of metropolitan interests in municipal water supply.

These illustrations suggest that a variety of informal arrangements may be available for negotiating basic policies among local government agencies in a metropolitan area. Such arrangements are vital in negotiating common interests among them. The larger public is taken into account in an informally constituted political community. These arrangements work effectively only so long as substantial unanimity can be reached, for formal implementation of such decisions must be ratified by each of the appropriate official agencies, including the state government when changes in state law or administrative policies are involved.

Higher levels of government may also be invoked in seeking the resolution of conflict among local governments in metropolitan areas. Again recourse is sought to a more inclusive political community. Under these circumstances, conflict tends to centralize decision-making and control. The danger is that the more inclusive political community will not give appropriate recognition to the particular public interests at issue and tend to inject a variety of other interests into settlements of local controversies.

Appeal to central authorities runs the risk of placing greater control over local metropolitan affairs in agencies such as the state legislature, while at the same time reducing the capability of local governments for dealing with their problems in the local context. Sensitivity over the maintenance of local control may produce great pressure for the subordination of differences while conflicting parties seek a common position approximating unanimity. A substantial investment in informal negotiating and decision-making arrangements can be justified from the perspective of the local authorities if such arrangements can prevent the loss of local autonomy to higher levels of government.

Ironically but logically, this effort to avoid recourse to conflict and the consequent centralization of decision-making tends also to reduce the local autonomy or degree of independence exercised by the local governing boards. Pressure for agreement on a common approach to some metropolitan problem limits the choices available to any particular local government. However, this range of choice may still be greater than that which would result from a settlement by a central authority. Negotiation among independent agencies allows the use of a veto against any unacceptable position. Agreement must be negotiated within the limits of the various veto positions if the alternative of recourse to an external authority at a higher level of political jurisdiction is to be avoided.

To minimize the costs of conflict to their power positions, administrators of local government agencies in metropolitan areas have tended to develop an extensive system of communication about each other's experience and to negotiate standards of performance applicable to various types of public services. Professional administrative standards may, thus, operate to constrain the variety of experience in local government agencies. Information about areas of difference and of potential conflict tend to be repressed under these circumstances. The negotiations about common problems through informal agencies are apt to be conducted in secrecy, and careful control may be developed over sensitive information.

These pressures to avoid the costs of conflict and seek agreement about metropolitan problems reflect the importance to local governments of resolving general public problems by negotiation at the local level in a metropolitan community. To the extent that these pressures are effective, the patterns of local government in a metropolitan area can only be understood by attention to the variety of formal and informal arrangements that may exist for settling area-wide problems.

Contrary to the frequent assertion about the lack of a "metropolitan framework" for dealing with metropolitan problems, most metropolitan areas have a very rich and intricate "framework" for negotiating, adjudicating and deciding questions that affect their diverse public interests. . . .

ROBERT C. WOOD

Metropolis Against Itself

What emerges from [a] review of the accomplishments and failures of metropolitan governments is not a prediction of catastrophe
or of governmental bankruptcy. The governments have attended to
the minimum needs of their citizens well enough to prevent any
fundamental breakdown. Indeed, the whole history of metropolitan
reform, or more properly, the failure of reform movements, reveals
that the regions' population have not become dissatisfied with the
existing conditions to the point of supporting major reorganizations.

What does emerge is the conclusion that metropolitan governments which retain allegiance to autonomy and diversity can discharge effectively only one major responsibility — the provision of
minimum urban services and facilities. The efforts required to sustain an adequate volume of public investment for ordinary service
activities, and the complicated arrangements necessary to provide
minimum standards throughout the metropolitan areas, preclude any
real possibility of developing coordinated regional services or per-
fecting institutions for regional policy-making. The present pattern
of metropolitan government can keep house; it cannot make and
carry out plans for any substantial remodeling or new construction.

This state of affairs, it should be pointed out, does not necessarily
commit the metropolitan governments to continued operations at a
subsistence level, nor to growing inequities and disparities. As the
process of economic growth goes on, it seems reasonable to expect
that the pressures on even the most hard pressed jurisdiction will
lighten. If the diffusion of commercial establishments continues, for

Reprinted from *Metropolis Against Itself* (New York: Committee for Economic Development, 1959), pp. 39-44, with the permission of the author
and the Committee for Economic Development.

example, their activities will locate where their customers are most closely congregated and their markets largest. Thus, they will bring tax resources in excess of service demands to the residential suburban municipalities most urgently in need of revenue. Similarly, industrial plants, in their search for elbow room, are likely to be attracted to the newest municipalities where the rate of population growth is fastest, and the get-going costs of community development most severe. As these migrations continue, more municipalities will receive the "windfalls" of shopping centers, amusement areas, medical buildings, and industrial parks, and tax revenues will be augmented accordingly.

Even the central city need not necessarily despair at the course of present economic trends. A substantial proportion of the growing service industry still needs to locate in the core — for example, advertising agencies, banks, law firms, and consultants. So do the home offices where communication, "the knowledge of the industry," gossip of the trade and face-to-face confrontations are prerequisites for doing business. So does the growing category of specialized and unstandardized manufacturing processes. Small firms which offer intermediate component products to a number of industries, which require unstandardized inputs or produce unstandardized products, and which maintain irregular schedules, find external economies downtown which few suburbs can supply.

The implication for the central city is, of course, that the businesses so engaged are relatively insensitive to tax changes. Existing levies can be increased, new taxes on earnings and incomes imposed, and the firms will still "stay put." The advantages of communication, proximity to client and competitor, fractional use of transportation facilities, rented space, a larger labor market, and close inventory control, outweigh the tax penalties involved. Thus, the city may be able to obtain substantially higher revenues to meet the challenge of obsolescence than it — or its businesses — have formerly supposed.[1]

These trends of economic growth are not the only evidence indicating that the present pattern of governments can continue to endure against mounting pressures and avoid making a serious attack on regional problems. There is, after all, a firm ideological basis for the belief that "keeping house" is all a local government *should*

[1] For a more extended examination of these trends, see the author's "The New Metropolis: Green Belts, Grass Roots or Gargantua?", *American Political Science Review*, LII:1 (March, 1958).

294   ROBERT C. WOOD

do. The traditional American theory of local government holds that
a municipality is "nothing but a bundle of services," that administrative problems and service problems and tax problems are the
only problems at the local level. The old saw runs that "there is no
Republican or Democratic way to pave a street," and this doctrine
persists despite the ideological content of housing and renewal programs, health activities and zoning ordinances. So long as this doctrine exists, few citizens will seriously look to their local governments to tackle the renewal problem, the transportation crisis, the
urban sprawl in a thoroughgoing manner.

Even if the public comes to demand these more positive programs, it is unlikely to be willing to pay the price for a thoroughgoing reorganization and reform. Linked to the "bundle of services"
philosophy is the even stronger conviction that the government
closest to home governs best. Autonomy is valued for the democratic
benefits it bestows: the opportunity for direct popular participation,
the chance to know public officials personally, and the fact that local
issues are concrete and understandable. City services combined with
grass-roots governments have a persuasive appeal in the modern
metropolitan region — and the values of this union are not likely to
be rapidly abandoned.

Indeed, the grass roots appeal is so persuasive that the very inequities created by the present pattern of government have their
defenders. The existence of a number of little governments in a single area, it is sometimes argued, provides each citizen with an array
of alternatives in ways of living and in levels of public services. Thus
Professors Banfield and Grodzins see the modern metropolitan region as allowing "spheres of free choice for individuals and community groups"; "wide options to be exclusive and expressive." They
believe a large number of governments is desirable because "the
consumer is in the position to know what combination of goods and
services — trees and sidewalks as against food and clothing, for example — will give him the greatest satisfaction.[2]

Yet, if the present system of metropolitan government can be supported by economic trends and defended philosophically, it still produces by-products which must be recognized and which, in the long

[2] Edward C. Banfield and Morton Grodzins, *Housing Policy and the
Government of Metropolitan Areas*, special report prepared for *ACTION*,
1956.

run, may be unpalatable. A single-minded fixation on the service concept of government, an insistence on the preservation of political autonomy and multiplicity, mean, first of all, that it is impossible to have a vision of what the metropolitan regions might become. When each jurisdiction goes on its separate way, urban sprawl continues, with its companions of spreading blight, cheap commercial developments along major highways, inadequate parks, congested schools, mediocre administration, smog, traffic jams, recurrent crises in mass transportation, and the hundred and one irritations of undirected growth. The "gray belt" which Raymond Vernon has so graphically described continues to expand, and the municipalities caught directly in its path are left to grapple with its consequences, one by one. In place of a coordinated attack on the less attractive by-products of urbanization, each jurisdiction tries to avoid the conditions it regards as unpalatable, to protect its own, and to let its neighbors fend for themselves. When local government disclaims responsibility for the regional environment, the capacity to realize the potential of that environment is irrevocably lost.

Second, it must be recognized that under the present system, not all the citizens of the region — nor even the majority — can exercise the freedom of choice which the multiplicity of jurisdictions may offer. Though bright islands of residential suburbs exist, there is a high price on their homes, and for many people there are no real alternatives except the backwaters of the city and the suburban-development house on the quarter-acre lot. Even the individual who can choose his home where he wishes may be disillusioned. Once settled, he has to accept his tastes as frozen, or resign himself to the ineffective position of the minority group — or move each time his values and opinions change.

A third consequence of the present state of affairs is that, as local governments disclaim any responsibility for regional services and for policy-making, this responsibility moves upstairs. The Federal government comes to exercise predominant influence over certain decisions — as it does today in redevelopment and highway construction. The State government calls the tune in recreation and public health, and in some ways, even in education. Or the "non-political" authorities arrive at some sort of compromise agreement, at the lowest common denominator, of what the shape and future of the region should be. The local governments of the region, by refusing to make policy, by attending strictly to the business of providing services, by defending local autonomy in the legal sense, forfeit the real authority to control and direct their own affairs.

Finally, so long as the present system of government exists, the regional economic system itself functions less effectively. Lacking a mechanism for regional policy-making, the metropolitan political system is unable to use planning, zoning, redevelopment, and transportation programs to assist the processes of production and distribution. Instead, as Kirk R. Petshek has pointed out, since the governments cannot take into account the new facts of regional economic life, they make these processes less efficient. Their mistakes in investment and regulatory programs, their competitive attitude toward their neighbors, mean extra costs for private business.[3] Thus when redevelopment authorities do not assign space to appropriate economic uses, when the transportation system fails to provide easy access to work or bypasses sub-areas otherwise suitable for development, when water is not available at attractive industrial sites, the economy assumes additional burdens. Public investments and decisions made at the wrong time, in the wrong place, and in the wrong way, serve, in Petshek's words, to "counteract the trend or 'mainstream' of development," and thus are "completely ineffectual, or act in such a way that the whole economic structure is rendered less efficient." At a time when rapidity of growth seems a critical factor in national survival, this tendency of government to work at cross purposes to the economic system may well be the most serious consequence of all.

If these consequences seem undesirable, and if their deficiencies appear to outweigh the advantages of diversity and insularity, then quite obviously a new and different philosophy of government is in order. The requirements of policy-making will have to take precedence over the requirements of simply maintaining some semblance of organized community existence. The carefully devised structure to permit a tolerable flow of public investment will have to give way to a structure which has the authority to make decisions about the region's transportation network, its broad pattern of land use, its common recreational facilities, the renewal of its obsolete sections, the contamination of its air and streams, and the preservation of nature's amenities. The system of representation — of individual

[3] Kirk R. Petshek, *Address* to the NAHRO Research Meeting on Urban Renewal and the Changing Urban Structure, May 15, 1958.

citizens looking directly to one small government or to no government at all — will have to be replaced by a system which uses parties, pressure groups, professional politicians and executives and legislators elected on a regional basis — in short, by a modern democratic system. . . .

But this can happen only if the residents of the metropolitan area change their concept of local government and are prepared to accept a philosophy of positive and coordinated action in place of a "business as usual" and essentially competitive philosophy. Not until such a change in attitudes and convictions occurs can local governments adapt to the metropolitan age and grapple seriously with the problems of metropolitan growth. The customary criticisms that the present structure is administratively inefficient, financially inequitable, poorly organized, and unnecessarily expensive, are not sufficient to bring about this change in outlook. Only a recognition of the new responsibilities of local government will go to the heart of the difficulty: the fact that big governments and policy-minded governments are essential companions of big and complex economic systems.

Throughout this century, people have debated the question of whether or not the American political system could countenance an unbridled laissez-faire economy — whether it did not have to intervene by selective measures to redress the balance of competition, at times to preserve it, and at times to guide it. But in the modern metropolitan region, the question is reversed. The issue is whether or not a modern economic system, requiring positive stimulation and selective aid and direction by public authority, can tolerate an unbridled laissez-faire profusion of governments which systematically avoid any responsibility for these matters.

6

THE METROPOLIS
AND THE FEDERAL SYSTEM

In the American federal system, no metropolitan area constitutes a self-contained political system. Fiscal and jurisdictional inadequacies, the monopoly of the formal powers of government by the higher levels, and the local base of the American political system combine to involve the polycentric metropolis in a complex web of relationships with state and federal government. From the state capital come the legal framework of the metropolitan area's local governments, money and personnel to plan and build its highway network, and funds to offset a growing proportion of the burgeoning educational expenses of its constituent units, to mention only the most important of the state's multiplying activities in the metropolis. Washington underwrites home mortgages, finances the massive federal-aid highway system, and assists local governments with a lengthening list of urban problems, ranging from air and water pollution, mass transportation, and open spaces, through poverty, public housing, and urban renewal.

Constitutional, jurisdictional, financial, and political considerations underlie the growing commitments of state and federal governments in metropolitan areas. Legal and constitutional factors are particularly important in the case of the states. The basic units of the federal system are the states and the nation; the Constitution does not mention local government. Thus, the legal framework of the metropolitan political system is a product of the state legislature, which grants powers to municipalities and other subdivisions of the state, sets standards for incorporation and annexation, creates special districts and authorities, sanctions interlocal agreements and contract arrangements, and provides enabling legislation for metropolitan planning agencies and regional units of government. Because of the dependent legal position of the localities, state involvement in the metropolis automatically increases as local units of government proliferate and their tasks multiply in the wake of urban growth and change.

Jurisdictional advantages also draw the states into the political arenas of the metropolis. Legal powers encompassing all or, in interstate regions, large portions of the metropolis permit the state to overcome some of the difficulties caused by the fragmentation of the metropolitan political system. By basing aid to education on need formulas the state legislature can partially redress the fiscal imbalances in suburbia which result from the differentiation of the metropolis into communities with wide disparities in resources. As might be expected, much of the pressure for increased state school assistance comes from the less affluent and the rapidly growing suburbs where the increase in number of children tends to outrun the addition of new ratables to the tax rolls. The state's jurisdictional advantages also can provide the benefits of regional government without disturbing the political status quo. If there were no state highway department with the power to plan and build an areawide system of arterial roadways, the metropolis would have to create a regional highway agency, perhaps at greater peril to local political and fiscal autonomy than the present system of state control. However, metropolitan areas pay a rather heavy price to secure the benefits of the state's jurisdictional scope. Robert C. Wood's account of New Jersey's efforts to find water for its portion of the New York area shows how state involvement dilutes metropolitan influence in the resolution of urban problems. The water issue was dealt with in the frame of reference of state politics, was bandied about for years by a legislature which over-represented rural counties, and finally was resolved by the electorate of the entire state.

Another attraction of the state is its superior fiscal resources, at least when compared to those of local government. In general, state income, sales, and excise taxes provide greater flexibility, equity, and growth potential than the real property tax, the chief financial prop of local government. Faced with rapidly rising demands and growing resistance to skyrocketing property taxes, mayors, councils, and school boards in the metropolis have turned with increasing frequency to the state capital for assistance. Few state exchequers have proved equal to the challenge. Demands from cities and suburbs for new and enlarged state programs have overwhelmed budget makers in every urban state. The focal point of the pressures for and against new programs and taxes is the governor, the state official most responsive to the restive urban majority. From the moment he takes office, the governor of an urban state is caught in a crossfire between two antithetical majorities, one demanding more from the state and the other opposed to increased state taxation. The fact that many voters, particularly in the metropolis, are in both camps only increases the governor's dilemma, as well as helping to explain the high political mortality rate of governors in the postwar years.

State fiscal difficulties also have contributed to the deepening involvement of the national government in the problems of the metropolis. Constitutional and jurisdictional considerations have been much less important than money in broadening the federal government's metropolitan role. In almost every respect, the federal tax base is superior to the revenue systems of state and local government. Unlike the property levy and most state taxes, the federal income tax cannot be evaded by moving across a local or state boundary. Since federal income tax revenues grow at a faster rate than the gross national product, Washington's financial problems in the prosperous

1960's have been quite different from those of the non-national governments. Instead of joining their state and local colleagues in the politically perilous search for new sources of revenue, federal officials have been faced recently with an embarrassment of riches. Eyeing these mounting federal revenues, the metropolitan areas, and particularly the hard-pressed cities, have successfully lobbied for an expanding set of federal commitments.

Of all the factors which shed light on the increased activity of the higher levels in the metropolis, none is more important than the urbanization of American politics. With urban growth has come a steady increase in the influence of cities and suburbs in the state capitals and along the banks of the Potomac. With over half of the states having a majority of their electorate in metropolitan areas, a growing proportion of the nation's governors and U. S. Senators are responsive to urban demands. The potent role of the large urban states in the national conventions and the Electoral College has made the presidency particularly sensitive to the needs of the metropolis. Finally, reapportionment in the wake of a historic series of decisions by the U. S. Supreme Court beginning with *Baker v. Carr* in 1962 is providing cities and suburbs with a fairer share of the seats in state legislatures and in the House of Representatives.

Growing state and federal involvement in metropolitan areas has rekindled the hopes of those who are dissatisfied with the spreading metropolis and its decentralized politics. Might not the constitutional and jurisdictional powers of the states be used to restructure the fragmented political system? Couldn't state and federal aid be conditioned on the creation of regional instrumentalities? Given their growing urban investments and superior jurisdictional and fiscal capabilities, shouldn't the higher levels take the lead in developing and implementing plans which will insure a less disruptive and costly pattern of metropolitan development? In the second selection in this chapter, the Council of State Governments argues forcefully that "the key to solving the complex difficulties that make up the general problem of urban regional growth lies with state government." The Council rests its case for state leadership in guiding and controlling the forces of urban development on the constitutional powers and jurisdictional advantages of the state, which it calls "an established regional form of government."

In concentrating on the state's potential, however, the advocates of state leadership tend to overlook the state's past performance in the metropolis. State government is not a sleeping giant which is about to awake and revitalize the urban world. Instead, the state has played a major role in creating the sprawling, fragmented, differentiated metropolis and in developing the modes of accommodation which sustain the decentralized system. Through its powers over annexation, incorporation, and the creation of special districts, the state has facilitated geographic and functional proliferation. Few states have used their jurisdictional or fiscal capabilities to promote regional approaches to urban problems. The two most important state activities in metropolitan areas, highways and education, encourage urban sprawl. By concentrating on roads and ignoring public transportation, the state highway departments have played a major role in the outward march of suburbia. Because state school aid usually is skewed in favor of the suburbs, it tends to widen the educational disparity between the city and the suburbs, a gap which is a major cause in the flight of the white middle class from the older cities.

Underlying the failure of the states to achieve their metropolitan potential are the same political forces which have doomed almost every effort to create areawide government. As Harold Herman indicates in his analysis of state-metropolitan relations in New York, the diverse interests of the fragmented metropolis are well-represented in the state legislature. Given the dearth of spokesmen for the metropolitan area as a whole, the pressures on the governor and other state officials come from cities, suburbs, special districts, and other sub-regional constituencies. As a consequence, state action inevitably reflects and reinforces the values of the dominant interests of the metropolis. By fostering functional accommodation to the problems of urban growth and change, New York, like most states, preserves the institutional status quo, relieves the pressures for more basic changes in the system of local government, and promotes continued functional and geographic proliferation.

Federal activities in the metropolis have had the same effect as those of the states. Robert C. Wood points out that federal programs tend to follow rather than guide decisions made in the marketplace. In the absence of an overall national strategy for metropolitan development, federal efforts tend to be uncoordinated and functionally autonomous. As a result, federal policy, like that of the states, encourages urban diffusion, facilitates accommodation, and helps maintain the fragmented political system. In Wood's opinion, however, the prospects for reversing the drift of federal policy are good. To do so, he believes, Washington must come to grips with the basic problem of policy-making in the metropolis — the decentralized political system. Increased federal spending and the creation of a cabinet-level department of urban affairs, the two most frequently advanced proposals for enhancing the federal role in urban development, he argues, fail to deal with this basic deficiency. Wood's alternative is a national policy for metropolitan areas based on employing federal programs and assistance to promote areawide planning and policy-making.

A reorientation of federal policy objectives in the metropolis, however, is likely to be considerably more difficult than Wood anticipates. The basic obstacle is the absence of consensus among the many metropolitan interests represented in Washington. Michael N. Danielson's study of federal-metropolitan relations on the mass transportation issue demonstrates that the influence of the fragmented institutional base on political behavior is as pervasive in the nation's capital as in the political arenas of the metropolis and the state. Differing interests, goals, and capabilities among cities, suburbs, and states produce a wide range of urban views and activities on a metropolitan issue contested in Washington. Like the state legislator from the metropolis, the average urban congressman rarely represents a district that encompasses the metropolitan area. Since his constituents do not view their urban problems in

a regional frame of reference, neither does the congressman. Thus, Danielson's conclusions on federal-metropolitan politics parallel those of Herman on the role of the
state: in a locally-based representative system, the higher
levels tend to be tightly constrained by the values and perceptions of the politically fragmented and differentiated
grass roots.

ROBERT C. WOOD

The Halfway House of State Government

In New Jersey, the historic pattern of each municipality's "going
it alone" in developing water facilities has prevailed . . . The state
has sizable potential reserves within its own borders; but no single
water system, not even that of Newark, has developed those reserves sufficiently to be able easily to share water with its neighbors.
A North New Jersey Water Supply Commission has made progress
in bringing about coordinated arrangements and a State Water
Policy and Supply Council has worked since the 1930's to establish
general plans. Still, metropolitan New Jersey has depended upon
thirty-six separate systems, under both public and private management, to service the counties within the Region. Comparatively
small in size and independent in action, these systems have been
unable to secure and develop sufficient reserves to meet the growing demands in Northern New Jersey.[1]

[1] New Jersey Taxpayers Association, "Series of Informational Memo-
randa on the Water Supply Problem," submitted to the Legislative Commission on Water Supply, mimeographed, 1956, Memorandum #3.

Reprinted by permission of the publishers from *1400 Governments*,
Robert C. Wood (Cambridge, Mass.: Harvard University Press), Copyright, 1961, by Regional Plan Association, Inc.

Thus, though warnings of impending trouble have been sounded in every one of the more than a hundred studies and reports which have been made on the water problem in Jersey since 1900, no major acquisitions of new sites were completed before 1950. By that time, the dimensions of the problem threatened residential and industrial expansion. For the state as a whole, water consumption rose between 1940 and 1953 from 390 million gallons per day to 593 million and the number of residents "per inch of average rainfall" increased from 93,000 to 104,000. For the nine New Jersey counties within the Region, water consumption in 1953 was 420 million gallons daily, compared to an estimated "safe yield" of 415 million. Engineers projected an even greater disparity for the future, requirements being estimated as 620 million in 1980 and 750 million in the year 2000.[2]

With little prospect for expanding supplies through action of individual municipalities, New Jersey in recent years has been receptive to more comprehensive river-basin arrangements. But a 1950 proposal by the Interstate Commission of the Delaware River Basin for interstate allocations of Delaware water among four states (of which New Jersey was one) was abandoned after New York City took unilateral action to develop its own Upper Delaware supplies. Sporadic bilateral negotiations between New Jersey and Pennsylvania also failed to produce an agreement to construct the so-called Wallpack Bend.[3]

Almost as a last resort, New Jersey's state government itself assumed immediate responsibility for providing more water for its northern counties. This alternative has proved to be an uncertain halfway house, occupied by a welter of conflicting interests and procedures. It is an expedient apparently ill-designed to arrive at a quick decision. Unlike a municipality, the state cannot speak only for water-users anxious for a larger supply from whatever source. Unlike a larger Regional enterprise, it cannot stand aloof from the state electorate — or call on interstate or federal resources or embark on a comprehensive program designed to offer a broad range of benefits. Instead, it had to resolve the conflict of interests between urban water-users and rural water-suppliers within its own legislature — and the water problem was only one of a series of issues on the political agenda. For five years, each proposal for a new site ran the gamut of partisan, ideological, and economic interests, not

[2] Taxpayers Association, Memorandum #5.
[3] Taxpayers Association, Memorandum #3.

always relevant to the problem at hand, but always important to the question of who controlled the government. In the end, the state adopted, with modifications, the same plan with which it began — sufficient in the judgment of George Shanklin, state water expert, to meet the area's needs through 1975.[4]

When the plan was first put forward it appeared straightforward enough. In 1953, on the advice of the State Water Supply Council, Governor Robert Meyner recommended the outlay of about $90 million to acquire and develop the site called Round Valley in Hunterdon County, which would supply an estimated 200 million gallons daily.[5] Hunterdon, bordering the Delaware River, is west of the New York Metropolitan Region. After some deliberations, Republican and Democratic members of the legislature reached tentative agreement on this proposal, as well as on plans for water development in southern New Jersey. Early in 1954, legislation was introduced to provide a referendum for a bond issue of $150 million and to establish a new state agency to undertake development.[6]

Partisan agreement was not tantamount to geographical agreement. Though acceptable to the Governor, and initially to both parties in the legislature, the bill did not find favor with the representatives of the areas in which the reservoirs would be built. Senators from five western counties adjacent to Round Valley were concerned lest recreational activities in their lakes and resorts would be eliminated and lest their cranberry industry would suffer. In a 21-man Senate, their opposition swung the balance between party divisions and defeated the bill. A compromise measure, providing for the purchase of the Round Valley site but delaying its development until after further study, passed both houses but in different versions which could not be reconciled in the conference committee of the Assembly and Senate. The Governor's appeals for reconsideration were unsuccessful. The legislature adjourned without taking action. Governor Meyner then called it back for a special session, but it refused to consider any proposal.[7]

In the 1955 legislative session, partisanship joined localism as a prime factor in the struggle over a water program. Governor Mey-

----

[4] "Crises of Growth in North Jersey," *New York Times* (Jan. 31, 1960).

[5] Taxpayers Association, Memorandum #4.

[6] *New York Times* (March 28, 1954). In general the account of legislative action is based on *Times* reports, as specified in that newspaper's index.

[7] *Ibid.* (Sept. 19, 1954), p. 16.

ner called again for action on Round Valley. The caucus of Republicans in the Assembly countered with proposals for a new study and for a Round Valley acquisition bill. The Assembly carried out the caucus plan and passed both measures. But the Senate, again because of opposition from the five western counties, sidetracked the Round Valley bill. It did approve the six-man study commission, of which the Governor was authorized to appoint but a single member. In July the new commission, on recommendation of a professional engineering firm, offered an alternative to Round Valley — the development of the Chimney Rock reservoir in Somerset County. In the judgment of the engineering firm, this site could be developed more cheaply and could utilize water drawn entirely from within the state.[8]

Since the new proposal introduced a new location, it engendered new local opposition; and since it was adjacent to Democratic territory, it changed the partisan battle lines. Opposition arose in the affected cities, the North Jersey Water Supply Commission, and private water companies of the areas. These sources offered a counter-proposal that eight municipalities undertake development of Round Valley, and the Democratic members of the legislature expressed their opposition to Chimney Rock.[9]

At this juncture, the classic legislative problem of conscience versus constituency introduced still another complication. Though all public expression in Somerset County seemed dead set against the Chimney Rock plan, the Republican Senator from Somerset declared himself in favor of the proposal. Given his declaration of intent, the legislature enacted a bill over Democratic opposition, providing for a $60 million bond issue to construct the Chimney Rock reservoir, make additional provisions to maintain water levels in the Raritan Canal, and erect smaller systems. Legislative action alone was not sufficient, however. A referendum was required to add the public at large as a final party in interest. The public proceeded to defeat the Chimney Rock project by 593,000 to 362,000. The rejection was attributed by the *New York Times* to an "anti-borrowing trend, faulty management of the bill, sectionalization, and lack of Democratic enthusiasm."[10]

With the development of internal sites stalemated, the state gov-

[8] *Ibid.* (July 25, 1955), p. 15.
[9] *Ibid.* (Aug. 23, 1955), p. 25.
[10] *Ibid.* (Sept. 10, 1955), p. 26.

ernment in 1956 turned to an attempt to tap out-of-state supplies in the Delaware River. Few Jerseyites objected to the notion of a reservoir in someone else's backyard, and the legislature authorized the purchase of Round Valley for $3 million, subject to the limitation that only out-of-state Delaware River water could be used to fill its reserves. On paper, the plan was attractive to Jerseyites. Unfortunately, as Governor Meyner pointed out, the other states in the Delaware Basin had not agreed to the project, and the Supreme Court had not authorized such interstate water allocations. Political consensus within the state structure had been achieved: the only difficulty was that no water was forthcoming.

In 1957, three major projects having been considered and rejected, and a half-dozen subsidiary schemes proposed and filed away, the state turned back to its own resources. A special advisory group formed by the State Water Resources Advisory Commission and the Department of Conservation and Economic Development presented a new plan designed to provide a basis for compromise. The group recommended the development of still another set of water storage facilities: a reservoir in Hunterdon County and another at Stony Brook, near Princeton in Mercer County, drawing water from the Raritan Canal.[11]

This plan effectively dampened Hunterdon opposition because no local lake water would be used. But it provoked a public explosion from Princeton residents, and by August the legislature had retreated to what now seemed a standard practice of authorizing a special study committee, this time composed of members of the legislature — two Republicans and one Democrat. The committee was instructed to report in 1958, and to make recommendations concerning the development of Round Valley (now without restriction to Delaware River water), and the possibility of compensation to Hunterdon County for losses in its property tax base if Round Valley appeared to be an appropriate site.[12]

At first, this 1957 assignment seemed essentially one of raking old coals and fanning old flames. Before the year had ended, however, nature took a hand. Little rain had fallen throughout the summer, and by September when the committee settled down to work, New Jersey was in the midst of the most severe drought in at least a generation. Trenton's water supply stood at 57 per cent of its reservoir

[11] *Ibid.* (June 2, 1956), p. 21.
[12] *Ibid.* (May 5, 1957), p. 78.

capacity; Jersey City's supply was below 50 per cent; and nine other cities had the lowest reserves ever recorded. The North Jersey Water Supply Commission considered special action to tap the Passaic River; Jersey City's officials talked darkly of rationing water and of bringing it in by tank trucks and milk cartons. Municipalities began to enter into cooperative agreements as their own supplies ran out.[13]

Against this background, the study committee lost little time in proposing a $37 million bond issue, including $21 million for Round Valley, $6 million for a project at Spruce Run, and $3 million to $4 million for Stony Brook.[14] In December the legislature convened in a spirit described as one of urgency and recognition of emergency conditions, and authorized a $40 million bond issue to be voted upon by the people.[15] Two days later rain fell in torrents across the state.

In the following month — January 1958 — Governor Meyner proposed an additional $40 million bond issue. The Senate would not grant this request, but it did raise the total issue to about $46 million including $25 million for Round Valley, and the Assembly concurred. With a flurry of support from organizations of such diverse outlooks as the Congress of Industrial Organizations and the New Jersey Taxpayers Association, the campaign for public approval was launched. In November 1958, New Jersey voters approved the proposed issue.[16]

From one perspective this five-year chronicle of a state in search of a reservoir can be viewed as standard operating procedure for an American state government that is wrestling with a controversial and expensive project. Different interests were differently affected; local sportsmen and recreationists had to come to terms with municipal and industrial water-users; competing state and local agencies had to evaluate proposals according to their future prospects for survival; the two parties had to judge the impact of any given plan on their future strength. The Governor, accountable to a statewide electorate, adopted an attitude quite different from a legislature responsible to a bundle of local constituencies. Since there were a number of separate plans to choose from, and since there existed the possibility of reaching outside the state entirely and thereby avoiding the painful prospect of dispossessing Jersey voters, one

[13] *Ibid.* (Sept. 11, 1957), p. 19.
[14] *Ibid.* (Nov. 16, 1957), p. 11.
[15] *Ibid.* (Dec. 17, 1957), p. 37.
[16] *Ibid.* (Nov. 5, 1958), p. 27.

might consider it natural that the resolution of the issue took time. It is even not surprising that the chronicle ended where it began, at Round Valley — although with important modifications and reservations attached. The participants, the channels of influence, the process of negotiation are familiar components of American state politics.

From the perspective of the New York Metropolitan Region, however, the resolution of the Jersey water problem is best seen as a study of the current pattern of water politics in metropolitan areas. It demonstrates the extent of temporizing which can take place under conditions in which local actions no longer suffice and regional or river-basin institutions are not available. In New Jersey, the halfway house of state government had to deal with an emerging water shortage in essentially non-Regional terms. People outside the New York Metropolitan Region made the key decisions; an electorate much broader than the Region delivered the final approval. Viewed this way, the provision of water to one part of the Region becomes the responsibility of a governmental system which touches only tangentially on Regional problems, and which offers little firm assurance about when and how new facilities will become available.

COUNCIL OF STATE GOVERNMENTS

The States' Role in Urban Development

Every level of government has a vital role to perform in resolving problems growing out of a dynamic urban society. Our federal system has been described as a government of "shared functions," in which many activities and responsibilities involve federal, state and

This selection, originally titled "The States' Role," is reprinted from *State Responsibility in Urban Regional Development* (Chicago: Council of State Governments, 1962), pp. 16-22, with the permission of the Council of State Governments.

local government.[1] In no place are the problems of intergovernmental relations so difficult as in urban areas. Solutions to countless
urban regional development problems now confronting the nation
can only be accomplished through joint governmental effort.

Although the roles of local governments and the national government are indispensable, the key to solving the complex difficulties
that make up the general problem of urban regional growth lies
with state government. There is a setting that must exist before urban development problems can effectively be resolved; and state
government, more than any other government, possesses the im-
plements to mold this setting. There are clear reasons for this.

The ability of local governments to meet critical development
problems is largely conditioned by the state. The tools the localities
can utilize, the money they spend and the powers they exercise,
are to a great extent determined by a wide assortment of state constitutional, statutory and administrative regulations. Even given
the independence that is afforded localities by home rule, the state
still controls and delimits local government functions.

Responsibility for providing a workable pattern of local government in metropolitan areas, with variations as circumstances require,
is clearly a state responsibility, all the more so because the present
complex pattern is its handiwork. Local governments in metropolitan areas face numerous obstacles. These range from deficiencies in
authority and funds to problems that transcend the corporate boundaries of local governments yet deeply affect their capacity for sound
development. There is no doubt that if localities are to function well,
the state must provide the proper framework and many of the
means for them to do so.

State government possesses singular qualifications to make profound and constructive contributions to urban regional development
practice. The state is, in fact, an established regional form of government. It has ample powers and financial resources to move broadly
on several fronts. Far-ranging state highway, recreation, and water
resource development programs, to name a few, have had and will
continue to have great impact on the development of urban and
regional areas. Moreover, the state occupies a unique vantage point,
broad enough to allow it to view details of development within its
boundaries as part of an interrelated system, yet close enough to

[1] Morton Grodzins, "The Federal System." In *Goals for America* (The
American Assembly, Columbia University, 1960), pp. 265-282.

enable it to treat urban regional problems individually and at first hand.

Strong state leadership will in the long run determine its role within the federal system in influencing the character of development within its boundaries. In the past, the extent to which local governments, especially in metropolitan areas, have leapfrogged the states to seek federal assistance for urban renewal, planning, and area redevelopment purposes, suggests that many states have been slow to respond to this challenge.

The need for prompt action applies regardless of whether a state is in the throes of accelerated urban growth or is experiencing the first, faint signs of urban sprawl. On the whole, the record shows that the states now most active in working for solutions are those with the most severe development problems. They have everything they can do, however, to keep up with the rapid pace of growth. On the other hand, states relatively detached from the tumult of mass transit woes, giant subdivisions, freeway swaths, and fast disappearance of open spaces, are in an excellent position to begin laying a solid foundation for good physical development within their boundaries. By charting long-range comprehensive programs, which illuminate the direct and indirect ways action can be taken in the critical area of urban development, these states can prepare themselves in advance for exercising intelligent future leadership.

The Advisory Commission on Intergovernmental Relations has recommended that the states play a more direct and effective part in meeting the problems generated by the growth of metropolitan areas. Their proposals can be classified under the following general summaries.

1. The states should provide an arsenal of remedial weapons to be drawn upon by governments in metropolitan areas.

2. The states should undertake a variety of direct actions to assist local governments in the exercise of their responsibilities.

3. The states should impose certain controls on the activities of local governments in the instances in which localities, acting independently of one another, cannot reach effective agreement.

The nature of state activity, however, necessarily will vary area by area. The principal task may be to equip local governments with a wide assortment of permissive powers, to be utilized as they see fit. More direct assistance of a technical and financial nature may be warranted. State government may supplement the above approaches by exerting greater regulatory and administrative control, coupled with expansion of state development programs in such fields as recreation, transportation and water supply.

The breadth of the state role vis-a-vis local governments thus is extensive, covering a wide range of possible actions. In one sense, the state's potential role can be viewed on a continuum extending from relatively indirect to markedly direct actions. In another sense, its activities can be interpreted on the basis of how permissive or how regulatory they are. Actions open to a state in dealing with local governments include the following:

1. The state may enable existing cities and counties to plan, spend money, raise funds, acquire land, and construct projects for urban development purposes. The state, at a minimum, has the responsibility to see that localities have the basic powers with which to make an intelligent start toward solutions of urban problems. In most instances, localities have these powers, although specific authority to plan or raise funds for a specific function may not always be included within the general statutory authorization.

2. The state may enable localities to collaborate, join together through cooperative arrangements, or consolidate to provide needed services that are difficult to handle satisfactorily on the individual local level. Such arrangements and devices as city-county consolidation, transfer of functions from city to county or vice-versa, the urban county, metropolitan study commissions, multi-purpose functional districts, and metropolitan planning agencies fall into this category. The state's aim would be to foster the enlargement or consolidation of local governments so that these units, in turn, will be more capable of facilitating metropolitan and regional growth. The initiative for adopting any one of the indicated devices, however, is left in the hands of local government.

3. The state may grant technical assistance to localities to help them fulfill their development responsibilities. An arrangement whereby a state planning agency provides staff service to a local government in preparing a comprehensive physical plan or a special planning study is only one of many ways in which such technical aid can be provided. More than likely, the state would require localities to meet minimum standards of performance as a condition for receiving technical aid.

4. The state may extend financial assistance to localities in the form of loans, grants, or tax concessions, in order to broaden the

fiscal base the localities may use to attack urban problems. Financial assistance takes various forms. New Jersey, for example, has a program of issuing grants-in-aid to communities over a five-year period to help carry out continuing planning. Several northeastern states provide funds to cities to help them meet their shares of urban renewal costs. A growing number of states are taking a more active part in metropolitan open-space programs by authorizing funds for localities to purchase the fee or an interest in the fee on land to be utilized for open space. In most cases state financial aid is extended to secure an adequate standard of local governmental performance. State aid often implies state standards, and thus results in a more pervasive influence by state government.

5. The state may regulate or administer certain activities of local government that have area-wide implications. It may move directly to resolve disputes among local units of government in a metropolitan area, especially disputes that cannot be resolved at the local level by mutual agreement, or are of such moment as to impede the effective performance of governmental functions in the area. Another form of direct state action would be to establish rigorous statutory standards for the creation of new municipal corporations within the geographical boundaries of metropolitan areas, and to provide further for the administrative review and approval of such proposed new incorporations by an appropriate state unit. In any case, this form of state action assumes that it is difficult for localities to take effective measures in these matters, so that the state is required to step in to protect the interests of the greater regional community.

6. The state may expand the scope of its activity in areas traditionally the responsibility of local government. State acquisition of land and purchase of easements for open space in metropolitan areas is an example of this form of direct action. Such measures may be precipitated primarily by the inability of localities to act as quickly as essential in the face of rapid growth.

7. The state may itself exercise local functions — but it doubtless will wish to do so only if local resources are completely inadequate for the task, or if the function cannot be performed efficiently by the locality even with state financial aid.

Determination of how far and in what directions a state should go depends on several factors. One is its historical experience in dealing with urban development problems. Some state highway departments, for example, traditionally have played a role in local highway development which leaves many of the decisions up to the discretion of counties and cities. Because this pattern is well established, the states in question may choose to continue this arrangement, rather than assert more direct control over highway development, as is common in most states. The degree of local initiative often is affected by the historical pattern of state financial aid. Some states have a long-standing policy of granting considerable funds to localities for general operations. State standards governing the use of these funds must be met, and thus state guidance over local policy is significant. In other states the major portion of local revenue is derived from local sources.

Another key factor that influences the course of state action is the relative intensity of metropolitan problems. If the supply of metropolitan open space is being devoured too quickly, or if the transportation system is not meeting area-wide needs for the movement of people and goods, the state may conclude that local government is responding too slowly, and that more direct state action is necessary.

Finally, what are the limits beyond which a state should not go in these matters, in order to avoid permanently impairing local autonomy? At what point is state activity excessive? At what point is local government incapable of providing solutions to area-wide problems?

Such questions may have bearing, for example, on the extent of state fiscal aid offered to local governments. State grants-in-aid are often criticized because they are viewed as acts of central government frustrating to local democracy. If policy makers decide that this is so, then the state's role will be limited. On the other hand, the state may reason that state aid actually preserves local governments by giving them the means to provide and maintain activities demanded of them. The argument is made that state financial aid, even while necessitating minimum service standards, utilizes a more effective tax base than the local base, and yet prevents the wholesale transfer of local functions to the state level. In the absence of such aid, localities might be forced to drop important services, thus placing pressures on the state to assume functions which properly should be carried out and administered on the local level.

Another determinant of how far the state should go involves a judgment on whether or not the multiplicity of local governments is causing a loss of local control over local problems of the metropolitan area. Some contend that many services are needlessly duplicated by local governments. They argue that such services could better be provided by a larger unit of government. Others affirm that the states must recognize the basic reluctance of residents in metropolitan areas to give up their local system of government for the sake of achieving the economy and efficiency that is associated with federated or consolidated metropolitan government. In the long run, some of the suburban residents may be willing to pay more for services that could be handled more cheaply at the metropolitan level, in order to retain their local autonomy. Consequently, the system of numerous, small, competing local governments in metropolitan areas may be difficult to alter.

Each state, however, needs to adopt a unified set of development objectives which can become guidelines for the many supervisory, regulatory, and development actions its own administrative agencies initiate or perform. Too often a state has worked at cross purposes within itself in its dealings with local governments. In part, this may be attributed to excessive diffusion of supervisory responsibility within a single field, such as water resources, and, in part it may result from conflicting policies among state agencies responsible for separate operating programs. State agencies are already making a significant impact upon urban development as regards highways, public health, social welfare, planning, urban renewal, recreation, parks, and water resources. But in many states there is no coordinating agency to prevent duplication of effort and conflict among operating programs.

The notable efforts of a few states in setting up offices of local affairs can go a long way toward achieving better coordination of activities on the state level. But something more is needed. In order to achieve effective coordination, the state must have the background upon which to make intelligent judgments. There is a definite need for unifying principles and policies to serve as a framework to guide urban and regional growth. The state can provide this unifying dimension — pulling together facts and information, making statewide projections of economic, social and physical development trends, and formulating imaginative, well-thought-out development goals.

The growing number of comprehensive state planning programs testifies to the heightened awareness of state government of the need to provide some overall, comprehensive direction to the pattern of development within state boundaries. Through such programs, the states can formulate long-range, general recommendations for orderly, coordinated growth. The policies thus established serve a threefold purpose: local governments will have benchmarks to chart their own development programs; state development activities can be more closely integrated; and federal government decisions can reflect development intentions of states before their programs affecting urban regional development are implemented.

In exercising leadership, the state also should act more aggressively in taking the first step to accelerate or cause a change in the development policies of public agencies and private institutions, for the benefit of the people of the state. The state can do this indirectly, without recourse to its extensive regulatory or administrative powers. The work of the numerous state legislative study commissions on metropolitan area problems is illustrative of the role state government can perform. Many practical and useful ideas have flowed from the concerted efforts of these study commissions. Their ideas have served as the basis for state policies on urban regional development, with important effect as well on the thinking of local and federal government. In some cases, state government has been instrumental in mobilizing the best academic minds to apply their findings to problems of an urban society; the Research Triangle of North Carolina is a case in point. Recently, the State of Wisconsin took the initiative to arrange a forthcoming meeting with federal officials for the purpose of achieving more effective coordination of federal-state programs as they apply to urban areas. Many other instances could be cited to show how the state functions or can function to change public and private thought and effort in this field. Common to all the experiences just cited, however, is the fact that state governments have taken the initiative and have provided active leadership.

HAROLD HERMAN

Limitations on State Action:
The View from Albany

Between 1957 and 1960, New York's Joint Legislative Committee
on Metropolitan Areas Study came to the conclusion that solutions
to the problems of metropolitan areas rest eventually with local governments. Although the committee noted the need for some state
action, for the most part, it regarded the state's role as facilitative
and only occasionally stimulative to local innovation. The legislature
has signified its general agreement with the committee's position by
its actions. In effect, the state appears to be following a course long
advocated by Home Rule enthusiasts, acting usually only upon the
request of local authorities. Leadership for metropolitan integration
in New York State rests where it probably must, at the local level.

To expect otherwise is more than unrealistic. Even though their
constituencies are larger, state political leaders are subject to the
same pressures that commit their local counterparts to continued
metropolitan governmental fragmentation. These pressures cannot
be interpreted merely in terms of self-seeking distrust on the part of
politicians to any change that threatens to upset the political systems in which their interests are vested. All too often, this simple
explanation is used to rationalize the defeat of proposals for metropolitan reorganization, attributing their defeat to recalcitrant politicians rather than general unpopularity. On the contrary, political
opposition to reorganization suggests that democracy is in fact working. The divisions in community interest that hinder local integra-

Reprinted from *New York State and the Metropolitan Problem* (Philadelphia: University of Pennsylvania Press, 1963), pp. 178-188, with the permission of the author and the publisher.

tion are accurately reflected in the state legislature, whose members are no more nor less able to reconcile their differences than local leaders.

But are local interests adequately represented in Albany? New York has not been free from criticism on the grounds of legislative malapportionment. Is imbalanced rather than accurate representation of urban interests responsible for New York's reluctance to deal squarely with the metropolitan problem?

The positions of Long Island Republican leaders with regard both to the distribution of state aid to education in 1960 and to congressional reapportionment in 1962 would indicate that, in their eyes at least, malapportionment is less a hindrance to the achievement of their objectives than the possible consequences of a Democratic majority's being seated in the legislature. They were willing to suffer some monetary loss in compromising with rural Republicans over state aid to education rather than form a coalition with the Democratic minority. In congressional apportionment, their voices have yet to be raised in demand for deserved increases in suburban representation. They seem to prefer the present security of the Republican caucus to the instability that might result from opening wide urban-rural cleavages.[1] . . .

Retaining Republican control of state policy machinery is a primary goal of upstate Republican leaders and even of some Democrats; for its alternative is Democratic control, which to many is synonomous with control of the state by New York City. This goal, in turn, is dependent upon maintaining the strength of the local roots of the Republican Party. There is then an element of self-protection in the legislature's hesitancy to tamper with local political institutions. It is operative, however, only in so far as area residents continue to believe that their limited integrative objectives are adequately being served by presently constituted political organizations. There is no evidence at this time to suggest that they feel otherwise.

Leadership is rarely expected from legislative bodies anyway. This quality is usually attributed to the Governor. Is he able to offer more positive leadership in metropolitan affairs? Those who see in

[1] David R. Derge documents the preference for party- rather than constituency-oriented legislative voting in "Metropolitan and Out-State Alignments in Illinois and Missouri Legislative Delegations," *American Political Science Review,* LII, No. 4 (December, 1958), pp. 1051-1065.

the electoral basis upon which he gains office a source of strength that is denied legislators individually and collectively usually over-estimate his ability to act independently of political influence and almost always place too much emphasis on the effect of legislative malapportionment. No less a leader than Governor Rockefeller has found it extremely difficult to do anything but equivocate on metro-politan policy.

In one respect, the Governor of New York is constrained from taking too strong a position on metropolitan issues even more than are other state chief executives. The shadow of the White House, so often pointed to as a factor in his favor, tempers whatever inclina-tion he might have to chance provoking local political leaders in both New York and the nation at large. Their support is vital to his future political ambitions, particularly in New York, where nomina-tions for key state and federal offices are decided by convention.

In short, the state's political leaders are ill equipped to champion measures for far-reaching change in local government in the face of continuing evidence of local preference for the *status quo*. Conse-quently, they have adopted an attitude consistent with the [Joint Legislative] Committee's belief that change will occur when local pressures for uniformity of service become undeniable.

If the political branches of state government are not providing general leadership for metropolitan integration, they are at least participating significantly in the process of adapting local govern-mental operations to newer problems of urbanism. At times, such participation amounts to gentle prodding and persuasion. More of-ten it takes the form of offering municipalities the opportunity to evolve their own methods of dealing with local problems. In a sense, New York is providing a type of leadership which is, if not as vigor-ous as that called for by the Council of State Governments and more recently by the Advisory Commission on Intergovernmental Rela-tions, at least more realistic.[2]

The leadership called for by the council and the commission is about as operationally definable as their concepts of the metropoli-tan problem. Both have taken great pains to stress their practicabil-

[2] In a report submitted to the House Committee on Government Opera-tions, the Advisory Commission on Intergovernmental Relations cites fa-vorably and comes to the same general conclusions as the Council of State Governments. *Governmental Structure, Organization, and Planning in Metropolitan Areas* (Washington: U.S. Government Printing Office, July, 1961).

ity, yet throughout their reports lies the suggestion that a problem
more deep-rooted than that which can be solved by annexation,
functional transfer, and special authority is involved in metropolitan
areas. But of course, they are not recommending the formation of
metropolitan governments.

New York State's position is more forthright. There is no single
governmental problem in metropolitan areas, but rather a number
of difficulties surrounding the provision of selected public services,
which existing local institutions can continue to perform with some
minor adjustments. Through different reasoning, at the same time
absolving itself from the responsibility for providing leadership,
New York has arrived at many of the policies advocated by the proponents of more direct state leadership: the interlocal agreement,
the special authority, the encouragement of expanded county activities, and most of all the sharing of state resources with local units
have typified metropolitan policy in New York State.

In the development of this policy, however, New York's leaders
have consistently held to a functional outlook toward metropolitan
problems and their solutions. Where general legislation has been
called for to permit or encourage intermunicipal cooperation, the
creation of special districts, or, as the commission put it, the building of "an 'arsenal' of remedial weapons" available to metropolitan
areas, New York has preferred to deal with metropolitan problems
with both geographic and functional selectivity. In one respect, it
has surpassed most recommendations for dealing generally with
local governments. In 1946, a per capita block grant to all local units
was initiated. Critics regard this non-conditional sharing of state
resources on the one hand as the best method of helping localities
help themselves, on the other as the surest means of encouraging
the retention of inefficient, marginal units of local government. The
choice of positions is largely a matter of personal prediliction. Even
were techniques of measurement available, the grant's size is as yet
too small to warrant drawing any conclusions.

In pursuing its functional course, the state has virtually ignored
exploring annexation as a metropolitan alternative. New York's annexation laws, in addition to the usual complexity, are extremely
protective to unincorporated territories. Considering the extent of
fringe-area development that has taken place in highly urban New
York . . . and the general opinion that annexation's usefulness is
quite limited, its application to New York is highly questionable.

Again consistent with its over-all policy, New York has continued to extend the scope of its Home Rule law. Constitutional amendments in 1959 considerably broadened the range of county discretion and for the first time included urban towns within the scope of Home Rule. Village officials at this time were particularly apprehensive of the irresponsibility and isolationism that might thus have been encouraged. Their attitude reflects the changing light in which Home Rule has come to be viewed. At one time, it was held to be the answer to most, if not all, local ills. Today it is regarded with some misgivings. The Advisory Commission on Intergovernmental Relations seems to be echoing the early [New York] Tax Commissions' search for formulas delineating governmental responsibilities when it recommends

> local home rule for strictly local problems; metropolitan home rule for area-wide problems, but with the state free to legislate and otherwise act with respect to problems which transcend county boundaries and which are not soluble through interlocal cooperation.[3]

Conceivably, definition of the problem may become more difficult politically than its treatment!

Home Rule in New York has never served to prohibit the state from intervening, when it wanted to, in what are presumably matters of local "property, affairs, and government." The legislature and the courts have seen to that. Moreover, Home Rule has constantly been served up with conditions and procedural requirements that limit the freedom apparently offered.

The County Home Rule Amendment approved by the electorate in 1959 is illustrative of the hesitant one-step-forward, two-steps-back pace that characterizes progress in New York State. The legislature had introduced the amendment in part to formalize the considerable degree of county independence operationally developed and in part to enable counties to adjust themselves to their newer metropolitan responsibilities. It offered considerable local discretion in organizing county governments, but at the same time it restored the requirement of a double-majority approval (a majority in any city and a majority in areas outside of cities) that had been dropped from the constitution by the 1938 convention. The provision requiring a triple majority for proposed transfers of functions to coun-

[3] *Ibid.*, p. 20.

ties (majorities in cities, outside areas, and all units affected by the transfer) was retained in its entirety. . . .

The interplay of local preference and state policy has resulted in the state's offering and local units' choosing forms of metropolitan action least damaging to the territorial and functional integrity of local political institutions. What has been their combined effect on metropolitan integration . . . ?

The state must be credited with contributing to the process of metropolitan integration through fostering an awareness of areal need and encouraging local cooperation in tackling selected problems on a metropolitan scale. Departmental officials have been especially active in promoting awareness of the areal aspects of local activities. The legislature, in addition to making cooperative means of local action available, has at times taken further steps to stimulate their employment through the offer of grant inducements. While not always effective, their joint efforts have assisted in breaking down previous barriers to intermunicipal cooperation. Not to be overlooked is the fact that such cooperation has successfully reduced some of the problems of transportation, water supply, sewage disposal, public health, and others. Metropolitan areas are not falling apart at the seams.

Although the state is helping alleviate some of the most evident manifestations of the metropolitan problem and although it is contributing to integration, defined as a process involving the development of metropolitan consciousness, it has not assisted, primarily because it has not wanted to, integration conceived as the creation of institutional mechanisms for organizing and coordinating policy making in metropolitan areas. There is good reason to believe that state and local concentration on individual service problems is, in fact, hindering metropolitan integration thus defined.

Government is more than a provider of services; it is a political institution of social organization and control. As an integrative institution, government in metropolitan areas should perform the task of eliciting expressions of interest and reconciling differences. To a significant degree, the state itself is now performing this task in metropolitan areas, but none of the current service-oriented undertakings of the state or local governments appears to be contributing to the creation of local institutions for this purpose. The state's functional approach to metropolitan problems appears to be furthering additional metropolitan fragmentation along functional, rather than geographical, lines. Paradoxically, this is occurring at the very time that the county, partly as a result of state policy, is beginning to show a potential capacity to act as an integrative institution.

The cumulative effect of functional policies has been gradually to expand the scope of county responsibility and activity. A remodeled county government could well serve as the agency of metropolitan policy making and administration. Single counties presently include most of these portions of metropolitan areas experiencing the problems of urbanism. The county represents both the largest service unit and the largest unit of local self-government. It has gained in popular stature and respect with its increased responsibilities. The New York county enjoys an advantage in structure lacking in many other states that increases its attractiveness when compared with other proposals for metropolitan government. This traditional unit of government is already federally organized, although quite often disproportionately.

State policy does not, however, look toward the eventual employment of counties for metropolitan government. For the most part, the county has "just growed." Although the state has encouraged expansion of their activities, it has done so with no general scheme of development in mind. In the past, the state usually sought to limit county authority to unincorporated areas whenever possible. Although county-wide authority is today preferred for many functions, the change in attitude has been justified on administrative grounds, with little concern for the county as an institution for governing. The state's opinion of the role of counties in metropolitan-area government might well be summed up by Pope's couplet: "that which is best administered is best."

Functionalism adds a new dimension to metropolitan fragmentation. It poses a problem of integration perhaps more difficult than the mere proliferation of units of government. It fosters intracommunity divisions in interest and leadership, adding these to divisions already founded on jurisdictional lines.

Throughout the state, leadership in metropolitan areas has come to be associated with particular functions. To the extent that opportunities to exercise general leadership still exist in pluralistic American society, they are lessened by increasing isolation of functional responsibilities and horizontal division of these among several units of government. Even traditionally strong mayors have succumbed to the trend toward functional specialization and exclusiveness.

They have seized upon urban renewal as their specialty, leaving other aspects of municipal leadership to other specialists and their interest groups.

Functional division of government has a dual impact on the citizen. It provides yet another obstacle to his understanding and participating in governmental decisions affecting him. Yet, it also offers him security, leading him to believe that there is really nothing wrong with local government (of this he needs little convincing) that a few more sewers or roads won't cure.

State and federal programs reinforce the functional-service definition of the metropolitan problem. They single out problems for treatment, holding out hopes that each successive project they encourage will bring an end to the metropolitan area's ills. One has only to read the glowing newspaper accounts of "how we solved our metropolitan problem" or "how our metropolitan area is progressing" that follow the announcement of new urban renewal, highway, or treatment-plant projects for visual evidence of their lulling effect. Functionalism thus tends to impede not only governmental integration but the development of metropolitan consciousness as well. When a problem has been solved there is little reason to continue to be concerned for the metropolitan area. Moreover, there is no evidence of a carry-over of metropolitan awareness from one specific problem to another.

Proponents of metropolitan action wage their campaigns within their respective fields of functional competence and rarely concern themselves with other problems, let alone with "the metropolitan problem." Each proposal for metropolitan action is considered on its own merits, with little apparent reliance on experience gained from other functional solutions, except where these have produced bitterness and resentment of "interference" and "domination." Metropolitan consciousness is as functionally oriented as metropolitan leadership.

Perhaps no amount of state activity can substitute for the local initiative necessary to progress toward metropolitan integration. Undoubtedly, metropolitan integration cannot occur until such time as the public is prepared to take a critical look at local government as a form of government, not merely as a dispenser of services. Can Albany hasten this day?

It can do so only by admitting that the metropolitan-area problem is political not administrative and that it involves the very nature of local government. It must discard the search for techniques of problem solving and concentrate on developing responsible and representative policy-making agencies in metropolitan areas. No number of functional jointures and agreements will ever provide a suitable governmental (and necessarily democratic) mechanism for planning and controlling the distribution of physical and human resources within a metropolitan area. Administration is not lacking in metropolitan areas; government is. There is little indication that New York will be prepared to adopt such a change in attitude in the foreseeable future.

_____

ROBERT C. WOOD

A Federal Policy for Metropolitan Areas

Season of the Urban Discontent

This is a paper concerned with defining the national interest in metropolitan areas. As such, it has a limited scope and purpose. We will not here tarry long with a description of urban and metropolitan affairs in the United States today; nor examine present Federal programs one by one, nor look into the future of urban America. We will take much for granted; we will make sizeable assumptions; and we will indulge in sweeping generalizations. But we take all these short-cuts for a single purpose — to focus on what goals the Federal government should pursue in carrying out public activities in metropolitan areas and in stimulating public policy there.

The departure point for this analysis is the assumption that events since World War II have inescapably involved the national government in metropolitan problems. . . . While the "metropolitan com-

Reprinted from _The Federal Government and the Cities_ (Washington: George Washington University, 1961), pp. 51-59, with the permission of the author and the publisher.

plex" and "open spaces" are not yet as popular terms as "missile gap" and "growth rate" here, most Washington officials now nod knowingly when the whisper of "gray area" runs through a cocktail party. Indeed, ever since the Ford Foundation began its ten million dollar investment to bring about a "coalition of interests" on urban problems, all signs have pointed to a continued growth of public concern and an apparently inexorable involvement of the national government.

Given this discontent and ferment, it seems appropriate to examine the extent and direction of the Federal effort and to ask what its purpose is. In these respects, I will advance and try to make plausible three propositions. I will suggest first, that present Federal activities are not directed to the basic deficiency in metropolitan areas: The reorientation and restructuring of local governmental institutions. I will argue, second, that in addition to being misdirected, the present activities exacerbate the basic deficiencies – by underwriting going economic, social and political systems and by camouflaging real difficulties. I will try to demonstrate last that while it is not fore-ordained that the Federal government will correct these errors, it is by no means infeasible for it to do so. While cries of grass-roots and local autonomy are often fearsomely ear-shaking, the plain fact is that the Federal government traditionally has been in the process of revamping and reordering the federal system. All the paragraphs that follow suggest that, so far as the metropolitan areas are concerned, Washington now proceeds consciously, deliberately and with some subtlety to pay more attention to acres than people. If it does so, the outcome will, I think, be better – and more democratic – urban living.

The Dynamic System on Dead-Center

The net effect of the operations of the metropolitan economic, social and political systems seems to be a stand off. To be sure, plans for metropolitan reform will still be drafted by what Norton Long calls "the intellectuals of local government," and the banner of metropolitan improvement will still be carried by business leaders tiptoeing into politics. When and where serious problems in public services, revenue and policy-making occur, adjustments will undoubtedly be forthcoming. Yet so will rejections of adjustments. We are painfully ignorant of voter behavior on issues of metropolitan reorganization, but so far the trend in electoral behavior on metropolitan issues has not been encouraging. And, while we know more about the motivations and aspirations of the other participants — the would-be governor in search of an issue, the civic-minded businessman grown weary of the United Community Fund — we are entitled to wonder how enduring their interest in the reasonably subtle values of metropolitan organization will be and how articulate, sophisticated, and effective strategists they will become. In short, it is relatively easy in economic, social, and political terms to project the continuation of the present structure of urban life in the United States. It is more difficult to contemplate a violent wrench in the operations of the present system without the intervention of some outside force.

The most obvious outside force to disrupt the present equilibrium of mediocrity and to encourage the development of governments of competent jurisdiction and policy orientation is, of course, the Federal government. Conceivably, Federal programs could rearrange the ordering of space in metropolitan areas, shape urban institutions and behavior patterns, and powerfully influence the kinds and quality of public services provided at the urban level. Yet quite clearly this is not Federal policy today. Instead, Federal activities operate in the opposite direction: To support business as usual in metropolitan areas, to make urban life tolerable but not good, to postpone the efforts of reorganization and reform. . . .

The specific deficiencies of the array of present Federal programs seem to me to be three: First, within broad areas of national activity, there is no definition of the national interest at all; there is simply support for whatever the private sector of the economy seems to require. Second, where there is policy, it is conflicting policy — the authorization of activities designed to satisfy particular clienteles which set one part of each metropolitan area against another; suburb against city and county against municipality. Third, in place of policy, there is emerging a kind of organizational shell game which mistakes activity for progress. Let me indicate briefly the dimension of each difficulty.

In Search of a National Policy

(1) *A House Is Not a Home.* Perhaps the most disturbing paradox in present Federal activity is that the programs most capable of having and carrying out a national interest in metropolitan areas

are most devoid of purpose. Potentially the most powerful instrument for Federal influence in metropolitan development are the various activities we lump under the name of housing. These possess today the vital characteristics of tradition, flexibility and deep involvement with the pattern of urban land use which make them capable of major influence. They also possess at least inarticulated sentiments in favor of improving urban life. Ever since World War I days and more particularly since the New Deal, the housing tradition in the United States has always been an urban one. Over the years, advocates of the cities and of urbanism have tended to cluster in loose confederation around and within the Housing and Home Finance Agency just as the spokesmen for state governments have found a special hospitality first in the Federal Security Agency and then in the Department of Health, Education and Welfare.

Yet, for all this sympathy, the housing program has never influenced qualitatively the course of metropolitan growth. Fundamentally, it remains a prop to the private market place, a powerful contributor to the volume of new housing in the United States, but not especially to the pattern of housing location. Though the quest for a "decent home" has become a search for a "decent environment," Federal goals are typically limited to improvements in housing design and standards of workmanship. Though a mounting concern with the interrelation of the impact of people, shelter, and space has appeared, the guiding star of the program is the family unit, not the community, and never the metropolitan area. Lenders, bankers, and home-owners receive aid and comfort from VA and HHFA mortgage operations, but not public officials or the public at large when these activities stimulate growth in areas already receiving too much too soon.

It is not impossible, of course, to conceive of the present mortgage programs as something more than a passive support for private construction activities wherever and whenever they choose to appear. With fair rapidity in recent months, the proposal to use these programs as a positive instrument for the selective encouragement of growth has appeared. One version of this concept would seek to encourage renewal activities by establishing preferential terms and conditions for particular types of mortgages. Another would establish criteria of land development applied to withhold or to liberalize Federal support in particular land areas. A third would tie mortgage programs to metropolitan planning, seeking to have the formulation of local and regional land-use goals precede the granting of Federal credit. Whatever the version, the underlying principle is the same — the perfection of instruments that assure not just houses for people, under appropriate interest rate conditions, but houses constructed with a regard for the complex pattern of social and economic relations which characterizes a metropolitan region.

Much the same kind of reformulation can be envisioned for the urban renewal program. Despite the substantial legislative and administrative progress achieved over the last few years, the fundamental limitation of municipal rather than metropolitan orientation remains. To be sure, the present program encourages metropolitan planning and collaborative municipal efforts in the field of land use controls, but these seem tentative steps in view of the magnitude of the problem. If it is fashionable renewal philosophy today to junk the old-style public housing and to emphasize open land residential development or paralleling renewal activity, then a municipality-by-municipality approach will be increasingly unsatisfactory. Like the insurance programs, redevelopment appears to make sense only as a part of a general plan of metropolitan development. Like the insurance programs again, it does not speak today to the fundamental of governmental adjustment and adaptation.

(2) *The Best Things in Life Cost Money.* If one deficiency in national policy-making for metropolitan areas is that in certain critical activities there is no real policy at all, a second is equally obvious. Where the need for public action is recognized and authorized, there is no assurance that any *common* policy exists. Highway engineer, conservationist, sanitary engineer, recreationist, renewal administrator move off in different directions and at different times. Frequently their activities cancel each other out and work in one program negates the other. The assumption is that if the clientele of a particular agency is served and satisfied, the responsibility of the agency is discharged.

The favorite whipping-boy here, of course, is the Federal highway program — in my judgment, somewhat overwhipped. Difficulties have appeared in relating automobiles and mass transportation, in making the painful choice between building more roads where the land is cheapest or less roads where the motorist is more plentiful, in meshing highway construction to renewal and recreational programs. These difficulties are by now a familiar story. And among the transportation intelligentsia the cry now goes up for the "systems approach" for design and interrelation of facilities which will optimize some community values instead of making the motorist an unchallenged consumer king.

There are more offenders than the much maligned engineer. Since the hectic war years of the Lanham Act down to the present day the public health officer, the park planner, the soil conservationist, and the housing administrators have yet to coordinate their work effectively in any single region. While we speculate the redesign of transportation networks, we could also think about emphasizing within our existing national conservation programs the development of urban rather than unsettled areas — of giving top priority to the acquisition of open spaces near metropolitan centers, and of more rapid development of camp and recreational facilities there. In such apparently unrelated fields as the disposal of surplus government land, we could consider asking what new uses are contemplated before we sell to the highest bidder.

We have, of course, one kind of common policy in all these programs — but it seems too easy an escape hatch. Out of the stampede of economists from the private to the public sector these days, the cry goes up that money is all we need to build a better metropolitan world. To many, in the redemption of an affluent society, the existence of talent, organization, and objectives apparently appear as almost irrelevant. Give us the cash, one hears state and local officials cry, and we will do the job.

This answer, I think, is far too shallow an estimate of the problem. Money, quite clearly, has not brought the highway program to the solution of its critical issue: What kind of city should a transportation network stimulate. Money will not answer the question of what we should put in renewal areas we clear. Money will not resolve the terribly difficult question of what we should do with our gray areas even if we decide to make them public reservations. In short, as attractive as the solution may seem to use the Federal government as a revenue base, putting cash in the hands of public officials without offering guidelines for their purchases, it can be as irritating to our fundamental problem as no policy at all.

(3) *Don't Think, Organize.* A companion proposal to the suggestion that we spend our way out of a metropolitan sprawl is that we organize our way to a better urban life. In its typical form, this proposal is a highly limited one; the organization contemplated is restricted to a reorganization plan for Federal agencies with major

responsibility in the field. The assumption apparently is that a national hierarchy of staff and line would develop such interactions that, quickly and inevitably, a policy would emerge full-blown from the depths of the administrative process. Or, the assumption is that somewhere within the Washington labyrinth a policy is already there — but it will take cabinet status for urban and metropolitan affairs before the national interest can see the light of day.

Now there is nothing very harmful in proposals of these sorts unless they are offered in lieu of policy-making. Greater efficiency, order, and rationality is always to be encouraged in the Executive Branch. A voice at the summit is always a valuable instrument, assuming the voice says something. But it is a dubious proposition to argue that organization is a prerequisite before policy can be implemented. Certainly a straightforward history of the Department of Agriculture does not support the thesis that in unity and cabinet status there are always clear answers to vexing public programs. And it is equally difficult to demonstrate a positive correlation between organizational standing and an agency's capacity to implement its objectives. The Corps of Engineers and the Federal Bureau of Investigation do not appear to have been seriously handicapped by their relatively low position on the executive organization chart. Just as clearly, a seat on the President's Cabinet has not resulted in the voice of Labor speaking always with vigor and effect. The real forces which push policy problems up for top-level attention, one senses, are other than administrative or organizational in character.

The problem with these reform proposals, then, is that they may obscure the absence of policy or the misdirection of policy in existing programs. Confident in the belief that once we assemble a better machine for the conduct of metropolitan affairs, we will know where to go, we stand in danger of never addressing ourselves to the real issue of what destination we originally had in mind.

The Politics of National Goal-Making

An analysis that the national interest in urban affairs calls for more attention to the political and social organizations in metropolitan areas and the arrangements of space than the people who inhabit them: that it is being ill served by present programs and not much better served by new proposals, invites the counter-charge of "academic." Policies are not born, the rejoinder frequently comes;

they are painfully made in an atmosphere of conflict and competition. A recommendation that the Federal government help its local counterparts put their houses in order cavalierly overrides factors of tradition, political and bureaucratic stakes in the present structure, the inevitable imperfections of administration and programming. Prudence dictates, one is told, or stern reality makes inevitable, compromises so that one offers carrots but never sticks, prizes but never penalties in the readjustment of our federal system.

Now it is certainly true that national goals rarely appear in the form of decrees and it may be true that the sign of the grassroots is invincible. Perhaps the fatal flaw of America's liberalism is that its citizens think most easily of themselves as individuals bent on personal betterment and rarely as participants in a community which itself liberates and ennobles. But this is a proposition which has never been adequately tested, it seems to me, especially in the urban context. Americans may not like cities because we have so few real ones here. Americans may accept black-top culture as they have mass developed homes because they have had no alternative choices.

At any rate, I tend to be skeptical of the political realists in local affairs, for at least three reasons which seem also practical. One is that the readjustment in Federal programs required to emphasize the environment in metropolitan development, rather than the personal fortunes of the residents, is not a major readjustment. . . . Federal agencies in the history of urban programs have scarcely considered trying to influence local organization. . . . We might borrow the workable program idea from urban renewal and apply it for many programs on a metropolitan basis. What is involved is not the violent rearrangement of local institutions but the development of a professional, comprehensive and competent plan undertaken and carried out under local auspices for metropolitan growth.

Given such a plan, a number of Federal instruments come to bear to persuade local governments to follow its broad outlines. One could imagine, for example, a Federal contribution of three-fourths of the write-down costs for a project in a metropolitan redevelopment program in contrast to the established two-thirds ratio. One could construct a sliding scale for insurance and guarantees in residential construction depending on the priority assigned in a general plan for the particular area in question. One could see similar dividends assigned in pollution control assistance, community facility grants and the disposal of surplus property. The point is that the introduction of Federal standards derived from land use planning is not an especially dramatic innovation, nor is it so nearly a feeble weapon as is often supposed. It is not the blunderbuss of spend-it-up for every local service — but it may be the rifle for selective direction which we so badly need today.

There is a second reason for optimism. Not only is no revolution called for, but the political obstacles involved seem often grossly overstated. The quick reaction to Federal requirement for metropolitan planning is usually "we have trouble enough working in a single municipality. Make us try to coordinate city and suburb and we're through." This has just the tone of cynicism to sound practical, but I doubt if supporters of this view have been in touch with local politics of late.

What we can piece together on urban metropolitan decision-making these days suggests that three characteristics predominate. One, the general public is either profoundly apathetic on development of issues or when the issue is carefully presented, inclined to go along. Metropolitan government in its most formal and flamboyant fashion may not be fashionable, but less dramatic adjustments appear to be acceptable.

Second, whenever we can discover a "metropolitan elite," it is tumbling over itself to be in the vanguard of orderly growth. Witness the extraordinary union of displaced New Dealers and reputable businessmen who are joining forces in the wave of economic base studies now sweeping the country. Third, when the elite doesn't appear (as is most frequently the case) the real power wielder is, peculiarly enough, the formal office holder. Within his own system, the rewards may be optimized, but interject Federal incentives and one may be surprised at the changes office holders themselves can make. "On the metropolitan planning bill," a Massachusetts legislator told me recently, "there is no mystery why it's not moving. There's no hidden opposition to bottle it up. There's just nobody who said he wants it." In these circumstances, if the Federal government is disposed to try, it may discover that the sturdy local American communities are in fact Potemkin villages.

There is a final reason why I think a national interest in guiding, influencing, and helping direct physical land development is not beyond the bounds of reality. However overbearing the initial position of the Federal government may appear, the national interest here defined supports rather than threatens local government in the

United States. If the long and tedious process of evolution of metropolitan institutions is brought off by consistent national encouragement, our federal system emerges stronger at the local and perhaps state levels than the national. The chronic structural weaknesses are corrected and the local agencies equipped with resources to match capacities all their own.

I think that it is not unreasonable to believe that the American people can come to understand and to support this definition of the national interest. At least it seems that every suburban *exposé* and central city defense in recent years has revealed an extraordinary popular concern with the quality of every-day life and government. Given a clear statement of domestic national purpose and given an outline of what our cities might become, the great beast Public Opinion does not seem formidable. On the contrary, the odds seem to be at least equal that Americans would prefer a Federal government vigorously guiding the processes of urban growth than underwriting a life with which they are already deeply discontented.

———————————

MICHAEL N. DANIELSON

The Pattern of Federal-Metropolitan Politics

Federal-metropolitan politics is a natural extension of the fragmented political system of the metropolis. Since the metropolitan
area commonly lacks regional institutions, legal recognition, and
public officials with areawide constituencies, the focus for political
activity is submetropolitan or supermetropolitan. Regional issues are
contested in terms of the interests of the central city, the suburbs,
the authorities, and the states. From a welter of conflicting constituency interests comes a metropolitan political process in which the
participants "are committed . . . to particular solutions of particular
problems. What results is a competitive scramble for available resources and power. The notion that there might be common goals
and resources becomes lost in the struggle."[1]

The mass transportation issue provides ample evidence of the
pervasive influence of particularism on federal-metropolitan politics.
When the commuter crisis first stimulated efforts to influence Washington, metropolitan actors from the New York area sought to save
northern New Jersey's commuter service, safeguard New York State's
tax relief program, secure federal aid for the New Haven Railroad,
pacify constituents in Bergen or Morris County, shield New York
City from new mass transportation financial burdens, or achieve
some other limited goal. Enlisting federal help for the improvement
of public transportation on a comprehensive regional basis tended
to be ignored, particularly by state and suburban interests, until
much later.

[1] Robert C. Wood, *Metropolis Against Itself* (New York, Committee for
Economic Development, 1961), p. 32.

Reprinted from *Federal-Metropolitan Politics and the Commuter Crisis*
(New York: Columbia University Press, 1965), pp. 183-189, with the
permission of the publisher.

Regional interests are represented at the federal level by various metropolitan actors, each of whom perceives regional problems in the perspective of its particular institutional base and none of whom possesses a regional mandate. Each participant brings to federal-metropolitan politics a set of values and resources which differ little from those governing its behavior in the internal politics of the metropolis. Thus, suburbia seeks federal help preoccupied with local problems, inadequately equipped for effective action beyond its borders, and fearful of proposals· which threaten autonomy or unequal costs and benefits. As for the regional congressman, his position in the larger metropolitan areas resembles that of the local politician. Since his district embraces only a portion of the metropolis and his constituents rarely perceive their problems as regional, the congressman is reluctant to devote his limited resources to complex metropolitan problems. State relations with the national government on regional problems are conditioned by the pressure of mushrooming urban demands on limited state fiscal resources and the necessity of the urban governor to function in a supermetropolitan constituency in which the rural sector traditionally has been overrepresented. Dedicated to preserving the urban core, the central city comes to Washington with an areawide frame of reference and a willingness to use the region's most potent aggregate of political resources for revisionist purposes, particularly with respect to public finance.

The mass transportation issue illustrates how these differences in regional perspective and in influence at the national level interact with the traditional positions of the states, cities, and suburbs in intergovernmental relations to produce characteristic attitudes toward the involvement of the federal government in metropolitan affairs. All these factors — outlook on regional matters, capabilities in the federal arena, and orientation toward federal-metropolitan relations — combine to provide each metropolitan actor with a distinctive set of interests and goals in his Washington ventures. Different goals, such as the crisis-inspired endeavor of the New Jersey suburbanites to amend the Transportation Act, the states' efforts to save commuter service on the New Haven, or the central-city coalition's campaign to secure support for mass transportation, require distinct kinds of resources, investments, and influence. Activities in pursuit of these goals, in turn, shape the patterns of participation by the suburb, by the state, by the central city, and by the urban congressman in federal-metropolitan politics.

Since the federal government is not an important factor in suburban politics, participation in federal-metropolitan relations at the suburban grass roots tends to be sporadic, crisis-stimulated, and concerned primarily with the short-run local aspects of a problem. . . . [E]ven the commuter, often cited as the most cosmopolitan of the suburbanites by virtue of his daily journey across the metropolitan landscape, usually views his transportation dilemma in a localistic and remedial perspective. In pursuing their limited objectives in Washington, suburbanites are hampered by the meager political resources afforded by their fragmented institutional base, the absence of national suburban pressure groups, and their heavy dependence on the local congressman.

Like the suburbs, most urban states have a limited and negative orientation toward federal involvement in urban affairs. The mutual interest of state and suburb in federal-metropolitan politics springs from partisan ties, as well as from a common fear of financial involvement in regional arrangements, a shared antipathy toward the city, and a mutual interest in resisting the extension of federal-city links. This last factor is particularly important since the states are extremely sensitive to the threat that direct federal aid programs pose to their role in local affairs. The behavior of New York and New Jersey illustrates clearly the typical state posture in federal-metropolitan politics: little interest in the development of long-term federal urban commitments, opposition to direct federal-local relations, and insistence that federal aid be channeled through the states.

The role of the central city in federal-metropolitan relations contrasts sharply with that of the suburbs and the states. Money, political realities, and the adverse impact of the decentralization of the metropolis on the urban core have made the central city the major force behind the involvement of the national government in urban problems. Onerous burdens have been placed on the city by the need to build expensive highways, to maintain sagging public transport systems, to replace spreading slums, to revitalize deteriorating downtowns, and to meet the burgeoning demands of an increasingly lower-class and non-white population on the local treasury. Suburban dedication to the fragmented political and fiscal system prevents the city from tapping much of the wealth of the metropolis. Help from the statehouse, where rural forces are commonly overrepresented and exchequers are chronically overburdened, is rarely adequate. As a result, argue the mayors, the cities are "the unwelcome stepchildren of the counties and the state" and "have no other choice than to journey to Washington."[2] Here the political process is more responsive to urban needs, here assistance can be obtained on terms favorable to the cities, and here the suburbanite can be tapped indirectly through the federal income tax.

Superior capabilities, an ability to mobilize interests from all parts of the nation, and a sustained interest in broadening the federal government's urban responsibilities make the central city the most influential participant in federal-metropolitan politics. In their efforts to enhance their alliance with Washington, city leaders can employ the many resources of the region's major unit of government, the influence of its most prominent political and economic figures, particularly the mayor, the help of the nation's great metropolitan dailies, and the efforts of the national urban lobbies. On the mass transportation issue, a combination of these assets first forged the urban-rail alliance. Then the geographical base of support was widened; as an official of the American Municipal Association noted in 1961, "Two years ago interest in federal help for commuter railroads was centered almost entirely on the eastern seaboard. But now we have west coast cities, like Los Angeles and San Francisco, and even southern cities behind us."[3] Next, the familiar central-city alliance of Democratic politicians, downtown economic interests, commuter railroad and transit operators, metropolitan newspapers, planners, professors, and regionally oriented civic groups was reproduced at the national level in support of the federal transit legislation.[4]

Suburban, state, and central-city perspectives, as well as those of the city's various districts, are reflected in the behavior of the congressional delegations from metropolitan areas. Since House districts encompass few metropolitan areas with more than half a million residents, the average urban congressman, like most other metropolitan actors, views the metropolis from a subregional institutional base and in the light of the particularist demands of his city or suburban constituents. For most congressmen, identifications with their

[2] Ben West, "Federal-City Relations from the Cities' Point of View," in George Washington University, *The Federal Government and the Cities* (Washington, 1961), p. 21.

[3] Statement of Patrick McLaughlin, *Wall Street Journal*, May 2, 1961.

[4] By 1964 the central-city forces supporting the mass transit bill had organized an Urban Passenger Transportation Association, composed of representatives of the AMA, the U.S. Conference of Mayors, the Institute of Rapid Transit, the Railway Progress Institute, and the American Transit Association; for an account of the activities of the association in attempting to steer the bill through the House of Representatives, see Newark *Sunday News*, May 24, 1964.

district, party, faction, and committee far outweigh any nebulous obligations arising from the fact that they represent part of a metropolitan area. Another factor inhibiting congressional involvement in metropolitan issues is the limited capability of the average urban representative for effective action in an area of emerging federal legislative concern. Efforts in the House on the mass transportation issue highlight the restrictions imposed by committee assignments, seniority, the lower chamber's conservative leadership, party loyalties and rewards, personal interests and abilities, and limited staff resources. Whether in response to constituency pressures or for broader reasons, most forays on the part of the urban congressman are both nominal and ineffective.

Compared with his colleague in the House, the urban senator is more likely to bring to federal-metropolitan politics a regional outlook and an opportunity to affect the consideration of urban issues. The statewide constituency and the six-year term foster a broader perspective on the metropolis than is afforded the House member. On the other hand, the senator's Washington sphere of operations liberates him in large part from the constraints that the state institutional base imposes on the urban activities of the governor. A good example of the difference between the gubernatorial and senatorial role in federal-metropolitan politics is provided by Abraham Ribicoff of Connecticut. While governor he followed Rockefeller's lead and largely ignored the movement to develop a federal-urban mass transportation program, but after his election to the Senate in 1962 he moved to the forefront of those in Congress advocating federal assistance for metropolitan transit systems.[5] Mass transportation politics also illustrate the senator's superior capabilities for action on urban issues. Senators Case and Williams were more successful than Representatives from the New York area because they served in a smaller, less hierarchical, more liberal chamber, in which individual members have greater prestige, more committee posts, adequate staff assistance, and far greater opportunities for influence and leadership.

All these factors help explain the characteristic behavior of the various urban participants in federal-metropolitan relationships. As the many facets of the mass transportation issue emphasize, however, national forces also play a crucial role in shaping the pattern of federal-metropolitan politics. The variables affecting the outcome of federal-metropolitan interaction are national rather than local, re-

[5] In fact, Ribicoff made his maiden speech in the Senate in defense of the Kennedy administration's mass transit bill.

gional, or state. The need for widespread urban support and national alliances is clear in the failure of the Transportation Act amendments compared with the success of the mass transit legislation. And because national considerations are the key to victory, leadership on federal-metropolitan issues is exercised more successfully by those urban actors who can mobilize for effective action at the national level.

The complexity of the national government and the multiplicity and magnitude of its tasks also shape federal-metropolitan relations. The federal government is hardly the monolithic entity that its critics decry. Rather it is "a government of separated institutions sharing powers."[6] Within and among these institutions exists a dynamic pattern of conflict and consensus, competition and cooperation. Based on a national constituency, the federal executive is more responsive to urban needs than Congress is. But, as the 1961 mass transit controversy indicates, interagency conflict, budgetary constraints, and the inexorable pressures of foreign policy and national defense limit the effectiveness of the Presidency in defense of urban interests. Another critical national influence on federal-metropolitan politics is the scattering of responsibilities for parts of problems such as transportation and urban development among a host of executive agencies, independent bodies, and congressional committees. This lack of focus multiplies and entangles the channels of information and influence to federal decision-makers. While widening the choice of urban claimants, this diffusion of responsibilities also invites competition, delay, and stalemate.

The result is a system in which the many pathways to the national capital attract numerous metropolitan actors, each motivated by a different perspective of the urban landscape and none representing the metropolis as a whole. From a constellation of federal agencies, commissions, committees, and individuals, most seek particular remedies for the maladies of their particular fragments of the metropolis. Few of the federal participants can satisfy urban demands independently, but most can block action unilaterally. In this scramble, capabilities and influence are unequally distributed; perceptions, attitudes, interests, constituency concerns, and goals vary widely. From the interplay of these many variables comes the characteristic pattern of federal-metropolitan politics.

[6] Richard E. Neustadt, *Presidential Power* (New York, Wiley, 1960), p. 33.

7

THE FUTURE METROPOLIS

Nothing is more certain in urban America than the prospect of change. The demographic, social, economic, and technological forces which have created the spreading metropolis and its decentralized political system show no sign of abating. By 1980, there will be 80 million more Americans than there were in 1960. Most of this growth will occur in metropolitan areas, which by the end of the century should contain close to 90 per cent of the nation's population. Metropolitan growth in the coming decade will exceed the combined 1960 populations of the three largest metropolitan areas — New York with 14.8 million, Chicago with 6.8 million, and Los Angeles with 6.0 million. All available evidence points to an acceleration of the decentralizing trends which between 1950 and 1960 almost doubled the amount of urbanized land in the United States, while nearly halving the metropolitan population density.

Distress over the failure of most metropolitan areas to develop areawide institutions of government has led some urban commentators to conclude that the socially and economically dynamic metropolis is politically static. However, as the readings in the previous chapters amply document, the transformation of the metropolitan political system has been no less sweeping because the prevail-

343

ing pattern of adjustment has been evolutionary rather than revolutionary. If local government had been static in the face of the political pressures generated by urban growth and change, it undoubtedly would have been replaced by some form of metropolitan government. Instead, the system of local government in the metropolis has been in a constant state of flux. The product of this continuing process of adjustment to the forces of urban dispersion is the politically decentralized metropolis. One need only compare the complex mosaic of local governments, inter-local agreements, special districts, and federal-state-local relationships with the relatively self-contained politics of the nineteenth century city to see the extent of the changes in local government and urban politics in the age of the metropolis.

Given the sustained outward growth of the metropolis, the weight of the evidence presented in this volume clearly indicates a continuation of the main trends of contemporary metropolitan politics. With most new urban development expected to occur at the outer reaches of the metropolis, the familiar political pattern of suburbanization should repeat itself countless times. The search for local control over land, taxes, and schools will promote proliferation of small scale, autonomous governments, while the quest for self-sufficiency and social status can be expected to foster continued differentiation. Lacking adequate jurisdictional and fiscal capabilities to meet burgeoning demands for a widening range of public goods and services, the many governments of the spatially expanding metropolis will tread the well-worn path of accommodation. In order to preserve their autonomy, local governments will continue to relinquish control over numerous activities, as they create special districts, forge interlocal agreements, and seek greater state and federal involvement in the solution of their problems.

While much of the recent political history of the metropolis will be re-enacted, especially along the urban frontier, the future will not be a carbon copy of the past, particularly in the developed suburbs and the older cities. Of growing significance for politics in the metropolis will

be the changing nature of suburbia. As more urban dwellers acquire the means to purchase homes, the class and
ethnic base of suburbia broadens. To be sure, the politics
of differentiation tend to make individual suburbs relatively homogeneous, but suburbia as a whole becomes
more heterogeneous. Commercial and industrial development also is widening the spectrum of suburban politics.
With shopping centers and industrial parks come a new
set of economic leaders, an expanding range of issues, and
greater possibilities for conflict in the formerly consensual
political arenas of suburbia. Diminished in the process is
the influence of the typical suburban activist whose political concerns center on the protection of residential property values and the maintenance of a superior educational
system. Even more traumatic changes face the inner suburbs as low-income and non-white city dwellers move out
from the urban core in search of better housing closer to
the new suburban industrial and commercial jobs. Clarence Dean's article illustrates some of the effects of these
demographic and economic shifts on party politics in the
suburbs of New York. As he notes, symptomatic of the
changes in suburbia is the erosion of the once monolithic
Republican strongholds of Westchester, Nassau, Bergen,
and Fairfield counties. Democrats no longer are social
outcasts in suburbia; they even win elections!

For the older cities, the future almost certainly will
bring greater dependence upon the federal government.
Few cities will share in the new development; all will
continue to face the most intractable consequences of
urban growth and change. Resources exceeding those
available to the cities will be needed to halt the spreading
slums, the flight of commerce and industry, the exodus of
the middle class, the declining schools, the deterioration
of transit systems, rising unemployment, and mounting
welfare burdens. Little help can be expected from the
cities' traditional antagonists in suburbia and the state
capitals who studiously avoid financial commitments to
solving the costly problems of the city. As indicated in the
previous chapter, Washington both has the money and is
responsive to the needs of the cities, which in turn are

well-organized for action in the national political arenas. The alliance between the federal government and the cities is particularly effective when the Democrats are in power in Washington. Since 1961, it has produced significant increases in federal urban renewal funds, a new program of transit assistance, a federally-financed war on poverty aimed largely at the urban poor, and a massive program of federal aid to education which, unlike state school assistance, will benefit cities more than suburbs.

In the opinion of Charles H. Percy, the unsuccessful Republican candidate for governor in Illinois in 1964, the federal-city axis is a "sinister alliance" designed to preserve the power of the declining cities. Percy's contention that federal aid to the cities is inimical to the interests of the suburbs, the states, and the Republican Party is likely to become a familiar refrain during campaigns in the years ahead. State leaders, particularly among Republicans, will play upon suburbia's fear of both the city and the federal "monolith" in an effort to retain the allegiance of suburban voters, whose influence will be greatly magnified in the coming decade by legislative reapportionment. Highway, education, and other state programs in the metropolis undoubtedly will continue to be skewed in favor of suburban needs. The probable result will be a reinforcement of the political and programmatic ties between the suburbs and state government parallelling the development of closer relations between the cities and Washington.

Regardless of what alliances emerge, however, the investments of the cities, suburbs, states, and the federal government in metropolitan areas will continue to mount. Few of these decisions have been guided by comprehensive strategies for regional development. Like the political system which it serves, planning in the metropolis is geographically and functionally fragmented. As the pace of metropolitan development quickens and the levels of urban public investment steadily rise, the lack of coordination and common purpose in the public sector attracts increasing attention. During the past decade, the worsening political prospects of areawide government have moved metropolitan planning to the forefront of the remedies proferred for the growing pains of the metropolis. In an excerpt from a report prepared for the U. S. Senate Subcommittee on Intergovernmental Relations, Charles M. Haar and his associates at the Joint Center for Urban Studies argue that comprehensive regional planning is essential for a more beneficial pattern of urban development in the future.

To date, the 140-odd metropolitan planning agencies have made a modest contribution toward the comprehensive planning and coordinated development envisaged by Haar and his associates. As with other efforts seeking to integrate policy-making in the metropolis, the stumbling block to effective metropolitan planning is the fragmented political system and its hypersensitivity to perceived threats to the autonomy of its components. State legislation authorizing the creation of metropolitan planning agencies invariably reflects the opposition of the dominant interests of the metropolis to coercive areawide planning. In every state that authorizes it, regional planning is advisory and participation by local governments voluntary. Nowhere can a metropolitan planning agency compel compliance with its plans; nor are they generally close advisers to federal, state, and local policymakers. As a consequence, the metropolitan planners rarely fulfill their potential for leadership and guidance. Instead, they become another participant in the already crowded metropolitan political system. Lacking power to enforce their plans and having no programs of their own to implement, the planners have far less influence on regional development than the local governments which tax, spend, and zone, or the functional agencies which shape land use patterns with their highways, water lines, and other facilities.

By and large, the metropolis has ignored the periodic calls for the rescue of metropolitan planning from the doldrums. Like the urban reformers who are its most ardent advocates, those with an interest in the institutional status quo view effective regional planning as the Trojan Horse of areawide government. Were it not for the federal government, the prospects for an appreciable increase in the influence of metropolitan planning agencies on the development of the future metropolis would be negligible. Washington, however, has been smitten with the idea of metropolitan planning in recent years, largely because of growing unhappiness over the haphazard impact of federal programs on urban development in the decentralized metropolis. Since 1960, the emphasis in federal planning policy has shifted from the promotion of metropolitan planning through grants-in-aid to the far more thorny objective of securing compliance with metropolitan plans on the part of local, state, and federal agencies. Jerry Landauer's account of the early stages of the federal campaign for a planned metropolis underscores the obstacles facing Washington in its latest venture into the wilds of the politically fragmented and functionally autonomous metropolis.

Metropolitan planning and federal aid programs conditioned on areawide plans certainly will influence urban decision-making in the future. But an expectation that planning or federal assistance will radically alter the nature of regional development or the workings of the political system ignores the underlying lessons that emerge from the study of metropolitan politics. As long as power remains geographically and functionally fragmented, cooperation, compromise, and accommodation to the political values of the existing system will characterize regional ventures. Instructive in this respect is the experience of the metropolitan councils, another device designed to foster regional perspectives and coordinated policy-making. Roscoe C. Martin's analysis of one of these voluntary associations of government officials demonstrates how political realities restrict the sphere of regional cooperation. While not without accomplishments, the Metropolitan Washington Council of Governments must limit itself to non-controversial, self-executing programs that disturb neither the political nor fiscal status quo.

Cooperation among the many geographic and functional units of the future metropolis may not be as tightly constrained as has been the case with the Washington council. But the basic principle will remain the same. Mutual interest is the essential ingredient in any joint undertaking in a unit veto system. As long as the components of the metropolis retain their autonomy and their influence at the higher levels, metropolitan plans, regional councils, and state and federal programs will accommodate to the interests of the decentralized system. To survive, the polycentric metropolis will have to continue to meet the service demands of a growing population. To date this has been the system's great strength. Perhaps the modes of accommodation are untidy and inefficient, yet they have been sufficient to foreclose revolution and are likely to remain so. The glaring weakness of the system will continue to be its lack of concern for the general welfare, particularly in the wornout neighborhoods of the cities and older suburbs. In these complex problem areas, federal aid increasingly will fill the gaps produced by the social irresponsibility of the metropolis.

A final question remains: How much difference would area-wide government make to the development of the future metropolis? Judging from the experience of Toronto, not nearly as much as the advocates of metropolitan reform would have us believe. Since its inception in 1953, the Municipality of Metropolitan Toronto has made impressive strides in the fields of water supply, sewage disposal, school construction, parks, and expressways. On the basis of these achievements, Frank Smallwood concludes that Toronto's experiment in metropolitan government has been a success. However, as Smallwood notes in the final reading, Toronto's metropolitan government has been far less effective when it has dealt with social problems like housing or issues such as transit which involve unequal costs and benefits. In other words, metropolitan government has worked well when serving as a multifunctional special district dealing with the service problems which most metropolitan areas find a way to resolve without areawide government. Metro is likely to falter, however, when it faces the issues that divide the many interests of the typically unstructured metropolis. Regional government probably can provide a more efficient instrument for the resolution of common service problems, but, as the Toronto experience indicates, the existence of an areawide government does not automatically foster a sense of regional community and an enhanced concern for the general welfare of the metropolis. In fact, the creation of a formal metropolitan political arena may only serve to intensify the political differences and conflicts produced by urban growth and change.

CLARENCE DEAN

The Changing Political Pattern
in the Suburbs

Every polling place in Westchester and Nassau Counties will be opened tomorrow because of countywide contests within the Republican party. Such evidence of disunity among the long-dominant and well-disciplined suburban Republicans would have been unthinkable in former years.

The nature of political organization and leadership in the suburbs has changed, as have other elements of the suburban power structure. Fragmentation and dilution of power characterize the change. Omnipotent political bosses are disappearing. The Republican monopoly on suburban votes is declining. Being a Democrat is now respectable.

New sources of power have come into being. The bedroom communities of yesteryear now house, or have nearby, large industrial organizations and vast highway shopping centers. The power of the banking industry has been altered by widespread mergers and by the multiplication of branches, some of them from New York City. The single local bank no longer is the financial pillar of the community.

All these aspects of the evolving suburbs are reflected in the change in the nature of political leadership. The era has passed when the late William L. Ward could rule Westchester as a benevolent Republican despot from his roll-top desk in Port Chester, or when J. Russel Sprague, now 77 years old and ailing, was the unquestioned leader in Nassau. Mr. Ward a wealthy manufacturer of nuts and bolts, a Quaker and a man of unquestioned probity, had no aversion to being identified as the boss of Westchester. For 37 years he was. He filled county offices without hesitation, sometimes quite informally as he sat on the spacious porch of his home on a Sunday morning. He built the county's parks and its parkways and ruled out the proposed extension of the city's subways to Westchester. The county, he decreed, was to be "class instead of mass" — and so it has remained.

The present Republican chairman of Westchester is no such patriarch. A quiet-mannered apple grower from Yorktown, Theodore Hill, Jr. accepted the position with some reluctance; he felt, he says, he was needed there. One of the attributes that led to Mr. Hill's appointment was his talent, demonstrated as a member of the State Assembly for 23 years, in diplomacy and conciliation. "In politics today," he says, "you have to kiss your way along." As chairman, Mr. Hill succeeded Edwin G. Michaelian, who was also the County Executive. Dissension had arisen within the party over Mr. Michaelian and his dual office.

Another political power in Westchester today is the Democratic county chairman. A liberal, urbane in mien, William F. Luddy commutes to New York, where he operates a news service for retailers. He personifies the social acceptability that Democrats now enjoy in the suburbs.

In Nassau County, where Mr. Sprague, a lawyer and a master of political strategy, held the reins for 24 years, the change is visible, too. The Republican leader now is Joseph F. Carlino, a handsome, immaculately groomed 46-year-old lawyer from Long Beach. Nassau is not Mr. Carlino's only political interest. In Albany he serves as Speaker of the Assembly, and some of his critics say his heart is in the capital. But even at home Mr. Carlino does not enjoy the unchal-

lenged authority that belonged to Mr. Sprague. Nassau now has its
first Democratic County Executive, Eugene F. Nickerson. Mr. Nickerson reflects the change not only in being a Democrat, but also in
his person. Ivy League, 45 years old, Mr. Nickerson is a former corporation lawyer. Since his election in 1961, he has established a record of improved county government. His prospects for re-election
this fall are considered bright. Allied with Mr. Nickerson is John
F. English, the county Democratic chairman. Mr. English is 38, a
lawyer and a tough in-fighter whose Irish blood boils readily.

Elsewhere in the suburbs, also, the political titans of the old era
have passed without leaving counterparts — Supreme Court Justice
Arthur S. Tompkins in Rockland, R. Ford Hughes and W. Kingsland
Macy in Suffolk. Even in Jersey's staunchly Republican Bergen
County, Walter H. Jones, the county chairman, does not approach
the power held by his predecessors, John Dickerson and Walter
Winne, whose regime collapsed in the gambling scandals of the early
nineteen-fifties.

As strong political control has diminished in the suburbs, new
sources of power have arisen through the development of industry
and commerce. Long Island has the aircraft industry, Westchester
has industrial giants like I.B.M. and General Foods, Bergen has Ford
and Curtiss-Wright. Huge highway shopping centers have come to
the suburbs. In Paramus, Bergen Mall and Garden State Plaza represent a total assessed valuation of $41.5 million. All of these, in some
degree, exercise power and influence, but it is diffused and fragmented — in part because of absentee ownership of the enterprises.
There is a parallel in banking. The movement toward merger of
banks and the rapid development of branches — Nassau has more
banks per capita than New York City — has made the locally owned
suburban bank a rarity. Competition is sharp, and the mortgage
seeker who once had no choice in banks now can shop around.

In all this change, a few vestiges of the old order remain, especially in the New Jersey suburbs. In Hudson County there is the
taciturn, remote John V. Kenny, who broke the back of the notorious
Frank Hague machine in 1949 and who has remained the Democratic helmsman ever since. And in Essex County there is Dennis F.
Carey, described by friends and foes alike as a throwback to another
era. He was elected last month to his 11th term as Democratic chairman of the county, which includes not only Newark, New Jersey's
largest city, but also such well-heeled suburbs as Short Hills, Mont-

clair and West Orange. Now 60, Mr. Carey has been politically active for 40 years. The suggestion that his influence is very considerable he modestly disclaims, but *The Newark News* and others have
been assailing him for years — unavailingly — as the county's boss.
Mr. Carey prefers to describe himself as "a business type of politician." He spends full time in his modest office on the 16th floor of
the National State Bank building in Newark. Aspiring postmasters,
and others, can be found waiting in the anteroom. Ruddy, white-
haired and dapper, Mr. Carey can be imperious and ingratiating in
turn. He is given to aphorisms: "If you don't tell a lie, you don't
have to remember so much." "It's better to say 'no' and have a 10-
minute argument than to say 'yes' and have six months of grief."

In Mr. Carey's domain, the party organization turns out the vote
with block-by-block precision. A problem is developing, however,
with the rapid growth of Newark's Negro population, now estimated
at 36 to 50 per cent of the city. An all-Negro slate was entered in the
last election under the label "New Frontiers" and polled 10,000
votes. While Mr. Carey's strength is pre-eminently in Newark, he
and the Democratic party have been helped in such areas as Mont-
clair by a development common to all the suburbs, the increasing
respectability of being a Democrat. "I remember the time when corporations wouldn't be found dead with a Democrat," Mr. Carey says.
"Now they're in my office."

Nassau provides the conspicuous example in its election of a
Democratic County Executive. A dozen years ago, Republican control in the county was so tight that new residents moving out from
the city, many of them Democrats, were told pointedly they would
be well advised to register as Republicans. Many did. Democratic
respectability has grown in status-conscious Westchester too. Mr.
Luddy, the county chairman, believes it was forwarded greatly here
by the eminent acceptability of the late President Kennedy and his
wife. Local elections reflect the trend. The city of Rye, in Westchester, elected two Democratic councilmen this year for the first
time. Yorktown named a Democratic supervisor and two Democratic
councilmen for the first time in 60 years. In state and national elections, Republican pluralities of 85,000 were once commonplace in
the county; in recent years, they have been closer to 40,000.

The drift away from a monopoly Republican power structure in
the suburbs is illustrated, although perhaps enigmatically, in Fairfield County, Connecticut. The home of many well-to-do commuters,

Fairfield has long been a Republican bastion of Connecticut. But the voter registration figures now indicate 111,000 Republicans, 84,000 Democrats and 130,000 listed as "independent." The growth in the number of unaffiliated voters, which seems to have accompanied the decline in Republican allegiance and the increasing Democratic respectability, has engaged the attention of many political professionals in the suburbs.

John Regan, secretary of the Board of Elections in Bergen County and former Mayor of Edgewater, describes the change this way: "People tend not to commit themselves to parties any more. The electorate is more sophisticated, and people realize that there is no clear-cut delineation of either major party. There are liberal and conservative elements in both." Other professionals, like Robert L. Bliss of New Canaan, Fairfield County Republican chairman, believe that the transiency that characterizes much of the suburbs is a factor. "People are transferred here by their companies for a while and then move on," he says. "They don't bother to affiliate with a political party."

Another element in the weakening of one-party power appears to be the decline in patronage opportunities. The era of tremendous development in the suburbs is past, most of the roads are built and the sewers laid. Municipal jobs are increasingly on a Civil Service basis, and the general prosperity has diminished the lure of moderately paid elective offices.

The diffusion and the dilution of power, politically and economically, that has come into the suburbs — the evolution of a predominantly rural and residential society into one increasingly urban — has led such students of the suburban power structure as Dr. Marvin A. Rapp, vice president and executive dean of the Nassau Community College, to conclude that the structure no longer has clearly visible dimensions. "We are in a transitional period," Dr. Rapp feels. "The old power structure is passing and a new one is developing." "If there is a dominant power in the suburbs today, it is probably government. And because of an increasingly sophisticated, independent electorate, suburban government today is more democratically based than ever before."

CHARLES H. PERCY

Washington and the Cities:
The Sinister Alliance

. . . Because the quality of state government has not been maintained at a sufficiently high level to retain the public trust, our American Federal system of government is in jeopardy. We are witnessing today a growing alliance between the national administration and the mayors of our biggest cities, attempting to by-pass the state governments as much as possible. The pending Federal mass transportation bill is a stunning example of this tendency. The continuing pressure by Mayor Daley and other leading Democrats to create a new Federal Department of Urban Affairs, is further evidence of this unholy alliance.

It is probably not a coincidence that the National administration and the mayors of our biggest cities are of the same party. Underlying this threat to the American Federal System, the unique and proud accomplishment of our Founding Fathers, is a disturbing partisan power struggle.

The justification that is given for this power-play move is that about 70 per cent of all Americans now live in urban areas and an even larger percentage will be concentrated in the great metropolitan areas in another ten or fifteen years. They say, therefore, that it is proper for the cities to go directly to the national government for the help they need in dealing with their problems when the states will not give them satisfaction.

From an address to the Republican Legislative Nominating Convention (Springfield, Ill., June 1, 1964). This selection appears in the book, *Percy of Illinois* (Chicago: Robinson Associates, 1964) and is reprinted here by permission of the author.

What is omitted from this argument is that the big cities proper are not growing, and some are declining not only relatively but absolutely. The growth is in the suburbs. By 1980, there will be more people living *and working* in the suburbs than in the cities themselves. And the mayors of major cities have no legitimate claim for absolute rule over the citizens of the suburbs.

To suggest the underlying struggle going on, I need only point to the well-known fact that the occupant of the White House, whoever he might be, usually owes his election to the votes from the big cities. But the majorities in the cities and the majorities in the suburbs have rarely supported the same party. The alliance of big-city politicians and the national executive branch has, therefore, sinister implications for the Republican Party. I suggest that they are rushing to complete this alliance for a power monopoly because the source of their power to accomplish it is declining. The big cities are losing population relative to the suburbs, and they are trying to freeze the power and retain it while time still remains. It is their major hope for political survival. . . .

CHARLES M. HAAR AND ASSOCIATES

The Promise of Metropolitan Planning

City planning has come into widespread acceptance in the United States. Community plans and their related zoning ordinances, subdivision controls, and capital improvement programs influence the nature and timing of much of our urban development. The planning that is now under way is primarily planning for individual cities and

Reprinted by permission of the author and the U.S. Congress, Senate, Committee on Government Operations from *The Effectiveness of Metropolitan Planning* (Washington: U.S. Government Printing Office, 1964), pp. 3-8.

towns, however, rather than planning for entire urban areas. Experience so far suggests that while much is being achieved through such planning, important opportunities are also being lost through a lack of areawide planning. Metropolitan planning is still in its infancy, but the inability of individual communities to cope with metropolitan-wide problems is becoming increasingly apparent.

In the absence of well-developed metropolitan plans, the urban patterns that are emerging today are a random collection of local plans and policies designed to meet local objectives. Yet each community, in seeking an optimum solution to its own problems, does not necessarily work in the interests of the people in the larger metropolitan area. Many suburban towns, for example, have chosen to promote the development of single-family houses on large lots as a means of forestalling costly investments in new utility systems. From their own point of view, these strategies have often been effective. But when large numbers of communities in an area limit their development in this way, the net result has often been to force a vast outward movement of people to the fringes of metropolitan areas, creating a need for new and expensive utility systems in the peripheral communities, and forcing long commuting trips to the central cities. A pattern of development that is economical for many individual suburbs can be very costly for the metropolitan area and for the Nation at large. Suburban growth since World War II has indeed required tremendous capital investment and operating expenses for new highways, schools, and utility systems. A recent study estimates that the cost of these major urban services increased by $5 billion from 1953 to 1957,[1] after adjustments for population growth and higher levels of service. The same study calls attention to the significant effects of urban growth costs in diverting capital investments from industry to these service facilities, and suggests that our expensive pattern of metropolitan development has slowed the rate of national ecoonmic growth.

Local planning is generally far removed from these broader regional and national concerns. A typical community plan focuses on activities that can be controlled within the local jurisdiction. The plan will specify what kinds of development are to be encouraged — types of housing, industry, and retailing — as well as the general locations and quantities of each. The location and programing of

[1] Henry B. Schechter, "Cost-Pust of Urban Growth," *Land Economics,* XXXVII (February 1961), 18-31.

local services — parks, streets, schools, utilities — are an important part of community plans. The objectives guiding community plans are likely to include promoting a harmonious mixture of activities, supplying public services to accompany private development, and keeping the public costs of new development within local fiscal capacity.

Metropolitan planning differs both in its point of view and in the activities with which it is concerned. It focuses mainly on facilities that serve large segments of the metropolitan population: major highways, transit lines, airports, flood and pollution controls, regional water and sewerage systems, large parks, regional shopping centers, and large industrial centers. Metropolitan plans for such facilities are guided by considerations of efficiency, consistency between the location of population and the location of major service facilities, economy in the extension of utilities and services, the adequacy of transportation and other facilities to meet present and future regional demands, the reservation of sites to meet future metropolitan needs, and the overall range of development in the light of the area's total requirements for housing, jobs, recreation, and services.

Metropolitan planning objectives. — Some of the objectives of metropolitan plans are similar to those of local plans, but with a broader geographic base. Such goals as the compatibility of specific developments with surrounding activities, the provision of adequate services, and the programing of public investments with a view to fiscal capacity are common to both community and metropolitan planning. In each case the content of the plans will differ according to whether the facilities are local or metropolitanwide in character.

Metropolitan plans, however, often seek to achieve objectives that are beyond the reach of local communities. In the Pittsburgh area, for example, high levels of unemployment have posed a special problem for some time. No single community within the region can cope effectively with this areawide problem, but the region at large has organized an effort to expand job opportunities. The economic study of the Pittsburgh region is a regional approach to common economic problems.[2] Its findings are intended in part to guide the physical

[2] This study was begun in 1959, sponsored by the Pittsburgh Regional Planning Association, and financed by the Ford Foundation, the Regional Industrial Development Corp., and the Commonwealth of Pennsylvania. Its main purpose is to support planning and economic improvements in the Pittsburgh area.

planning of the Pittsburgh metropolitan area in order to provide appropriate sites and services to promote business and industrial expansion.

The transportation problems that beset our urban areas are also beyond the scope of individual community plans, but they have spurred metropolitan planning efforts in many parts of the country. The Penn-Jersey transportation study, Chicago area transportation study, and similar projects in Detroit, Los Angeles, Pittsburgh, Seattle, Hartford, and Milwaukee — to name only a few — have produced areawide transportation plans to cope with the problems of congestion and the need to maintain good accessibility throughout rapidly expanding urban regions.

Metropolitan planning addresses itself also to the recreational needs of urban areas. As early as the turn of the century, the Boston area's metropolitan district commission acquired land for parks according to a well-conceived plan to reserve land for future recreational use. The Regional Plan Association of New York has long been active in the same field, studying the changing needs for recreational land and open space, and drawing up proposals for continuing land acquisition and park development. State and metropolitan agencies in other parts of the country are performing the same function on an areawide basis. The new federally sponsored open-space program has already begun to strengthen these efforts; the Federal legislation calls explicitly for a metropolitan program as a prerequisite for assistance in public land acquisition.

Assuring an adequate supply of decent housing has long been a problem in America's urban areas. Numerous Federal and local programs have been aimed at maintaining a high level of new residential construction, conserving the existing stock of sound housing, and eliminating obsolete and substandard structures. Despite notable progress to date, much remains to be done in order to achieve the congressional goal of a decent home for every American family. It has become increasingly clear that continued progress will require a coordinated approach within metropolitan areas, rather than a series of unrelated housing programs within the many communities that comprise a metropolitan housing market. Tax considerations frequently lead to local housing policies intended to discourage the building of moderate-cost houses, and to promote the use of buildable land for high-value property only. When such restrictive policies cover large portions of a metropolitan area, the result may be a shortage of land for inexpensive housing and a slowdown of new building for families with moderate incomes. The urban renewal policies of separate municipalities may also work counter to the housing needs and resources of the total region. People displaced by slum clearance or rehabilitation in one community will seek other housing within a large market area that crosses local governmental boundaries. Unless relocation programs are planned on a metropolitan basis, the housing gains of the community undertaking renewal may be matched by overcrowding and housing shortages elsewhere in the region.

Metropolitan planning agencies are giving increasing attention to housing needs. The Northeastern Illinois Metropolitan Area Planning Commission is now studying the future housing needs of the Chicago region; the Regional Plan Association of New York has completed elaborate projections of housing and population distribution; and similar efforts are under way elsewhere. Federally aided "community renewal programs" in a number of large cities are also covering the metropolitanwide housing market in their studies and projections.

Economic development, transportation, recreation, and housing are four major concerns that require a metropolitan approach for effective planning. Other illustrations can also be cited, particularly in such areas as water supply and distribution, waste disposal, flood control, and the control of air and water pollution. In large urban areas, water must often be carried from distant sources through elaborate systems of trunklines and local branches to serve residential and industrial areas. The cost of developing separate reservoirs and aqueducts for each community within an area can be enormous; the economies obtained by sharing water supply systems constitute powerful incentives for joint planning and cooperative action. For optimum use of regional water supply systems, coordination of land-use planning is also necessary. Typically, some branch lines will operate far below their technical capacity, while others will be used to full capacity. In the interest of overall economy in water supply, it is often desirable to guide new industrial and residential development to locations where there is excess water capacity, and to plan for a systematic expansion of branch lines as the region continues to grow. Metropolitan planning can make its contribution both in the advance planning of a water supply system, and in alerting local governments to the impact of their development controls upon the use and cost of the system.

The situation is similar with respect to waste disposal. Economies of scale in the operation of sewage treatment plants often promote cooperative action among local communities. Land-use controls then have an important influence on the use of the system, for the location and density of development can result either in optimum use of collector lines, or in underutilization of investments in some sewage lines and premature demands for sewer extensions.

Flood control measures, and the control of air and water pollution, also require cooperative planning by many communities if they are to be effective. In the absence of a coordinated effort, the plans of one community may be negated by the inaction of others. In the case of flood control, urbanization often creates new problems as land development removes trees, levels the contours of the ground, and covers the ground surface with structures and pavement. All these factors increase the rate of runoff of rainwater into streams and rivers, so that streambeds may no longer be able to contain the drainage resulting from a heavy rainfall. Local efforts either to restrict development in vulnerable flood plains or to enlarge river channels may be useless if neighboring communities do not take similar action. The same is true of local efforts to control stream pollution, which can be undone by the failure of upstream communities to set up corresponding controls. Local controls over air pollution are equally subject to neighboring influences; winds and air currents cross jurisdictional boundaries as freely as rainfall and rivers.

The protection of agricultural land is another problem of urbanization that local communities cannot handle on an individual basis. Prime farmland is rapidly being developed for urban purposes in many areas. Orange County, Calif., is a well-known example where new housing developments are replacing some of the most productive agricultural tracts in the country. Local governments can try to retard this process by means of special agricultural assessment policies (as in Santa Clara County, Calif.), but an effective solution requires making alternative locations elsewhere in the region equally attractive for urban development, to forestall development pressures on farmland. Diverting development to other areas depends upon building highways to provide good access, extending water and sewer lines, and zoning the land appropriately — all of which require action by many governments within the metropolitan region.[3]

In all these fields, there may be general consensus on regional objectives — a healthy economy, good transportation system, adequate water supply, suitable recreation facilities and open space, and decent housing for everyone — but local planning alone is not effective in moving toward these regional goals. First, many of them require action either by a number of local governments, or by levels of government other than the local community alone. Problems of housing, economic development, water and sewerage, pollution control, and preservation of farmland all illustrate the weakness of independent local action, and the clear advantages of joint local planning. Other areas of concern require not only interlocal cooperation but joint action by higher levels of government. Highways, for example, are typically designed and built by State highway departments, and must meet Federal standards if they are to receive Federal aid in financing. Large parks and land reserves are generally acquired and managed by State agencies or special district commissions. Effective guidance of metropolitan development almost always depends upon an intricate coordination of action by local and State governments, often involving Federal agencies as well, and upon sensitive adjustments of governmental policies to meet changing conditions of private development. Metropolitan planning can be an instrument for bringing about this kind of coordination within urban areas.

Conflicting interests. — A second reason why local planning alone cannot achieve metropolitan objectives is the difference in point of view between local governments and the metropolitan areas at large. Although all localities in an area may see the need for regional parks, many will resist having large public parks within their own boundaries, fearing inundation of local roads by out-of-town visitors or hoping to use their open land for high-value development. New highways may be welcome — if they are just across the border in the

[3] Recent studies have indicated in more detail the need for areawide planning or performance of certain functions, as for example, Advisory Commission on Intergovernmental Relations, "Performance of Urban Functions: Local and Areawide," Washington 1963, and made more specific recommendations for Federal aid. Advisory Commission on Intergovernmental Relations, "Intergovernmental Responsibilities for Water Supply and Sewage Disposal in Metropolitan Areas," Washington, D.C., 1962; "Intergovernmental Responsibilities for Mass Transportation Facilities and Services in Metropolitan Areas," Washington, D.C., 1961.

next town. All communities may see the desirability of industrial expansion — provided that heavy industry locates in another part of the region and only research laboratories develop nearby. It will be generally conceded that moderate-cost housing is needed for workers and their families, but many local plans discourage it.

Conflicts exist in regional development, and they must be recognized. Metropolitan planning will not eliminate conflicting interests among different communities, but it will try to prevent these conflicts from interfering with the sound development of the region. Competition to attract new industry is a case in point. A metropolitan area typically has a limited amount of land that is suitable for modern industrial development, with adequate access and utilities, proper drainage and soil conditions, is priced reasonably and is available in large enough parcels. The metropolitan area at large has an interest in the best use of this land, for new jobs and increased incomes benefit the entire region directly or indirectly. Individual communities have a narrower interest in industrial development because the property tax income from a new factory goes to the community where it is located. Competition for new industry may lead to a wasteful use of industrial land: scarce in-town sites may be used for plants that could as well locate in the suburbs, so that firms later requiring central location may have nowhere to go in the region; or suburban towns may discourage certain industries from building on their vacant land because they hope for a higher tax yield from other types of firms in the future, and the region may lose a chance to strengthen its overall industrial base. A recent study of industrial renewal prospects for the Utica, N.Y., urban area[4] underlined this danger in narrowly competitive local industrial policies and urged a statesmanlike regional approach to maintain and expand employment for the entire area. Metropolitan planning can help competing localities coordinate their efforts and work for the advantages that result from economic growth anywhere in the region.

A metropolitan planning agency will speak for areawide interests when government policies are formulated and when program decisions are made. When conflicting interests are acknowledged openly, and when the regional point of view is presented clearly, it may be

[4] Chester Rapkin, "Industrial Renewal: Determining the Potential and Accelerating the Economy of the Utica Urban Area" (New York: New York State Division of Housing and Community Renewal and Urban Renewal Administration, U.S. Housing and Home Finance Agency, 1963).

possible to work out agreements to resolve the conflicts in a particular situation. Localities can compromise and bargain. If the regional plan that will best promote economic growth leaves certain communities with little likelihood of industrial development for many years, regional representatives may agree to support other measures to help these communities finance local services, such as revisions in State school-aid allocations. Or the plan itself may attempt to promote the region's development in ways that will strike a balance between tax resources and service needs in each jurisdiction; thus, the community that is to obtain little industry may instead provide a location for a major shopping center, or may have its service demands limited by using its vacant land for a regional park rather then new housing.

A metropolitan planning agency will alert local governments to the regional implications of their decisions, and will work to encourage informed decisionmaking in place of fragmented policies that plan for the region more by accident than by choice. An effective planning agency will also help to resolve conflicts between localities and the larger region, when these conflicts prejudice the development of the region. Metropolitan planning can make an important contribution in these situations of conflict merely by posing the issues and analyzing the effects of alternative courses of action. More complete information, highlighting the regional implications of local actions, will enable local decisonmakers to see beyond immediate parochial advantages and to consider alternatives more beneficial in the long run — and to justify such alternatives to their constituents.

JERRY LANDAUER

Shaping the Metropolis with Federal Money

Federal officials from President Johnson on down are hammering away on the need for better, broader planning as a prerequisite for building the Great Society in urban America. But a sizable contingent of skeptics is questioning both the realism of the Administration's approach to urban problems and the qualifications of Uncle Sam in the planning field.

What the Federal Government hopes to do is use its mighty power of the purse to wheedle or push big cities and their suburbs, sometimes located in different states, into adopting what Mr. Johnson calls "unified long-range policies for the entire metropolitan region."

Generally, such policies entail agreement by cities and neighboring counties and towns on a land-use plan to coordinate transportation utilities, public buildings, parks, schools, urban renewal projects and privately financed construction. The main goals are to cure decay in central cities, control suburban sprawl and serve the most people at lowest cost and with least violence to aesthetics.

Despite the deep doubts of many that achievements can possibly match these grand aspirations, there is no denying that the Government holds many whips over localities — and that more hands are grasping for them. While Washington can't by fiat require cooperation by a core city and its surrounding communities, in his housing message due to go to Congress this week the President will emphasize that various Federal aids will be withheld from urban areas that haven't drafted comprehensive development plans.

For example, grants under a proposed $100 million program to help build water and sewer lines in fast-growing places will be available only for projects that fit into a metropolitan development plan.

Reprinted by permission from *The Wall Street Journal*, February 17, 1965.

Starting July 1, moreover, Federal money for new highway projects will supposedly be withheld from urban areas not engaged in a "continuing comprehensive transportation planning process" which devotes "due consideration" to the plan's probable impact on community growth. One official in the Bureau of Public Roads expects as many as 50 areas may fail to qualify by the deadline. Few officials, however, think the bureau would actually plug its money spigot suddenly.

In the housing message or in extra appropriations requests to Congress soon, the President also will suggest a new program of dollar inducements for states to plunge deeper into planning or let their urban areas plan together. Texas, among other states, hasn't authorized general planning by metropolitan areas; in many other states, localities require special permission from legislatures before they can execute plans for mass transit, water supply, pollution control or other area-wide projects.

Mr. Johnson also may accept a suggestion by Housing Administrator Robert Weaver to station emissaries from Washington at "metro desks" in big-city areas to help local officials make better use of, and impose sense upon, 43 Federal grant and loan programs available to urban areas; the money flows from several dozen bureaus and divisions within five Cabinet-level departments and eight "independent" agencies.

Further, the President wants Congress to start financing an already-authorized Federal-state program to supply urban areas with expert advice on community development; Mr. Weaver views this as an embryo "urban extension service" akin to an existing program of advice to farmers. Mr. Johnson envisions great accomplishments eventually arising from it.

But certain officials who deal daily with urban problems regard the Johnsonian vision as unrealistic. The agricultural extension program succeeded, it's felt, because expert agents backed by university research worked directly with farm families; it would be a gigantic undertaking to transfer this concept wholesale to city life. In fact, the Administration plan is quite modest: Working through states and universities, the urban service would offer fact-finding, research and training aids to city governments and to local housing and planning councils.

In part, the comprehensive planning which Washington increasingly will demand is supposed to impose order on the rapidly proliferating and sometimes contradictory Federal aid programs. Mr. Weaver hopes the proposed Cabinet-level Department of Housing and Urban Development, working with comprehensive planners below, will "unite the Federal thrust in the urban area."

But no plan that takes all the anti-decay, low-cost, anti-sprawl objectives into account will easily gain approval from politicians, businessmen and citizens groups. The Federal thrust which Mr. Weaver seeks to unite may actually aggravate controversy, as some experience with Washington's various prongs in metropolitan areas suggest.

Even now, some local officials complain, the Farmers Home Administration and the Community Facilities Administration are undermining uplift efforts by the Nashville-Davidson County metropolitan government in Tennessee. In the surrounding counties, asserts Herbert Bingham, executive secretary of the Tennessee Municipal League, the two Federal agencies have issued or backed loans to utility districts for small-gauge water lines utterly inadequate for the urban-type development that surely will creep outward toward these utilities. Equally bad, he charges, Federally financed farm-to-market roads are being built uncomfortably close to metropolitan boundaries; these, he's sure, will shortly become substandard foundations for suburban streets.

"These Federal agencies have no idea of what they're doing," Mr. Bingham concludes. "They're financing development that will have to be bailed out some day at gigantic cost to all levels of government."

Federal officials, however, contend Mr. Bingham's fears are exaggerated. They argue it's tremendously hard to draw a boundary between country and city; a placid rural place today may become suburban tomorrow. Following a policy promulgated two years ago, the Community Facilities Administration says it won't finance water supply or sewerage lines if they don't conform to a local planning objective.

In West Orange, N. J., Mayor James Sheeran is no less angry than Mr. Bingham at apparent lack of forethought or coordination in Government planning. He sees a Federally aided partly elevated freeway built on dirt fill moving on a path that will split two desirable residential sections, and he fears that blight soon will hit neighborhoods near the freeway. Some day, he predicts, Washington will spend in his town more millions for renewal that could have been saved by depressing the entire freeway below ground at higher cost now. A future mayor, Mr. Sheeran adds, may well apply for a Federal "open space" grant to compensate for a playground which the freeway will consume in part.

There also are growing local grumbles about lack of coordination or consistency in Government policies for paying moving costs of those displaced by Federally aided construction projects; it's estimated that more than 60,000 families and 6,000 businesses will be displaced this year.

For the businessman particularly, luck chiefly determines reimbursement. Should an interstate highway rip through, moving costs up to $3,000 may be allowed. Displacement by urban renewal may yield as much as $25,000. But if the business man is sufficiently unlucky to be ousted by a new Federal court house, he isn't entitled to a dime for moving.

"Some day the President will grab hold of this thing and make Congress make sense of it," a ranking policy-maker hopes. "But it will take a while. So we'll just keep muddling along as we have."

More fundamental doubts persist about the effectiveness of local planning unless Washington tightens its own aid operations or reconsiders certain well established policies. Some urban affairs specialists maintain planning won't restrain sprawling megalopolis as long as the Federal Housing Administration and the Veterans Administration, by insuring mortgage loans, encourage the pursuit of a house in suburbia by every family.

Equally discouraging to the planners, a recent report by the Federal-state-local Advisory Committee on Intergovernmental Relations found an increase in conflict-creating racial and income disparities between city and suburb. Some experienced urban hands believe metropolitan area planning simply elevates to a higher level the rivalries that couldn't be settled by neighboring jurisdictions in the area.

But Washington tends to answer complaints of poor planning by suggesting more planning, particularly of the comprehensive kind. Last month, in its annual report, the President's Council of Economic Advisers proclaimed that planning objectives can't be achieved unless "there is some method of taking an area-wide comprehensive point of view, which brings together all levels of government and pertinent private organizations to evolve a metropolitan area plan."

So far, this sort of mechanism remains elusive. Coordinating councils of elected officials function in just seven of the 140 places engaged in metropolitan area planning.

Examples of cooperative planning aren't exactly rare: The town of Cary, N. C., to take one homely example, was persuaded by a planning commission to reverse the flow of its proposed sewer system to coordinate with nearby Raleigh's. But in most places political support is lacking to translate controversial plans into action.

In part, that's why hundreds, possibly thousands, of carefully prepared, brightly colored plans lie unheeded in state capitals, city halls and county councils. For this and other reasons, Norman Beckman, the Advisory Commission's assistant director, finds a widespread belief among planners themselves "that something is rotten in the state of the art."

Nonetheless, the planning boom keeps inflating. In 1963-64, 10 more states authorized their urban areas generally to plan together; three others, Illinois, Michigan and Maryland, granted such authority to specified areas. More requests for permission to plan are high on the agenda of several legislatures this year.

By now, planning jobs far exceed the manpower supply. So the Administration will ask Congress to train more planners; a coming money request will call for a modest sum to finance two-year fellowships for city planners and other urban specialists.

"The planners have taken over," grieves William Widnall, ranking Republican on the House Banking Committee, which handles housing legislation. But, in general, the new planning has escaped the connotation of "social engineering" that made it a rather dirty word among conservatives in New Deal days. Today planning built into Federal grants programs is popular with many anti-spending Congressmen; they hope the time-consuming planning process will stanch the Federal money flow.

But when pressure builds to generate jobs through Government spending or to refill the pork barrel, members of Congress and administrators alike tend to shade or ignore the requirements. Under the Area Redevelopment Act, distressed communities were eligible for aid only after they had drawn "over-all economic development plans." But then came the accelerated public works program; it offered funds to any designated area so long as the aid wasn't inconsistent with an existing development plan.

"When Congress gets skeptical about a program, we'll put in some planning," a candid policy-maker explains. "But when it wants to shovel out dough fast, naturally Congress wants less planning."

ROSCOE C. MARTIN

The Natural Limits of Cooperation:
The Metropolitan Washington
Council of Governments

Washington, D. C., the seat of the Metropolitan Washington Council of Governments, ranks 10th in size among the Nation's standard metropolitan statistical areas. In at least three important respects it is typical of the larger metropolitan areas. First, it is growing rapidly in population: From a recorded 1 million in 1940 and 2 million in 1960 to a projected 3 million in 1980 and 5 million in 2000. Second, Washington's suburbs are growing at a much faster rate than is the central city. The Washington metropolitan area was contained largely within the District of Columbia until 1920, when the growth of the suburbs began in earnest. At present somewhat more than one-third of the area's 2 million inhabitants reside in the District, almost exactly one-third in Maryland, somewhat less than a third in Virginia. This means, as a corollary, that Washington resembles other metropolitan areas in yet a third respect, in that many governments have a hand in the public affairs of the area.

In two additional particulars, however, the Washington area is different. In one it is so different as to be unique, for no other metropolitan area contains the Nation's Capital and none has a central city whose government even faintly resembles that of the District of Columbia. What the Federal Government wishes to do the Federal Government may do with regard to the government of the District. But the District is only a third (or a little more) of the metropolitan

Reprinted from *Metropolis in Transition* (Washington: U.S. Housing and Home Finance Agency, 1964), pp. 39-50, with the permission of the author and the U.S. Housing and Home Finance Agency.

area, which outside its limits looks, behaves, and is governed like any other metropolitan area. Here then is a sort of centaur among metropolitan areas, with two-thirds of the beast looking like almost any other large area but one-third resembling nothing found elsewhere throughout the broad domain of local government. In a second respect, too, Washington is different; for if public responsibilities there are divided among many governments, the number nevertheless is not so great as is found in most of the large metropolitan areas. In 1962 the Chicago area had 1,060 governments; Philadelphia had 963, New York 555, and San Francisco 398. Washington had 69 governments; St. Louis, the next larger area in population (1960 census), had 439, and Cleveland, the next smaller, had 135.[1] None would argue that, with respect to number of governments, Washington is in good shape because it has fewer units than its sister areas; but in any event the problem of fragmentation is not as serious there as elsewhere. The fact that the Federal Government controls an area containing more than a third of the metropolitan population is at once a complicating and a simplifying factor.

Background of Intergovernmental Cooperation

As in every metropolitan area, the governments of the Washington area have experimented for many years with arrangements designed to alleviate metropolitan pressures. Over a long period there have indeed been established as many as a dozen agencies designed with this end in view. [The table on page 372] reveals some pertinent facts about these agencies.[2] In every case save one the purpose of the agency is defined in terms of a paramount functional activity. The table therefore emphasizes the functions performed or the services rendered by the several agencies.[3]

[1] 1962 Census of Governments, "Governmental Organization," passim.
[2] The standard metropolitan statistical area (SMSA) as employed by the Bureau of the Census does not include Loudon and Prince William Counties, Va., which may more accurately be described as part of the emergent metropolitan area. Both counties, however, are generally considered to be part of Metropolitan Washington, and are member governments in several of the regional organizations.
[3] "Metropolitan Washington Council of Governments," 1962 (Washington: The Council, 1962) presents (at p. 9) a summary of most of the organizations listed. This is the annual report of the council for 1962. The "U.S. Government Organization Manual, 1962-63" (Washington, 1962) also offers (passim) summaries of those organizations in which the Federal Government is a participant.

ORGANIZATIONS PROVIDING REGIONAL AND SUBREGIONAL SERVICES IN THE WASHINGTON METROPOLITAN AREA, 1962

ORGANIZATION PROVIDING INTERGOVERNMENTAL SERVICE	LEGAL BASIS AND YEAR ESTABLISHED	Water supply	Sewage disposal	Pollution abatement	Planning	Land use	Transportation	Public safety	Social services	District of Columbia	Montgomery County (Md.)	Prince Georges County (Md.)	Arlington County (Va.)	Fairfax County (Va.)	Alexandria (city) (Va.)	Falls Church (city) (Va.)	Fairfax (city) (Va.)	Prince William County (non-SMSA)	Loudon County (non-SMSA)
Washington Aqueduct Corps of Engineers.	Federal Statute, 1852.	×								×			×	×		×	×		
District of Columbia Department of Sanitary Engineering.	Federal Statute, 1932.		×							×									
Washington Suburban Sanitary Commission.	Maryland Statute, 1918.	×	×								×	×							
Maryland-National Capital Park and Planning Commission.	Maryland Statute, 1927.				×	×					×	×							
Interstate Commission on the Potomac River Basin.	Interstate Compact, 1941.			×						×	×	×	×	×	×	×	×	×	×
Northern Virginia Regional Planning and Economic Development Commission.	Virginia Statute, 1948.				×								×	×	×	×	×	×	×
National Capital Planning Commission.	Federal Statute, 1952.				×					×	×	×	×	×	×	×	×	×	×
National Capital Regional Planning Council.	Federal Statute, 1952.				×					×	×	×	×	×	×	×	×	×	×
Northern Virginia Regional Park Authority.	Virginia Statute, 1958.					×							×	×	×	×	×	×	×
Washington Metropolitan Area Transit Commission.	Interstate Compact, 1961.						×			×	×	×	×	×	×	×	×	×	×
National Capital Transportation Agency.	Federal Statute, 1960.						×			×	×	×	×	×	×	×	×	×	×
Metropolitan Washington Council of Governments.	None, 1957.									×	×	×	×	×	×	×	×	×	×

TYPE OF SERVICE PROVIDED; JURISDICTION IN WHICH PROVIDED (Maryland, Virginia).

As it is so frequently in an urban setting, water supply was the first function to command areawide attention. As early as 1852 the Washington aqueduct was created to supply the District of Columbia with water, and as the suburbs have developed their governments have contracted with the District for most or all of their water requirements. This story is far from finished, for it became obvious some time ago that the existing water supply would not prove adequate to the needs of the area in the event of a long drought. Of recent years the Corps of Engineers has completed a survey of the Potomac River Basin, with recommendations for water supply structures. These recommendations, currently under consideration, carry far-reaching implications for the Washington metropolitan area.

A second major functional field in which intergovernmental cooperation was early found advantageous is sewage disposal. The table indicates that a number of governments purchase waste disposal service from the District of Columbia Department of Sanitary Engineering. This is facilitated in the case of the two largest suburban areas by the Washington Suburban Sanitary Commission, which was created by the State of Maryland more than 40 years ago. In a related area the Interstate Commission on the Potomac River Basin, created by interstate compact in 1941, has been active in the control of pollution in the Potomac.

Planning (with which may be associated control of land use) is a third major functional field which has received interjurisdictional attention. Maryland was first on the scene with its Maryland-National Capital Park and Planning Commission, created in 1927 to meet the need for planning in Montgomery and Prince Georges Counties. The commission not only serves as a joint planning agency for the two counties but also operates a joint park program. More than 20 years later the local governments of suburban Virginia created the Northern Virginia Regional Planning and Economic Development Commission. Ten years later yet there was created a Northern Virginia Regional Park Authority, under which Arlington and Fairfax Counties, together with the city of Falls Church, are developing a joint park system.

Meanwhile the Federal Government, though slow to start, had moved into the planning field. The first step was taken in 1924 with the creation of the National Capital Park Commission, whose mission was expanded in 1926 by the addition of planning functions. A third major act, passed in 1952, created the present National Capital Planning Commission. The NCPC is the central planning agency for the Federal and District Governments in the National Capital region. The same act (1952) established the National Capital Regional Planning Council to meet the needs for overall planning for the development of the region. The members of the council are in part ex officio, in part appointed on nomination by the appropriate local planning agencies. The act makes the NCPC responsible for providing staff for the regional planning council.

It was 1956 before transportation asserted itself in a manner to command regional attention. In that year the National Capital Planning Commission and the regional planning council, together with a joint transportation commission created by parallel legislation passed by the Legislatures of Maryland and Virginia and the U.S. Congress, initiated a mass transportation study. This study, completed in 1959, made a number of significant recommendations regarding transportation and mass transit in the metropolitan area. Two important steps have been taken to date in pursuance of these recommendations. First, Congress in 1960 established the National Capital Transportation Agency and charged it with responsibility for planning and developing a transportation system for the area. Its attention was directed particularly to the problems of financing and administering a rapid transit system. Second, an interstate compact creating a Washington Metropolitan Area Transit Commission passed by the two States was approved by Congress in 1961. During its first 2 years, the commission has succeeded in persuading the area transit companies to introduce interjurisdictional express bus service, through fares, and integrated schedules.

As matters stood in the mid-1950's, then, Metropolitan Washington had had considerable experience of intergovernmental cooperation, and more particularly of interjurisdictional services. The arrangements which had been devised for meeting metropolitan needs were, however, deficient in several respects. First, they had been adopted piecemeal over the years in reaction to specific needs; second, each organization (or operation) was defined in functional terms. These approaches of necessity resulted in uneven responses to regional needs, for if some needs were reasonably well met, others were not; and many, not having reached the critical point, were ignored altogether. Third, the jurisdictions of several agencies were defined in subregional rather than in regional terms. It was almost inevitable that this should be so, seeing that three major governments shared responsibility for identifying and taking common action on areawide problems. Fourth, most agencies with regional (or subregional) responsibilities were underfinanced. Fifth, none of the agencies was genuinely representative of the region and its governments, let alone its people. On the contrary, each was an administrative organ created (normally) by one government and operating at second or third remove in terms of representativeness. Sixth and finally, there was no public body or viable combination of public bodies with anything approaching general government responsibility for the region as a whole. In all these respects, be it observed, Washington's lot was not materially different from that of most metropolitan areas.

Emergence of the Metropolitan Washington Council of Governments

As early as 1952 it was recognized by some of the Washington area's political leaders that there were many metropolitan needs which could not be met by the existing machinery of government. A possible solution was seen in an organization which would permit the area's governments to act in concert. In that year F. Joseph Donahue, President of the Board of Commissioners of the District of Columbia, called together a group representative of the governing bodies in the region with the intention of setting up an informal continuing organization. He left office shortly thereafter, and his effort proved abortive. The idea was to lie dormant until 1957 when Robert E. McLaughlin, likewise President of the District Board of Commissioners, revived the concept of an areawide agency. He invited representatives of the governing bodies of the suburban jurisdictions, and of the general Assemblies of Maryland and Virginia as well, to meet at the District building on April 11, 1957. The group met several times, and by November 1957 an organization called the Washington Metropolitan Regional Conference had evolved. The conference adopted a charter which outlined its purpose and organization, and which emphasized as the basic guiding principle of the new body its voluntary character.

In its initial years the metropolitan regional conference avoided controversial issues while building strength through gradual increase in mutual understanding. Its most important early activities had to do with promotion of the area transit commission compact. It was also active in the fields of water supply and pollution abatement. By 1959 the organization had developed to the point where it was willing (and able) to adopt a budget and hire a permanent staff. In 1962 the conference changed its name to Metropolitan Washington Council of Governments, sometimes abbreviated as COG.

The conference was encouraged in its early years by the warm endorsement it received from the newly created congressional Joint Committee on Washington Metropolitan Problems. That committee, created like the conference in 1957, prepared a series of reports on metropolitan needs and suggested a variety of steps, organizational and otherwise, designed to alleviate metropolitan problems. A principal recommendation called for strengthening the metropolitan regional conference, in which the committee found high promise as an agency for identifying metropolitan problems and moving, through consensus among existing governments, toward their alleviation.[4]

The council of governments has not changed in any important particular since its creation in 1957. The bylaws, adopted in 1960 and at semiannual meetings subsequently, are substantially identical with the original charter approved in the earlier year. They stress the council's voluntary character: That body's purpose is to promote a sense of harmony and cooperation among the governments of the area, and to seek the alleviation of metropolitan problems through action which, mutually arrived at, will be generally agreeable. Beyond the power to advise and recommend, the COG has no authority.

The council has two governing bodies. The first, a general deliberative body, is the 68-member conference, which meets semiannually. The conference includes all the members of the governing bodies of the six counties and three independent cities in the suburban areas; the mayors of two of the larger cities in addition; two members each from the General Assemblies of Maryland and Virginia appointed by the respective Governors; the three Commissioners of the District of Columbia; and one member each appointed by the District of Columbia Committees of the Senate and the House of Representatives.

---

[4] Joint Committee on Washington Metropolitan Problems, 85th Cong., 2d sess. (1958), "The Governing of Metropolitan Washington" (Washington, 1958), especially pp. 81 ff. This is a joint committee print of a staff study made for the committee.

A 19-member executive board, which meets monthly, has the power to make decisions in the name of the conference. The board includes those members of the conference who represent the General Assemblies of Maryland and Virginia and the Congress of the United States; the three members of the District Board of Commissioners; two members each representing Montgomery and Prince Georges Counties; and one representative from each local jurisdiction in northern Virginia.

In the fall of 1962 the COG had a staff of five, including an executive secretary, an assistant executive secretary, a research assistant, and two secretaries. . . . [T]he council's staff resources are multiplied several times over through its ability to coopt technical personnel as needed from the participating governments.[5]

Two types of committees which are utilized by the council play a vital role in its work. First are six policy committees which, drawn from the members of the conference, deal with transportation, water supply and pollution abatement, land use, public safety, health and welfare, and internal operations. It will be observed at once that each committee (excepting only the last) is oriented toward a major functional field. Assisting the policy committees are several technical advisory committees made up of staff officials from the various participating governments. These committees deal with such subjects as sanitation, police, fire protection, building codes, civil defense, health, welfare, air pollution, transportation, finance, and procurement. One advisory committee, to illustrate, is the regional transportation advisory board, which was the 10-year old metropolitan area traffic council until it was amalgamated with the COG in 1962. Another advisory committee, made up of managers and chief administrative officers, advises the council with regard to general administrative problems.[6] It goes without saying that these committees are not all equally active or productive.

The activities of the council are paid for by voluntary assessments assumed by the several participating governments. The assess-

[5] Legally, for administrative convenience, the staff of the council of governments is a section of the Executive Office of the District of Columbia. Its members are paid partly from the regular District budget and partly from a trust fund to which the cooperating governments make contributions.

[6] The council's 1962 annual report (cited above) summarizes (at p. 10) the committee structure.

ments are determined by a formula which is based primarily on population.

The Council's Program

The scope of the council's program interests is indicated by the names of five of its six policy committees. [The table on page 372] also suggests the nature and breadth of its program activities. The table stresses services provided, which in the case of the council of governments is something of a misnomer. The council does not render services direct, but rather serves as adviser to the agencies which do provide services. Its role is that of negotiator, facilitator, arranger. Indeed it might more appropriately be considered a forum than an organization in any institutional sense. Its staff, symbolized in the person of its executive secretary, is a staff in the true sense of the word.[7]

The council early identified traffic congestion as the areawide problem most clearly deserving of attention. The Mass Transportation Survey of 1959 predicted that traffic volume in the region would increase by almost three times by 1980, and recommended the establishment of the National Capital Transportation Agency and the Washington Metropolitan Area Transit Commission. The council has played an important part in the work of both agencies, which were established in 1960. Through its transportation policy committee (which has had the assistance of the appropriate technical advisory committee, called in this instance the Regional Transportation Advisory Board) it has made a number of recommendations to the relevant agency. Further, it has pursued on its own responsibility a number of activities designed to complement those of the official agencies. It has, for example, been active in traffic safety education, and in the promotion of antiair pollution devices for use on automotive vehicles. Finally, the council has sought to promote coordination of their various programs through regular monthly meetings of the regional transportation agencies. There are those who feel that this has been the council's most significant contribution in the field of transportation. At the same time it is not difficult to find others who, citing the continued differences among these agencies, discount the activities of the council.

With respect to waste disposal the COG, working through its re-

[7] For a succinct statement of council activities, see ibid., pp. 4-8.

gional sanitary advisory board, has developed a master sewer and waste water disposal plan which has recently been released. The advisory board has obtained agreements from Maryland and Virginia regarding sewage control installations in the Potomac River. Studies of the disposal of solid wastes were underway at the time of writing. On the supply side, the council's appropriate committee has in progress a review of the water needs of the area and potential sources of supply. This will involve an evaluation of the plan recently released by the Corps of Engineers for the development of the Potomac River Basin. Central to this review, as indeed to all council undertakings, is the development of understanding and consensus among the governments participating in its deliberations.

In the social service domain — health, welfare, juvenile delinquency, unemployment slums, physical amenities — the council of governments has pursued a wide range of activities. These have been under the general direction of its health and welfare committee, with the technical assistance of the appropriate advisory committees. Among these activities may be noted the establishment, with the cooperation of the (Federal) Department of Health, Education, and Welfare, of the Metropolitan Washington Health Facilities Planning Council. Federal funds for a study of the need for and the location of health facilities in the metropolitan area have been allocated to this agency. In addition, the COG was instrumental in the formation of a Commission on Mental Retardation, which will address the problem of the coordination of regional facilities to meet the needs in that field.

A further activity, undertaken on council initiative, is a network of air pollution sampling stations operated by the local governments of the region with the technical assistance of the U.S. Public Health Service. As an outgrowth of interest in this subject, a model air pollution control ordinance has been prepared for adoption by local governments.

Last among social service activities the COG has joined with a number of organizations, including the health and welfare council and the Washington Center for Metropolitan Studies, to design an agency to be called the United Planning Organization for Human Services. Foundation support is being sought for the proposed organization, which is expected to do in the social service realm what the standard planning agency does in the physical.

It has long been commonplace that neither fires nor criminals —

and we may now add potential enemy bombs — have respect for political boundaries. Local governments have of course taken protective action in recognition of this verity for perhaps a hundred years; now such action is further encouraged by the civil defense program. It was, indeed, primarily the civil defense impetus which prompted the council of governments to establish its public safety committee. This committee is backstopped by a technical committee which, composed of local, State, and National civil defense officers, has undertaken to develop an areawide plan for emergency action. Civil defense impinges, of course, on local law enforcement, and this has led to renewed emphasis on the work of the technical committee of police chiefs. This committee has developed an agreement for a regional police teletype system, which is in the process of being set up. In addition, it has addressed itself to the complex problem of jurisdictional overlap in police activities. Civil defense also impinges on fire protection, and this has led the council's public safety committee to encourage a technical committee of fire chiefs to develop plans for fire protection on a regional basis.

A final activity in the domain of public safety concerns the work of a newly organized technical committee on codes and regulations. This committee, which is composed of both public officials and interested private citizens, seeks to determine whether a greater degree of uniformity in construction requirements would be of advantage in terms of public safety and convenience.

Yet another field in which the COG has been active has to do with land use. The National Capital Planning Commission and the National Capital Regional Planning Council have drawn up and published "The Year 2000 Plan." The plan lays emphasis on the very intergovernmental cooperation which is the council of governments' reason for being. The council has undertaken responsibility for developing the consensus among local governments necessary to the formulation of a unified regional policy regarding the plan. Reflecting its concern for sound area growth, the COG has joined with other interested agencies to establish a joint open space committee. This committee, charged to develop a plan and an action program to govern land use, had chosen a director and begun work at the time of writing.

Miscellaneous activities pursued by the council of governments include the encouragement of joint purchasing of supplies and equipment, which in other areas has yielded considerable advantages, including substantial savings through standard specifications, mass buying, and inspection of items purchased. Another recent proposal called for launching a metropolitan statistical program under which governments without statistical or computer equipment would be furnished data otherwise available only through expensive installations. Such data, it is believed, would prove useful in assisting in the identification and solution of both local and regional problems.

The doctrine behind the council of governments allows for contributions of several kinds. First, there is the matter of identifying and nominating for consideration problems of a regional character. Its organizational structure gives it an advantage in respect of breadth of view not enjoyed by any other agency. Second, there is the service which the COG performs in assisting to solve, or to alleviate, the problems identified. Here, as has been noted, it operates as a staff agency, extending aid to the governments which in the end must take the necessary action. Third, the council affords a vehicle through which the member governments can make known their views respecting area problems — in the matter, for example, of proposed Federal legislation affecting the region. Fourth, the COG can initiate studies and (within limits) raise money for their support. Its contributions here are generally held to have been substantial. Finally, the council's method of operation might be thought to result in some benefit to the region even where no observable positive action ensues. Its standard procedure involves exhaustive discussions: Within the staff, within the policy committees, within the technical advisory committees, within and among the governing bodies themselves, and finally in the public forum. Nowhere does the council or any of its agents have sanctional powers; instead it must rely wholly on persuasion. This places a high premium on education, for it is only through voluntary acceptance of a common goal and a plan for united action that a regional policy can evolve. The tangible value of general discussion is as difficult to establish here as elsewhere, but one committed to the educational process as a way of improving the human lot would scarcely argue that it is not useful.

The Future of the Council

In view of the general feeling among those most closely associated with it that the council of governments has accomplished much during its 5 years' life, one is somewhat astonished to learn that there is also a widespread impression that the achievements have not been as great as might have been expected. Stated positively, many feel that a few relatively modest changes would make of the council a more effective instrument than it now is. This attitude was given added point by the National Transportation Act of 1960 which, it may be recalled, directed the National Capital Transportation Agency to make recommendations regarding a permanent organization to carry on the work it had begun. The discussions conducted in behalf of that agency indicated both a need for a new organization and a possible opportunity for the council of governments to develop into that organization.

Prerequisite to any such development, many say, is the necessity for the council to rethink both its organization and its strategy. For all the good deeds performed by the council, its critics point out, decisionmaking in the area remains as badly fragmented as ever. The metropolitan problems chosen for attention have been defined in functional terms; and emphasis on individual services, however justifiable pragmatically, lends small encouragement to thinking about general metropolitan solutions. The council of governments, though aspiring to the role of general spokesman for the region's governments, lacks authority not only over the governments (this is inherent in its philosophy) but also over the several regional agencies. Further, it is inadequately supported, and its decisionmaking apparatus is defective in that voting powers in its executive board are inequitably allocated.

One line of thinking developed in the council maintains that, while that body must remain a joint instrumentality of the participating governments, it must at the same time be given more authority than it has enjoyed in the past. And since planning is widely held to be the key to the form and direction of metropolitan development in the future, that is the area in which the council's authority should be expanded.[8] One recalls here the liaison between the Puget Sound Governmental Conference and the Puget Sound Regional Planning Council as an illustration of the arrangement suggested for the National Capital Council. This, however, brings on more talk, for presumably the agency (or agencies) to be affected by the proposed increase in council authority will have something to say on that sub-

[8] The staff study titled "The Governing of Metropolitan Washington" (cited above) recommended that the council of governments and the National Capital Regional Planning Council be brought together. Joint Committee on Washington Metropolitan Problems, op. cit., p. 91.

ject. The director of the cognate agency, the National Capital Regional Planning Council, has in fact made a counterproposal: That his agency be clothed with enforcement powers. If this does not block the suggested absorption of metropolitan planning by the council of governments, it will at least slow the drive. The council is not the only aspirant to regional hegemony.

Meanwhile the organization is beset from another direction. The Montgomery County Council has voted to withdraw that county from COG participation July 1, 1963, thus breaching a hitherto solid front. The blow is not softened by the fact that it was delivered by a newly elected council which is said to be antimetropolitan and economy minded. Who is to speak critically of Montgomery's action, for these or any other reasons? It is one of the conference movements' cardinal tenets that association together in a metropolitan council is purely voluntary, and that a participating government may withdraw at any time. The question of reason is not relevant, for it is not necessary for a defector even to cite a reason. Still it is hard on the regional conference when a member elects to act on this tenet, for it raises the stark question of council survival.

It is clear that those most closely associated with the council of governments view that body as a highly appropriate agency for considering problems of regional scope which are beyond the reach of individual governments. They conceive the council as being in business to stay. If its managers reach out for new functions and responsibilities for the council, their reasoning goes, that is because the individual-function approach to regional problems is of limited utility and because the COG is the only general-purpose agency with areawide jurisdiction. And if in the process of adjustment the agency should be nudged ever so slightly along the road toward regional government, it would nevertheless remain a joint instrumentality of the area's governments — that and, for the present, nothing more. Its supporters regard the council as an experimental body, one which, though successful over its 5-year life, is nevertheless susceptible of improvement. What steady, conscious, and self-directed improvement of the council of governments may mean for government in the Washington metropolitan area in the future only time can tell. The basic question is whether the modest adaptations acceptable to existing governments will blunt the edge of metropolitan disjunction sufficiently to forestall (or indefinitely postpone) the need for more drastic action.

The Conference Approach: Concluding Comment

. . . The first metropolitan conference of governments was launched in 1954, and there were at the time of writing (late 1962) only eight such organizations in existence. Considering its youth and the modest number of its adherents to date, the conference movement commands extraordinarily widespread interest. It is the subject of speeches galore, of many essays and articles in magazines designed for popular and light professional reading, of countless newspaper stories. Of the professional associations of local governments and officials, and of those whose primary purpose is citizen education as well, none would think of scheduling a program meeting these days without a good stout session on voluntary associations of governments. References to the annual conference programs for 1961 and 1962 of the American Municipal Association, the National Association of Counties, and the National Municipal League, together with the literature of those organizations, will bear out these observations.

So far as the record shows, formal organizational notice of "voluntary multipurpose regional organizations" was first taken at the American Municipal Association's American Municipal Congress held in Seattle in August 1961. There a workshop session examined the conference movement in some detail.[9] Sensing from the general interest manifested in the subject, and in particular from the reaction to the Seattle workshop discussion, that the voluntary regional council idea was worthy of further exploration, the American Municipal Association and the National Association of County Officials (since late 1962 the National Association of Counties) united to provide a Joint Service to Encourage Voluntary City-County Regional Cooperation.[10] The announcement of this service also revealed plans on the part of the two organizations to sponsor joint workshops on the subject at their national conferences. The workshop program, to be held annually at the organizations' national conference on an alternating basis, was inaugurated with a session held July 10, 1962, in

[9] The discussion was summarized in a report mimeographed and distributed by the American Municipal Association. See "Summary of Discussion, Workshop on 'Voluntary Multipurpose Regional Organizations'," American Municipal Congress, Seattle, Wash., Aug. 27, 1961 (Washington: American Municipal Association, 1961; mimeographed).

[10] The mimeographed announcement of this service, made available by the Washington office of the American Municipal Association, is dated May 25, 1962.

connection with the NACO meeting in New York. The AMA will sponsor the second joint workshop at its annual conference to be held in Houston in August 1963. One product of the 1962 discussion was a mimeographed summary outlining the services which AMA–NACO was prepared to render voluntary regional councils.[11]

Official sponsorship of the conference approach by AMA and NACO indicates the intent of those organizations, and presumably of the mass of local officials and local governments as well, to give full support to the voluntary council as a device for alleviating the pressures of metropolitan problems. The summaries of the two workshops held thus far (at Seattle and New York) reveal clearly the nature of the voluntary council as it is understood by council participants. One speaker after another in the two discussion sessions viewed the council as a means of preserving local government while at the same time taking action to ameliorate metropolitan problems within the framework of that government. A number also pointed to what they regarded as the logical alternative to voluntary cooperation, namely a metropolitan "supergovernment."

A metropolitan conference of governments is, by confession of its adherents, an alliance among member units. It is, moreover, the weakest kind of alliance conceivable, one which has no sanctional authority with regard to its members, one from which a participant may withdraw without citing cause. It is not a body politic or corporate, nor could it by any reasonable definition of the term be called a government. Yet it is not to be written off as a futile exercise. On the contrary, it has demonstrated a capacity to achieve some alleviation of those metropolitan problems which lie within the purview of existing governments — and there are many such. It may well represent as much by way of affirmative approach to metropolitan issues as may reasonably be expected from traditional governments. The case can be made that, within limits, it serves a good and positive purpose.[12]

[11] "First Joint AMA–NACO Voluntary Regional Association Workshop Meeting Held" (Washington: AMA–NACO, July 18, 1962; mimeographed).

[12] Not all would accept even this qualified endorsement. Thus one observer, who persists in the ancient heresy that metropolitan problems should be dealt with by a metropolitan government, questions (in a recent letter to the author) whether the conference of governments is a really good way to approach regional problems or "merely a good enough way to forestall a better and more permanent solution." It may, of course, be both: As good a way for some purposes as is available "and" good enough to relieve the pressure for more drastic action.

It is not to be doubted, however, that the limits are both more numerous and more restrictive than some have thought them. They appear most clearly when the conditions for successful conference action are analysed. The prospects for success are best when:

1. The problem to be solved is noncontroversial: That is, when all participating governments agree on both the definition and the solution of the problem at hand, and when the danger of political repercussion is not great.

2. The proposed solution will not disparage in anywise the scope of action, or the status or reputation, of any member government.

3. The proposed decision is self-executing: That is, when it does not require positive action by the member governments for its implementation.

4. The course of action proposed to be taken costs the member governments little or nothing.

Clearly these conditions while not ironclad nevertheless are such as to set severe limits to the usefulness of the conference of governments as a method for dealing with regional issues.

There are metropolitan problems which, whether for want of power, or of resources, or of imagination, or of incentive, are beyond the ken of traditional local governments. With these an association of governments is powerless to deal, and it may be expected to pass them by. Others are off limits from political considerations. Others still simply will not yield to the lowest-common-denominator measures available under the requirements of voluntary agreement and unanimous consent among existing governments. It follows therefore that other arrangements for metropolitan adaptation must be searched out, explored, and improved upon in practice. . . .

FRANK SMALLWOOD

Toronto: The Problems of
Metropolitan Unity

When the "Cumming Report" was issued in 1953, it noted the
"serious cleavage of interest" that existed between the City of Toronto and the twelve other municipalities, and expressed the hope
that a "better spirit of metropolitan unity" would be realized in future years.

Perhaps if one of the Report's major organizational recommendations had been followed, the development of this spirit of unity
could have been expedited. . . . [T]he Report proposed that the
City of Toronto should have four members on the new Metropolitan
Council, while the twelve suburbs should have an equal number of
members drawn from four suburban "divisions," each of which
would appoint one councillor. Although this arrangement would not
have alleviated any potential city-versus-suburbs split, it at least represented a step in the direction of breaking down narrow local identities within the suburban community. When the Provincial Legislature rejected this proposal in favor of a 24 member constituency-unit
system of representation (i.e. one representative for each of the
twelve suburban municipalities plus twelve for the City of Toronto),
it both helped and hindered the future development of the new metropolitan government.

. . . [T]he help came from the fact that such an arrangement
tended to minimize the potentialities of an external attack upon the
new governmental body by local political leaders. Because these

Reprinted from *Metro Toronto: A Decade Later* (Toronto: Bureau of
Municipal Research, 1963), pp. 28-39, with the permission of the author
and the Bureau of Municipal Research, Toronto, Canada.

leaders were involved in the formulation of Metro policies, they understood what these policies were all about, and they were in a position to translate the significance of the policies to their local communities. In essence, the Toronto arrangement provided the means for a close liaison between the new Metro Council and the existing local municipalities. Yet the price the Council has been forced to pay for such potential liaison has been a very severe one.

In effect, the representative arrangements adopted by the Province have tended to turn the new metropolitan government into a very real 'Assembly of Sovereign States.' Since the Metro Council members are the actual Mayors, Reeves or other local political leaders of their constituent councils, it has been virtually impossible for these members to ignore parochial interests in approaching their Metro responsibilities. Under the circumstances, Council deliberations can easily turn into bargaining sessions, in which local representatives tend to place more emphasis upon their respective constituencies than upon the larger needs of the metropolitan community taken as a whole.

The appearance of such a conflict is not a new problem unique to the Toronto Council. Despite Edmund Burke's historic plea for the broad exercise of representative judgement, political man has always experienced considerable difficulty reconciling the tug of local demands with some larger concept of community interest, even under the very best of circumstances. Yet by placing local leaders (who have been elected to oversee the interests of their individual communities) upon its Council, Toronto's metropolitan government has tended to magnify this already difficult problem to the breaking point. It is hard enough to serve one master well, much less two, and perhaps the best insight that can be gained into the true nature of the Toronto Councillors' dilemma is to visualize a Canadian Parliament made up solely of Provincial Premiers, or a United States Congress consisting of fifty State Governors.

This potential drift towards parochialism has been reinforced by the pattern of the area's population growth during the past ten years. [See table on page 389.]

The basic result of this growth has been to increase further the population inequities of a previously inequitable representative arrangement. By 1963, North York, with some 17% of the area's total population, had one representative on the Metropolitan Council, while Swansea, with considerably less than 1% of the population,

POPULATION GROWTH (1953-63)[1]

	1953	1963	% Increase
City of Toronto	665,502	644,358	− 3.2%
"Inner Ring"			
York	100,463	126,511	+ 25.9%
East York	65,736	71,300	+ 8.5%
Forest Hill	17,719	21,513	+ 21.4%
Leaside	15,910	18,853	+ 18.5%
Mimico	12,301	17,989	+ 46.2%
New Toronto	11,190	12,924	+ 15.5%
Long Branch	9,140	11,091	+ 21.3%
Weston	8,374	9,832	+ 17.4%
Swansea	8,344	9,249	+ 10.8%
"Outer Ring"			
North York	110,311	286,446	+160 %
Scarborough	78,803	230,338	+192.3%
Etobicoke	70,209	165,001	+135 %
Totals	1,174,002	1,625,405	+ 38.4%

also retained its one member. The seven smallest municipalities, contained only 5% of the total area population but almost 30% of the seats on the Council. A similar, although not as dramatic imbalance was becoming apparent with respect to the City's position. Whereas in 1953, the City had to be given half the Council seats on the grounds that it contained 57% of the area's total population, by 1961 the City had dropped to 40% of the area's total population, yet it still retained its twelve Council seats.

While the most obvious implication of this situation has been a growing representative imbalance on the Council, its more subtle manifestation has taken the form of a more parochial approach towards Council deliberations. Representatives of the smaller municipalities, realizing that they are the beneficiaries of a representative system that defies any logical justification, can hardly help being tempted to adopt an increasingly defensive and protective attitude toward their existing position. Representatives of the larger suburban units, looking on themselves as the victims of an injustice, are equally tempted to adopt an increasingly more aggressive pursuit of their own local interests. These psychological attitudes have tended to split the smaller and the larger suburban communities on a number of issues. Yet, the Council has always operated under the threat that the twelve suburbs would, in fact, be able to realize a total

[1] "Metropolitan Toronto 1953-1963: 10 Years of Progress," Annual Brochure issued by the Metropolitan Toronto Council, June, 1963, p. 11.

alignment of forces and thus produce a complete deadlock in the
form of a basic city-versus-suburbs split.

During earlier years, the appearance of any such division was
forestalled by Chairman [Frederick] Gardiner's forceful leadership
("I only put the axe to their heads when everything else fails"[2]),
coupled with the ability of the twelve City representatives to organize themselves as a unit, and thus carry the day by picking up
one or two 'strays' from the initially disorganized suburbs. As a result, the only serious early City-suburban break occurred in the
form of a bitter fight over water rate charges, with the issue not
being resolved until Chairman Gardiner had twice cast his tie-
breaking vote. A second major break threatened to occur in late 1961
when Toronto Mayor Nathan Phillips made a major push for his total amalgamation scheme, but the Council rejected this idea decisively by an 18 to 5 vote, with six of the City representatives
deserting their Mayor.

Yet, while surface appearances may have indicated a relatively
mild degree of City-suburban infighting, beneath this surface tensions were building up to a point where only a very slight nudge was
needed to split the Council wide apart. Such a nudge appeared in
the 1963 session in the form of the Toronto Transit Commission subsidy issue, and the basic stakes were largely economic in their underlying impact.

Despite the fact that its revenues have been barely able to cover
the costs of its operating budget alone, by 1963 the T.T.C. was paying $4 million in interest and debt installments for its first major sub-
way line (Yonge Street), plus another $1.1 million in interest
charges on a recently opened second line extension (University
Avenue). Within a few years, the Commission can look forward to
another $6.4 million burden in annual debt charges to cover the cap-
ital costs of a new, east-west (Bloor-Danforth Street) subway that is
scheduled to open in 1966.

The only consistent action the T.T.C. has followed in an attempt
to resolve this financial dilemma has been the periodic fare increase.
Fares were raised in 1954, 1956 and 1960, and the result has been a
decrease in revenue passengers from 320 million in 1954 to 269 million in 1962. In short, during the past ten years, the Commission's
passenger load has dropped 16% while the area's total population has
increased 38%.

[2] J. LeBlanc, "He Uses The Axe As Last Resort," Canadian Press Staff
article, January 20, 1961.

During the early winter months of 1963, it became obvious that the Commission was destined to go far into the red in its projected current year budget, and it announced that, unless it received outside financial assistance, it would increase fares again on May 1st. The Metropolitan Council held a preliminary debate on the question in March, with two virtually solid phalanxes emerging. The City favoured a T.T.C. subsidy (the subway lines are located wholly within its boundaries), and the suburbs were against it (unless there was a new fare structure that would, in effect, give cheaper rides to suburban residents). The division was clear-cut and simple; so simple in fact that Toronto's new Mayor, Donald Summerville, complained, "Metro Toronto is getting like a kindergarten."[3]

Although Toronto's three daily newspapers, *The Star, The Globe and Mail, and The Telegram** warned that "The Metro Split Widens," little could be done to head off the impending clash that lay ahead. The die was cast when the Provincial Legislature removed all previous restrictions on the Council, permitting it to grant direct operating subsidies to the T.T.C. if it elected to do so. The Council considered the issue in late April and although a majority of its members supported a $2.5 million T.T.C. subsidy, it failed to secure the necessary two-thirds vote. The final count was 13 to 11, with all twelve City representatives (plus one suburbanite) supporting the subsidy and the remaining eleven suburban members lined up solidly against it. The City's reaction was immediate and bitter, with Mayor Summerville charging that Toronto was being milked by the suburbs through metropolitan government.[4]

On May 1st the Transit Commission raised its fares, thus setting into motion a further series of bewildering procedural and parliamentary maneuvers that defy easy description. The net result was that the Metropolitan Council once again reconsidered the issue at a series of meetings in early May, before finally approving the $2.5 million subsidy.

If the City's previous reaction to its initial defeat had been bitter, its reaction was mild compared with the explosion that marked the suburbs' approach to this second switch in policy. Indeed, two of the "outer ring" giants, North York and Etobicoke, were so incensed as

[3] Quoted in "The Metro Split Widens" (edit) Toronto Daily Star, March 19, 1963.
* All of whom are critical of the current federation concept and favor some form of complete amalgamation of the thirteen municipalities into one united metropolitan city.
[4] Quoted in Toronto Globe and Mail, April 30, 1963, p. 5.

to set off a chain of events that may well lead to the disintegration of the basic metropolitan federation concept as it is presently organized.

Spearheaded by North York's Reeve, Norman Goodhead, these two communities filed suit against the Metropolitan Council, challenging the legality of its action and attempting to have the subsidy declared null and void. Both sides have retained special counsel to handle their cases and the litigation promises to be both protracted and bitter.

This latest action has had a two-fold impact on Metro. First, it has represented a new phase in the deterioration of relations within the Council itself. For the first time two of the Council's more powerful members have launched a direct, and massive assault upon the metropolitan body, and in the words of the Council's new Chairman, William R. Allen, there can be "no real winners" in the legal battle that lies ahead.

In addition, the Council's handling of the entire subsidy issue appears to have tarnished its public image quite severely. The newspapers, in stepping up their campaign for total metropolitan amalgamation, have launched especially vitriolic attacks upon the current organization — witness the following sample from *The Telegram*[5]

> . . . Ad hocery, government by gimmick, decision by intrigue, policy-making by playing one faction against another, back scratching and saw-offs — these are the built-in weaknesses of Metro politics . . . Metro is a balkanized state where each municipality subordinates the interests of the whole to its own interests. . . .

Whether or not it survives its current political and legal woes, it is obvious that Toronto's federated government is now in deep trouble. Whatever else it may or may not have been able to accomplish in the past decade, the federation approach has made very little headway towards the realization of the "spirit of metropolitan unity" that the "Cumming Report" so wistfully contemplated some ten years ago. Indeed, the most alarming aspect of the whole situation is that the relations between Council members appear to be growing worse, rather than better, with the passage of years.

The parochial strains within Metro have tended to inhibit the Council's program in a number of distinct ways. First, there have

---

[5] Toronto Telegram, "Metro's Ad Hocery" (edit), May 8, 1963.

been occasions when the more affluent municipalities have demonstrated a reluctance to share their wealth with the area's less fortunate communities. The resistance encountered in raising the level of maintenance assistance grants in the field of education, . . . serves as an apt illustration of this development.

Second, and on the opposite side of the coin, there have also been cases where the less wealthy communities have balked against accepting increased responsibilities on the grounds that it would further jeopardize their already precarious financial positions. The field of public housing provides a dramatic example of this problem.

The Toronto public housing program represents a tangled web of overlapping governmental jurisdictions and its current woes are certainly not due to any problems of local financial inequities alone. Yet it is just as obvious that these local inequities have contributed additional complications to an already complex situation.

The greatest difficulty of all is the simple fact that too many separate agencies share responsibilities for public housing in the Toronto metropolitan area. One specialized program, which is managed by a quasi-independent commission known as the Metropolitan Toronto Housing Company Ltd., oversees the construction of low-rental apartment developments for senior citizens (i.e. age 60 and older). This group, which was founded in 1954, has been able to complete some 1,474 low-rental units in eleven locations. It has an additional 392 units presently under construction.

A second separate program is operated by the City of Toronto. Due to a general lack of public interest and initiative in urban renewal throughout the inner core area, the City has been able to accomplish little in the field of public housing during recent years, although to its great credit, it did manage to initiate the 1,397 unit Regent Park North project prior to the inception of Metro. In addition, the City of Toronto Limited Dividend Housing Corporation, which serves as an arm of the City government, has completed some 366 units of moderate rental family housing and is presently constructing a 900 unit Moss Park project.

The major low-rental housing organization in Metropolitan Toronto is a third body known as the Metropolitan Toronto Housing Authority, which was created in 1955 to construct and operate general public housing projects throughout the Metro area. Despite the "Metropolitan" nomenclature, this authority does not fall directly under the Metro Council, but rather operates as a quasi-Metro organization under the direction of an independent nine-man board appointed by the Province.

The Authority's program represents a literal inter-governmental maze, involving Federal, Provincial, Metro and individual local authorities, as well as its own nine-member board. Although the Metro Council set a theoretical goal of 1,000 new public housing units per year in May 1958, the Authority has been able to complete only three projects — Lawrence Heights (1,081 units), South Regent Park (732 units) and Scarlettwood (150 units). Hence, despite the proliferation of housing authorities throughout the metropolitan area, metropolitan Toronto has witnessed the completion of only 5,000 units of public housing during the past decade.[6]

While much of this delay must be blamed on the problems of red tape and intergovernmental confusion resulting from the complicated housing organizational structure, another problem has been the marked reluctance on the part of local municipalities, most especially the three "outer ring" suburbs, to absorb additional public housing programs. The rationale for this obstinancy is primarily economic:

> Metro wants to build 100 units of low-rental housing in Scarborough. But Scarborough says, in effect, "We've got enough now; go build somewhere else."
>
> Etobicoke Council is stalling on the approval of a 1,100 unit Metro low-rental project in its Thistletown area.
>
> Still another project — 300 units in North York — is hung up in a complicated wrangle.
>
> . . . The Scarborough project was approved by Metro Council in 1958. But the Township said no. It still says no. "We've got about half of all the limited dividend low-rental apartments in Metro," says Reeve Albert Campbell. "Our per capita assessment is the lowest in Metro. Until we get it up, we won't take on any more public housing. It will be up to the other municipalities."
>
> Scarborough's main worry is school costs. It has found that the average low-rental housing project has four times the community average of school children. Two years ago, Metro began discussion of a method of compensating municipalities with public housing for their additional school costs. But the idea was later dropped. . . .[7]

[6] Data on numbers of housing units taken from "Metropolitan Toronto: 10 Years of Progress," op. cit., 37-40.

[7] Michael Best, "Our Public Housing Paradox," Toronto Daily Star, May 7, 1963, p. 7.

The above observation indicates the depth of the impact that local financial inequalities can have on a major component of the Metro program. If public housing is to move forward in metropolitan Toronto, it will have to depend upon the co-operative support of the three "outer ring" suburbs since these three communities contain the only major blocs of undeveloped land remaining within the present Metro boundaries. Yet resistance to accept such housing has characterized the attitude of all three communities, with Scarborough arguing most adamantly that its present financial problems preclude the absorption of additional housing projects. Scarborough's attitude serves as a fitting illustration of the second limitation which has affected Metro's growing inability to act decisively — the reluctance of the less wealthy communities to accept increased responsibilities for major new projects on the basis that such action would further jeopardize their already difficult financial problems.

The third sphere where Metro has displayed considerable indecision is not solely economic in its underlying origins. Instead, it appears to be the outgrowth of a highly pragmatic leadership philosophy that has shaped the Metro operation from its very inception.

There is little doubt that Metro's great leadership strength to date has been in its response to the more dramatic physical service crises that have exerted the loudest demands for immediate and sustained attention. Metro has realized its greatest accomplishments in tackling such drastic situations as those that were to be found in the water supply, sewage disposal, school construction, and transportation services. Although this effort has required a massive organizational and financial capability, it has not placed too many subtle, or even controversial, demands on the Metro Council members because both the nature of these problems and the nature of the actions necessary to realize their solution have been relatively obvious. During its formative years, Metro's basic raison d' etre has been reasonably apparent to all. Faced with a staggering backlog of previous neglect in a variety of public areas, the Metropolitan Council has had little choice but to emphasize the "steamshovel approach" to its job in order to build the miles of new sewers and the myriad of new schools necessary to preserve metropolitan Toronto as a going, and growing, concern.

Largely as a result of the pragmatic nature of this initial mandate, the Council has tended to adopt a highly pragmatic approach to all spheres of its operations that has meshed very closely with the personal philosophical orientation of its first chairman, Frederick Gardiner. Stated quite simply, Metro has often been inclined to operate more as a business than as a governmental organization — the more as a gigantic construction company operating under a metropolitan-wide mandate, than as a political body responsible for a wide range of social, as well as physical obligations. Ten years' cumulative experience indicates that the Metropolitan Council has been consistently aggressive in tackling the so-called "hard core" problems where results are concrete and obvious, and considerably less assertive in meeting some of the "softer," more socially-oriented issue areas where results are usually less tangible and more controversial. An analysis of some of the particular fields where Metro's record of response has not been particularly aggressive indicates the true nature of this dichotomy.

Three such fields are public housing, planning and the publicity and information functions that are involved in carrying Metro's story to the public. The lack of assertiveness that has characterized the field of public housing has already been described in enough detail to indicate that Metro's record of accomplishments here falls far short of its more spectacular achievements in the water supply, water pollution control and related public works fields.

Planning represents another field where a disturbing lack of resolution has tended to characterize the Council's position. This is not to assert that Metro has suffered from any lack of adequate planning guidance at the staff level. The Metropolitan Toronto Planning Board and a second quasi-independent body, the Metropolitan Toronto and Region Conservation Authority, have both formulated some excellent open space, recreational and general planning proposals that promise to add a great deal to the future well-being of the metropolitan Toronto area. Yet it is significant to note that while the Planning Board has prepared a general master plan for Metro Toronto, this plan still remains in the draft stage. During ten years of existence, the Metropolitan Council has never got down to the difficult business of approving a formal Official Plan to guide the growth of the metropolitan Toronto area.

While it might be argued that the existence of a draft master plan makes any such formal action unnecessary, this is a debatable contention at best. A plan is not only designed to serve as a guideline for future growth, but also as an official policy commitment on the part of its sponsoring agency. Through the adoption of a formal Official Plan, Toronto's Council would actually be forcing itself to hammer out its future development policies and priorities for the entire metropolitan area. In the process it would be formulating a comprehensive guideline that could help to provide a sense of central cohesion to the entire Metro operation. This is precisely the task which the new Winnipeg Metropolitan Corporation has viewed as constituting its primary obligation. Yet while the Winnipeg Corporation is attempting to work out its long-range planning projections as its first order of business, the Toronto Council has permitted ten years to pass without bothering to adopt a formal plan. The Council's record here has been far from decisive.

A comparable lack of decisiveness has characterized the Council's approach to its public information responsibilities. In all fairness, it must be noted that Metro's new Chairman, William Allen, has been making a major effort to emphasize Metro's public education role during the past two years through an increasingly heavy program of speaking engagements and other public commitments. Yet it is highly questionable whether one man's efforts can fill the organizational void that exists in this area. During more recent years, Metro's major public information document has been an attractive annual brochure which summarizes the Council's key achievements to date. It is interesting to note, however, that responsibility for producing this brochure has been assigned to an already busy operating unit, the Metropolitan Planning Board. In effect, the Metropolitan Council has viewed its public information effort as an "added chore" that is to be relegated to an existing operational unit that is already attempting to discharge a full-time responsibility of its own. As is the case with its research and central intelligence responsibilities, which have been relegated without any major staff commitment to the Treasury Department, the Metropolitan Council has not regarded its public information role as being of enough importance to warrant its own central staff organization.

This general lack of decisiveness in the planning, the research and the public information fields becomes highly relevant if one views the major components of the political leadership role in its totality. In addition to its responsibility to respond to existing crisis situations, any strong leadership agency must be prepared to anticipate future developments and to educate the public with regard to their implications. This is especially true in a democratic society which places a high premium on the existence of an informed public opinion. Metro's forte to date, however, has most decidedly been an emphasis upon response to already apparent crisis situations to an extent where the other components of the leadership process, most especially public information and education, have been largely ignored.

Perhaps the Toronto Council has not been unique in this regard. Urban America's current unpreparedness to deal with a rising civil rights crisis that has been a long time in the making serves as another telling indication of the tendency of our political institutions to limit themselves to the rudimentary elements of a basic stimulus and response pattern — in short, these institutions are all too often unable, or unwilling, to act until after obvious crisis situations are already crashing about their ears. Yet this is a rather dismal picture at best, and indeed, tell-tale signs are now emerging in the Toronto area that raise the question of whether the Metropolitan Council can follow any such course in the future.

These signs are the outgrowth of some basic environmental changes that are now taking place in Metropolitan Toronto, many of which appear to be the result of Metro's own initial successes. As this new governmental organization has resolved many of the most immediate crisis problems that have plagued Greater Toronto in the past, the area's basic service demands have been shifting gradually from the larger public works' priorities of the past to the considerably more complex, and subtle, considerations of social and economic accommodation. Metro itself, or at least the Metropolitan Planning Board which prepared the Council's Tenth Anniversary Report, has begun to indicate a fundamental awareness of this changing environmental context:

> The changing nature of the metropolitan problem is perhaps best reflected in the shifting focus of metropolitan concern. Where emphasis in the first 10 years has of necessity been largely on the basic and essential physical services, that of the next 10 years will be increasingly on social and community welfare. In the first 10-year capital works program adopted by Metro in 1955, the projected expenditure . . . was allocated on the basis of 76% to roads, sewers and water supply; 21% to education; and only 3% to all of the other services and facilities, such as housing, welfare, conservation and parks, and the administration of justice.
>
> The 10-year capital program adopted in 1963 . . . presents a far

different picture: 36% on roads, sewers and water; 28% on education; 30% on public transit; and 6% on the other Metropolitan services.[8]

Although the major forces of change at work here have been largely self-generating (i.e. Metro, though its own initial successes has been working itself into new jobs), certain external factors have tended to magnify the impact of these shifting priorities. The most dramatic of these factors has been a very high degree of foreign immigration into the metropolitan area during the past decade. The City of Toronto Planning Board estimates that Metropolitan Toronto has absorbed some 385,000 immigrants between 1951 and 1960. While English, Germans and Italians comprise the major portion of this new influx, the Planning Board lists no less than thirty different nationalities as migrating to the Toronto area in the past ten years.[9] Although this changing cosmopolitan population contains the promise of a rich mixture of cultural vitality, it also contains difficult challenges of social adjustment, as efforts are made to integrate these groups fully into the daily patterns of metropolitan life. Here, once again, there is a strong indication that Metro's mandate is now shifting from the physical to the social challenges of urban living. Under the circumstances, the Metro organization will have no choice but to pay increasing attention to some of the less glamorous problems of social accommodation that it has tended to subordinate to its higher priority public works goals of the past.

It is this final observation that relates back to the earlier analysis of the widening economic inequalities that are now becoming more apparent in the original metropolitan federation framework as it was first devised in 1953. During its formative years, one of the reasons Metro has been able to achieve a considerable degree of consensus among its member municipalities is due to the fact that the basic problems that have represented its primary fields of concern have been relatively obvious in their priorities and relatively non-controversial in their implications. While these different member municipalities may have been subjected to widely divergent fluctuations in their own local resources, it was hardly difficult for them to agree that a modern metropolitan community must have an adequate water supply system if it is to survive. As Metro now places

[8] "Metropolitan Toronto: 10 Years of Progress," *op. cit.*, pp. 5-6.
[9] City of Toronto Planning Board, A Report on the Ethnic Origins of the Population of Toronto, September 12, 1961, p. 4.

increasing emphasis on such fields as welfare, housing, recreation and the like, the considerably more contentious nature of these newer priorities (complete with all their implications of "unnecessary frills") promises to place increasing strains upon the original federation framework. In short, Metro has been suffering from a growing lack of resolution during its first decade in precisely those fields that will demand an increasing amount of its attention during the next decade. It is highly debatable whether the existing Metro municipalities will be able to achieve a degree of consensus on these newly emerging issues of social reform that will be comparable to the degree of consensus they have been able to achieve in the past when considering the more tangible, "hard core" problems that have monopolized Metro's first decade.